Mastering SQL Server 2017

Build smart and efficient database applications for your
organization with SQL Server 2017

Miloš Radivojević
Dejan Sarka
William Durkin
Christian Coté
Matija Lah

BIRMINGHAM - MUMBAI

Mastering SQL Server 2017

First Published: August 2019

Production Reference: 1140819

Published by Packt Publishing Ltd.
Livery Place, 35 Livery Street
Birmingham, B3 2PB, U.K.

ISBN 978-1-83898-320-8

www.packtpub.com

Contributors

About the Authors

Miloš Radivojević is a database consultant in Vienna, Austria. He is a data platform MVP and specializes in SQL Server for application developers and performance/ query tuning. Currently, he works as a principal database consultant in Bwin (GVC Holdings)—the largest regulated online gaming company in the world. Miloš is a co-founder of PASS Austria. He is also a speaker at international conferences and speaks regularly at SQL Saturday events and PASS Austria meetings.

Dejan Sarka, MCT and Microsoft Data Platform MVP, is an independent trainer and consultant who focuses on the development of database and business intelligence applications. Besides projects, he spends about half his time on training and mentoring. He is the founder of the Slovenian SQL Server and .NET Users Group. He is the main author or co-author of many books about databases and SQL Server. The last three books before this one were published by Packt, and their titles were SQL Server 2016 Developer's Guide, SQL Server 2017 Integration Services Cookbook, and SQL Server 2016 Developer's Guide. Dejan Sarka has also developed many courses and seminars for Microsoft, SolidQ, and Pluralsight.

William Durkin is a data platform architect for Data Masterminds. He uses his decade of experience with SQL Server to help multinational corporations achieve their data management goals. Born in the UK and now based in Germany, William is a regular speaker at conferences around the globe, a Data Platform MVP, and the founder of the popular SQLGrillen event.

Christian Coté has been in IT for more than 12 years. He is an MS-certified technical specialist in business intelligence (MCTS-BI). For about 10 years, he has been a consultant in ETL/BI projects. His ETL projects have used various ETL tools and plain code with various RDBMSes (such as Oracle and SQL Server). He is currently working on his sixth SSIS implementation in 4 years.

Matija Lah has more than 15 years of experience working with Microsoft SQL Server, mostly from architecting data-centric solutions in the legal domain. His contributions to the SQL Server community have led to the Microsoft Most Valuable Professional award in 2007 (data platform). He spends most of his time on projects involving advanced information management, and natural language processing, but often finds time to speak at events related to Microsoft SQL Server where he loves to share his experience with the SQL Server platform.

Packt Is Searching for Authors Like You

If you're interested in becoming an author for Packt, please visit authors.packtpub.com and apply today. We have worked with thousands of developers and tech professionals, just like you, to help them share their insight with the global tech community. You can make a general application, apply for a specific hot topic that we are recruiting an author for, or submit your own idea.

`mapt.io`

Mapt is an online digital library that gives you full access to over 5,000 books and videos, as well as industry-leading tools to help you plan your personal development and advance your career. For more information, please visit our website.

Why Subscribe?

- Spend less time learning and more time coding with practical eBooks and Videos from over 4,000 industry professionals

- Improve your learning with Skill Plans built especially for you

- Get a free eBook or video every month

- Mapt is fully searchable

- Copy and paste, print, and bookmark content

Packt.com

Did you know that Packt offers eBook versions of every book published, with PDF and ePub files available? You can upgrade to the eBook version at `www.packt.com` and as a print book customer, you are entitled to a discount on the eBook copy. Get in touch with us at `customercare@packtpub.com` for more details.

At `www.packt.com`, you can also read a collection of free technical articles, sign up for a range of free newsletters, and receive exclusive discounts and offers on Packt books and eBooks.

Table of Contents

Preface

Mastering SQL Server 2017 brings in the power of R and Python for machine learning and containerization-based deployment on Windows and Linux. By knowing how to use the features of SQL Server 2017 to your advantage, you can build scalable applications and easily perform data integration and transformation.

After a quick recap of the features of SQL Server 2017, this Learning Path shows you how to use Query Store, columnstore indexes, and In-Memory OLTP in your applications. You'll then learn to integrate Python code in SQL Server and graph database implementations for development and testing. Next, you'll learn how to design and build SQL Server Integration Services (SSIS) data warehouse packages using SQL server data tools. You'll also learn to develop SSIS packages designed to maintain a data warehouse using data flow and other control flow tasks.

By the end of this Learning Path, you'll have the required information to easily design efficient, high-performance database applications. You'll also have explored on-premises big data integration processes to create a classic data warehouse.

This Learning Path includes content from the following Packt products:

- SQL Server 2017 Developer's Guide by Miloš Radivojević, Dejan Sarka, William Durkin
- SQL Server 2017 Integration Services Cookbook by Christian Coté, Dejan Sarka, Matija Lah

Who This Book Is For

Database developers and solution architects looking to develop ETL solutions with SSIS, and who want to learn the new features and capabilities in SSIS 2017, will find this Learning Path very useful. It will also be valuable to advanced analysis practitioners, business intelligence developers, and database consultants dealing with performance tuning. Some basic understanding of database concepts and T-SQL is required to get the best out of this Learning Path.

What This Book Covers

Chapter 1, *Introduction to SQL Server 2017*, very briefly covers the most important features and enhancements, not just those for developers. The chapter shows the whole picture and points readers in the direction of where things are moving.

Chapter 2, *SQL Server Tools*, helps you understand the changes in the release management of SQL Server tools and explores small and handy enhancements in **SQL Server Management Studio (SSMS)**. It also introduces RStudio IDE, a very popular tool for developing R code, and briefly covers **SQL Server Data Tools (SSDT)**, including the new **R Tools for Visual Studio (RTVS)**, a plugin for Visual Studio, which enables you to develop R code in an IDE that is popular among developers using Microsoft products and languages. The chapter introduces Visual Studio 2017 and shows how it can be used for data science applications with Python.

Chapter 3, *JSON Support in SQL Server*, explores the JSON support built into SQL Server. This support should make it easier for applications to exchange JSON data with SQL Server.

Chapter 4, *Stretch Database*, helps you understand how to migrate historical or less frequently/infrequently accessed data transparently and securely to Microsoft Azure using the **Stretch Database (Stretch DB)** feature.

Chapter 5, *Temporal Tables*, introduces support for system-versioned temporal tables based on the SQL:2011 standard. We explain how this is implemented in SQL Server and demonstrate some use cases for it (for example, a time-travel application).

Chapter 6, *Columnstore Indexes*, revises columnar storage and then explores the huge improvements relating to columnstore indexes in SQL Server 2016: updatable non-clustered columnstore indexes, columnstore indexes on in-memory tables, and many other new features for operational analytics.

Chapter 7, *SSIS Setup*, contains recipes describing the step by step setup of SQL Server 2016 to get the features that are used in the book.

Chapter 8, *What Is New in SSIS 2016*, contains recipes that talk about the evolution of SSIS over time and what's new in SSIS 2016. This chapter is a detailed overview of Integration Services 2016, new features.

Chapter 9, *Key Components of a Modern ETL Solution*, explains how ETL has evolved over the past few years and will explain what components are necessary to get a modern scalable ETL solution that fits the modern data warehouse. This chapter will also describe what each catalog view provides and will help you learn how you can use some of them to archive SSIS execution statistics.

Chapter 10, *Dealing with Data Quality*, focuses on how SSIS can be leveraged to validate and load data. You will learn how to identify invalid data, cleanse data and load valid data to the data warehouse.

Chapter 11, *Unleash the Power of SSIS Script Task and Component*, covers how to use scripting with SSIS. You will learn how script tasks and script components are very valuable in many situations to overcome the limitations of stock toolbox tasks and transforms.

Chapter 12, *On-Premises and Azure Big Data Integration*, describes the Azure feature pack that allows SSIS to integrate Azure data from blob storage and HDInsight clusters. You will learn how to use Azure feature pack components to add flexibility to their SSIS solution architecture and integrate on-premises Big Data can be manipulated via SSIS.

Chapter 13, *Extending SSIS Tasks and Transformations*, talks about extending and customizing the toolbox using custom-developed tasks and transforms and security features. You will learn the pros and cons of creating custom tasks to extend the SSIS toolbox and secure your deployment.

Chapter 14, *Scale Out with SSIS 2017*, talks about scaling out SSIS package executions on multiple servers. You will learn how SSIS 2017 can scale out to multiple workers to enhance execution scalability.

To Get the Most out of This Book

1. In order to run all of the demo code in this book, you will need SQL Server 2017 Developer or Enterprise Edition. In addition, you will extensively use SQL Server Management Studio.
2. You will also need the RStudio IDE and/or SQL Server Data Tools with R Tools for Visual Studio plug-in
3. SQL Server 2017 Developer or Enterprise Edition.
4. In addition, you will extensively use SQL Server Management Studio.

5. Other tools you may need are Visual Studio 2015, SQL Data Tools 16 or higher and SQL Server Management Studio 17 or later.
6. In addition to that, you will need Hortonworks Sandbox Docker for Windows Azure account and Microsoft Azure.

Download the Example Code Files

You can download the example code files for this book from your account at `http://www.packtpub.com`. If you purchased this book elsewhere, you can visit `http://www.packtpub.com/support` and register to have the files e-mailed directly to you. You can download the code files by following these steps:

1. Log in or register to our website using your e-mail address and password.
2. Hover the mouse pointer on the **SUPPORT** tab at the top.
3. Click on **Code Downloads & Errata**.
4. Enter the name of the book in the **Search** box.
5. Select the book for which you're looking to download the code files.
6. Choose from the drop-down menu where you purchased this book from.
7. Click on **Code Download**.

You can also download the code files by clicking on the **Code Files** button on the book's webpage at the Packt Publishing website. This page can be accessed by entering the book's name in the **Search** box. Please note that you need to be logged in to your Packt account. Once the file is downloaded, please make sure that you unzip or extract the folder using the latest version of:

- WinRAR / 7-Zip for Windows
- Zipeg / iZip / UnRarX for Mac
- 7-Zip / PeaZip for Linux

The code bundle for the book is also hosted on GitHub at `https://github.com/PacktPublishing/Mastering-SQL-Server-2017-`. We also have other code bundles from our rich catalog of books and videos available at `https://github.com/PacktPublishing/`. Check them out!

Download the color images

We also provide a PDF file that has color images of the screenshots/diagrams used in this book. You can download it here: `https://static.packt-cdn.com/downloads/9781838983208_ColorImages.pdf`.

Conventions Used

In this book, you will find a number of text styles that distinguish between different kinds of information. Here are some examples of these styles and an explanation of their meaning. Code words in text, database table names, folder names, filenames, file extensions, pathnames, dummy URLs, user input, and Twitter handles are shown as follows: "The last characters CI and AS are for case insensitive and accent sensitive, respectively." A block of code is set as follows:

```
USE DQS_STAGING_DATA;
SELECT CustomerKey, FullName, StreetAddress, City, StateProvince,
CountryRegion, EmailAddress, BirthDate, Occupation;
```

CodeInText: Indicates code words in text, database table names, folder names, filenames, file extensions, pathnames, dummy URLs, user input, and Twitter handles. Here is an example: "The simplest query to retrieve the data that you can write includes the SELECT and the FROM clauses. In the SELECT clause, you can use the star character (*), literally SELECT *, to denote that you need all columns from a table in the result set."

A block of code is set as follows:

```
USE WideWorldImportersDW;
SELECT *
FROM Dimension.Customer;
```

When we wish to draw your attention to a particular part of a code block, the relevant lines or items are set in bold:

```
USE WideWorldImporters;
CREATE TABLE dbo.Product
(
    ProductId INT NOT NULL CONSTRAINT PK_Product PRIMARY KEY,
    ProductName NVARCHAR(50) NOT NULL,
    Price MONEY NOT NULL,
    ValidFrom DATETIME2 GENERATED ALWAYS AS ROW START NOT NULL,
    ValidTo DATETIME2 GENERATED ALWAYS AS ROW END NOT NULL,
    PERIOD FOR SYSTEM_TIME (ValidFrom, ValidTo)
)
WITH (SYSTEM_VERSIONING = ON);
```

Any command-line input or output is written as follows:

```
Customer                        SaleKey  Quantity
-----------------------------   -------- -----------
Tailspin Toys (Aceitunas, PR)   36964    288
Tailspin Toys (Aceitunas, PR)   126253   250
Tailspin Toys (Aceitunas, PR)   79272    250
```

Bold: Indicates a new term, an important word, or words that you see onscreen. For example, words in menus or dialog boxes appear in the text like this. Here is an example: "Go to **Tools | Options** and you are then able to type your search string in the textbox in the top-left of the **Options** window."

Warnings or important notes appear in a box like this.

Tips and tricks appear like this.

Get in Touch

Feedback from our readers is always welcome.

General feedback: Email feedback@packtpub.com and mention the book title in the subject of your message. If you have questions about any aspect of this book, please email us at questions@packtpub.com.

Errata: Although we have taken every care to ensure the accuracy of our content, mistakes do happen. If you have found a mistake in this book, we would be grateful if you would report this to us. Please visit www.packtpub.com/submit-errata, selecting your book, clicking on the Errata Submission Form link, and entering the details.

Piracy: If you come across any illegal copies of our works in any form on the Internet, we would be grateful if you would provide us with the location address or website name. Please contact us at copyright@packtpub.com with a link to the material.

If you are interested in becoming an author: If there is a topic that you have expertise in and you are interested in either writing or contributing to a book, please visit authors.packtpub.com.

Reviews

Please leave a review. Once you have read and used this book, why not leave a review on the site that you purchased it from? Potential readers can then see and use your unbiased opinion to make purchase decisions, we at Packt can understand what you think about our products, and our authors can see your feedback on their book. Thank you!

For more information about Packt, please visit packtpub.com

Introduction to SQL Server 2017

SQL Server is the main relational database management system product from Microsoft. It has been around in one form or another since the late 80s (developed in partnership with Sybase), but as a standalone Microsoft product, it's been here since the early 90s. In the last 20 years, SQL Server has changed and evolved, gaining newer features and functionality along the way.

The SQL Server we know today is based on what was arguably the most significant (r)evolutionary step in its history: the release of SQL Server 2005. The changes that were introduced allowed the versions that followed the 2005 release to take advantage of newer hardware and software improvements, such as: 64-bit memory architecture, better multi-CPU and multi-core support, better alignment with the .NET framework, and many more modernizations in general system architecture.

The incremental changes introduced in each subsequent version of SQL Server have continued to improve upon this solid new foundation. Fortunately, Microsoft has changed the release cycle for multiple products, including SQL Server, resulting in shorter time frames between releases. This has, in part, been due to Microsoft's focus on their much reported Mobile first, Cloud first strategy. This strategy, together with the development of the cloud version of SQL Server Azure SQL Database, has forced Microsoft into a drastically shorter release cycle. The advantage of this strategy is that we are no longer required to wait 3 to 5 years for a new release (and new features). There have been releases every 2 years since SQL Server 2012 was introduced, with multiple releases of Azure SQL Database in between the *real* versions.

While we can be pleased that we no longer need to wait for new releases, we are also at a distinct disadvantage. The rapid release of new versions and features leaves us developers with ever-decreasing periods of time to get to grips with the shiny new features. Prior versions had multiple years between releases, allowing us to build up a deeper knowledge and understanding of the available features, before having to consume new information.

Following on from the release of SQL Server 2016 was the release of SQL Server 2017, barely a year after 2016 was released. Many features were merely more polished/updated versions of the 2016 release, while there were some notable additions in the 2017 release.

In this chapter (and book), we will introduce what is new inside SQL Server 2017. Due to the short release cycle, we will outline features that are brand new in this release of the product and look at features that have been extended or improved upon since SQL Server 2016.

We will be outlining the new features in the following areas:

- Security
- Engine features
- Programming
- Business intelligence

Security

The last few years have made the importance of security in IT extremely apparent, particularly when we consider the repercussions of the Edward Snowden data leaks or multiple cases of data theft via hacking. While no system is completely impenetrable, we should always be considering how we can improve the security of the systems we build. These considerations are wide ranging and sometimes even dictated via rules, regulations, and laws. Microsoft has responded to the increased focus on security by delivering new features to assist developers and DBAs in their search for more secure systems.

Row-Level Security

The first technology that was introduced in SQL Server 2016 to address the need for increased/improved security is **Row-Level Security (RLS)**. RLS provides the ability to control access to rows in a table based on the user executing a query. With RLS it is possible to implement a filtering mechanism on any table in a database, completely transparently to any external application or direct T-SQL access.

The ability to implement such filtering without having to redesign a data access layer allows system administrators to control access to data at an even more granular level than before. The fact that this control can be achieved without any application logic redesign makes this feature potentially even more attractive to certain use-cases. RLS also makes it possible, in conjunction with the necessary auditing features, to lock down a SQL Server database so that even the traditional *god-mode* sysadmin cannot access the underlying data.

Dynamic data masking

The second security feature that we will be covering is **Dynamic Data Masking (DDM)**. DDM allows the system administrator to define column level data masking algorithms that prevent users from reading the contents of columns, while still being able to query the rows themselves. This feature was initially aimed at allowing developers to work with a copy of production data without having the ability to actually *see* the underlying data. This can be particularly useful in environments where data protection laws are enforced (for example, credit card processing systems and medical record storage). Data masking occurs only at query runtime and does not affect the stored data of a table. This means that it is possible to mask a multi-terabyte database through a simple DDL statement, rather than resorting to the previous solution of physically masking the underlying data in the table we want to mask. The current implementation of DDM provides the ability to define a fixed set of functions to columns of a table, which will mask data when a masked table is queried. If a user has the permission to view the masked data, then the masking functions are not run, whereas a user who may not see masked data will be provided with the data as seen through the defined masking functions.

Always Encrypted

The third major security feature to be introduced in SQL Server 2016 is Always Encrypted. Encryption with SQL Server was previously a (mainly) server-based solution. Databases were either protected with encryption at the database level (the entire database was encrypted) or at the column level (single columns had an encryption algorithm defined). While this encryption was/is fully functional and *safe*, crucial portions of the encryption process (for example, encryption certificates) are stored inside SQL Server. This effectively gave the owner of a SQL Server instance the ability to potentially gain access to this encrypted data—if not directly, there was at least an increased surface area for a potential malicious access attempt. As ever more companies moved into hosted service and cloud solutions (for example, Microsoft Azure), the previous encryption solutions no longer provided the required level of control/security.

Always Encrypted was designed to bridge this security gap by removing the ability of an instance owner to gain access to the encryption components. The entirety of the encryption process was moved outside of SQL Server and resides on the client side. While a similar effect was possible using homebrew solutions, Always Encrypted provides a fully integrated encryption suite into both the .Net Framework and SQL Server. Whenever data is defined as requiring encryption, the data is encrypted within the .NET framework and only sent to SQL Server after encryption has occurred. This means that a malicious user (or even system administrator) will only ever be able to access encrypted information should they attempt to query data stored via Always Encrypted.

Microsoft has made some positive progress in this area of the product. While no system is completely safe and no single feature can provide an all-encompassing solution, all three features provide a further option in building up, or improving upon, any system's current security level.

Engine features

The Engine features section is traditionally the most important, or interesting, for most DBAs or system administrators when a new version of SQL Server is released. However, there are also numerous engine feature improvements that have tangential meanings for developers too. So, if you are a developer, don't skip this section—or you may miss some improvements that could save you some trouble later on!

Query Store

The Query Store is possibly the biggest new engine feature to come with the release of SQL Server 2016. DBAs and developers should be more than familiar with the situation of a query behaving reliably for a long period, which suddenly changed into a slow-running, resource-killing monster. Some readers may identify the cause of the issue as the phenomenon of *parameter sniffing* or similarly through *stale statistics*. Either way, when troubleshooting to find out why one unchanging query suddenly becomes slow, knowing the query execution plan(s) that SQL Server has created and used can be very helpful. A major issue when investigating these types of problems is the transient nature of query plans and their execution statistics. This is where Query Store comes into play; SQL Server collects and permanently stores information on query compilation and execution on a per-database basis. This information is then persisted inside each database that is being **monitored** by the Query Store functionality, allowing a DBA or developer to investigate performance issues after the fact.

It is even possible to perform longer-term query analysis, providing an insight into how query execution plans change over a longer time frame. This sort of insight was previously only possible via handwritten solutions or third-party monitoring solutions, which may still not allow the same insights as the Query Store does.

Live query statistics

When we are developing inside SQL Server, each developer creates a mental model of how data flows inside SQL Server. Microsoft has provided a multitude of ways to display this concept when working with query execution. The most obvious visual aid is the graphical execution plan. There are endless explanations in books, articles, and training seminars that attempt to make *reading* these graphical representations easier. Depending upon how your mind works, these descriptions can help or hinder your ability to understand the data flow concepts—fully blocking iterators, pipeline iterators, semi-blocking iterators, nested loop joins... the list goes on. When we look at an actual graphical execution plan, we are seeing a representation of how SQL Server processed a query: which data retrieval methods were used, which join types were chosen to join multiple data sets, what sorting was required, and so on. However, this is a representation after the query has completed execution. Live Query Statistics offers us the ability to observe during query execution and identify how, when, and where data moves through the query plan. This live representation is a huge improvement in making the concepts behind query execution clearer and is a great tool to allow developers to better design their query and index strategies to improve query performance.

 Further details of Live Query Statistics can be found in `Chapter 2`, *SQL Server Tools*.

Stretch Database

Microsoft has worked a lot in the past few years on their Mobile First, Cloud First strategy. We have seen a huge investment in their cloud offering, Azure, with the line between on-premises IT and cloud-based IT being continually blurred. The features being released in the newest products from Microsoft continue this approach and SQL Server is taking steps to bridge the divide between running SQL Server as a fully on-premises solution and storing/processing relational data in the cloud.

One big step in achieving this approach is the new Stretch Database feature with SQL Server 2016. Stretch Database allows a DBA to categorize the data inside a database, defining which data is *hot* and which is *cold*. This categorization allows Stretch Database to then move the *cold* data out of the on-premises database and into Azure Cloud Storage.

The segmentation of data remains transparent to any user/application that queries the data, which now resides in two different locations. The idea behind this technology is to reduce storage requirements for the on-premises system by offloading large amounts of archive data onto cheaper, slower storage in the cloud.

This reduction should then allow the smaller *hot* data to be placed on smaller capacity, higher performance storage. The *magic* of Stretch Database is the fact that this separation of data requires no changes at the application or database query level. This is a purely storage-level change, which means the potential ROI of segmenting a database is quite large.

 Further details of Stretch Database can be found in `Chapter 4`, *Stretch Database*.

Database scoped configuration

Many DBAs who support multiple third-party applications running on SQL Server can experience the difficulty of setting up their SQL Server instances per the application requirements or best practices. Many third-party applications have prerequisites that dictate how the actual instance of SQL Server must be configured. A common occurrence is a requirement of configuring the *Max Degree of Parallelism* to force only one CPU to be used for query execution. As this is an instance-wide setting, this can affect all other databases/applications in a multi-tenant SQL Server instance (which is generally the case). With Database Scoped Configuration in SQL Server 2016, several previously instance-level settings have been moved to a database-level configuration option. This greatly improves multi-tenant SQL Server instances, as the decision of, for example, how many CPUs can be used for query execution can be made at the database-level, rather than for the entire instance. This will allow DBAs to host databases with differing CPU usage requirements on the same instance, rather than having to either impact the entire instance with a setting or be forced to run multiple instances of SQL Server and possibly incur higher licensing costs.

Temporal Tables

There are many instances where DBAs or developers are required to implement a change tracking solution, allowing future analysis or assessment of data changes for certain business entities. A readily accessible example is the change in history on a customer account in a CRM system. The options for implementing such a change tracking system are varied and have strengths and weaknesses. One such implementation that has seen wide adoption is the use of triggers, to capture data changes and store historical values in an archive table. Regardless of the implementation chosen, it was often cumbersome to be able to develop and maintain these solutions.

One of the challenges was in being able to incorporate table structure changes in the table being tracked. It was equally challenging creating solutions to allow for querying both the base table and the archive table belonging to it. The intelligence of deciding whether to query the *live* and/or *archive* data can require some complex query logic.

With the advent of Temporal Tables, this entire process has been simplified for both developers and DBAs. It is now possible to activate this *change tracking* on a table and push changes into an archive table with a simple change on a table's structure. Querying the base table and including a temporal attribute to the query is also a simple T-SQL syntax addition. As such, it is now possible for a developer to submit temporal analysis queries, and SQL Server takes care of splitting the query between the live and archive data and returning the data in a single result set.

 Further details of Temporal Tables can be found in Chapter 5, *Temporal Tables*.

Columnstore indexes

Traditional data storage inside SQL Server has used the row-storage format, where the data for an entire row is stored together on the data pages inside the database. SQL Server 2012 introduced a new storage format: columnstore. This format *pivots* the data storage, combining the data from a single column and storing the data together on the data pages. This storage format provides the ability of massive compression of data; it's orders of magnitude better than traditional row storage.

Initially, only non-clustered columnstore indexes were possible. With SQL Server 2014, clustered columnstore indexes were introduced, expanding the usability of the feature greatly. Finally, with SQL Server 2016, updateable columnstore indexes and support for In-Memory columnstore indexes have been introduced. The potential performance improvements through these improvements are huge.

 Further details of columnstore indexes can be found in `Chapter 6`, *Columnstore Indexes*.

Containers and SQL Server on Linux

For the longest time, SQL Server has run solely on the Windows operating system. This was a major roadblock for adoption in traditionally Unix/Linux based companies that used alternative RDBM systems instead. Containers have been around in IT for over a decade and have made a major impression in the application development world. The ability to now host SQL Server in a container provides developers with the ability to adopt the development and deployment methodologies associated with containers into database development. A second major breakthrough (and surprise) around SQL Server 2017 was the announcement of SQL Server being **ported** to Linux. The IT world was shocked at this revelation and what it meant for the other RDBM systems on the market. There is practically no other system with the same feature-set and support network available at the same price point. As such, SQL Server on Linux will open a new market and allow for growth in previously unreachable areas of the IT world.

This concludes the section outlining the engine features. Through Microsoft's heavy move into cloud computing and their Azure offerings, they have had increased need to improve their internal systems for themselves. Microsoft has been famous for its *dogfooding* approach of using their own software to run their own business and Azure is arguably their largest foray into this area. The main improvements in the database engine have been fueled by the need to improve their own ability to continue offering Azure database solutions at a scale and provide features to allow databases of differing sizes and loads to be hosted together.

Programming

Without programming, a SQL Server isn't very useful. The programming landscape of SQL Server has continued to improve to adopt newer technologies over the years. SQL Server 2017 is no exception in this area. There have been some long-awaited general improvements and also some rather revolutionary additions to the product that changes the way SQL Server can be used in future projects. This section will outline what programming improvements have been included in SQL Server 2017.

Transact-SQL enhancements

The last major improvements in the T-SQL language allowed for better processing of running totals and other similar window functions. This was already a boon and allowed developers to replace arcane cursors with high-performance T-SQL. These improvements are never enough for the most performance conscious developers among us, and as such there were still voices requesting further incorporation of the ANSI SQL standards into the T-SQL implementation.

Notable additions to the T-SQL syntax include the ability to finally split comma-separated strings using a single function call, `STRING_SPLIT()`, instead of the previous *hacky* implementations using loops or the **Common Language Runtime (CLR)**.

The sensible opposing syntax for splitting strings is a function to aggregate values together, `STRING_AGG()`, which returns a set of values in a comma-separated string. This replaces similarly *hacky* solutions using the XML data type of one of a multitude of looping solutions.

Each improvement in the T-SQL language further extends the toolbox that we, as developers, possess to be able to manipulate data inside SQL Server. The ANSI SQL standards provide a solid basis to work from and further additions of these standards are always welcome.

JSON

It is quite common to meet developers outside of the Microsoft stack who look down on products from Redmond. Web developers, in particular, have been critical of the access to *modern* data exchange structures, or rather the lack of it. JSON has become the de facto data exchange method for the application development world. It is similar in structure to the previous *cool-kid* XML, but for reasons beyond the scope of this book, JSON has overtaken XML and is the expected payload for application and database communications.

Microsoft has included JSON as a native data type in SQL Server 2016 and provided a set of functions to accompany the data type.

 Further details of JSON can be found in `Chapter 3`, *JSON Support in SQL Server*.

In-Memory OLTP

In-Memory OLTP (codename Hekaton) was introduced in SQL Server 2014. The promise of ultra-high performance data processing inside SQL Server was a major feature when SQL Server 2014 was released. As expected with version-1 features, there were a wide range of limitations in the initial release and this prevented many customers from being able to adopt the technology. With SQL Server 2017, a great number of these limitations have been either raised to a higher threshold or completely removed. In-Memory OLTP has received the required maturity and extension in feature set to make it viable for prime production deployment.

SQL Server Tools

Accessing or managing data inside SQL Server and developing data solutions are two separate disciplines, each with their own specific focus on SQL Server. As such, Microsoft has created two different tools, each tailored towards the processes and facets of these disciplines.

SQL Server Management Studio (SSMS), as the name suggests, is the main management interface between DBAs/developers and SQL Server. The studio was originally released with SQL Server 2005 as a replacement and consolidation of the old Query Analyzer and Enterprise Manager tools. As with any non-revenue-generating software, SSMS only received minimal attention over the years, with limitations and missing tooling for many of the newer features in SQL Server. With SQL Server 2016, the focus of Microsoft has shifted and SSMS has been de-coupled from the release cycle of SQL Server itself. This decoupling allows both SSMS and SQL Server to be developed without having to wait for each other or for release windows. New releases of SSMS are created on top of more recent versions of Visual Studio and have seen almost monthly update releases since SQL Server 2016 was released into the market.

SQL Server Data Tools (SSDT) is also an application based on the Visual Studio framework. SSDT is focused on the application/data development discipline. SSDT is much more closely aligned with Visual Studio in its structure and the features offered. This focus includes the ability to create entire database projects and solution files, easier integration into source control systems, the ability to connect projects into automated build processes, and generally offering a developer-centric development environment with a familiarity with Visual Studio. It is possible to design and create solutions in SSDT for SQL Server using the Relational Engine, Analysis Services, Integration Services, Reporting Services, and of course the Azure SQL database.

> Further details of SQL Server Tools can be found in Chapter 2, *SQL Server Tools*.

This concludes the overview of programming enhancements inside SQL Server 2016. The improvements outlined are all solid evolutionary steps in their respective areas. New features are very welcome and allow us to achieve more while requiring less effort on our side. The In-memory OLTP enhancements are especially positive, as they now expand on the groundwork laid down in the release of SQL Server 2014. Please read the respective chapters to gain deeper insight into how these enhancements can help you.

Business intelligence

Business intelligence is a huge area of IT and has been a cornerstone of the SQL Server product since at least SQL Server 2005. As the market and technologies in the business intelligence space improve, so must SQL Server. The advent of cloud-based data analysis systems as well as the recent buzz around *big data* are driving forces for all data platform providers, and Microsoft is no exception here. While there are multiple enhancements in the business intelligence portion of SQL Server 2016, we will be concentrating on the feature that has a wider audience than just data analysts: the R language in SQL Server.

R in SQL server

Data analytics has been the hottest topic in IT for the past few years, with new niches being crowned as the pinnacles of information science almost as fast as technology can progress. However, IT does have a few resolute *classics* that have stood the test of time and are still in widespread use. SQL (in its many permutations) is a language we are well aware of in the SQL Server world. Another such language is the succinctly titled **R**. The R language is a data mining, machine learning, and statistical analysis language that has existed since 1993.

Many professionals such as data scientists, data analysts, or statisticians have been using the R language and tools that belong in that domain for a similarly long time. Microsoft has identified that although they may want all of the world's data inside SQL Server, this is just not feasible or sensible. External data sources and languages like R exist and they need to be accessible in an integrated manner.

For this to work, Microsoft made the decision to purchase Revolution Analytics (a commercial entity producing the forked *Revolution R*) in 2015 and was then able to integrate the language and server process into SQL Server 2016. This integration allows a *normal* T-SQL developer to interact with the extremely powerful R service in a native manner and allows more advanced data analysis to be performed on their data.

Release cycles

Microsoft has made a few major public-facing changes in the past 5 years. These changes include a departure from longer release cycles in their main products and a transition towards subscription-based services (for example, Office 365 and Azure services). The ideas surrounding continuous delivery and agile software development have also shaped the way that Microsoft has been delivering on its flagship integrated development environment Visual Studio, with releases occurring approximately every six months. This change in philosophy is now flowing into the development cycle of SQL Server. Due to the similarly constant release cycle of the cloud version of SQL Server (Azure SQL Database), there is a desire to keep both the cloud and on-premises versions of the product as close to each other as possible. As such, it is unsurprising to see that the previous release cycle of every three to 5 years is being replaced with much shorter intervals. A clear example of this is that SQL Server 2016 released to the market in June of 2016, with a **Community Technology Preview (CTP)** of SQL Server 2017 being released in November of 2016 and the **Release To Market (RTM)** of SQL Server 2017 happening in October 2017. The wave of technology progress stops for no one. This is very clearly true in the case of SQL Server!

Summary

In this introductory chapter, we saw a brief outline of what will be covered in this book. Each version of SQL Server has hundreds of improvements and enhancements, both through new features and through extensions on previous versions. The outlines for each chapter provide an insight into the main topics covered in this book and allow you to identify which areas you may like to dive into and where to find them.

So let's get going with the rest of the book and see what SQL Server 2017 has to offer.

2
SQL Server Tools

As developers, we are accustomed to using **Integrated Development Environments (IDEs)** in our software projects. Visual Studio has been a major player in the IDE space for many years, if not decades, and it has allowed developers to use the latest software development processes to further improve quality and efficiency in software projects. Server management, on the other hand, has generally been a second-class citizen for many products in the past. In general, this fact can be understood, if not agreed with. IDEs are tools that design and create software that can generate revenue for a business, whereas management tools generally only offer the benefit of some sort of cost-saving, rather than direct revenue generation.

The SQL Server Tools of the past (pre-SQL 2005) were very much focused on fulfilling the requirements of being able to manage and query SQL Server instances and databases but received no great investments in making the tools *comfortable* or even enjoyable to use. Advanced IDEs were firmly in the application development domain and application developers know that databases are a storage system at best and therefore require no elegant tooling to be worked with.

Luckily for us, the advent of SQL Server 2005, along with the release of the .NET Framework, encouraged some people at Microsoft to invest a little more time and resources in providing an improved interface for both developers and DBAs for database and data management purposes. The **SQL Server Management Studio (SSMS)** was born and unified the functionality of two legacy tools: **Query Analyzer** and **Enterprise Manager**. Anyone who has worked with SQL Server since the 2005 release will recognize the application regardless of whether they are using the 2005 release or the latest 2016 build.

There have been several different names and releases of the second tool in this chapter, **SQL Server Data Tools (SSDT)**, going back to SQL Server 2005/2008 where the tool was known under the name **Visual Studio Database Projects** (that is, **Data Dude**). The many incarnations of this tool since SQL Server 2005 have been focused on the development of database projects. The SSDT has many of the tools and interfaces known to Visual Studio users and allows a seasoned Visual Studio user to quickly familiarize themselves with the tool. Particularly interesting is the improved ability to integrate database and business intelligence projects into source control and continuous integration and automated deployment processes.

In this chapter, we will be exploring:

- Installing and updating SQL Server Tools
- New SSMS features and enhancements
- SQL Server Data Tools
- Tools for developing R and Python code

Installing and updating SQL Server Tools

The very beginning of our journey with SQL Server is the installation process. In previous versions of SQL Server, the data management and development tools were delivered together with the SQL Server installation image. As such, if a developer wanted to install SSMS, the setup of SQL Server had to be used to facilitate the installation.

As of SQL Server 2016, Microsoft made the very smart decision to separate the management tools from the server installation. This is not only a separation of the installation medium but also a separation of the release process. This separation means that both products can be developed and released without having to wait for the other team to be ready. Let's take a look at how this change affects us at installation time.

In the following screenshot, given as follows, we see the **SQL Server Installation Center** screen. This is the first screen we will encounter when running the `SQL Server setup.exe` shown in the installation screenshot. After choosing the **Installation** menu point on the left, we are confronted with the generic installation options of SQL Server, which have only minimally changed in the last releases. The second and third options presented on this screen are **Install SQL Server Management Tools** and **Install SQL Server Data Tools**. If we read the descriptions of these options, we note that both links will redirect us to the **Downloads** page for either SSMS or SSDT. This is the first clear indication that the delivery of these tools has now been decoupled from the server installation:

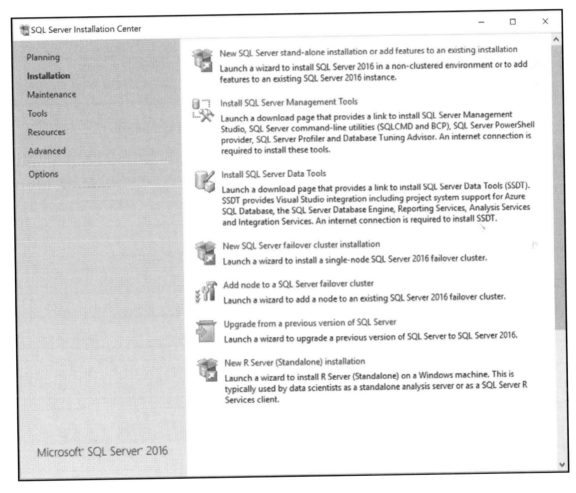

SQL Server Installation Center

After clicking **Install SQL Server Management Studio**, you should be redirected to the **Downloads** page, which should look like the following screenshot:

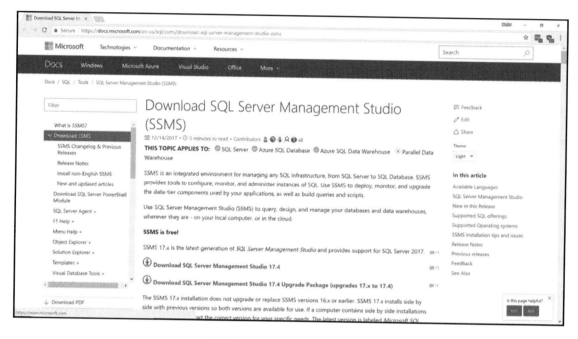

SQL Server Management Studio download page

The **Downloads** page offers us the latest production version of SSMS on the main page, together with any upgrade packages for previous versions of the software. We are also able to see details on the current release and view, download previous releases, and find information on change logs and release notes on the left of the web page:

RELEASE 16.5.1
Microsoft SQL Server Management Studio

Welcome. Click "Install" to begin.

By clicking the "Install" button, I acknowledge that I accept the License Terms and Privacy Statement.

SQL Server Management Studio transmits information about your installation experience, as well as other usage and performance data, to Microsoft to help improve the product. To learn more about SQL Server Management Studio data processing and privacy controls, see the privacy statement link above.

Install   Close

SQL Server Management Studio setup dialogue

After downloading the desired version of SSMS, we can run the installation just the same way as with previous versions of the tool. The next immediately noticeable difference to previous versions is the installation program itself. SSMS 2016.x and higher is based on Visual Studio 2015 Isolated Shell, and as such uses similar color schemes and iconography to Visual Studio 2015.

Once the installation has completed, we can start SSMS and are greeted with a familiar starting screen as in all previous versions of SSMS. The subtle differences in the application is exactly that, subtle. The splash-screen at application start shows that the SSMS is now *powered by Visual Studio*; otherwise there are no major indications that we are working with a tool based on Visual Studio. The interface may feel familiar, but the menus and options available are solely concentrated on working with SQL Server.

Previously, SQL Server and the SQL Server Tools were packaged together. This led to bug fixes and featured additions to the tools having to be bundled with **Cumulative Updates (CU)** and **Service Packs (SP)**, or general version releases of the SQL Server product.

Through the decoupling of the applications SSMS and SSDT from SQL Server, we no longer have to wait for CUs and SPs, or version releases of SQL Server, before we can receive the required/requested features and fixes for SSMS and SSDT. The SQL Server Tools team has taken immediate advantage of this and has made regular releases for both SSMS and SSDT since the general release of SQL Server 2016. The initial release of SSMS 2016.x was in June 2016 and there have been subsequent update releases in July 2016, August 2016, September 2016, and December 2016. The change to version 17.x followed in 2017 and the releases were less rapid, as the port from SQL Server releases and integration into the Visual Studio 2015 shell matured and the preparations for the release of SQL Server 2017 were ramping up. Each release has included a range of bug fixes and featured additions which are much more rapidly deployable when compared to the previous versions of SQL Server and SSMS.

A further advantage of the separation of the data tools from the server product is the reduced overhead of managing the installation and updating the tools in a network. The process of updating an already installed SSMS installation is demonstrated in the following screenshot, where we see that a **Check for Updates** option has been included in the **Tools** menu of SSMS:

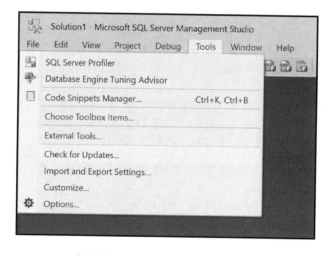

Checking for updates in SQL Server Management Studio

Further to this, the separation of the tools as a standalone installer will reduce the administrative overhead in larger organizations where software is deployed using centralized management software. Where previously the larger ISO image of an SQL Server installation was required, now a smaller standalone installer is available for distribution.

We also have the option to request that SSMS automatically checks for updates at application start. This will create a notification balloon message in Windows if a new version is available. A sample notification on a Windows 10 machine can be seen in the following screenshot:

Update notification for SQL Server Management Studio

Once the update check has been opened, SSMS connects to the update systems of Microsoft and performs checks against the currently installed version and the latest downloadable release of the software. If updates have been found, these will be offered using the update mechanism, as shown in the following screenshot. We are also able to decide if the automated update check should be performed or not:

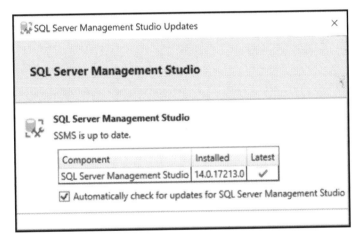

SQL Server Management Studio Update Checker

These enhancements to the installation and update process are not mind-blowing, especially considering that these features have been available in other products for years or even decades. However, these are the first main improvements that have to do with the switch from a standalone application to an application based on the extremely successful Visual Studio Framework.

New SSMS features and enhancements

As we saw with the installation process, there are already a few enhancements in the installation and updating process for SSMS. Through the migration of the SSMS application to the Visual Studio 2015 Isolated Shell, there are a number of additions into SSMS that will be familiar to application developers that use Visual Studio 2015 (or one of its derivatives). While some of these are simple improvements, these additions can be of help to many SQL developers who have been isolated inside SSMS 16.x and higher.

Autosave open tabs

The first improvement is the option to choose whether SSMS should prompt to save unsaved tabs when you decide to close SSMS. This is a simple change, but if you use SSMS to run many ad hoc queries and do not want to constantly close out and save each tab, this is now an option. The default is for SSMS to prompt when closing a window, but by unchecking the checkbox marked as shown in the following screenshot you can force SSMS to silently close these windows:

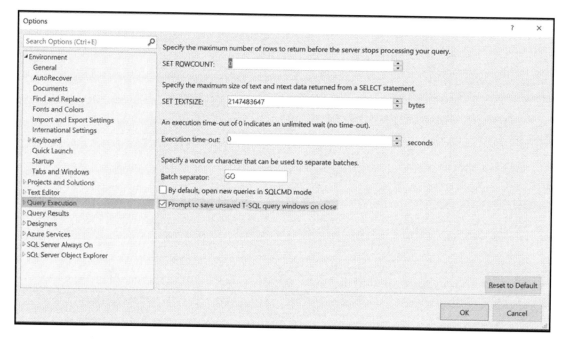

Options window in SQL Server Management Studio—prompt to save unsaved work

Searchable options

The next usability or productivity enhancement comes with the Visual Studio 2015 Isolated Shell features. The **Options** menu inside Visual Studio, and SSMS, are jam-packed with features and functionalities that can be configured. Unfortunately, these options are so numerous that it can be difficult to navigate and find the option you are interested in. To aid us in the search for the settings we are interested in, we are now able to quickly search and filter in the **Options** menu. The following screenshot explains the ability to quickly search through the options for settings using text search without having to memorize where the settings are hidden. Go to **Tools** | **Options** and you are then able to type your search string in the textbox in the top-left of the **Options** window. In the following screenshot, the search term execution has been entered, the results filtered as the word is typed into the search form:

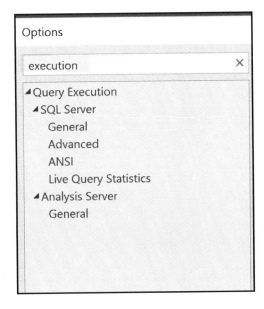

Options window—search/filter

Enhanced scroll bar

A further improvement that will be used on a much more regular basis is the enhanced scroll bar in the **T-SQL editor** tab. In the following screenshot, we can see an example of a T-SQL stored procedure that has been opened for editing:

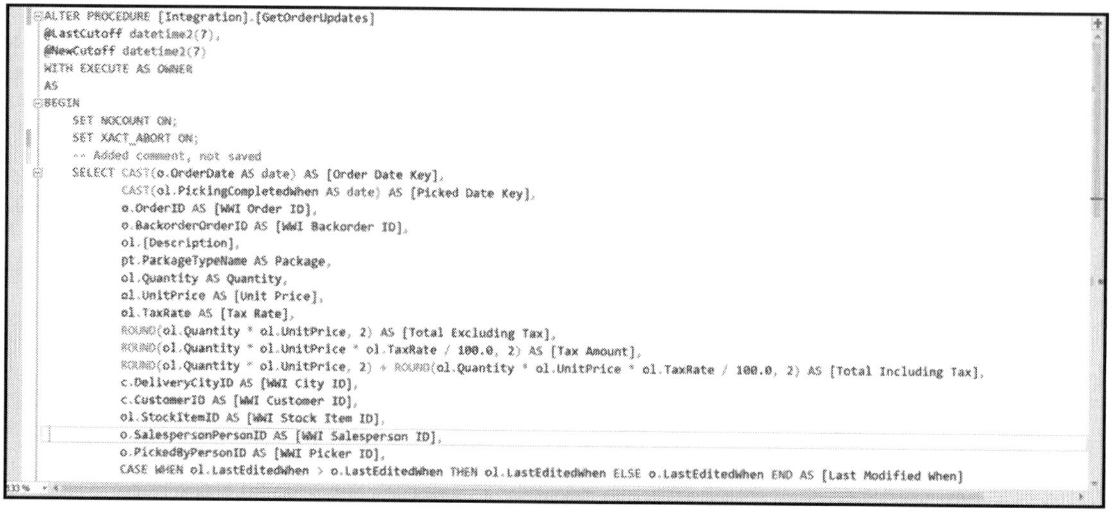

SQL Server Management Studio scroll bar enhancements

The main points to pay attention to are: the margin on the left-hand side of the screen and the scroll bar on the right-hand side of Management Studio. The enhancement here allows us to easily identify a few details in our script window, namely:

- **Green blocks** show changes made in the editor have been saved to the file currently being edited
- **Yellow blocks** show changes that have not yet been saved
- **Red blocks** show code that is invalid or has syntax errors (native IntelliSense must be enabled for this feature to work)
- The **blue marker** on the scroll bar shows the location of the cursor

These subtle changes are further examples of the Visual Studio base providing us with further enhancements to make working inside SSMS easier. Knowing what code has been changed or is defective at a syntax level allows us to quickly navigate through our code inside SSMS.

Execution plan comparison

Refactoring and improving the performance of code is a regular occurrence in the working day of a developer. Being able to identify if a particular query refactoring has helped improve an execution plan can sometimes be difficult. To help us identify plan changes, SSMS 16.x and higher now offers the option to compare execution plans.

By saving the execution plan and the T-SQL of our initial query as a `.sqlplan` file, we can then run our redesigned query and compare the two plans. In the following screenshot we see how to initiate a plan comparison:

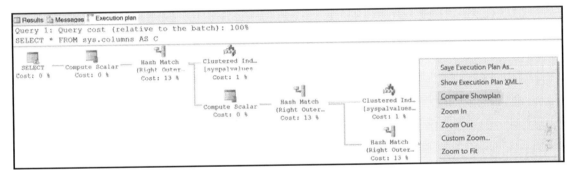

Activating a plan comparison session

Upon activation, we must choose which `.sqlplan` file we would like to use for the comparison session. The two execution plans are loaded into a separate **Compare Showplan** tab in SSMS and we can evaluate how the plans differ or how they are similar. In the following screenshot we see a plan comparison where there are only slight differences between the plans:

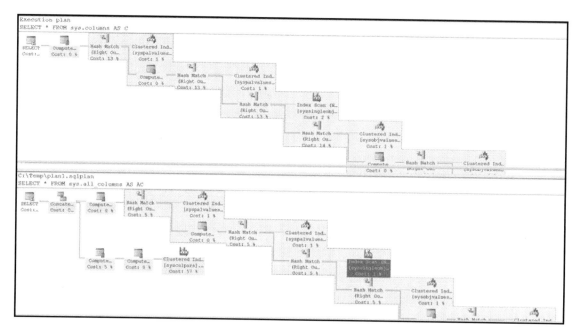

Showplan comparison tab

The nodes of the execution plans in the preceding screenshot that are similar have a red background, while nodes that are different have a yellow background.

If we click the nodes inside one of the plans, the matching node in the comparison plan will be highlighted and we can then investigate how they are similar and how they differ.

Once we have chosen the node in our execution plan, we will be able to view the properties of the node we wish to compare, similar to the details shown as follows:

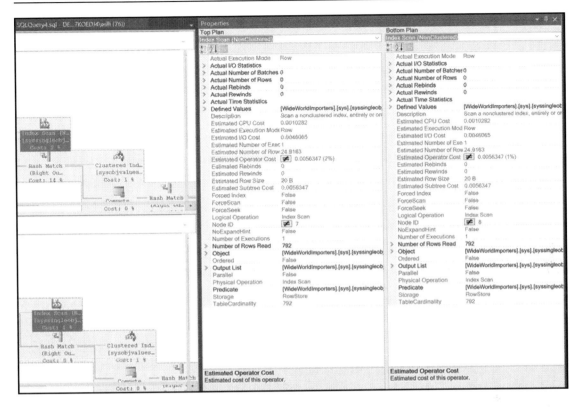

Showplan comparison—node properties

The **Properties** tab shows clearly which parts of the node are different. In the preceding screenshot we can ignore the lower inequality, which is stating the Node ID is different; this will occur wherever our query has a slightly changed plan. Of interest in this case is the **Estimated Operator Cost** property, which is showing a difference. This example is very simple and the differences are minimal, but we are able to identify differences in a very similar plan with a few simple clicks. This sort of support is invaluable and a huge time saver, especially where plans are larger and more complex.

Live query statistics

Following on from the plan comparison feature, we have one of the more powerful features for a developer. **Live Query Statistics (LQS)** does exactly what the name says—it provides us with a live view of a query execution so that we can see exactly how data is flowing through the query plan. In previous versions of SQL Server and SSMS we have been able to request a static graphical representation of a query execution plan. There have been multiple books, blogposts, videos, and training seminars designed and delivered to thousands of developers and DBAs around the world in an attempt to improve people's abilities to understand these static execution plans. The ability of a developer to read and interpret the contents of these plans rests largely on these resources. With LQS we have an additional tool at our disposal to be able to more easily identify how SQL Server is consuming and processing the T-SQL query that we have submitted to it.

The *special sauce* in LQS is that we don't get a static graphical representation, but rather an animation of the execution. The execution plan is displayed in SSMS and the arrows between the plan nodes move to show the data flowing between the nodes. In the following screenshot we see how to activate LQS inside SSMS for a particular **Query** tab:

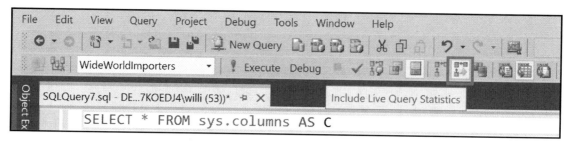

Activating Live Query Statistics

As LQS shows a moving image, we are at a distinct disadvantage in a book! However, when we run a query with LQS activated, it is still possible to see an example of how LQS looks while running, as we can see in the following screenshot:

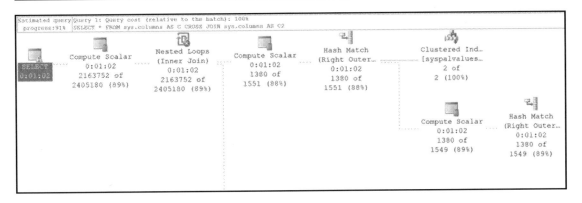

Live Query Statistics—query execution

In the preceding screenshot, we can see that the execution plan image that we are used to has been extended slightly. We now see a few extra details. Starting in the top left of this image, we see the **Estimated query progress** in percent. As with anything to do with query execution and statistics, SQL Server is always working with estimations. Estimations that are based on table and index statistics, which is a topic worthy of an entire book! We also see an execution time displayed beneath each node that is still actively processing data. Also, beneath each node is a display of how many rows are still left to be processed (these are also based on estimations through statistics). Finally, we see the arrows connecting each node; solid lines are where execution has completed, dotted lines (which also move during execution) show where data is still flowing and being processed.

You can try out the same query shown in the preceding screenshot and see how LQS looks. This is a long-running query against `sys.objects` to produce a large enough result set that LQS has time to capture execution information. The following code shows a sample query function:

```
SELECT * FROM
SYS.OBJECTS AS o1
CROSS JOIN sys.objects AS o2
CROSS JOIN sys.objects AS o3
```

This sample query should run long enough to allow LQS to display an animated query plan long enough to understand how LQS makes a query plan easier to understand. It should also be clear that LQS can only display a useful animation for queries that run longer than a few seconds, as the animation only runs for the duration of the query.

This moving display of data flow allows us as developers to understand how SQL Server is processing our query. We are able to get a better insight into where execution is spending the most time and resources and also where we may need to consider rewriting a query or applying different indexing to achieve better results. LQS, coupled with query plan comparisons, will allow us as developers to design better database solutions and better understand how SQL Server processes our queries. In particular, how SQL Server must wait for certain nodes in an execution plan to complete before continuing onto the next node.

However, we must not forget that running LQS is similar to running a trace, and it requires a certain set of permissions and also consumes resources on the server. We should be approaching our queries with LQS at a development stage and attempting to write optimal code before we deploy into production. LQS should therefore be used primarily in your development work on a test environment and *not* on your production environment.

Importing flat file Wizard

SSMS was designed to make regular tasks of DBAs and developers easier. Wizards were built for many different tasks to guide users to a quicker solution. There was one area that remained frustrating: the simple task of importing a flat file (CSV or TXT file). This seemingly basic functionality was mired by a clumsy and irritating **Import and Export Wizard**, which often made the task of importing data *more* difficult rather than easier.

With SSMS 17.3 came some relief! The **Import Flat File Wizard** removes much of the earlier unnecessary complexities of importing flat files into SQL Server. The wizard can be found using a right-click on a desired database name, then under the menu **Tasks**, as shown in the following screenshot:

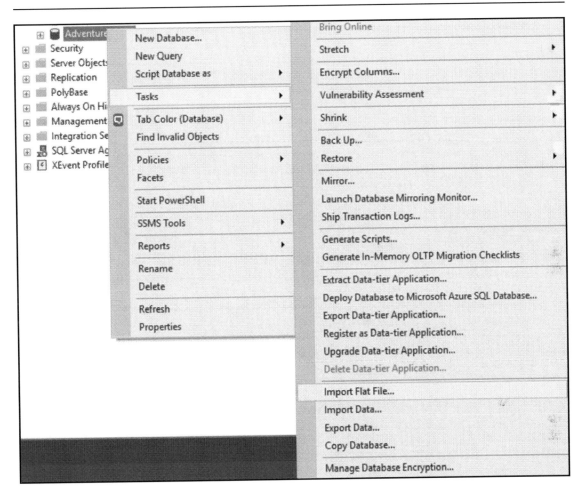

Import Flat File Wizard

The wizard that appears guides the user through a handful of steps to easily import flat files into a target table inside SQL Server.

Now, let's see the steps to import Flat File Wizard:

1. The flat file is chosen from the filesystem, with the wizard automatically suggesting a table name based on the filename. The schema for creating/storing the table must be chosen from the schemas already available in the target database, as shown in the following screenshot:

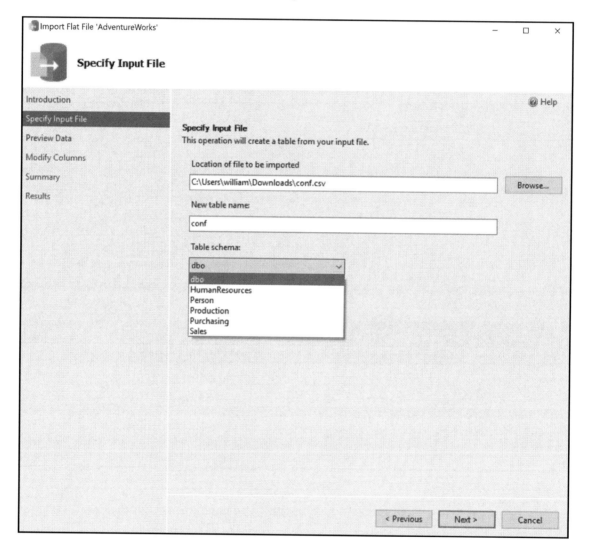

Import Flat File Wizard

2. The next step of the wizard provides a preview of the first 50 rows of data in the flat file. The wizard parses the data and shows the columns that have been identified in the file, as shown in the following screenshot:

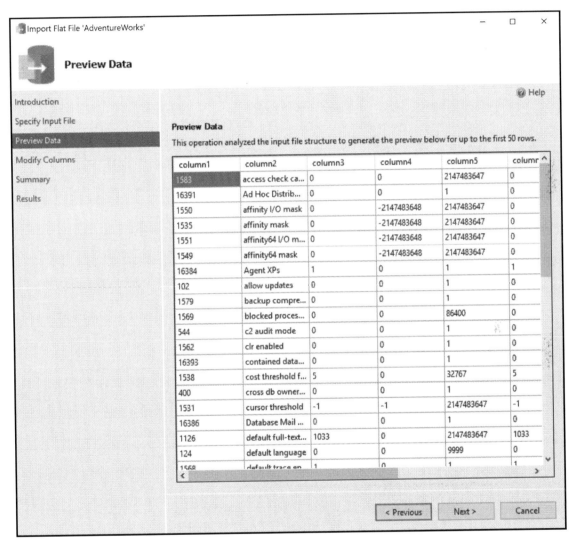

Import Flat File—data preview

3. The data preview shows how the wizard has interpreted the rows and columns; if this analysis is incorrect, the schema of the new target table can be altered in the next step of the wizard, as shown in the following screenshot:

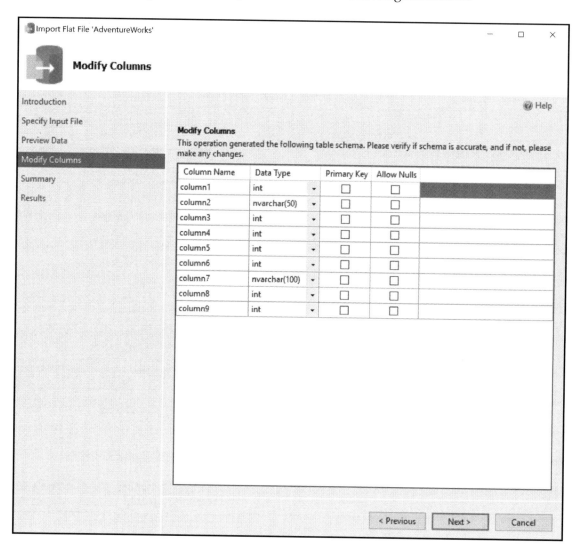

Import Flat File—Modify Columns

Once we are happy with the target schema, the import is summarized and then started by the wizard. The flat file data is rapidly imported into the new table and the import process completes. This is a big step forward from the previous incarnation of an import wizard and should make it easier to import data into SQL Server with much less hassle.

Vulnerability assessment

The regular headlines of security breaches, along with increasing pressure from governments to hold companies accountable for the breaches, are making more developers (and their managers) pay more attention to security in their IT solutions.

Automated code analysis for application code is nothing new, but database code analysis has been behind the curve for many years.

Microsoft introduced the SQL **Vulnerability Assessment (VA)** feature in SSMS 17.4 in December 2017. The idea behind the feature is to easily scan your database(s) for standardized security best practices. The rules of the scan are supplied by Microsoft and (at the time of writing) don't allow for user-designed rules to be implemented. Microsoft states that they are working on multiple improvements, as well as adding to the number of security checks that the tool performs.

In its current state, the tool runs from the SSMS installation and requires no internet connection. The rules that are used for the scan are installed locally to the SSMS installation and are only updated when an update for SSMS is installed.

A vulnerability scan can be performed on any database (including system databases) on any instance from SQL Server 2012 and higher (including Azure SQL Database). The scan is extremely lightweight and generally runs in seconds. The scan is also completely read-only and does not make any changes to a scanned database.

Starting a vulnerability scan is simple. Right-click on a desired database, choose the **Task** menu, and navigate to **Vulnerability Scan**. The options available are to run a new scan or open the report from a previous scan. A scan that is run will store the results in a user-defined location, but it defaults to the user's default documents location. The following screenshot illustrates the process:

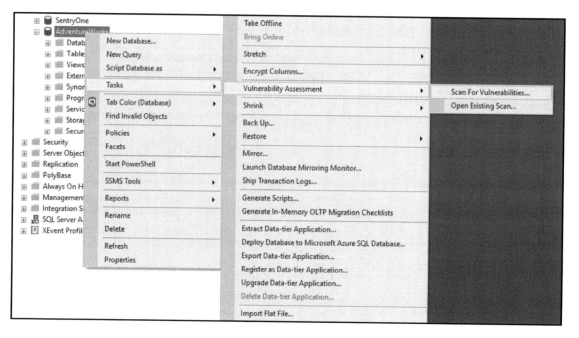

Vulnerability scan

Once a scan is completed, SSMS will automatically open the generated report and display it inside SSMS. At the time of writing, it is not possible to automatically export the results in a different format (for example, Word or Excel). The basis of the report is a JSON file, so any further processing would require waiting for an export functionality from Microsoft or require your ingenuity in parsing the JSON file.

The resulting report displayed in SSMS allows for further analysis of the security threats that may have been found. In the following screenshot, we can see an example scan of an `AdventureWorks` database:

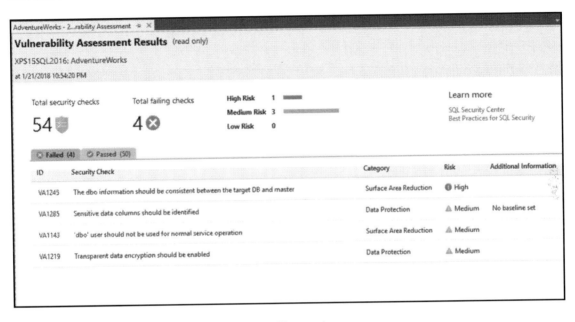

Vulnerability scan results

The scan indicates that the database has passed **50** tests and failed **4**. By clicking on one of the tests we can see more details about the failure/pass.

The following screenshot shows the details of the failed check ID **VA1219**, which states that a database should have **Transparent data encryption** activated:

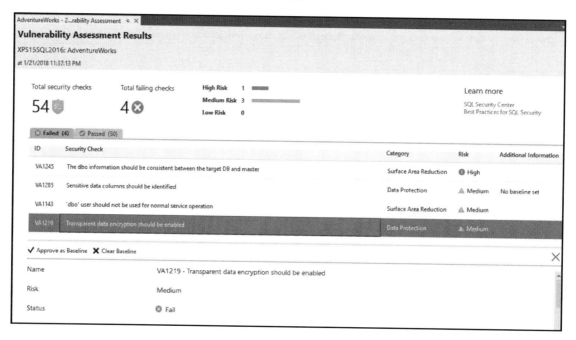

Vulnerability scan—failed TDE

Each check is accompanied with a range of information, including the query that was run against the scanned database. This allows us to see whether the check is correct for our database/environment.

Should a certain check be irrelevant for a database/environment, the **Approve as Baseline** button can be clicked. This will override the check outcome to ensure that a future scan against this database will deem the overridden check to be a pass rather than a failure.

Upon marking the failing TDE check as an acceptable value, a second scan of the AdventureWorks database provides us with **51** passes and **3** failures. The TDE check is now listed as a passing check, with the extra information being set as a custom baseline value. The following screenshot illustrates the baseline:

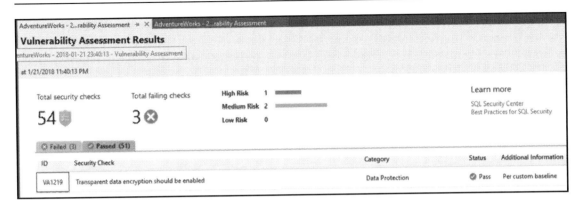

Vulnerability scan custom baseline

The Vulnerability Assessment is by no means a perfect tool, currently *only* covering a limited set of scenarios. It does, however, provide a good start to assessing the security threats inside a database. The tool will continue to receive updates (especially to the rules that are checked against). A further tool to help improve the security of database systems should always be welcomed.

SQL Server Data Tools

As with the installation of SSMS, SQL Server Data Tools is also offered as a separate download. This can be found using the SQL Server setup screen shown at the beginning of the chapter. Clicking on **Install SQL Server Data Tools** will launch a web browser, directing you to the **Downloads** page for SSDT. This **Downloads** page offers the latest stable build and also the latest release candidate of the next version of SSDT (with the usual warning of a release candidate not being production ready). SSDT is delivered with the same Visual Studio Integrated Shell as SSMS, and can be installed as a standalone tool. However, SSDT is aimed at developers and the workflows associated with developing database solutions as a team member. This includes the processes of source control and the packaging of project deployments. With this in mind, it is also possible to install SSDT on a machine that has the full Visual Studio environment installed. Doing so will integrate SSDT into Visual Studio and incorporate the database development templates and workflows, allowing Visual Studio to remain in the development environment, instead of adding a separate environment just for database development.

If Visual Studio is already installed, the SSDTs update can be installed from inside Visual Studio. To download and install this update, navigate to **Tools | Extensions and Updates** and select the node **Updates** on the left side of the **Extensions and Updates** modal window, as shown in the following screenshot:

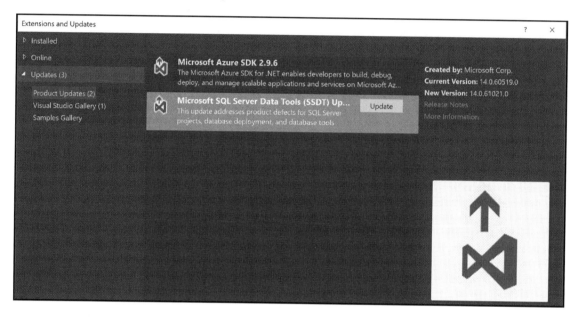

SSDT—extensions and updates

Once installed, SSDT (whether installed as a standalone tool or integrated into Visual Studio) provides four separate project templates to help jump-start development of SQL Server projects:

- **Relational databases**: This is a template designed for traditional relational database development and it supports SQL Server versions 2005 through to 2016 (although SQL Server 2005 is now a deprecated version). SSDT also supports on-premises installations and also Azure SQL Database projects (the Database as a Service solution hosted in Microsoft Azure). It is also possible to design queries (but not full projects) for Azure SQL Data Warehouse (the cloud-based data warehouse solution, hosted in Microsoft Azure).
- **Analysis Services models**: This template is designed to assist in the design and deployment of Analysis Services projects and it supports SQL Server versions 2008 through to 2016.

- **Reporting Services reports**: This template is designed to assist in the design and deployment of Reporting Services projects and it supports SQL Server versions 2008 through to 2016.
- **Integration Services packages**: This template is designed to assist in the design and deployment of Integration Services projects and it supports SQL Server versions 2012 through to 2016.

The template choice dictates what files and folders are automatically prepared at project creation time. Choosing **File | New Project** presents the new project dialogue shown in the following screenshot. There are two additions to the project type navigation tree. **Business Intelligence** groups **Analysis Services**, **Reporting Services**, and **Integration Services** projects together. The relational database project type is found under the **SQL Server** navigation node, as shown in the following screenshot:

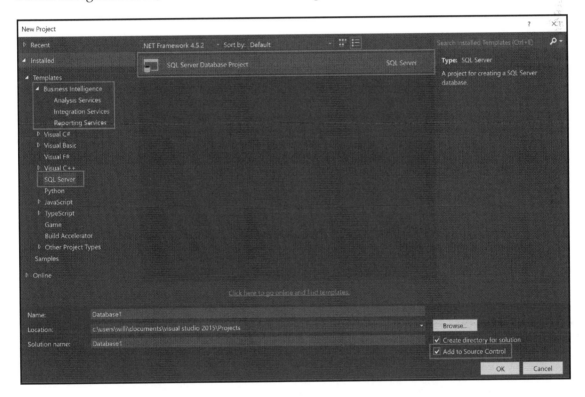

SSDT—new project dialogue

As shown in the preceding screenshot, a project folder is created and the option to add the project to a source control system is available. Visual Studio offers the option to natively access the source control system's Visual Studio Team Services (a hosted source control system from Microsoft) or alternatively to use a local source control system such as Git. Furthermore, source control systems can be added through the extensive extensions library offered through Visual Studio and they can be accessed through the **Tools | Extensions and Updates** menu described earlier in this section.

Working with SSDT and the aforementioned templates should be familiar to any developer that has used Visual Studio before. Upon creating a project, the next step is to begin by adding new items (tables, view, stored procedures, and so on). The dialogue for this is filtered down to the project type, and for an SQL Server database project, we have the option of creating items ranging from Application Roles to XML Schema Collections. Of note is the ability to create **SQL CLR** objects (C# based common language runtime objects), which provide the ability to create more complex calculations that are otherwise not possible (or perform poorly) in the T-SQL language:

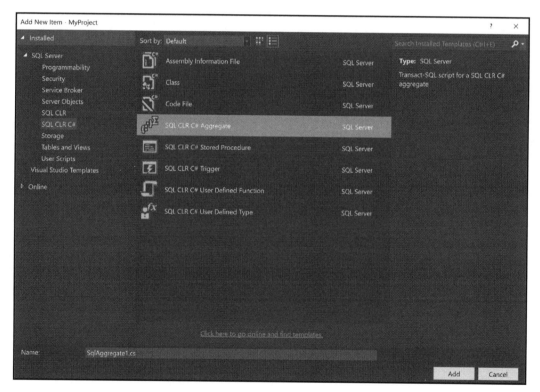

Adding new SQL CLR C# aggregate

The advantages of using SSDT over SSMS for developers is the focus on development workflows and the integrations in the program: source control integration, project structuring, and object templates. This developer focus is further strengthened through the possibility of connecting the source control system to a build system and the option to extend the build system to include **continuous integration/deployment (CI/CD)**. Both automated builds and CI/CD have become ubiquitous in application development circles in the past decade. This area has only seen limited support for database development until now, because databases also permanently store data. Now that application development environments have matured, the ability to introduce CI/CD to database projects has become a reality. Luckily, the foundation for CI/CD has long been laid for application development and so the work to implement CI/CD into a database project is greatly reduced. SSDT is therefore fully capable of integrating SQL Server database projects into a source control system and to extend those projects into automated build, test, and deployment workflows.

There is now a wealth of options to cover CI/CD in the SQL Server world. The tools TeamCity for continuous integration and Octopus Deploy are two products that have been proven to work well in conjunction with SSDT to provide a smooth process for CI/CD in SQL Server projects.

 An interesting and useful website to visit for more information on topics on SSDT is the Microsoft *SQL Server Data Tools Team Blog* at `https://blogs.msdn.microsoft.com/ssdt/`.

Tools for developing R and Python code

As you probably already know, SQL Server 2016 brings the support for the R language, and SQL Server 2017 adds support for the Python language. Of course, you need to have a development tool for the R code. There is a free version of the IDE tool called **RStudio IDE** that has been on the market for quite a long time. This is probably the most popular R tool. In addition, Microsoft is developing **R Tools for Visual Studio (RTVS)**, a plug-in for Visual Studio, which enables you to also develop R code in an IDE that is common and well known among developers that use Microsoft products and languages.

In this section, you will learn about:

- RStudio IDE
- R Tools for Visual Studio
- Using Visual Studio for data science applications

RStudio IDE

The first tool you get to write and execute the R code in is the **R Console**. The console presents the greater than (>) sign as the prompt to the user. In the console, you write commands line by line, and execute them by pressing the *Enter* key. You have some limited editing capabilities in the console. For example, you can use the up and down arrow keys to retrieve the previous or the next command in the buffer. The following screenshot shows the console, with the demo() command executed, which opens an Explorer window with a list of demo packages.

Because R is a functional package, you close the R Console with the q() function call. Anyway, you probably want to use a nicer, graphical environment. Therefore, it is time to introduce the RStudio IDE. The following screenshot shows the R console:

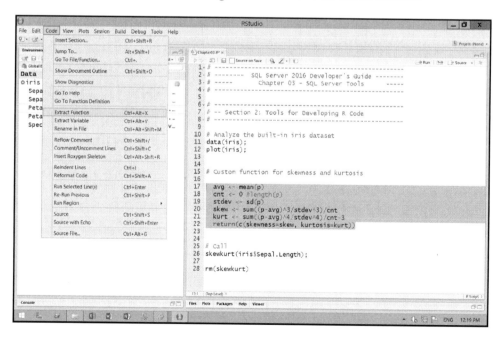

R Console

RStudio is a company that is dedicated to helping the R community with its free and payable products (`https://www.rstudio.com/`). Their most popular product is the RStudio IDE, or as most R developers used to say, just RStudio. RStudio is available in open source and commercial editions, in both cases for desktop computers or for servers `https://www.rstudio.com/products/rstudio/`. The open source desktop edition, which is described in this section, is very suitable for starting developing in R. Already this edition has the majority of features built-in for smooth and efficient coding. This edition is described in this section.

You can download the RStudio IDE from the RStudio company site. The IDE supports Windows, macOS, and Linux. Once you install it, you can open it through a desktop shortcut, which points to the `C:\Program Files\RStudio\bin\rstudio.exe` file, if you used the defaults during the installation.

The RStudio screen is usually split into four panes if you open an R script file, as shown in the following figure.

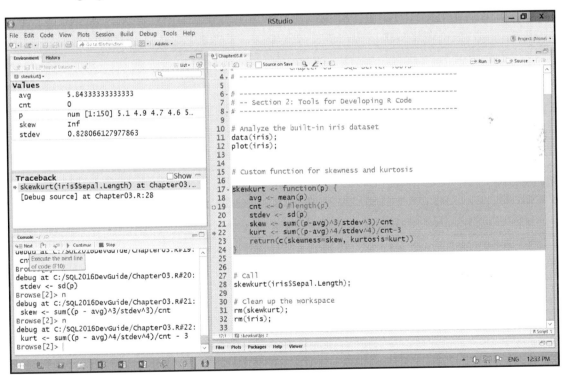

RStudio IDE

The bottom left pane is the **Console** pane. It works similarly to the R Console Command Prompt utility shipped with the R engine. You can write statements and execute them one by one, by pressing the *Enter* key. However, in RStudio, you have many additional keyboard shortcuts available. One of the most important keyboard shortcuts is the *Tab* key, which provides you with the code complete option. You can press the Tab key nearly anywhere in the code. For example, if you press it when you are writing function arguments, it gives you the list of the possible arguments, or if you already started to write a name of an object, all objects that start with the letters you have already written.

The top-left pane is the **Source** pane, the pane that is by default settings used for the R code script; therefore, this is your basic R code editor. Writing R code line by line in a console is simple, but not very efficient for developing a script with thousands of lines. The **Source** pane does not execute your R code line by line. You highlight portions of your code and you execute it by pressing the *Ctrl* and *Enter* keys simultaneously.

The top-right pane is the **Environment** pane. It shows you the objects in your current environment, the objects currently loaded in memory. However, this pane has more than one function. You may notice additional tabs at the top of the pane. By default, you see the **History** tab, the tab that leads you to the **History** pane, where you can see the history of the commands. The history goes beyond the commands in the current session and in the current console or script.

The bottom-right pane is also a multi-purpose pane. It includes the **Help** pane, **Plots** pane, **Files** pane, **Packages** pane, and **Viewer** pane by default. You can use the **Files** tab to check the files you saved in your RStudio account. With the help of the **Packages** tab you can get a list of all R packages you have access to in the current session. The **Help** tab brings you, of course, to R documentation and a help system. You can use the **Viewer** tab to get to the **Viewer** pane where you can see local web content that you can create with some graphical packages. The **Plots** pane shows you the plots you created by executing R code either in the **Console** or in the **Script** pane.

The following screenshot shows you all the four panes in action. You can see the usage of the *Tab* key in the **Source** pane to auto-complete the name of the dataset used in the `plot()` function. The dataset used is the `iris` dataset, a very well-known demo dataset in R. You can see the command echoed in the **Console** pane. The **Environment** pane shows the details about the `iris` dataset that is loaded in memory. The **Plots** pane shows the plots for all of the variables in the demo `iris` dataset:

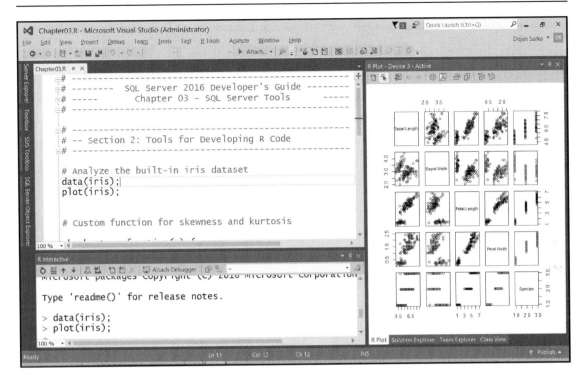

RStudio IDE in action

Note that you can zoom the plot and save it in different graphical formats from the **Plots** pane.

There are literally dozens of keyboard shortcuts. It is impossible to memorize all of them. You memorize them by using them. Nevertheless, you don't need to know all of the shortcuts before you start writing R code. You can always get a quick reference of the keyboard shortcuts by pressing the *Alt*, *Shift*, and *K* keys at the same time. The keyboard **Shortcut Quick Reference** cheat sheet appears, as shown in the following screenshot. You can get rid of this cheat sheet by pressing the *Esc* key.

Please note that, although exhaustive, even this cheat sheet is not complete. In the top-right corner of the cheat sheet you can notice a link to even more shortcuts. Finally, it is worth mentioning that you can modify the pre-defined shortcuts and replace them with your own ones.

You have access to many of the keyboard shortcuts actions through the menus at the top of the RStudio IDE window. For example, in the Tools menu, you can find the link to the keyboard shortcuts cheat sheet. In the Help menu, you can find, besides the help options you would expect, the links to various cheat sheets, for example to the complete RStudio IDE cheat sheet, a PDF document you can download from `https://www.rstudio.com/wp-content/uploads/2016/01/rstudio-IDE-cheatsheet.pdf` at the RStudio site. The following screenshot illustrates the keyboard shortcuts cheat sheet:

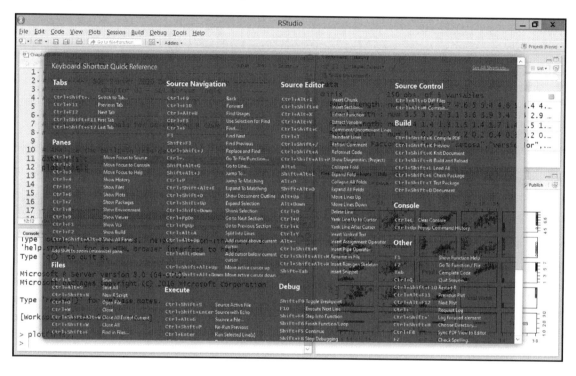

RStudio IDE keyboard shortcuts cheat sheet

Using the **Panes** menu, you can change the default layout of the panes. There are numerous options in the **Code** menu. For example, you can extract a function from the code. Figure *Extracting a function* shows an example where the **Source** pane is enlarged at the right side of the RStudio IDE window to show the path to the **Extract Function** option in the **Code** menu. The highlighted code is calculating the third and the fourth population moments for a continuous variable, the `skewness` and the `kurtosis`, as known from the descriptive statistics. When you extract a function from the code, you need to provide the name for the function, and RStudio extracts the necessary parameters from the code.

If you extract the function with the name **skewkurt** and test it using the `iris` dataset `Sepal.Length` variable, you get an infinite number for both skewness and kurtosis. Apparently, there is a bug in the code (you can see the bug from the inline comments in the code in the following screenshot). Fortunately, RStudio provides a debugger. You can just click at the left border of the **Source** pane at the line where you want the execution to stop, meaning to set a breakpoint at that line. Then you highlight the code and start debugging by clicking the **Source** button at the top right of the **Source** pane, or by using the keyboard shortcut *Ctrl*, *Shift*, and *S*:

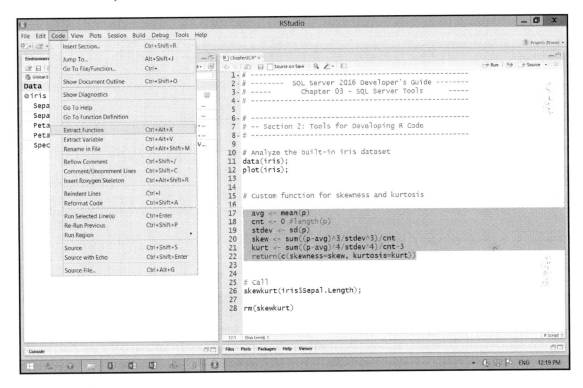

Extracting a function

When you execute the code in the debugging mode, the execution stops at the breakpoint. You can use the buttons in the **Console** pane to execute the code line by line, step into a function, execute the remainder of a function, and more. You can use the Traceback pane to see the full call stack to the code you are currently executing. In the **Environment** pane, you can watch the current values of the objects you are using.

The following screenshot shows a debugging session in RStudio IDE. In the **Source** pane at the right of the window, you can see a breakpoint in **line 19**, near the `cnt <- 0` code. You can see also the line that is just about to execute, in this case **line 22**, with the code `kurt <- sum((p-avg)^4/stdev^4)/cnt-3`. In the **Console** pane at the bottom-left of the screen, you can see the **Next** button highlighted. This button executes the next line of the code. In the middle-left of the screen you can see the **Trackback** pane, and at the top left the **Environment** pane. You can see that the value of the variable `cnt` is 0, and because this variable is used in the denominator when calculating the `skewness`, the skew variable has an infinite value:

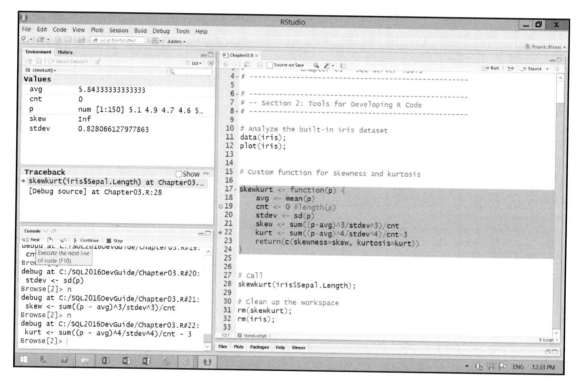

Debugging in RStudio IDE

After you find the error, you can stop debugging either from the **Debug** menu or with the *Shift* and *F8* keyboard shortcut. Correct the code and run it to test it.

R Tools for Visual Studio 2015

Microsoft is developing **RTVS** for those developers that are used to developing code in the most popular Microsoft IDE, Visual Studio. RTVS comes in two versions: as a free download for Visual Studio 2015 and already included in Visual Studio 2017. You can download RTVS for Visual Studio 2015 from `https://www.visualstudio.com/vs/rtvs/`. Visual Studio 2017 is covered in the next section of this chapter.

Once you install the RTVS you open the Visual Studio like you would open it for any other project. Of course, since SSDT is not a separate product-it is just another shortcut to the Visual Studio IDE-you can also open SSDT and get the R Tools menu besides other common Visual Studio menus.

With RTVS, you get most of the useful common panes of the RStudio IDE. You get the **Source** pane, the **Console** pane- which is called **R Interactive** in RTVS-and the **Plots** pane. The following figure shows the RTVS window with the **Source**, **R Interactive**, and the **Plots** pane open, showing the same plots for the variables from the `iris` demo dataset, shown in the figure *RStudio IDE in action* earlier in this section:

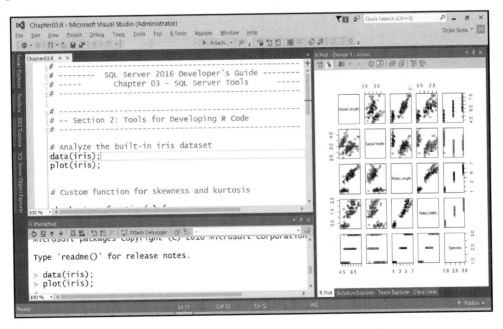

R Tools for Visual Studio

If you are familiar with the Visual Studio IDE, then you might want to test RTVS.

Setting up Visual Studio 2017 for data science applications

Here, Visual Studio 2017 is introduced. You can use either the Professional or free Community Edition (`https://www.visualstudio.com/downloads/`) to develop Python and R code.

When installing Visual Studio 2017, be sure to select Python development workload, and then data science and analytical applications, as the following screenshot shows. This will install Python language templates, including data science templates, and also R Tools for Visual Studio 2017:

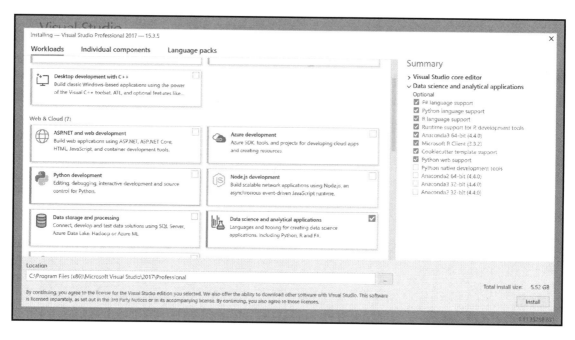

Visual Studio 2017 setup for data science

There you go, you are nearly ready. There is a small trick here. VS 2017 also installs its own Python interpreter. In order to use the scalable one installed with SQL Server, the one that enables executing code in the Database Engine context and includes Microsoft scalable libraries, you need to set up an additional Python environment, pointing to the scalable version of the interpreter. The path for this scalable interpreter is, if you installed the default instance of SQL Server, `C:\Program Files\Microsoft SQL Server\MSSQL14.MSSQLSERVER\PYTHON_SERVICES\python.exe`. You can see how to set up this environment in the following screenshot. Note that there is no need for any additional step for developing R code because VS 2017 also installs the Microsoft R Client, the open R engine that includes the Microsoft scalable libraries:

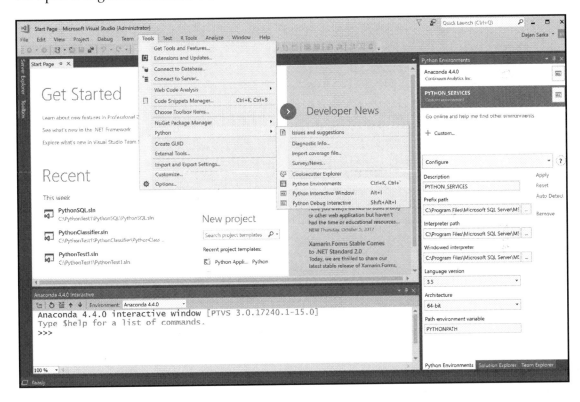

Setting up Python environments

That's it. You are ready to start Python programming. Just start a new project and select the **Python Application** template from the Python folder. You can also explore the **Python Machine Learning** templates, which include **Classifier**, **Clustering**, and **Regression** projects. If you selected the **Python Application** template, you should have open the first empty Python script with a default name, the same as the project name, and the default extension .py, waiting for you to write and interactively execute Python code.

Summary

In this chapter, we have taken a look at the new additions in the developer toolset for SQL Server 2017. There have been some long-awaited improvements made, especially the separation of SQL Server Management Studio from the release cycle of SQL Server itself. The accelerated release cycle of SSMS has brought a breadth of new features and support that will help developers in their daily work with SQL Server.

Some of the featured additions to SSMS are quite powerful and will allow us as developers to be more efficient. Live Query Statistics provides us with excellent insights into how our queries are *actually* processed, removing parts of the guessing game when trying to refactor or tune our queries. The Vulnerability Assessment tool should allow for quicker identification of potential security threats inside our databases. A safer database means a safer business!

For SQL Server developers, there are two new development environments for developing the R code. Of course, one of them, the RStudio IDE, is well-known among R developers. Because it is so widely used, it will probably be the first choice when developing R code, and also for SQL Server developers. Nevertheless, if you are used to and love the Visual Studio IDE, you might give R Tools for Visual Studio a try.

After this short excursion into the tools that are delivered with SQL Server 2017, now, it is time to check JSON support in SQL Server 2017.

3
JSON Support in SQL Server

In the last few years, JSON has been established as a standard format for data exchange among applications and services. XML is still the exchange standard (and will remain so), but many applications communicate by exchanging JSON data instead of XML documents. Therefore, the most important relational database management system products need to support JSON.

Two release cycles after the feature was requested by the community, Microsoft has implemented built-in JSON support in SQL Server 2016. The support is not as comprehensive as for XML, but for most databases and workloads, it will be quite fine.

This chapter explores how SQL Server stores and processes JSON data, with a comprehensive comparison between JSON and XML support in SQL Server.

The most important actions related to JSON data in SQL Server are demonstrated in detail:

- Formatting and exporting JSON data from SQL Server
- Converting JSON data to a tabular format
- Importing JSON data to SQL Server
- Validating, querying, and modifying JSON data

Finally, you will be made aware of limitations caused by missing JSON data types and indexes, and given advice on how you can improve the performance of JSON queries despite these limitations.

Why JSON?

The Microsoft Connect site is the place where you can leave your feedback, suggestions, and wishes for Microsoft products. The most popular feature request for SQL Server is the one for JSON support. It was created in June 2011 and at the time of writing (October 2017) it has 1,138 votes. The request is still open, as you can see in the following screenshot, and you will see later in this chapter, why it still makes sense to have it in the active state:

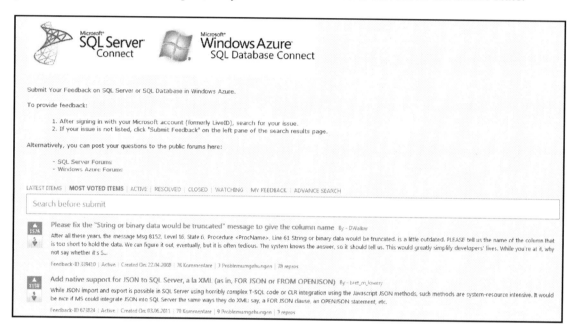

Highly ranked requests for SQL Server on the Microsoft Connect site (October 2017)

What arguments are used by community members to justify the request? They are as follows:

- JSON is already standard, and it should be supported, similar to XML.
- Other vendors support it (Oracle, PostgreSQL, and others)
- Due to the lack of JSON support, my customers want to move from SQL Server to other database systems supporting JSON.

As always with vox populi (the opinions or beliefs of the majority), some of the arguments and given examples represent development and business needs. Some of them, however, are very personal, sometimes guided by passion. But there is one thing upon which they agree and which is common in almost all comments: *a serious relational database management system should have significant support for JSON*. Almost five years after the item was created, Microsoft added JSON support in SQL Server 2016.

Of course, the number of votes on the Microsoft Connect site is not the only reason for this feature. The other competitors (PostgreSQL, Oracle, DB2, MySQL) have already introduced support for JSON; some of them, such as PostgreSQL, are very serious and robust. And if you want to still be a respectable vendor, you need to come up with JSON support.

What is JSON?

JavaScript Object Notation (JSON) is an open standard format for data exchange between applications and services. JSON objects are human-readable lists of key-value pairs. Although its name suggests otherwise, JSON is language-independent. It is specified in the ECMA-404 standard
(`http://www.ecma-international.org/publications/files/ECMA-ST/ECMA-404.pdf`).

ECMA International is an industry association founded in 1961 and dedicated to the standardization of **Information and Communication Technology (ICT)** and **Consumer Electronics (CE)**. You can find more information about it at `https://www.ecma-international.org`.

JSON is very simple and very popular. It is commonly used in AJAX applications, configurations, RESTful web services, apps from social media, and NoSQL database management systems such as MongoDB and CouchDB. Many developers prefer JSON to XML because they see JSON as less verbose and easier to read.

JSON support in SQL is defined in the latest SQL standard—SQL:2016. The standard describes how to store, publish, and query JSON data, and defines the SQL/JSON data model and path language. The specification document (*ISO/IEC TR 19075-6:2017*) is available at the following web address: `https://www.iso.org/standard/67367.html`.

Why is it popular?

JSON is a simple data format, but its simplicity is not the only thing that makes it a leading standard for exchanging data among web services and applications. The most important reason for its popularity is the fact that the JSON format is native for many programming languages, such as JavaScript. They can generate and consume JSON data natively, without serialization. One of the biggest problems in software development in recent years is object-relational impedance. The JSON data format is flexible and self-describing and allows you to use it effectively without defining a strict schema for data, which XML might need. This allows for the quick integration of data.

JSON versus XML

Both JSON and XML are simple, open, and interoperable. Since JSON usually contains less data, by using JSON, less data traverses through the network. Both formats are human-readable; JSON is a bit cleaner, since it contains less text. This is because the number of data formats supported by JSON is much smaller than with XML.

JSON is handy for sharing data. Data in JSON is stored in arrays and objects while XML documents form a tree structure. Therefore, data transfer is easier with JSON and native for many programming languages: JavaScript, Python, Perl, Ruby, and so on. On the other hand, XML can store more data types (JSON does not have even a data type for date); it can include photos, videos, and other binary files. XML is more robust and it is better suited for complex documents. XML also offers options for data representation, while JSON just transfers data, without suggesting or defining how to display it.

Generally, JSON is better as a data exchange format, while XML is more convenient as a document exchange format.

JSON objects

According to the ECMA specification, a JSON text is a sequence of tokens formed of Unicode code points that conforms to the JSON value grammar. A JSON value can be:

- **Primitive**: This is a string, number, true/false, or null value
- **Complex**: This is an object or an array

JSON object

A JSON object is a collection of zero or more key-value pairs called **object members**. The collection is wrapped in a pair of curly brackets. The key and value are separated by a single colon, while object members are separated with a comma character. The key is a string. The value can be any primitive or complex JSON data type. The structure of a JSON object is shown in the following figure:

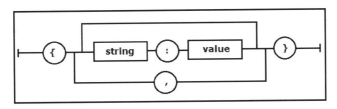

JSON object data type

The member name within a JSON object does not need to be unique. The following strings show a JSON text representing an object:

```
{
"Name":"Mila Radivojevic",
"Age":12,
"Instrument": "Flute"
}
{}
{
"Song":"Echoes",
"Group":"Pink Floyd",
"Album":{
"Name":"Meddle",
"Year":1971
}
}
{
"Name":"Tom Waits",
"Name":"Leonard Cohen"
}
```

Since the value can be any data type, including an object or an array, you can have many nested layers. This makes JSON a good choice for even complex data. Note that white spaces are allowed between the key and the value.

JSON array

A JSON array is an ordered list of zero or more values separated by commas and surrounded by square brackets. The structure is shown in the following figure:

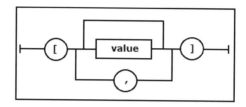

JSON array data type

Unlike JSON objects, here, the order of values is significant. Values can have different data types.

The following strings are JSON conform arrays:

```
["Benfica","Juventus","Rapid Vienna","Seattle Seahawks"]
["NTNK",3,"Käsekrainer","Sejo Kalac","political correctness",true,null]
```

Primitive JSON data types

JSON is designed to be lightweight and supports only four primitive data types:

- **Numbers**: This is a double-precision float
- **String**: Unicode text surrounded by double quotes
- **True/false**: Boolean values; they must be written in lowercase
- **Null**: This represents a null value

As you can see, there is no `date` data type. Dates are represented and processed as strings. A JSON string is a sequence of Unicode code points wrapped with quotation marks. All characters may be placed within the quotation marks, except for the characters that must be escaped. The following table provides the list of characters that must be escaped according to this specification and their JSON conform representation:

JSON escaping rules

Special character	JSON conform character
Double quote	\ "
Solidus	\ /

Reverse solidus	`\\`
Backspace	`\b`
Form feed	`\f`
New line	`\n`
Carriage return	`\r`
Tabulation	`\t`

In addition to this, all control characters with character codes in the range 0-31 need to be escaped too. In JSON output, they are represented in the following format: u<code>. Thus, the control character CHAR(0) is escaped as u0000, while CHAR(31) is represented by u001f.

The structure of a JSON string is shown in the following figure:

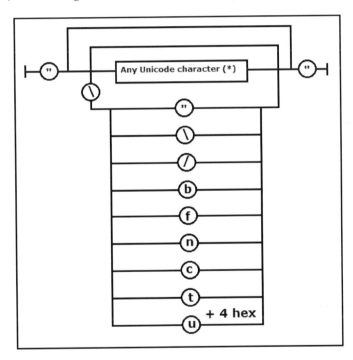

JSON string data type

JSON in SQL Server prior to SQL Server 2016

JSON has become established as a respectable and important data exchange format in the last 6-7 years. You read earlier in this chapter that JSON support in SQL Server was requested six years ago. Since this support was not provided prior to SQL Server 2016, developers had to implement their own solutions. They had to use either CLR or Transact-SQL to process and manipulate JSON data in SQL Server. This section will briefly discuss a few solutions.

JSON4SQL

JSON4SQL is a commercial CLR-based solution (with a trial version). It provides a fast, feature-rich binary JSON type for SQL Server. JSON4SQL stores JSON in a binary format ported from the JSONB format used in the PostgreSQL database. It is available at the following web address: `http://www.json4sql.com`.

JSON.SQL

JSON.SQL is a CLR-based JSON serializer/deserializer for SQL Server written by Bret Lowery, available at this address:
`http://www.sqlservercentral.com/articles/SQLCLR/74160/`. It uses a popular JSON framework—Json.NET.

Transact-SQL-based solution

There is also a Transact-SQL-only solution that does not use `.NET` functionality at all. It is written by Phil Factor and described in two articles:

- *Consuming JSON Strings in SQL Server:* You can find this article at `https://www.simple-talk.com/sql/t-sql-programming/consuming-json-strings-in-sql-server/`.
- *Producing JSON Documents from SQL Server queries via TSQL:* The article is available at `https://www.simple-talk.com/sql/t-sql-programming/producing-json-documents-from-sql-server-queries-via-tsql/`.

Since it processes text with Transact-SQL only, the solution is not performant, but it can be used to process small or moderate JSON documents.

Retrieving SQL Server data in JSON format

This section explores JSON support in SQL Server with a very common action: formatting tabular data as JSON. In SQL Server 2017, the clause FOR JSON can be used with the SELECT statement to accomplish this. It is analogous to formatting relational data as XML by using the FOR XML extension.

When you use the FOR JSON clause, you can choose between two modes:

- FOR JSON AUTO: The JSON output will be formatted by the structure of the SELECT statement automatically.
- FOR JSON PATH: The JSON output will be formatted by the structure explicitly defined by you. With JSON PATH, you can create a more complex output (nested objects and properties).

In both modes, SQL Server extracts relational data defined by the SELECT statement, converts SQL Server data types to appropriate JSON types, implements escaping rules, and finally formats the output according to explicitly or implicitly defined formatting rules.

FOR JSON AUTO

Use FOR JSON AUTO when you want to let SQL Server format query results for you. When you specify this mode, the JSON format is controlled by how the SELECT statement is written.

FOR JSON AUTO requires a table; you cannot use it without a database table or view. For instance, the following query will fail:

```
SELECT GETDATE() AS today FOR JSON AUTO;
```

Here is the error message:

```
Msg 13600, Level 16, State 1, Line 13
FOR JSON AUTO requires at least one table for generating JSON objects. Use
FOR JSON PATH or add a FROM clause with a table name.
```

To demonstrate how SQL Server automatically generates JSON data, use the `WideWorldImporters` SQL Server 2017 sample database. Consider the following query, which returns the first three rows from the `Application.People` table:

```
USE WideWorldImporters;
SELECT TOP (3) PersonID, FullName, EmailAddress, PhoneNumber
FROM Application.People ORDER BY PersonID ASC;
```

Here is the result in tabular format:

```
PersonID  FullName           EmailAddress                         PhoneNumber
--------  ----------------   -----------------------------------  -----------

1         Data Conversion Only  NULL                              NULL

2         Kayla Woodcock     kaylaw@wideworldimporters.com        (415) 555-0102

3         Hudson Onslow      hudsono@wideworldimporters.com       (415) 555-0102
```

First, you will recall how SQL Server converts this data automatically to XML. To generate an XML, you can use the `FOR JSON AUTO` extension:

```
SELECT TOP (3) PersonID, FullName, EmailAddress, PhoneNumber
FROM Application.People ORDER BY PersonID ASC FOR XML AUTO;
```

Here is the portion of XML generated by the previous query:

```
<Application.People PersonID="1" FullName="Data Conversion Only" />
<Application.People PersonID="2" FullName="Kayla Woodcock"
EmailAddress="kaylaw@wideworldimporters.com" PhoneNumber="(415) 555-0102"
/>
<Application.People PersonID="3" FullName="Hudson Onslow"
EmailAddress="hudsono@wideworldimporters.com" PhoneNumber="(415) 555-0102"
/>
```

Analogous to this, the simplest way to convert the result in JSON format is to put the `FOR JSON AUTO` extension at the end of the query:

```
SELECT TOP (3) PersonID, FullName, EmailAddress, PhoneNumber
FROM Application.People ORDER BY PersonID ASC FOR JSON AUTO;
```

The result is an automatically formatted JSON text. By default, it is a JSON array with objects:

```
[{"PersonID":1,"FullName":"Data Conversion
Only"},{"PersonID":2,"FullName":"Kayla
Woodcock","EmailAddress":"kaylaw@wideworldimporters.com","PhoneNumber":"(41
5) 555-0102"},{"PersonID":3,"FullName":"Hudson
Onslow","EmailAddress":"hudsono@wideworldimporters.com","PhoneNumber":"(415
) 555-0102"}]
```

As you can see, in **SQL Server Management Studio (SSMS)**, the JSON result is prepared in a single line. This is hard to follow and observe from a human-readable point of view. Therefore, you will need a JSON formatter. In this book, JSON output generated in SSMS is formatted by using the JSON formatter and validator that are available at `https://jsonformatter.curiousconcept.com`. The previous result looks better after additional formatting:

```
[
    {
        "PersonID":1,
        "FullName":"Data Conversion Only"
    },
    {
        "PersonID":2,
        "FullName":"Kayla Woodcock",
        "EmailAddress":"kaylaw@wideworldimporters.com",
        "PhoneNumber":"(415) 555-0102"
    },
    {
        "PersonID":3,
        "FullName":"Hudson Onslow",
        "EmailAddress":"hudsono@wideworldimporters.com",
        "PhoneNumber":"(415) 555-0102"
    }
]
```

As you can see, for each row from the original result set, one JSON object with a flat property structure is generated. Compared to XML, you see less text since the table name does not appear in the JSON output.

The difference in size is significant when you compare JSON with XML generated by using the ELEMENTS option instead of default RAW.

To illustrate this, you can use the following code; it compares the data length (in bytes) of XML-and JSON-generated output for all rows in the `Sales.Orders` table:

```
USE WideWorldImporters;
SELECT
   DATALENGTH(CAST((SELECT * FROM Sales.Orders FOR XML AUTO) AS
NVARCHAR(MAX))) AS xml_raw_size,  DATALENGTH(CAST((SELECT * FROM
Sales.Orders FOR XML AUTO,    ELEMENTS) AS NVARCHAR(MAX))) AS
xml_elements_size,  DATALENGTH(CAST((SELECT * FROM Sales.Orders FOR JSON
AUTO) AS    NVARCHAR(MAX))) AS json_size;
```

The preceding query generates the following results:

xml_raw_size	xml_elements_size	json_size
49161702	81161852	49149364

You can see that the XML representation of data when columns are expressed as XML elements is about 65% larger than the JSON representation. When they are expressed as XML attributes, JSON and XML output have approximately the same size.

The `FOR JSON AUTO` extension creates a flat structure with single-level properties. If you are not satisfied with the automatically created output and want to create a more complex structure, you should use the `FOR JSON PATH` extension.

FOR JSON PATH

To maintain full control over the format of the JSON output, you need to specify the `PATH` option with the `FOR JSON` clause. The `PATH` mode lets you create wrapper objects and nest complex properties. The results are formatted as an array of JSON objects.

The `FOR JSON PATH` clause will use the column alias or column name to determine the key name in the JSON output. If an alias contains dots, the `FOR JSON PATH` clause will create a nested object.

Assume you want to have more control over the output generated by `FOR JSON AUTO` in the previous subsection, and instead of a flat list of properties you want to represent `EmailAddress` and `PhoneNumbers` as nested properties of a new property named `Contact`. Here is the required output for the `PersonID` property with a value of 2:

```
{
    "PersonID":2,
    "FullName":"Kayla Woodcock",
    "Contact":
```

```
    {
        "EmailAddress":"kaylaw@wideworldimporters.com",
        "PhoneNumber":"(415) 555-0102"
    }
}
```

To achieve this, you simply add an alias to columns that need to be nested. In the alias, you have to use a dot syntax, which defines a JSON path to the property. Here is the code that implements the previous request:

```
SELECT TOP (3) PersonID, FullName,
EmailAddress AS 'Contact.Email', PhoneNumber AS 'Contact.Phone'
FROM Application.People ORDER BY PersonID ASC FOR JSON PATH;
```

Here is the expected result:

```
[
    {
        "PersonID":1,
        "FullName":"Data Conversion Only"
    },
    {
        "PersonID":2,
        "FullName":"Kayla Woodcock",
        "Contact":{
            "Email":"kaylaw@wideworldimporters.com",
            "Phone":"(415) 555-0102"
        }
    },
    {
        "PersonID":3,
        "FullName":"Hudson Onslow",
        "Contact":{
            "Email":"hudsono@wideworldimporters.com",
            "Phone":"(415) 555-0102"
        }
    }
]
```

By default, null values are not included in the output as you can see in the first array element; it does not contain the Contact property.

`FOR JSON PATH` does not require a database table. The following statement, which was not allowed in the `AUTO` mode, works in the `PATH` mode:

```
SELECT GETDATE() AS today FOR JSON PATH;
```

It returns:

```
[{"today":"2017-08-26T09:13:32.007"}]
```

If you reference more than one table in the query, the results are represented as a flat list, and then `FOR JSON PATH` nests each column using its alias. `JSON PATH` allows you to control generated JSON data and to create nested documents.

FOR JSON additional options

In both modes of the `FOR JSON` clause, you can specify additional options to control the output. The following options are available:

- **Add a root node**: This option allows you to add a top-level element to the JSON output.
- **Include null values**: This option allows you to include null values in the JSON output (by default they are not shown).
- **Remove array wrapper**: By using this option, you can format JSON output as a single object.

Add a root node to JSON output

By specifying the `ROOT` option in the `FOR JSON` query, you can add a single, top-level element to the JSON output. The following code shows this:

```
SELECT TOP (3) PersonID, FullName, EmailAddress, PhoneNumber
FROM Application.People ORDER BY PersonID ASC FOR JSON AUTO,
ROOT('Persons');
```

Here is the result:

```
{
    "Persons":[
        {
            "PersonID":1,
            "FullName":"Data Conversion Only"
```

```
        },
        {
            "PersonID":2,
            "FullName":"Kayla Woodcock",
            "EmailAddress":"kaylaw@wideworldimporters.com",
            "PhoneNumber":"(415) 555-0102"
        },
        {
            "PersonID":3,
            "FullName":"Hudson Onslow",
            "EmailAddress":"hudsono@wideworldimporters.com",
            "PhoneNumber":"(415) 555-0102"
        }
    ]
}
```

By specifying the root element, you have converted the outer array to a single complex property named `Persons`.

Include NULL values in the JSON output

As you can see in the preceding example, the JSON output does not map a column to a JSON property if the column value is NULL. To include null values in the JSON output, you can specify the INCLUDE_NULL_VALUES option. Let's apply it to our initial example:

```
SELECT TOP (3) PersonID, FullName, EmailAddress, PhoneNumber
FROM Application.People ORDER BY PersonID ASC FOR JSON AUTO,
INCLUDE_NULL_VALUES;
```

Let's observe the result:

```
[
  {
    "PersonID":1,
    "FullName":"Data Conversion Only",
    "EmailAddress":null,
    "PhoneNumber":null
  },
  {
    "PersonID":2,
    "FullName":"Kayla Woodcock",
    "EmailAddress":"kaylaw@wideworldimporters.com",
    "PhoneNumber":"(415) 555-0102"
  },
  {
    "PersonID":3,
    "FullName":"Hudson Onslow",
```

```
          "EmailAddress":"hudsono@wideworldimporters.com",
          "PhoneNumber":"(415) 555-0102"
      }
  ]
```

Now each element has all properties listed even if they don't have a value. This option is similar to the XSINIL option used with the ELEMENTS directive in the case of FOR XML AUTO.

Formatting a JSON output as a single object

The default JSON output is enclosed within square brackets, which means the output is an array. If you want to format it as a single object instead of an array, use the WITHOUT_ARRAY_WRAPPER option.

Even if a query returns only one row, SQL Server will format it by default as a JSON array, as in the following example:

```
SELECT PersonID, FullName, EmailAddress, PhoneNumber
FROM Application.People WHERE PersonID = 2 FOR JSON AUTO;
```

Although only one row is returned, the output is still an array (with a single element):

```
[
  {
    "PersonID":2,
    "FullName":"Kayla Woodcock",
    "EmailAddress":"kaylaw@wideworldimporters.com",
    "PhoneNumber":"(415) 555-0102"
  }
]
```

To return a single object instead of an array, you can specify the WITHOUT_ARRAY_WRAPPER option:

```
SELECT PersonID, FullName, EmailAddress, PhoneNumber
FROM Application.People WHERE PersonID = 2 FOR JSON AUTO,
WITHOUT_ARRAY_WRAPPER;
```

The output looks more convenient now:

```
{
    "PersonID":2,
    "FullName":"Kayla Woodcock",
    "EmailAddress":"kaylaw@wideworldimporters.com",
    "PhoneNumber":"(415) 555-0102"
}
```

Removing square brackets from the output allows us to choose between an object and an array in the output JSON. However, only square brackets guarantee that the output is JSON conforming. Without the brackets, JSON text will be valid only if the underlined query returns a single row or no rows at all.

To demonstrate this, include `PersonID` with a value of 3 in your initial query:

```
SELECT PersonID, FullName, EmailAddress, PhoneNumber
FROM Application.People WHERE PersonID IN (2, 3) FOR JSON AUTO,
WITHOUT_ARRAY_WRAPPER;
```

The output is expected, but invalid; there is no parent object or array:

```
{
    "PersonID":2,
    "FullName":"Kayla Woodcock",
    "EmailAddress":"kaylaw@wideworldimporters.com",
    "PhoneNumber":"(415) 555-0102"
},
{
    "PersonID":3,
    "FullName":"Hudson Onslow",
    "EmailAddress":"hudsono@wideworldimporters.com",
    "PhoneNumber":"(415) 555-0102"
}
```

But, wait! By specifying the `ROOT` option, you can wrap the output in an object, can't you? You saw this demonstrated earlier in this chapter. You can add a no-name root element to the preceding output:

```
SELECT PersonID, FullName, EmailAddress, PhoneNumber
FROM Application.People WHERE PersonID IN (2, 3) FOR JSON AUTO,
WITHOUT_ARRAY_WRAPPER, ROOT('');
```

This should add a top-level element, and with that change, the JSON output should be valid. Check this out in the output:

```
Msg 13620, Level 16, State 1, Line 113
ROOT option and WITHOUT_ARRAY_WRAPPER option cannot be used together in FOR
JSON. Remove one of these options.
```

A bitter disappointment! You cannot combine these two options! Therefore, use this option with caution; be aware that the JSON could be invalid.

Converting data types

As mentioned earlier, JSON does not have the same data types as SQL Server. Therefore, when JSON text is generated from relational data, a data type conversion is performed. The FOR JSON clause uses the following mapping to convert SQL Server data types to JSON types in the JSON output:

Conversion between SQL Server and JSON data types

SQL Server data type	JSON data type
Char, Varchar, Nchar, NVarchar, Text, Ntext, Date, DateTime, DateTime2, DateTimeOffset, Time, UniqueIdentifier, Smallmoney, Money, XML, HierarchyId, Sql_Variant	string
Tinyint, Smallint, Int, Bigint, Decimal, Float, Numeric	number
Bit	true or false
Binary, Varbinary, Image, Rowversion, Timestamp	encoded string (BASE 64)

The following data types are not supported: geography, geometry, and CLR-based user-defined data types. Thus, you cannot generate JSON output from tabular data if it includes columns of the aforementioned data types. For instance, the following query will fail:

```
SELECT * FROM Application.Cities FOR JSON AUTO;
```

Instead of returning a JSON output, it will generate an error with the following error message:

```
Msg 13604, Level 16, State 1, Line 282
FOR JSON cannot serialize CLR objects. Cast CLR types explicitly into one
of the supported types in FOR JSON queries.
```

The reason for the error is the `Location` column in the `Cities` table. Its data type is geography.

User-defined data types (UDT) are supported and will be converted following the same rules as underlined data types.

Escaping characters

Another action that is automatically performed when JSON is generated by using the FOR JSON clause is escaping special characters from text columns according to JSON's escaping rules. The rules are explained in detail in the *Primitive JSON data types* section earlier in this chapter.

Converting JSON data in a tabular format

Nowadays, JSON is a recognized format for data representation and exchange. However, most of the existing data still resides in relational databases and you need to combine them to process and manipulate them together. In order to combine JSON with relational data or to import it in relational tables, you need to map JSON data to tabular data, that is, convert it into a tabular format. In SQL Server 2016, you can use the OPENJSON function to accomplish this:

- OPENJSON is a newly added `rowset` function. A `rowset` function is a table-valued function and returns an object that can be used as if it were a table or a view. Just as OPENXML provides a rowset view over an XML document, OPENJSON gives a rowset view over JSON data. The OPENJSON function converts JSON objects and properties to table rows and columns respectively.
- It accepts two input arguments:
    - **Expression**: JSON text in the Unicode format.
    - **Path**: This is an optional argument. It is a JSON path expression and you can use it to specify a fragment of the input expression.

The function returns a table with a default or user-defined schema.

To use the OPENJSON function, the database must be in compatibility level 130. If it is not, you will get the following error:

```
Msg 208, Level 16, State 1, Line 78
Invalid object name 'OPENJSON'.
```

As mentioned, the returned table can have an implicit (default) schema or an explicit one, defined by the user. In the next two sections, both schemas will be explored in more detail.

OPENJSON with the default schema

When you don't specify a schema for returned results, the OPENJSON function returns a table with three columns:

- **Key**: This is the name of a JSON property or the index of a JSON element. The data type of the column is nvarchar, the length is 4,000, collation is Latin1_General_BIN2, and the column does not allow null values.
- **Value**: This is the value of the property or index defined by the key column. The data type of the column is nvarchar(max), it inherits collation from the input JSON text, and nulls are allowed.
- **Type**: The JSON data type of the value. The data type of the column is tinyint. Following table lists the possible values for this column and appropriate descriptions:

OPENJSON mapping of JSON data types

Type column value	JSON data type
0	null
1	string
2	number
3	true/false
4	array
5	object

OPENJSON returns only one table; therefore only first-level properties are returned as rows. It returns one row for each JSON property or array element. To demonstrate the different results provided by the OPENJSON function, use the following JSON data with the information about the album *Wish You Were Here* by the British band Pink Floyd. You will provide JSON data as an input string and call the function without specifying an optional path argument:

```
DECLARE @json NVARCHAR(MAX) = N'{
"Album":"Wish You Were Here",
"Year":1975,
"IsVinyl":true,
"Songs":[{"Title":"Shine On You Crazy Diamond","Authors":"Gilmour, Waters,
Wright"},
{"Title":"Have a Cigar","Authors":"Waters"},
{"Title":"Welcome to the Machine","Authors":"Waters"},
{"Title":"Wish You Were Here","Authors":"Gilmour, Waters"}],
"Members":{"Guitar":"David Gilmour","Bass Guitar":"Roger
Waters","Keyboard":"Richard Wright","Drums":"Nick Mason"}
}';
SELECT * FROM OPENJSON(@json);
```

The function has been invoked without the path expression; simply to convert the whole JSON document into a tabular format. Here is the output of this action:

key	value	type
Album	Wish you Were Here	1
Year	1975	2
IsVinyl	true	3
Songs	[{"Title":"Shine On You Crazy Diamond","Writers":"Gilmour, Waters, Wright" ...]	4
Members	{"Guitar":"David Gilmour","Bass Guitar":"Roger Waters","Keyboard":"Richard Wright","Drums":"Nick Mason"}	5

As you can see, five rows were generated (one row for each JSON property), property names are shown in the key column, and their values in the value column.

The input JSON expression must be well formatted; otherwise, an error occurs. In the following code, a leading double quote for the Year property is intentionally omitted:

```
DECLARE @json NVARCHAR(500) = '{
"Album":"Wish You Were Here",
Year":1975,
```

```
"IsVinyl":true
}';
SELECT * FROM OPENJSON(@json);
```

Of course, the optimizer does not forgive this small mistake and its reaction is very conservative:

```
Msg 13609, Level 16, State 4, Line 23
JSON text is not properly formatted. Unexpected character 'Y' is found at
position 34.
```

As already mentioned and demonstrated, only first-level properties are returned with the OPENJSON function. To return properties within complex values of a JSON document (arrays and objects), you need to specify the path argument. In this example, assume you want to return the Songs fragment from the initial Wish You Were Here JSON string:

```
DECLARE @json NVARCHAR(MAX) = N'{
"Album":"Wish You Were Here",
"Year":1975,
"IsVinyl":true,
"Songs":[{"Title":"Shine On You Crazy Diamond","Authors":"Gilmour, Waters,
Wright"},
{"Title":"Have a Cigar","Authors":"Waters"},
{"Title":"Welcome to the Machine","Authors":"Waters"},
{"Title":"Wish You Were Here","Authors":"Gilmour, Waters"}],
"Members":{"Guitar":"David Gilmour","Bass Guitar":"Roger
Waters","Keyboard":"Richard Wright","Drums":"Nick Mason"}
}';
SELECT * FROM OPENJSON(@json,'$.Songs');
```

The $ path expression represents the context item and $.Songs refers to the Songs property and actually extracts this fragment from the JSON document. The rest of the document must be valid; otherwise, the path expression cannot be evaluated.

Here is the result:

key	value	type
0	{"Title":"Shine On You Crazy Diamond","Writers":"Gilmour, Waters, Wright"}	5
1	{"Title":"Have a Cigar","Writers":"Waters"}	5
2	{"Title":"Welcome to the Machine","Writers":"Waters"}	5
3	{"Title":"Wish You Were Here","Writers":"Gilmour, Waters"}	5

You can see four entries for four elements in the JSON array representing songs from this album. Since they contain objects, their values are still in the JSON format in the column value.

When you do the same for the Members property, you get a nice list of properties with their names and values:

```
DECLARE @json NVARCHAR(MAX) = N'{
"Album":"Wish You Were Here",
"Year":1975,
"IsVinyl":true,
"Songs":[{"Title":"Shine On You Crazy Diamond","Authors":"Gilmour, Waters,
Wright"},
{"Title":"Have a Cigar","Authors":"Waters"},
{"Title":"Welcome to the Machine","Authors":"Waters"},
{"Title":"Wish You Were Here","Authors":"Gilmour, Waters"}],
"Members":{"Guitar":"David Gilmour","Bass Guitar":"Roger
Waters","Keyboard":"Richard Wright","Drums":"Nick Mason"}
}';
SELECT * FROM OPENJSON(@json,'$.Members');
```

Here is the result:

key	value	type
Guitar	David Gilmour	1
Bass Guitar	Roger Waters	1
Keyboard	Richard Wright	1
Drums	Nick Mason	1

Note that the returned type this time is **1** (*string*), while in the previous example it was **5** (*object*).

The function returns an error if the JSON text is not properly formatted. To demonstrate this, the initial string has been slightly changed: a leading double quote has been omitted for the element Drums (value Nick Mason). Therefore, the string is not JSON valid. Invoke the OPENJSON function for such a string:

```
DECLARE @json NVARCHAR(MAX) = N'{
"Album":"Wish you Were Here",
"Members":{"Guitar":"David Gilmour","Bass Guitar":"Roger
Waters","Keyboard":"Richard Wright","Drums":Nick Mason", "Vocal":"Syd
Barrett"}
}';
SELECT * FROM OPENJSON (@json,'$.Members');
```

Here is the result:

```
Msg 13609, Level 16, State 4, Line 15
JSON text is not properly formatted. Unexpected character 'N' is found at
position 417
```

key	value	type
Guitar	David Gilmour	1
Bass Guitar	Roger Waters	1
Keyboard	Richard Wright	1

You can see an error message, but also the returned table. The table contains three rows, since the first three properties of the complex `Member` property are JSON conforming. Instead of a fourth row, an error message has been generated and the fifth row is not shown either, although it is well formatted.

What would happen if the JSON path expression points to a scalar value or to a non-existing property? In the default JSON path mode (lax), the query would return an empty table; and when you specify strict mode, in addition to an empty table, an error message is shown (a batch-level exception is raised), as shown in the following examples:

```
DECLARE @json NVARCHAR(MAX) = N'{
"Album":"Wish you Were Here",
"Year":1975,
"IsVinyl":true,
"Songs" :[{"Title":"Shine On You Crazy Diamond","Writers":"Gilmour, Waters,
Wright"},
{"Title":"Have a Cigar","Writers":"Waters"},
{"Title":"Welcome to the Machine","Writers":"Waters"},
{"Title":"Wish You Were Here","Writers":"Gilmour, Waters"}],
"Members":{"Guitar":"David Gilmour","Bass Guitar":"Roger
Waters","Keyboard":"Richard Wright","Drums":"Nick Mason"}
}';
SELECT * FROM OPENJSON(@json, N'$.Members.Guitar');
SELECT * FROM OPENJSON(@json, N'$.Movies');
```

Both queries return an empty table:

key	value	type

The same calls with the `strict` option end up with error messages:

```
SELECT * FROM OPENJSON(@json, N'strict $.Members.Guitar');
```

The result for the preceding query is the first error message:

```
Msg 13611, Level 16, State 1, Line 12
Value referenced by JSON path is not an array or object and cannot be
opened with OPENJSON
```

The second query from the preceding example:

```
SELECT * FROM OPENJSON(@json, N'strict $.Movies');
```

The result for the preceding query is the second error message:

```
Msg 13608, Level 16, State 3, Line 13
Property cannot be found on the specified JSON path.
```

You can use OPENJSON, not only to convert JSON data into a tabular format, but also to implement some non-JSON related tasks.

Processing data from a comma-separated list of values

The following code example demonstrates how to use the OPENJSON rowset function to return the details of orders for IDs provided in a comma-separated list:

```
USE WideWorldImporters;
DECLARE @orderIds AS VARCHAR(100) = '1,3,7,8,9,11';
SELECT o.OrderID, o.CustomerID, o.OrderDate
FROM Sales.Orders o
INNER JOIN (SELECT value FROM OPENJSON('[' + @orderIds + ']' )) x ON
x.value= o.OrderID;
```

Here is the list of orders produced by the preceding query:

OrderID	CustomerID	OrderDate
1	832	2013-01-01
3	105	2013-01-01
7	575	2013-01-01
8	964	2013-01-01
9	77	2013-01-01
11	586	2013-01-01

In this example, the input argument is wrapped with square brackets to create a proper JSON text and the OPENJSON function is invoked without the path argument. OPENJSON created one row for each element from the JSON array and that is exactly what you needed.

Returning the difference between two table rows

Another example where you can use OPENJSON is to return the difference between two rows in a table. For instance, when you put application settings for different environments in a database table, you might need to know what is different in the settings between the two environments. You can accomplish this task by comparing values in each column, but this can be annoying and error prone if the table has many columns.

The following example returns the difference for database settings in the **master** and **model** database in an instance of SQL Server 2017:

```
SELECT
  mst.[key],
  mst.[value] AS mst_val,
  mdl.[value] AS mdl_val
FROM OPENJSON ((SELECT * FROM sys.databases WHERE database_id = 1 FOR JSON
AUTO, WITHOUT_ARRAY_WRAPPER)) mst
INNER JOIN OPENJSON((SELECT * FROM sys.databases WHERE database_id = 3 FOR
JSON AUTO, WITHOUT_ARRAY_WRAPPER)) mdl
ON mst.[key] = mdl.[key] AND mst.[value] <> mdl.[value]
```

Here is the list showing columns that have different values for these two databases.

key	mst_val	mdl_val
name	master	model
database_id	1	3
snapshot_isolation_state	1	0
snapshot_isolation_state_desc	ON	OFF
recovery_model	3	1
recovery_model_desc	SIMPLE	FULL
is_db_chaining_on	true	false
target_recovery_time_in_seconds	0	60

This is very handy and efficient; you don't need to know or write a lot of OR statements with column names. For instance, in the system view used in this example (sys.databases), there are 78 columns and you would need to include them all in the WHERE clause in a relational Transact-SQL statement.

OPENJSON with an explicit schema

If you need more control over formatting when it is offered by default, you can explicitly specify your own schema. The function will still return a table but with the columns defined by you. To specify the resultant table schema, use the WITH clause of the OPENJSON function. Here is the syntax for the OPENJSON function with an explicit schema:

```
OPENJSON( jsonExpression [ , path ] )
[
    WITH (
        column_name data_type [ column_path ] [ AS JSON ]
        [ , column_name data_type [ column_path ] [ AS JSON ] ]
        [ , . . . n ]
        )
]
```

When you use the WITH clause, you need to specify at least one column. For each column, you can specify the following attributes:

- column_name: This is the name of the output column.
- data_type: This is the data type for the output column.
- column_path: This is the value for the output column specified with the JSON path expression (it can be a JSON property or value of an array element); this argument is optional.
- AS JSON: Use this to specify that the property referenced in the column path represents an object or array; this argument is optional.

The best way to understand how the function works is to look at examples. The following code shows how to extract JSON properties as columns and their values as rows for JSON primitive data types:

```
DECLARE @json NVARCHAR(MAX) = N'{
"Album":"Wish You Were Here",
"Year":1975,
"IsVinyl":true,
"Songs" :[{"Title":"Shine On You Crazy Diamond","Writers":"Gilmour, Waters,
Wright"},
{"Title":"Have a Cigar","Writers":"Waters"},
{"Title":"Welcome to the Machine","Writers":"Waters"},
{"Title":"Wish You Were Here","Writers":"Gilmour, Waters"}],
"Members":{"Guitar":"David Gilmour","Bass Guitar":"Roger
Waters","Keyboard":"Richard Wright","Drums":"Nick Mason"}
}';
SELECT * FROM OPENJSON(@json)
WITH
```

```
(
  AlbumName NVARCHAR(50) '$.Album',
  AlbumYear SMALLINT '$.Year',
  IsVinyl    BIT '$.IsVinyl'
);
```

The result of the previous action is a table defined with the `WITH` statement:

AlbumName	AlbumYear	IsVinyl
Wish You Were Here	1975	1

You can add a fourth column to show band members. Here is the code:

```
SELECT * FROM OPENJSON(@json)
WITH
(
  AlbumName NVARCHAR(50) '$.Album',
  AlbumYear SMALLINT '$.Year',
  IsVinyl  BIT '$.IsVinyl',
  Members  VARCHAR(200) '$.Members'
);
```

Here is the resultant table:

AlbumName	AlbumYear	IsVinyl	Members
Wish You Were Here	1975	1	NULL

The result might be unexpected, but the value for the Members property is an object, and therefore the function returns NULL since the JSON path is in default lax mode. If you specified the strict mode, the returned table would be empty and an error would be raised. To solve the problem and show the value of the Members property you need to use the AS JSON option to inform SQL Server that the expected data is properly JSON-formatted, as shown in the following code:

```
SELECT * FROM OPENJSON(@json)
WITH
(
  AlbumName NVARCHAR(50) '$.Album',
  AlbumYear SMALLINT '$.Year',
  IsVinyl  BIT '$.IsVinyl',
  Members  VARCHAR(MAX) '$.Members' AS JSON

);
```

Now it should return the expected result, but it returns an error:

```
Msg 13618, Level 16, State 1, Line 70
AS JSON option can be specified only for column of nvarchar(max) type in
WITH clause.
```

As the error message clearly says, the `AS JSON` option requires a column with the `nvarchar(max)` data type. Finally, here is the code that works and returns the expected result:

```
SELECT * FROM OPENJSON(@json)
WITH
(
  AlbumName NVARCHAR(50) '$.Album',
  AlbumYear SMALLINT '$.Year',
  IsVinyl  BIT '$.IsVinyl',
  Members  NVARCHAR(MAX) '$.Members' AS JSON
);
```

AlbumName	AlbumYear	IsVinyl	Members
Wish You Were Here	1975	1	{"Guitar":"David Gilmour","Bass Guitar":"Roger Waters","Keyboard":"Richard Wright","Drums":"Nick Mason"}

To combine property values from different levels and convert them to a tabular format, you would need to have multiple calls of the `OPENJSON` function. The following example lists all songs and authors and shows the appropriate album name:

```
DECLARE @json NVARCHAR(MAX) = N'{
"Album":"Wish You Were Here",
"Year":1975,
"IsVinyl":true,
"Songs" :[{"Title":"Shine On You Crazy Diamond","Writers":"Gilmour, Waters,
Wright"},
{"Title":"Have a Cigar","Writers":"Waters"},
{"Title":"Welcome to the Machine","Writers":"Waters"},
{"Title":"Wish You Were Here","Writers":"Gilmour, Waters"}],
"Members":{"Guitar":"David Gilmour","Bass Guitar":"Roger
Waters","Keyboard":"Richard Wright","Drums":"Nick Mason"}
}';
SELECT s.SongTitle, s.SongAuthors, a.AlbumName FROM OPENJSON(@json)
WITH
(
  AlbumName NVARCHAR(50) '$.Album',
  AlbumYear SMALLINT '$.Year',
  IsVinyl BIT '$.IsVinyl',
```

```
    Songs   NVARCHAR(MAX) '$.Songs' AS JSON,
    Members NVARCHAR(MAX) '$.Members' AS JSON

) a
CROSS APPLY OPENJSON(Songs)
WITH
(
  SongTitle NVARCHAR(200) '$.Title',
  SongAuthors NVARCHAR(200) '$.Writers'
) s;
```

This time the result meets expectations. No hidden catch! Here is the result:

SongTitle	SongAuthors	AlbumName
Shine On You Crazy Diamond	Gilmour, Waters, Wright	Wish You Were Here
Have a Cigar	Waters	Wish You Were Here
Welcome to the Machine	Waters	Wish You Were Here
Wish You Were Here	Gilmour, Waters	Wish You Were Here

Import the JSON data from a file

Importing JSON data from a file and converting it into a tabular format is straightforward in SQL Server 2016. To import data from a filesystem (local disk or network location) into SQL Server, you can use the OPENROWSET (BULK) function. It simply imports the entire file contents in a single-text value.

To demonstrate this, use your knowledge from the previous section and generate content for a JSON file. Use the following query to create JSON data from the Application.People table:

```
USE WideWorldImporters;
SELECT PersonID, FullName, PhoneNumber, FaxNumber, EmailAddress, LogonName,
IsEmployee, IsSalesperson FROM Application.People FOR JSON AUTO;
```

You then save the resulting JSON text in a file named app.people.json in the C:Temp directory. Now import this JSON file into SQL Server.

By using the OPENROWSET function, the file is imported in a single-text column. Here is the code:

```
SELECT BulkColumn
FROM OPENROWSET (BULK 'C:\Temp\app.people.json', SINGLE_CLOB) AS x;
```

The following screenshot shows the result of this import action. The entire file content is available in the single-text column named BulkColumn:

Import JSON file into SQL Server by using OPENROWSET function

To represent a JSON file's contents in a tabular format, you can combine the OPENROWSET function with the OPENJSON function. The following code imports JSON data and displays it with the default schema (columns key, value, and type):

```
SELECT [key], [value], [type]
FROM OPENROWSET (BULK 'C:\Temp\app.people.json', SINGLE_CLOB) AS x
CROSS APPLY OPENJSON(BulkColumn);
```

The result is shown in the following screenshot. You can see one row for each element of a JSON array in the file:

	key	value	type
1	0	{"PersonID":1,"FullName":"Data Conversion Only","Lo...	5
2	1	{"PersonID":2,"FullName":"Kayla Woodcock","Logon...	5
3	2	{"PersonID":3,"FullName":"Hudson Onslow","LogonNa...	5
4	3	{"PersonID":4,"FullName":"Isabella Rupp","LogonNam...	5
5	4	{"PersonID":5,"FullName":"Eva Muirden","LogonName...	5
6	5	{"PersonID":6,"FullName":"Sophia Hinton","LogonNam...	5
7	6	{"PersonID":7,"FullName":"Amy Trefl","LogonName":"...	5
8	7	{"PersonID":8,"FullName":"Anthony Grosse","LogonNa...	5
9	8	{"PersonID":9,"FullName":"Alica Fatnowna","LogonNa...	5
10	9	{"PersonID":10,"FullName":"Stella Rosenhain","Logon...	5

Importing a JSON file into SQL Server and combining with OPENJSON with the default schema

Finally, this code example shows the code that can be used to import a JSON file and represent its content in tabular format, with a user-defined schema:

```
SELECT PersonID, FullName,PhoneNumber, FaxNumber, EmailAddress,LogonName,
IsEmployee, IsSalesperson
FROM OPENROWSET (BULK 'C:\Temp\app.people.json', SINGLE_CLOB) as j
CROSS APPLY OPENJSON(BulkColumn)
WITH
(
  PersonID INT '$.PersonID',
  FullName NVARCHAR(50) '$.FullName',
  PhoneNumber NVARCHAR(20) '$.PhoneNumber',
  FaxNumber NVARCHAR(20) '$.FaxNumber',
  EmailAddress NVARCHAR(256) '$.EmailAddress',
  LogonName NVARCHAR(50) '$.LogonName',
  IsEmployee  BIT '$.IsEmployee',
  IsSalesperson BIT '$.IsSalesperson'
);
```

The following screenshot shows the result of this import procedure:

	PersonID	FullName	PhoneNumber	FaxNumber	EmailAddress	LogonName	IsEmployee	IsSalesperson
1	1	Data Conversion Only	NULL	NULL	NULL	NO LOGON	0	0
2	2	Kayla Woodcock	(415) 555-0102	(415) 555-0103	kaylaw@wideworldimporters.com	kaylaw@wideworldimporters.com	1	1
3	3	Hudson Onslow	(415) 555-0102	(415) 555-0103	hudsono@wideworldimporters.com	hudsono@wideworldimporters.com	1	1
4	4	Isabella Rupp	(415) 555-0102	(415) 555-0103	isabellar@wideworldimporters.com	isabellar@wideworldimporters.com	1	0
5	5	Eva Muirden	(415) 555-0102	(415) 555-0103	evam@wideworldimporters.com	evam@wideworldimporters.com	1	0
6	6	Sophia Hinton	(415) 555-0102	(415) 555-0103	sophiah@wideworldimporters.com	sophiah@wideworldimporters.com	1	1
7	7	Amy Trefl	(415) 555-0102	(415) 555-0103	amyt@wideworldimporters.com	amyt@wideworldimporters.com	1	1
8	8	Anthony Grosse	(415) 555-0102	(415) 555-0103	anthonyg@wideworldimporters.com	anthonyg@wideworldimporters.com	1	1
9	9	Alica Fatnowna	(415) 555-0102	(415) 555-0103	alicaf@wideworldimporters.com	alicaf@wideworldimporters.com	1	0
10	10	Stella Rosenhain	(415) 555-0102	(415) 555-0103	stellar@wideworldimporters.com	stellar@wideworldimporters.com	1	0

Importing a JSON file into SQL Server and combining with OPENJSON with an explicit schema

As expected, the structure is identical to the one generated by the simple SELECT statement against the Application.People table.

JSON storage in SQL Server 2017

Since XML support was introduced in SQL Server 2005, the native XML data type has been implemented as well. SQL Server 2016 introduces built-in support for JSON but unlike XML, there is no native JSON data type. Here are the reasons that the Microsoft team gave for not introducing a new data type:

- **Migration**: Prior to SQL Server 2016, developers already had to deal with JSON data.
- **Cross-feature compatibility**: The data type `nvarchar` is supported in all SQL Server components, so JSON will also be supported everywhere (memory-optimized tables, temporal tables, and Row-Level Security).
- **Client-side support**: Even if a new data type were introduced, most of the client tools would still represent it outside SQL Server as a string.

They also noted that if you believe that the JSON binary format from PostgreSQL, or a compressed format, such as zipped JSON text, is a better option, you can parse JSON text in UDT, store it as JSONB in a binary property of CLR UTD, and create member methods that can use properties from that format. You can find more details about their decision at `https://blogs.msdn.microsoft.com/jocapc/2015/05/16/json-support-in-sql-server-2016`.

A part of the SQL Server community has expected a native data type in the SQL Server 2017 version, but the native JSON data type is still not provided.

Although the arguments mentioned make sense, a native JSON data type would be better, especially from a performance point of view. However, this requires more effort and time frames for development, and release of new features are shorter which should be also taken in account when you judge the feature. JSON support in SQL Server would be complete with a native data type, but built-in support is a respectable implementation and this is a very useful feature.

Since there is no JSON data type, JSON data is stored as text in `NVARCHAR` columns. You can use the newly added `COMPRESS` function to compress JSON data and convert it to a binary format.

Validating JSON data

To validate JSON, you can use the ISJSON function. This is a scalar function and checks whether the input string is valid JSON data. The function has one input argument:

- string: This is an expression of any string data type, except text and ntext.

The return type of the function is int, but only three values are possible:

- 1, if the input string is JSON conforming
- 0, if the input string is not valid JSON data
- NULL, if the input expression is NULL

The following statement checks whether the input variable is JSON valid:

```
SELECT
   ISJSON ('test'),
   ISJSON (''),
   ISJSON ('{}'),
   ISJSON ('{"a"}'),
   ISJSON ('{"a":1}'),
   ISJSON ('{"a":1"}');
```

Here is the output:

```
------  ------  ------  ------  ------  ------
0       0       1       0       1       0
```

ISJSON does not check the uniqueness of keys at the same level. Therefore, this JSON data is valid:

```
SELECT ISJSON ('{"id":1, "id":"a"}') AS is_json;
```

It returns:

```
is_json
-----------
1
```

Since there is no JSON data type and data must be stored as text, the `ISJSON` function is important for data validation before the text is saved into a database table. To ensure that a `text` column stores only JSON- conforming data, you can use the `ISJSON` function in the check constraint. The following code creates a sample table with a `JSON` column and an appropriate check constraint:

```
USE WideWorldImporters;
DROP TABLE IF EXISTS dbo.Users;
CREATE TABLE dbo.Users(
id INT IDENTITY(1,1) NOT NULL,
username NVARCHAR(50) NOT NULL,
user_settings NVARCHAR(MAX) NULL CONSTRAINT CK_user_settings CHECK
(ISJSON(user_settings) = 1),
CONSTRAINT PK_Users PRIMARY KEY CLUSTERED (id ASC)
);
```

To test the constraint, you will have to insert two rows in the table. The first `INSERT` statement contains a well-formatted JSON text, while in the second the value for the last property is omitted; thus the JSON text is invalid. Now, execute the statements:

```
INSERT INTO dbo.Users(username, user_settings) VALUES(N'vasilije', '{"team"
: ["Rapid", "Bayern"], "hobby" : ["soccer", "gaming"], "color" : "green"
}');

INSERT INTO dbo.Users(username, user_settings) VALUES(N'mila', '{"team" :
"Liverpool", "hobby" }');
```

The first statement has been executed successfully, but the second, as expected, generated the following error message:

```
Msg 547, Level 16, State 0, Line 12
The INSERT statement conflicted with the CHECK constraint
"CK_user_settings". The conflict occurred in database "WideWorldImporters",
table "dbo.Users", column 'user_settings'.
The statement has been terminated.
```

Ensure that you have dropped the table used in this exercise:

```
USE WideWorldImporters;
DROP TABLE IF EXISTS dbo.Users;
```

Extracting values from a JSON text

As mentioned earlier in this chapter, JSON has four primitive types (string, number, Boolean, and null) and two complex (structure) types: object and array. SQL Server 2016 offers two functions to extract values from a JSON text:

- JSON_VALUE: This is used to extract values of primitive data types.
- JSON_QUERY: This is used to extract a JSON fragment or to get a complex value (object or array).

JSON_VALUE

The JSON_VALUE function extracts a scalar value from a JSON string. It accepts two input arguments:

- **Expression**: This is JSON text in the Unicode format.
- **Path**: This is an optional argument; it is a JSON path expression and you can use it to specify a fragment of the input expression.

The return type of the function is nvarchar(4000), with the same collation as in the input expression. If the extracted value is longer than 4,000 characters, the function returns NULL provided the path is in lax mode, or an error message in the case of strict mode.

If either the expression or the path is not valid, the JSON_VALUE function returns an error explaining that the JSON text is not properly formatted.

The following example shows the JSON_VALUE function in action. It is used to return values for properties and an array element:

```
DECLARE @json NVARCHAR(MAX) = N'{
"Album":"Wish You Were Here",
"Year":1975,
"IsVinyl":true,
"Members":["Gilmour","Waters","Wright","Mason"]
}';
SELECT
  JSON_VALUE(@json, '$.Album') AS album,
  JSON_VALUE(@json, '$.Year') AS yr,
  JSON_VALUE(@json, '$.IsVinyl') AS isVinyl,
  JSON_VALUE(@json, '$.Members[0]') AS member1;
```

Here is the result of the previous query:

```
album                      yr    isVinyl   member1
------------------------   -----  ------   --------
Wish You Were Here         1975   true     Gilmour
```

Note that all returned values are strings; as already mentioned, the data type of the returned value is `nvarchar`.

The aim of the function is to extract scalar values. Therefore, it won't work if the JSON path specifies an array or an object. The following call with the JSON string in the previous example will return a NULL value:

```
DECLARE @json NVARCHAR(MAX) = N'{
"Album":"Wish You Were Here",
"Year":1975,
"IsVinyl":true,
"Members":["Gilmour","Waters","Wright","Mason"]
}';
SELECT
   JSON_VALUE(@json, '$.Members') AS member;
```

The JSON path `$.members` specifies an array and the function expects a scalar value. A NULL value will be returned even if the property specified with the path expression does not exist. As mentioned earlier, the JSON path expression has two modes: lax and strict. In the default lax mode, errors are suppressed and functions return NULL values or empty tables, while every unexpected or non-existing path raises a batch-level exception. The same call with the JSON path in strict mode would end up with an error:

```
SELECT
   JSON_VALUE(@json, 'strict $.Members') AS member;
```

Here is the error message:

```
Msg 13623, Level 16, State 1, Line 75
Scalar value cannot be found in the specified JSON path.
```

If the length of a JSON property value or string element is longer than 4,000, the function returns NULL. The next example demonstrates this by using two very long strings as values for two properties. The first one has 4,000 characters and the second is one character longer:

```
DECLARE @json NVARCHAR(MAX) = CONCAT('{"name":"', REPLICATE('A',4000),
'",}'),
@json4001 NVARCHAR(MAX) = CONCAT('{"name":"', REPLICATE('A',4001), '",}')
SELECT
  JSON_VALUE(@json, '$.name') AS name4000,
  JSON_VALUE(@json4001, '$.name') AS name4001;
```

The abbreviated result is here:

```
Name4000              name4001
------------------    ---------
AAAAAAAAAAAAAAAA...   NULL
```

You can see that 4001 is too much for JSON_VALUE, and the function returns NULL. If you specify strict in the previous example, the function returns an error:

```
DECLARE @json4001 NVARCHAR(MAX) = CONCAT('{"name":"', REPLICATE('A',4001),
'",}')
SELECT
  JSON_VALUE(@json4001, ' strict $.name') AS name4001;
```

Here is the error message:

```
Msg 13625, Level 16, State 1, Line 65
String value in the specified JSON path would be truncated.
```

This is a typical change in function behavior regarding the JSON path mode. Lax mode usually returns NULL and does not break the code, while strict mode raises a batch-level exception.

JSON_VALUE can be used in SELECT, WHERE, and ORDER clauses. In the following example, it is used in all three clauses:

```
SELECT
  PersonID,
  JSON_VALUE(UserPreferences, '$.timeZone') AS TimeZone,
  JSON_VALUE(UserPreferences, '$.table.pageLength') AS PageLength
FROM Application.People
WHERE JSON_VALUE(UserPreferences, '$.dateFormat') = 'yy-mm-dd'
  AND JSON_VALUE(UserPreferences, '$.theme') = 'blitzer'
ORDER BY JSON_VALUE(UserPreferences, '$.theme'), PersonID;
```

One important limitation of the `JSON_VALUE` function in SQL Server 2016 is that a variable as a second argument (JSON path) is not allowed. For instance, the following code won't work in SQL Server 2016:

```
DECLARE @jsonPath NVARCHAR(10) = N'$.Album';
DECLARE @json NVARCHAR(200) = N'{
"Album":"Wish You Were Here",
"Year":1975
}';
SELECT
   JSON_VALUE(@json, @jsonPath) AS album;
```

The query fails with the following error message:

```
Msg 13610, Level 16, State 1, Line 137
The argument 2 of the "JSON_VALUE or JSON_QUERY" must be a string literal
```

This was a significant limitation; you had to provide JSON path as a static value in advance and you cannot add or change it dynamically. Fortunately, this limitation has been removed in SQL Server 2017, and the preceding code in SQL Server 2017 provides the following result:

```
album
------------------
Wish You Were Here
```

 You can use variables for both arguments of the `JSON_VALUE` function in SQL Server 2017 even if the database is still in compatibility mode 130 (which corresponds to SQL Server 2016).

There are not many differences between JSON implementations in SQL Server 2016 and 2017; this is the most important one.

JSON_QUERY

The `JSON_QUERY` function extracts a JSON fragment from the input JSON string for the specified JSON path. It returns a JSON object or an array; therefore, its output is JSON conforming. This function is complementary to the `JSON_VALUE` function.

`JSON_QUERY` always returns JSON conforming text. Thus, if you want to suggest to SQL Server that the string is JSON formatted, you should wrap it with this function.

The function has two input arguments:

- **Expression**: This is a variable or column containing JSON text.
- **Path**: This is a JSON path that specifies the object or the array to extract. This parameter is optional. If it's not specified, the whole input string will be returned.

The return type of the function is `nvarchar(max)` if the input string is defined as `(n)varchar(max)`; otherwise, it is `nvarchar(4000)`. As already mentioned, the function always returns a JSON conforming string.

If either the expression or the path is not valid, `JSON_QUERY` returns an error message saying that the JSON text or JSON path is not properly formatted.

In the following self-explanatory examples, how to use this function with different JSON path expressions is demonstrated:

```
DECLARE @json NVARCHAR(MAX) = N'{
"Album":"Wish You Were Here",
"Year":1975,
"IsVinyl":true,
"Songs" :[{"Title":"Shine On You Crazy Diamond","Writers":"Gilmour, Waters,
Wright"},
{"Title":"Have a Cigar","Writers":"Waters"},
{"Title":"Welcome to the Machine","Writers":"Waters"},
{"Title":"Wish You Were Here","Writers":"Gilmour, Waters"}],
"Members":{"Guitar":"David Gilmour","Bass Guitar":"Roger
Waters","Keyboard":"Richard Wright","Drums":"Nick Mason"}
}';
--get Songs JSON fragment (array)
SELECT JSON_QUERY(@json,'$.Songs');
--get Members SON fragment (object)
SELECT JSON_QUERY(@json,'$.Members');
--get fourth Song JSON fragment (object)
SELECT JSON_QUERY(@json,'$.Songs[3]');
```

Here is the result of these invocations:

```
[{"Title":"Shine On You Crazy Diamond","Writers":"Gilmour, Waters,
   Wright"},
{"Title":"Have a Cigar","Writers":"Waters"},
{"Title":"Welcome to the Machine","Writers":"Waters"},
{"Title":"Wish You Were Here","Writers":"Gilmour, Waters"}]
```

```
{"Guitar":"David Gilmour","Bass Guitar":"Roger
  Waters","Keyboard":"Richard Wright","Drums":"Nick Mason"}
{"Title":"Wish You Were Here","Writers":"Gilmour, Waters"}
```

You can see that the returned values are JSON objects and arrays. However, if you specify a value that is not an array or object, the function returns NULL in lax mode and an error in strict mode:

```
--get property value (number)
SELECT JSON_QUERY(@json,'$.Year');
--get property value (string)
SELECT JSON_QUERY(@json,'$.Songs[1].Title');
--get value for non-existing property
SELECT JSON_QUERY(@json,'$.Studios');
```

All three calls return NULL, whereas strict mode raises a batch-level exception:

```
SELECT JSON_QUERY(@json,'strict $.Year');
/*Result:
Msg 13624, Level 16, State 1, Line 54
Object or array cannot be found in the specified JSON path.
*/
--get value for non-existing property
SELECT JSON_QUERY(@json,'strict $.Studios');
/*Result:
Msg 13608, Level 16, State 5, Line 60
Property cannot be found on the specified JSON path
*/
```

You can also use JSON_QUERY to ensure data integrity of JSON data in a table column. For instance, the following check constraint ensures that all persons in the People table have the OtherLanguages property within the CustomFields column if this column has a value:

```
USE WideWorldImporters;
ALTER TABLE Application.People
ADD CONSTRAINT CHK_OtherLanguagesRequired
CHECK (JSON_QUERY(CustomFields, '$.OtherLanguages') IS NOT NULL OR
CustomFields IS NULL);
```

The JSON_QUERY function has the same restrictions in SQL Server 2016 for the path argument as JSON_VALUE; only literals are allowed. In SQL Server 2017 you can use variables too.

Modifying JSON data

You might sometimes need to update only a part of JSON data. In SQL Server 2016, you can modify JSON data using the JSON_MODIFY function. It allows you to:

- Update the value of an existing property
- Add a new element to an existing array
- Insert a new property and its value
- Delete a property based on a combination of modes and provided values

The function accepts three mandatory input arguments:

- **Expression**: This is a variable or column name containing JSON text.
- **Path**: This is the JSON path expression with an optional modifier append.
- **new_value**: This is the new value for the property specified in the path expression.

The JSON_MODIFY function returns the updated JSON string. In the next subsections, you will see this function in action.

Adding a new JSON property

In the following code example, you add a new property named IsVinyl with the value true:

```
DECLARE @json NVARCHAR(MAX) = N'{
"Album":"Wish You Were Here",
"Year":1975
}';
PRINT JSON_MODIFY(@json, '$.IsVinyl', CAST(1 AS BIT));
```

You need to cast the value explicitly to the BIT data type; otherwise it will be surrounded by double quotes and interpreted as a string. Here is the result of the modification:

```
{
"Album":"Wish You Were Here",
"Year":1975,
"IsVinyl":true
}
```

Note that the JSON path expression is in default lax mode. By specifying strict mode, the function will return an error:

```
DECLARE @json NVARCHAR(MAX) = N'{
"Album":"Wish You Were Here",
"Year":1975
}';
PRINT JSON_MODIFY(@json, 'strict $.IsVinyl', CAST(1 AS BIT));
```

Strict mode always expects the property specified with the JSON path expression to exist. If it does not exist, it returns the following error message:

```
Msg 13608, Level 16, State 2, Line 34
Property cannot be found on the specified JSON path.
```

Be aware when you add a value that it is already JSON formatted. In the next example, assume you want to add a new property named `Members` and you have already prepared the whole JSON array:

```
DECLARE @json NVARCHAR(MAX) = N'{
"Album":"Wish You Were Here",
"Year":1975,
"IsVinyl":true
}';
DECLARE @members NVARCHAR(500) = N'["Gilmour","Waters","Wright","Mason"]';
PRINT JSON_MODIFY(@json, '$.Members', @members);
```

A new `Members` property has been added to the input JSON data, but our JSON conform value has been interpreted as text and therefore all special characters are escaped. Here is the modified input string:

```
{
"Album":"Wish You Were Here",
"Year":1975,
"IsVinyl":true,
"Members":"["Gilmour","Waters","Wright","Mason"]"
}
```

To avoid the escaping of JSON conforming text, you need to tell the function that the text is already JSON and escaping should not be performed. You can achieve this by wrapping the new value with the `JSON_QUERY` function:

```
DECLARE @json NVARCHAR(MAX) = N'{
"Album":"Wish You Were Here",
"Year":1975,
"IsVinyl":true
}';
```

```
DECLARE @members NVARCHAR(500) = N'["Gilmour","Waters","Wright","Mason"]';
PRINT JSON_MODIFY(@json, '$.Members', JSON_QUERY(@members));
```

As mentioned in the previous section, the JSON_QUERY function returns JSON conforming text and now SQL Server knows that escaping is not required. Here is the expected result:

```
{
"Album":"Wish You Were Here",
"Year":1975,
"IsVinyl":true,
"Members":["Gilmour","Waters","Wright","Mason"]
}
```

This is a drawback of the missing JSON data type. If you had it, it wouldn't be necessary to use JSON_QUERY and SQL Server would distinguish between JSON and string.

Updating the value for a JSON property

In the next examples, you will update the value of an existing property. You will start by updating the Year property from 1973 to 1975. Here is the code:

```
DECLARE @json NVARCHAR(MAX) = N'{
"Album":"Wish You Were Here",
"Year":1973
}';
PRINT JSON_MODIFY(@json, '$.Year', 1975);
PRINT JSON_MODIFY(@json, 'strict $.Year', 1975);
```

You invoked the function twice to demonstrate using both JSON path modes: lax and strict. Here are the output strings:

```
{
"Album":"Wish You Were Here",
"Year":1975
}
{
"Album":"Wish You Were Here",
"Year":1975
}
```

You can see that there is no difference between lax and strict mode if the property specified with the path exists.

The following example demonstrates how to update a value of an array element within a JSON text. Assume you want to replace the first element of the Members array (Gilmour) with the value (Barrett):

```
DECLARE @json NVARCHAR(MAX) = N'{
"Album":"Wish You Were Here",
"Year":1975,
"Members":["Gilmour","Waters","Wright","Mason"]
}';
PRINT JSON_MODIFY(@json, '$.Members[0]', 'Barrett');
```

Here is the expected result:

```
{
"Album":"Wish You Were Here",
"Year":1975,
"Members":["Barrett","Waters","Wright","Mason"]
}
```

If you want to add a new element to an array, you have to use append. In the following example, you simply add another element in the Members array:

```
DECLARE @json NVARCHAR(MAX) = N'{
"Album":"Wish You Were Here",
"Year":1975,
"Members":["Gilmour","Waters","Wright","Mason"]
}';
PRINT JSON_MODIFY(@json, 'append $.Members', 'Barrett');
```

Here is the result:

```
{
"Album":"Wish You Were Here",
"Year":1975,
"Members":["Gilmour","Waters","Wright","Mason","Barrett"]
}
```

If you specify an index that is out of range or if the array does not exist, you will get:

- **Strict mode**: This shows an error message and no return value (batch-level exception).
- **Lax mode**: This shows no error; the original input string is returned.

To update a value of a JSON property to NULL, you have to use a JSON path in strict mode. Use the following code to update the Year property from the input JSON string to a NULL value:

```
DECLARE @json NVARCHAR(MAX) = N'{
"Album":"Wish You Were Here",
"Year":1975,
"Members":["Gilmour","Waters","Wright","Mason"]
}';
PRINT JSON_MODIFY(@json, 'strict $.Year', NULL);
```

Here is the output.

```
{
"Album":"Wish You Were Here",
"Year":null,
"Members":["Gilmour","Waters","Wright","Mason"]
}
```

Removing a JSON property

To remove a property from the input JSON string, you have to use a JSON path expression in lax mode. You will repeat the preceding code, but this time in lax mode:

```
DECLARE @json NVARCHAR(MAX) = N'{
"Album":"Wish You Were Here",
"Year":1975,
"Members":["Gilmour","Waters","Wright","Mason"]
}';
PRINT JSON_MODIFY(@json, '$.Year', NULL);
```

When you observe the result of this action, you can see that the Year property does not exist anymore:

```
{
"Album":"Wish You Were Here",
"Members":["Gilmour","Waters","Wright","Mason"]
}
```

By taking this approach, you can remove only properties and their values. You cannot remove an array element. The following code will not remove the Waters element from the JSON array property Members; it will actually update it to NULL:

```
DECLARE @json NVARCHAR(MAX) = N'{
"Album":"Wish You Were Here",
"Year":1975,
```

```
"Members":["Gilmour","Waters","Wright","Mason"]
}';
PRINT JSON_MODIFY(@json, '$.Members[1]', NULL);
```

The result is as follows:

```
{
"Album":"Wish You Were Here",
"Year":1975,
"Members":["Gilmour",null,"Wright","Mason"]
}
```

If you want to remove the Waters element, you can use the following code:

```
DECLARE @json NVARCHAR(MAX) = N'{
"Album":"Wish You Were Here",
"Year":1975,
"Members":["Gilmour","Waters","Wright","Mason"]
}';
PRINT JSON_MODIFY(@json, '$.Members',
JSON_QUERY('["Gilmour","Wright","Mason"]'));
```

And finally, the expected result:

```
{
"Album":"Wish You Were Here",
"Year":1975,
"Members":["Gilmour","Wright","Mason"]
}
```

Multiple changes

You can change only one property at a time; for multiple changes you need multiple calls. In this example, you want to update the IsVinyl property to false, add a new property Recorded, and add another element called Barrett to the Members property:

```
DECLARE @json NVARCHAR(MAX) = N'{
"Album":"Wish You Were Here",
"Year":1975,
"IsVinyl":true,
"Members":["Gilmour","Waters","Wright","Mason"]
}';
PRINT JSON_MODIFY(JSON_MODIFY(JSON_MODIFY(@json, '$.IsVinyl', CAST(0 AS
BIT)), '$.Recorded', 'Abbey Road Studios'), 'append $.Members', 'Barrett');
```

Here is the output:

```
{
"Album":"Wish You Were Here",
"Year":1975,
"IsVinyl":false,
"Members":["Gilmour","Waters","Wright","Mason","Barrett"],
"Recorded":"Abbey Road Studios"
}
```

Performance considerations

One of the main concerns about JSON in SQL Server 2016 is performance. As mentioned, unlike XML, JSON is not fully supported; there is no JSON data type. Data in XML columns is stored as **binary large objects** (**BLOBs**). SQL Server supports two types of XML indexes that avoid parsing all the data at runtime to evaluate a query and allow efficient query processing. Without an index, these BLOBs are shredded at runtime to evaluate a query. As mentioned several times, there is no JSON data type; JSON is stored as simple Unicode text and the text has to be interpreted at runtime to evaluate a JSON query. This can lead to slow reading and writing performance for large JSON documents. The primary XML index indexes all tags, values, and paths within the XML instances in an XML column. The primary XML index is a shredded and persisted representation of the XML BLOBs in the XML data type column. For each XML **BLOB** in the column, the index creates several rows of data. The number of rows in the index is approximately equal to the number of nodes in the XML BLOB.

Since JSON is stored as text, it will always be interpreted. On JSON columns that are not larger than 1,700 bytes, you could create a non-clustered index, or use them as an included column without the limit.

Without a dedicated data type and storage, performance and options for JSON query improvements in SQL Server 2016 are limited: you can use computed columns and create indexes on them, or use the benefits of full-text indexes. However, you can expect performance problems during the processing of large amounts of JSON data in SQL Server 2016.

Indexes on computed columns

The following code example creates a sample table with a JSON column and populates it with values from the `Application.People` table:

```
USE WideWorldImporters;
DROP TABLE IF EXISTS dbo.T1;
CREATE TABLE dbo.T1(
id INT NOT NULL,
info NVARCHAR(2000) NOT NULL,
CONSTRAINT PK_T1 PRIMARY KEY CLUSTERED(id)
);

INSERT INTO dbo.T1(id, info)
SELECT PersonID, info FROM Application.People t1
CROSS APPLY(
  SELECT (
    SELECT t2.FullName, t2.EmailAddress, t2.PhoneNumber,      t2.FaxNumber
  FROM Application.People t2 WHERE t2.PersonID = t1.PersonID FOR      JSON
AUTO, WITHOUT_ARRAY_WRAPPER
  ) info
  ) x
```

Assume you want to return rows that have the `Vilma Niva` value for the `FullName` property. Since this is a scalar value, you can use the `JSON_VALUE` function. Before you execute the code, ensure that the actual execution plan will be displayed as well (on the **Query** menu, click on **Include Actual Execution Plan**, or click on the **Include Actual Execution Plan** toolbar button). Now execute the following code:

```
SELECT id, info
FROM dbo.T1
WHERE JSON_VALUE(info,'$.FullName') = 'Vilma Niva';
```

The execution plan for the query is shown in the following screenshot:

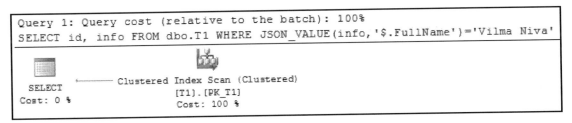

Execution plan without computed columns

The plan shows that a `Clustered Index Scan` was performed; SQL Server was not able to search for full names within the JSON column in an efficient manner.

To improve the performance of the query, you can create a computed column by using the same expression as in its `WHERE` clause and then using a non-clustered index on it:

```
ALTER TABLE dbo.T1 ADD FullName AS  JSON_VALUE(info, '$.FullName');
CREATE INDEX IX1 ON dbo.T1(FullName);
```

When you execute the same query again, the execution plan is changed:

```
SELECT id, info
FROM dbo.T1
WHERE JSON_VALUE(info,'$.FullName') = 'Vilma Niva';
```

A newly created index is used and the plan is more efficient, as shown in the following screenshot:

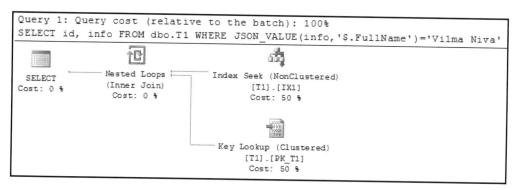

Execution plan using the index on the computed column

Of course, this will work only for a particular JSON path, in this case for the `FullName` property only. For the other properties, you would need to create additional computed columns and indexes on them. In the case of XML indexes, all nodes and values are covered; they are not related to particular values.

An important feature of JSON indexes is that they are collation-aware. The result of the `JSON_VALUE` function is a text value that inherits its collation from the input expression. Therefore, values in the index are ordered using the collation rules defined in the source columns.

By using indexes on computed columns, you can improve performance for frequently used queries.

Full-text indexes

One of the advantages of the fact that JSON data is stored as text in SQL Server is that you can use full-text search features. With computed columns, as demonstrated in the previous section, you can index only one property. To index all JSON properties (actually, to simulate this) you can use full-text indexes.

To demonstrate how full-text searching can improve JSON query performance, you first create a full-text catalog and index it in the sample table that you created earlier in this section:

```
USE WideWorldImporters;
CREATE FULLTEXT CATALOG ftc AS DEFAULT;
CREATE FULLTEXT INDEX ON dbo.T1(info) KEY INDEX PK_T1 ON ftc;
```

Now, after you have created a full-text index, you can execute JSON queries to check whether they can use full-text index benefits. You need to use the CONTAINS predicate; it can identify rows where a word is near another word. Here is the query:

```
SELECT id, info
FROM dbo.T1
WHERE CONTAINS(info,'NEAR(FullName,"Vilma")');
```

The execution plan for the query shown in the following screenshot clearly demonstrates that a full-text index was helpful for this query:

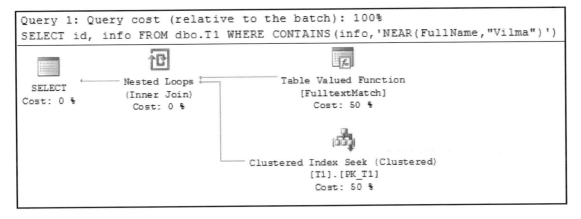

Execution plan with full-text index on the FullName property

To ensure that the same index can improve performance for JSON queries searching the other JSON properties and not only `FullName` (as in the case of the index on the computed column), let's execute another query that searches the `PhoneNumber` property:

```
SELECT id, info
FROM dbo.T1
WHERE CONTAINS(info,'NEAR(PhoneNumber,"(209) 555-0103")');
```

The execution plan is the same as for the previous query, as you can see in the following screenshot:

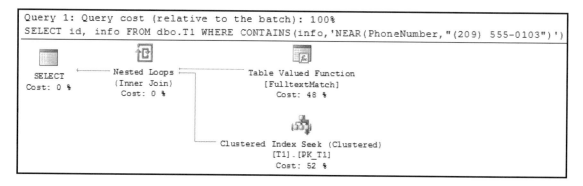

Execution plan with full-text index on the PhoneNumber property

The same index covers both queries. Unfortunately, JSON path expressions are not supported in the `CONTAINS` predicate; you can only search for property values, but it is better than scanning the whole table.

You can store and process small and moderate amounts of JSON data within SQL Server with good support of JSON functions and acceptable performance. However, if your JSON documents are large and you need to search them extensively, you should use a NoSQL solution, such as DocumentDB.

Ensure that you have dropped the table used in this exercise:

```
USE WideWorldImporters;
DROP TABLE IF EXISTS dbo.T1;
```

Summary

This chapter explored JSON support in SQL Server 2017. It is not as robust and deep as XML—there is no native data type, and no optimized storage, and therefore you cannot create JSON indexes to improve performance. Thus, we are talking about built-in and not native JSON support.

However, even with built-in support, it is easy and handy to integrate JSON data in SQL Server. For most of JSON data processing, it would be acceptable. For large JSON documents stored in large database tables, it would be more appropriate to use DocumentDB or other NoSQL based solutions.

In this chapter, you learned that SQL Server 2017 brings built-in support for JSON data; unlike XML, there is no native data type. You used the FOR JSON extension to generate JSON from data in a tabular format and converted JSON data into a tabular format by using the OPENJSON rowset function. You learned how to parse, query, and modify JSON data with a function and how to improve the performance of JSON data processing by using indexes on computed columns and full-text indexes. You also discovered the limitations of JSON implementation in SQL Server 2017.

In the next chapter, you will meet another promising SQL Server feature—*Stretch Databases.*

4
Stretch Database

Stretch Database (**Stretch DB**) is a feature introduced in SQL Server 2016 that allows you to move data or a portion of data transparently and securely from your local database to the cloud (Microsoft Azure). All you need to do is mark the tables that you want to migrate, and the data movement is done transparently and securely. The intention of this feature is to let companies store their old or infrequently used data on the cloud. Companies need to store data locally and operate with active data only, thus reducing the cost and using their resources more effectively. This feature is great and very promising, but there are many limitations that reduce its usability.

In this chapter, we will cover the following points:

- Stretch DB architecture
- How to enable Stretch DB
- How to select tables or part of tables for migration
- Managing and troubleshooting Stretch DB
- Under what circumstances should you use Stretch DB

Stretch DB architecture

When you enable `Stretch Database` for an on-premise SQL Server 2017 database, SQL Server automatically creates a new stretch database in MS Azure SQL Database as an external source and a remote endpoint for the database.

When you query the database, the SQL Server's database engine runs the query against the local or remote database, depending on the data location. Queries against stretch-enabled tables return both local and remote data by default. This is completely transparent to the database user. This means that you can use `Stretch Database` without changing Transact-SQL code in your queries, procedures, or applications. You can stretch an entire table or a portion of table data. The data migration is done asynchronously and transparently. In addition, Stretch Database ensures that no data is lost if a failure occurs during migration. It also has retry logic to handle connection issues that may occur during migration. The following figure illustrates the `Stretch Database` architecture:

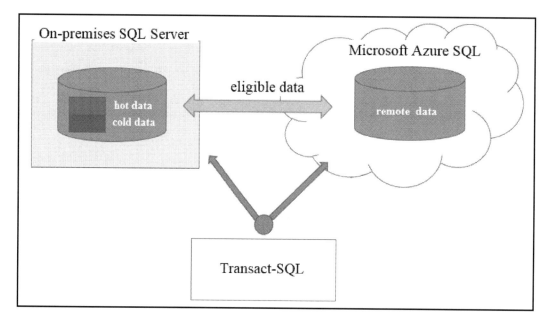

Stretch DB architecture

Data can be located in three stages:

- **Local data**: Local data is data in the table that remains in the on-premise instance. This is usually frequently used or hot data.
- **Staging (eligible data)**: Eligible data is data marked for migration but not migrated yet.
- **Remote data**: Remote data is data that has already been migrated. This data resides in Microsoft Azure SQL Database and is rarely used.

`Stretch Database` does not support stretching to another SQL Server instance. You can stretch a SQL Server database only to Azure SQL Database.

Is this for you?

When SQL Server 2016 RTM was released, there was the tool *Stretch Database Advisor*. This tool could be used to identify databases and tables that were candidates for the `Stretch DB` feature. It was a component of the *SQL Server 2016 Upgrade Advisor,* and by using it, you were also able to identify constraints and blocking issues that prevented the use of the feature.

However, this tool has been removed and replaced by the *Microsoft Data Migration Assistant*. But why I am mentioning this deprecated tool? The *Stretch Database Advisor* checked all tables in the database and creates a report showing the stretching capabilities of each table. I have used it to check which tables in the Microsoft sample SQL Server database `AdventureWorks` are ready for stretching. The results was very disappointing: there was no single table from the Microsoft official SQL Server sample database that this tool marked as recommended and ready for stretching! However, as you will see later in this chapter, this feature is not designed for all tables; it is for special ones.

Data Migration Assistant does not have a separate functionality for `Stretch DB` advises. It analyzes your database and helps you to upgrade it to a new SQL Server version or to Azure SQL Database by detecting compatibility issues that can impact database functionality on your new database version. It also recommends performance and reliability improvements for your target environment. In the Data Migration Assistant, `Stretch DB` is only one of the storage improvements. You can download Data Migration Assistant v3.4 from `https://www.microsoft.com/en-us/download/details.aspx?id=53595`.

Using Data Migration Assistant

In this section, you will use the *Data Migration Assistant* to see what you should expect for your databases when you migrate them to SQL Server 2017 or Azure SQL Database. This is a standalone program and you can run it by executing the `Dma.exe` file in the default install directory `C:\Program FilesMicrosoft Data Migration Assistant`. When you start the tool, you should see an intro screen, as shown in the following screenshot:

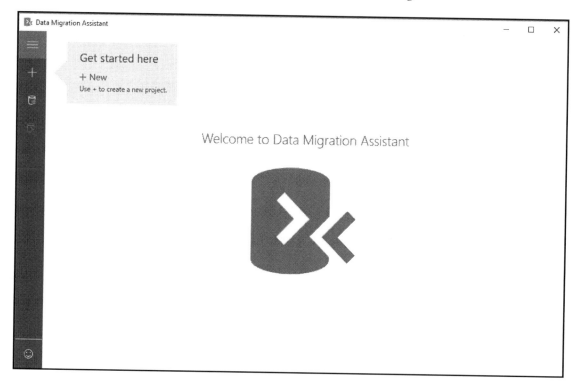

Data Migration Assistant introduction screen

To start a project, you need to click on the + symbol and the new project form appears. On the new project screen, choose **Assessment** as **Project type**, type AdvWorksStretchDB in the **Project name** field, and choose **SQL Server** as **Target server type** (**Source server type** is preselected to **SQL Server**), as displayed here:

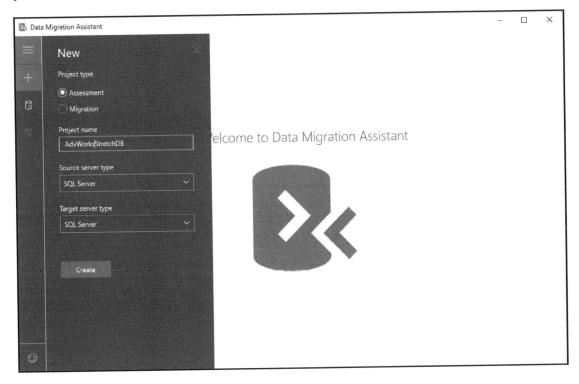

Data Migration Assistant—New Project

After you are done, click on the **Create** button and you will see the next screen, similar to the one shown in the following screenshot:

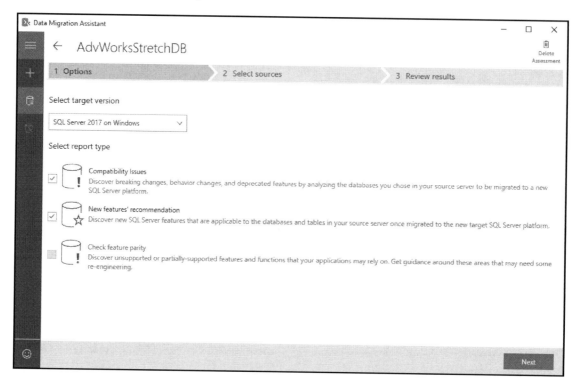

Data Migration Assistant—Select target version

On this screen, you can choose the target SQL Server version. In the dropdown, all versions from 2012 are available; you should, of course, choose **SQL Server 2017 on Windows**. In addition to this, you can select the report type. This time you will choose **New features' recommendation** since you want to see which new features *Data Migration Assistant* recommends to you and not potential compatibility issues.

You then need to click on the **Next** button, connect to a SQL Server 2014 instance, and select the desired databases. In this example, I have selected the Microsoft former standard sample databases `AdventureWorks` and `AdventureWorksDW` that I have restored. If you don't have these two databases, you can choose any other database, but you will most probably end up with different results.

After you have established the connection with the SQL Server 2014 instance, you need to choose the databases that should be analyzed by *Data Migration Assistant*. As mentioned, choose the `AdventureWorks2014` and `AdventureWorksDW2014` databases. You should see a screen like the following one:

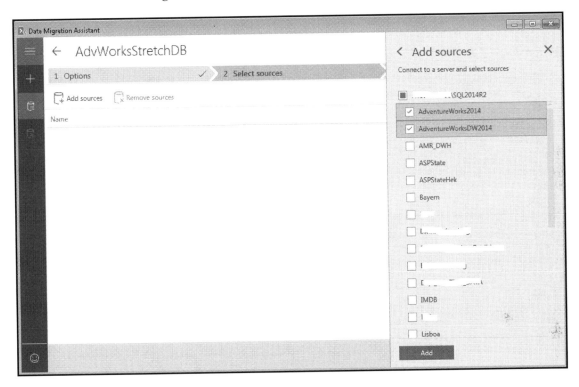

Data Migration Assistant - choose databases for analyzing

When you click the **Add** button, the selected databases are added to the sources collection. You'll get another screen, where you can start the assessment by clicking on the **Start Assessment** button:

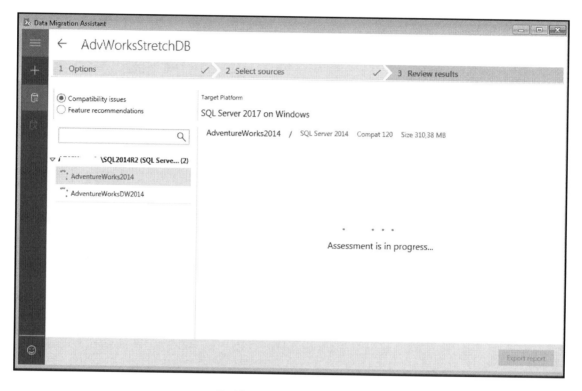

Data Migration Assistant—Start Assessment

The analysis takes less than a minute, and the next figure shows its results for the
`AdventureWorks2014` database:

Data Migration Assistant—Review results for the AdventureWorks2014 database

On the left radio-buttons, you need to choose the *Feature recommendations* option. `Stretch DB`-related recommendations are located under the **Storage** tab. In the case of the `AdventureWorks2014` database, two tables are listed as tables that would benefit from using the `Stretch DB` feature: `Sales.SalesOrderDetail` and `Production.TransactionHistory`.

However, both of them have properties that prevent the use of the `Stretch DB`, so you can conclude that this feature is irrelevant for the `AdventureWorks2014` database. The result of the analysis for the `AdventureWorksDW2014` looks a bit better, as shown in the following screenshot:

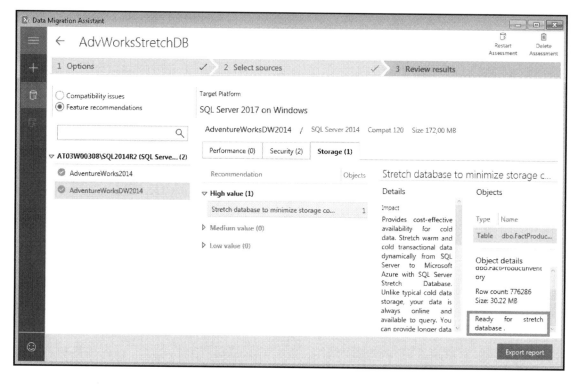

Data Migration Assistant—Review results for the AdventureWorksDW2014 database

Data Migration Assistant has found one table (`dbo.FactProductInventory`) that is ready to use the `Stretch DB` feature. It does not mention the other tables in the report—just three tables from two selected databases. At this point, I need to mention again that although this sample databases have a few very simple tables, with just a few rows, even for them you cannot use the `Stretch DB` feature. In data warehouse databases, tables seem to be more stretch-friendly, but according the tool, it is very hard to find a table that qualifies for stretching.

`Stretch Database` will give you benefits with your data warehouse databases, especially with historical data that is taking up space and is rarely used. On the other hand, this feature might not be eligible for your OLTP system due to the table limitations that your OLTP system has. Now, it is finally time to see in detail what these limitations are.

Limitations of using Stretch Database

As you saw in the previous section, there are many limitations when you work with Stretch Database. You can distinguish between limitations that the prevent usage of Stretch Database and limitations in database tables that are enabled for stretching.

Limitations that prevent you from enabling the Stretch DB features for a table

In this section, you will see the limitations that prevent you from using Stretch DB. They can be divided into table, column, and index limitations.

Table limitations

You cannot enable the `Stretch DB` feature for any SQL Server table. A table should have stretch-friendly properties. The following list shows the table properties that prevent the use of the `Stretch DB` feature:

- It is a memory-optimized table
- It is a file table
- It contains `FILESTREAM` data
- It uses `Change Data Capture` or `Change Tracking` features
- It has more than 1,023 columns or more than 998 indexes
- Tables referenced with a foreign key
- It is referenced by indexed views
- It contains full-text indexes

The list is not so short, but let's see how huge these limitations are in practice. Despite their power and a completely new technology stack behind them, memory-optimized tables are still not in use intensively. From my experience, I can say that most companies still don't use memory-optimized tables in production environments due to the lack of use cases for them, hardware resources, or even the knowledge required for their implementation and configuration. In addition to this, memory-optimized tables usually store hot data, data that is frequently needed and whose content is not intended to be sent to the cloud. Therefore, you cannot say that the first limitation is a huge one.

`File Table` and `FILESTREAM` tables appear frequently in the list of limitations for new SQL Server features. The same is true for tables using `Change Data Capture` or `Change Tracking` features. They are simply not compatible with many other features since they address specific use cases. Therefore, I am not surprised to see them in this list. Full-text indexes and indexed views also prevent Stretch DB usage. From my experience, in companies that I have worked with or where I was involved as a consultant, less than 10% of tables belong to these categories. According to all of these limitations, I would say that the potential of Stretch DB is slightly reduced, but not significantly. However, the most important limitation is that a table cannot be referenced with a foreign key. This is an implementation of database integrity and many tables are and should be referenced with foreign keys. Therefore, this is a serious limitation for Stretch DB usage and significantly reduces the number of potential tables that can be stretched.

 You should not disable foreign key relationships in order to use the Stretch DB feature! I would never suggest removing any database object or attribute that implements data integrity to gain performance or storage benefits.

However, this is just the beginning; more limitations will come in the next subsection.

Column limitations

Even if your table does not violate constraints from the preceding table of limitations, it is still far away from fulfilling the conditions for stretching. The following properties and characteristics of table columns don't support the Stretch DB feature:

- Unsupported data types: Deprecated large data types (`text`, `ntext`, and `image`), XML, `timestamp`, `sql_variant`, spatial data types (geometry and geography), `hierarchyId`, user-defined CLR data types
- Computed columns
- Default constraints
- Check constraints

Let's repeat a similar analysis of the reduced potential of `Stretch DB` for the items from this list. I think that Microsoft has a balanced approach with deprecated data types; they are not removed in order to prevent the breaking of changes in legacy code, but all new features don't support them. This is completely correct and it should not be considered a limitation.

The other unsupported data types are used rarely and do not represent a huge limitation.

 You can find user-defined CLR data types in a list of limitations for almost all SQL Server features in recent releases. This is also one of the reasons they are not so popular or frequently used.

However, the most important limitation in this list is that a table column in a Stretch Database cannot have a default or check constraint. This is a huge limitation and significantly reduces the usage and importance of the Stretch DB feature!

Also, as mentioned before, you should not remove database objects created to implement database integrity just to enable Stretch DB. Default constraints and foreign keys are the reasons why there is not a single table in the `AdventureWorks2014` database that is ready for stretching.

Limitations for Stretch-enabled tables

If your table survives these limitations and you have enabled it for stretching, you should be aware of these additional constraints:

- Uniqueness is not enforced for `UNIQUE` constraints and `PRIMARY KEY` constraints in the Azure table that contains the migrated data.
- You cannot `UPDATE` or `DELETE` rows that have been migrated or rows that are eligible for migration in a Stretch-enabled table or in a view that includes Stretch-enabled tables.
- You cannot `INSERT` rows into a Stretch-enabled table on a linked server.
- You cannot create an index for a view that includes Stretch-enabled tables.
- Filters on SQL Server indexes are not propagated to the remote table.

These limitations are not unexpected; the Azure portion of data is automatically managed and it should be protected from direct access and changes. Therefore, these limitations are acceptable, especially compared to all those listed in the previous sections.

Use cases for Stretch Database

With so many limitations, finding use cases for `Stretch DB` does not seem to be an easy task. You would need tables without constraints and rare data types that are not involved in relations with other tables and that don't use some special SQL Server features. Where to find them? As potential candidates for stretching, you should consider historical or auditing and logging tables.

Archiving of historical data

Historical or auditing data is commonly produced automatically by database systems and does not require constraints to guarantee data integrity. In addition to this, it is usually in large data sets. Therefore, historical and auditing data can be a candidate for using the `Stretch DB` feature. SQL Server 2016 introduced support for system-versioned temporal tables. They are implemented as a pair of tables: a current and a historical table. One of the requirements for historical tables is that they cannot have any constraints. Therefore, historical tables used in system-versioned temporal tables are ideal candidates for stretching. Temporal tables are covered in `Chapter 5`, *Temporal Tables*.

Archiving of logging tables

Sometimes, developers decide to store application and service logging information in database tables. Such tables usually have no constraints, since writing to log must be as fast as possible. They are also possible candidates for using the `Stretch DB` feature.

Testing Azure SQL database

Small or medium companies that are considering whether to use the cloud or to move data completely to it can use `Stretch DB` to start using Azure SQL database. They can learn about data management in Azure and collect experience and then decide whether they need to delegate more or their entire data to the cloud.

Enabling Stretch Database

Before you select tables for stretching, you need to enable the feature at the instance level. Like many other new features, it is disabled by default. To enable it, you need to execute the following statements:

```
EXEC sys.sp_configure N'remote data archive', '1';
RECONFIGURE;
GO
```

Actually, you have to allow remote data archiving; there is no enabling Stretch Database option. Anyway, after enabling it at an instance level, you can choose a database and enable the feature at the database level.

Enabling Stretch Database at the database level

If the feature is enabled at the instance level and you have enough database permissions (db_owner or CONTROL DATABASE), the next step is to enable Stretch DB at the database level. Of course, before you enable it, you need to have a valid Azure account and subscription. You also need to create and configure firewall rules to allow your Azure database to communicate with your local server. In this section, you will enable the Stretch DB feature for a new database. Use this code to create a database named Mila:

```
DROP DATABASE IF EXISTS Mila; --Ensure that you create a new, empty
database
GO
CREATE DATABASE Mila;
GO
```

Since the database is new and has no tables, it does not violate the limitations listed in the previous section. You can enable the Stretch Database feature at the database level by using wizard or with Transact-SQL.

Enabling Stretch Database by using wizard

You can use the **Enable Database for Stretch** wizard to configure a database for Stretch Database. To launch it, you need to right-click on the newly created Mila database in **SQL Server Management Studio (SSMS)**, and from the right-click context menu, select **Tasks | Stretch | Enable** respectively. When you launch the wizard, you should get the following screen:

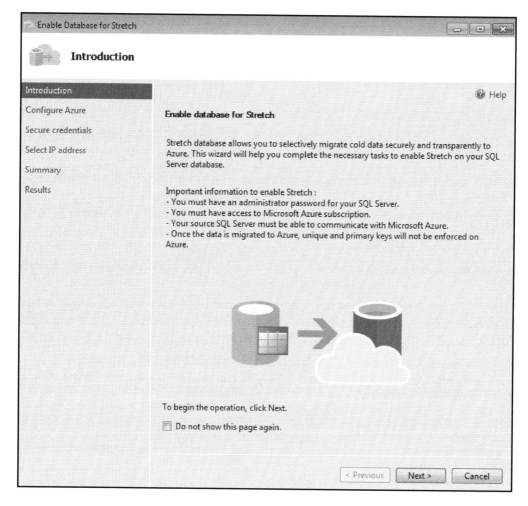

Enable Database for Search Wizard—Introduction page

You can see an intro screen that describes what you can achieve with the Stretch Database feature and what you need to use them. Since your database has no tables, the second section of the wizard is **Configure Azure**. You are asked to enter your Azure credentials and to connect to Azure:

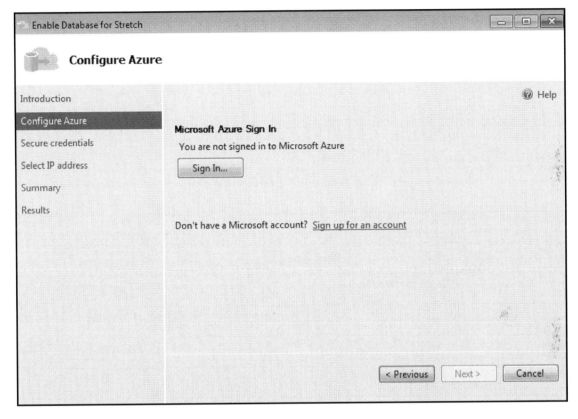

Enable Database for Search Wizard—Configure Azure page

After signing in to Azure, you should select one of your Azure subscriptions and an appropriate Azure region. Create a new or choose an existing Azure server, as follows:

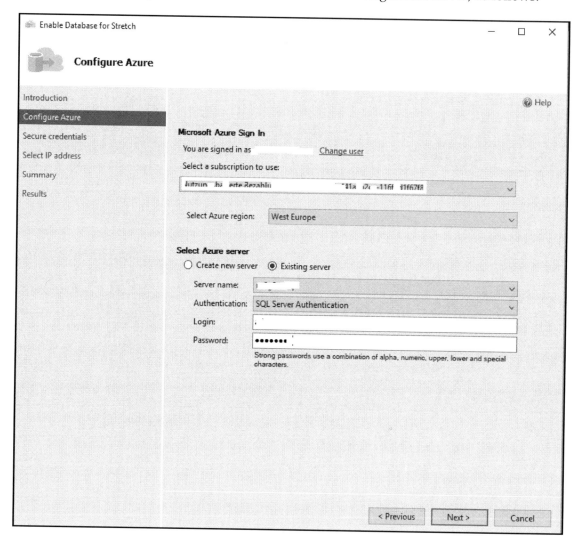

Enable Database for Search Wizard—Sign in to Azure and select subscription and server

The next part of the wizard is **Secure credentials**. The wizard lets you create a database master key (if your database does not have one) in order to protect the database credentials and connection information stored in your SQL Server database. Here is the screen where you can create a database master key:

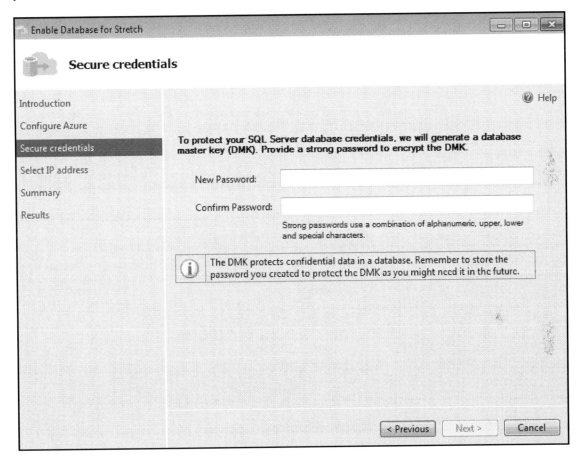

Enable Database for Search Wizard—Secure credentials

As already mentioned, you need to create Azure firewall rules to let your Azure SQL database communicate with your local SQL Server database. You can define a range of IP addresses with the **Enable Database for Stretch** wizard's page **Select IP address**:

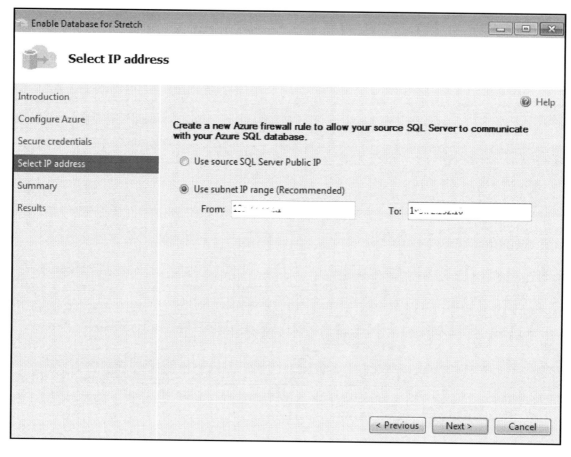

Enable Database for Search Wizard—Select IP address

And the tour is almost done. The next screen is **Summary** and it displays what you have already selected and entered, but it also provides an estimated price for the Stretch DB setup. The following screenshot shows the **Summary** screen:

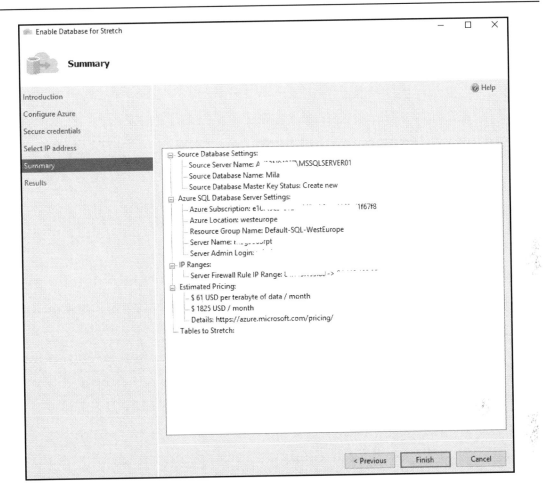

Enable Database for Search Wizard—Summary

As you can see, the **Summary** screen brings one very important piece of information to you: the estimated price for enabling the Stretch DB feature. The **Estimated Pricing** section in the summary report is a bit strange: it shows two prices: $61 per TB per month and $1,825 per month. If you enable Stretch DB for your database with no tables, you would need to pay at least $1,825 per month! It does not seem to be cheap at all for an empty database. However, there is also a third piece of information in that section—a link to the pricing page at Microsoft Azure—and you can find more details about pricing there. The pricing is covered later in this chapter, in the *SQL Server Stretch Database pricing* section. For now, it is enough to know that you don't need to pay a full month's cost if you remove your database from the cloud before that. The minimum period for payment is 1 hour.

However, this is not immediately clear, and even if you want to just try or play with the feature to find out how it works or to explore it, you need to pay for this or apply for a trial subscription (which involves giving credit card details). I expected a non-complicated trial version with limited functionalities but without required registration and payment data, where I can check and learn about the feature. Stretch DB as a new and promising feature should be easy to try. Now it is time to click on the **Finish** button to instruct the wizard to perform the final step in the process of enabling the Stretch DB feature. After the last wizard action is done, the stretch database is created in Azure. You can use SSMS to see that the action was successful. When you choose the database Mila, you will see a different icon near to the database name:

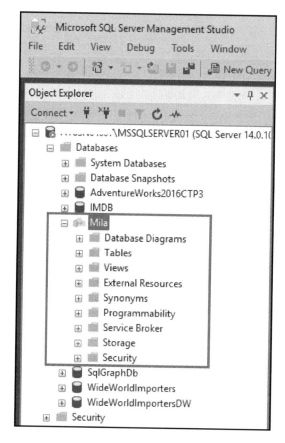

Database in SSMS with enabled Stretch DB feature

After the feature is enabled for your sample database, you should not expect anything, since there are no tables in it. You will create a table and continue to play with stretching later in this chapter.

Enabling Stretch Database by using Transact-SQL

You can enable the `Stretch DB` feature by using Transact-SQL only. As you saw in the previous section, to enable `Stretch DB`, you need to create and secure communication infrastructure between our local database and the Azure server. Therefore, you need to accomplish the following three tasks:

1. Create a database master key to protect server credentials
2. Create a database credential
3. Define the Azure server

The following code creates a database master key for the sample database `Mila`:

```
USE Mila;
CREATE MASTER KEY ENCRYPTION BY PASSWORD='<very secure password>'; --you
need to put your password here
```

Next, we create a credential. This is saved authentication information that is required to connect to external resources. You need a credential for only one database; therefore you should create a database-scoped credential:

```
CREATE DATABASE SCOPED CREDENTIAL MilaStretchCredential
WITH
IDENTITY = 'Vasilije',
SECRET = '<very secure password>'; --you need to put your password here
```

Now you can finally enable the Stretch DB feature by using the `ALTER DATABASE` statement. You need to set `REMOTE_DATA_ARCHIVE` and define two parameters: Azure server and just-created database scoped credential. Here is the code that can be used to enable the Stretch DB feature for the database `Mila`:

```
ALTER DATABASE Mila
    SET REMOTE_DATA_ARCHIVE = ON
        (
            SERVER = '<address of your Azure server>,
            CREDENTIAL = [MilaStretchCredential]
        );
```

With this action, you have created an infrastructure, necessary for communication between your local database and the Azure server that will hold the stretched data. Note that this action can take a few minutes. When I executed the command, it took more than three minutes:

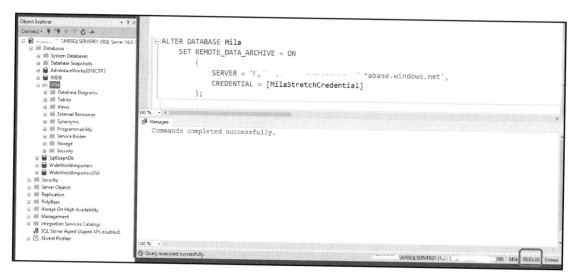

Enabling Stretch Database by using Transact-SQL

The next and final step is to select and enable tables for stretching.

Enabling Stretch Database for a table

To enable Stretch DB for a table, you can also choose between the wizard and Transact-SQL. You can migrate an entire table or just part of a table. If your cold data is stored in a separated table, you can migrate the entire table; otherwise you must specify a filter function to define which rows should be migrated. To enable the Stretch DB feature for a table, you must be a member of the db_owner role. In this section, you will create a new table in the Mila database, populate it with a few rows, and enable it for stretching. Use this code to create and populate the table:

```
USE Mila;
CREATE TABLE dbo.T1(
id INT NOT NULL,
c1 VARCHAR(20) NOT NULL,
c2 DATETIME NOT NULL,
CONSTRAINT PK_T1 PRIMARY KEY CLUSTERED (id)
);
```

```
GO
INSERT INTO dbo.T1 (id, c1, c2) VALUES
    (1, 'Benfica Lisbon','20180115'),
    (2, 'Manchester United','20180202'),
    (3, 'Rapid Vienna','20180128'),
    (4, 'Juventus Torino','20180225'),
    (5, 'Red Star Belgrade','20180225');
```

In the next sections, you will enable and use the Stretch DB feature for the T1 table. Assume that you want to move all rows from this table with a value in the c2 column that is older than *1st February 2018* to the cloud.

Enabling Stretch DB for a table by using wizard

You can create a new table with the Stretch DB feature enabled or enable it for an existing table using the **Enable Table for Stretch** wizard. To launch it, you need to navigate to the T1 table under the database Mila in SSMS. Then, after right-clicking, you need to select the option **Tasks/Stretch/Enable** respectively. You should get a following screenshot:

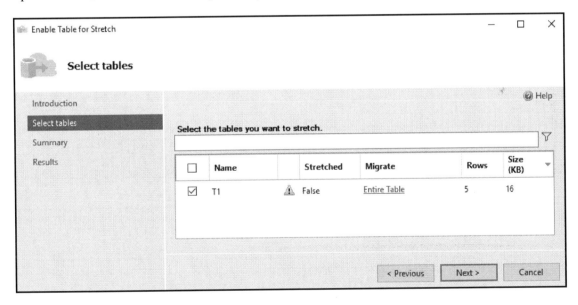

Enable Table for Stretch Wizard—Select tables

As you can see, T1 can be selected for stretching, since it meets the `Stretch DB` requirements discussed in the previous sections. You can choose to migrate the entire table or (by clicking on the link **Entire Table**) only a part of it. When you click on the link, you'll get this screen:

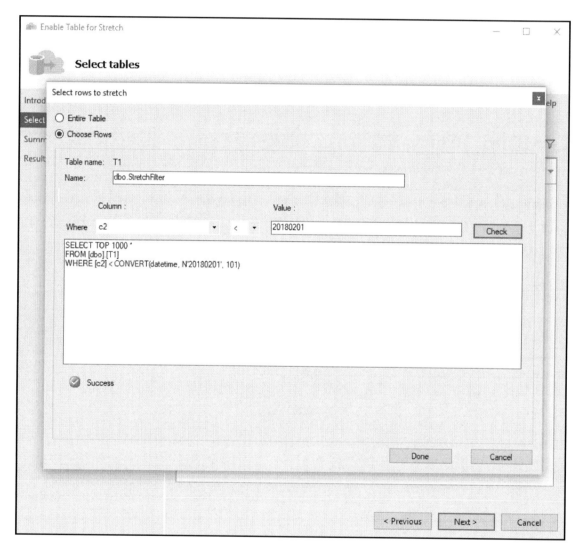

Enable Table for Stretch Wizard—Select rows to stretch

You see a query builder that can help you to write the correct filter function. Filter function is used to define which rows have to be migrated to the cloud. In this example, you are going to return all rows from the T1 table, where the value in the c2 column is less than *2018/02/01*.

However, developers find query builders a bit clumsy, and most of them prefer to work with Transact-SQL. In the next section, you will see how to use Transact-SQL to configure Stretch DB.

Enabling Stretch Database for a table by using Transact-SQL

In order to support table stretching, the CREATE and ALTER TABLE statements have been extended in SQL Server 2016. Here is the syntax extension for the ALTER TABLE statement that supports the Stretch DB feature:

```
<stretch_configuration> ::=
    {
      SET (
        REMOTE_DATA_ARCHIVE
        {
            = ON (  <table_stretch_options>  )
          | = OFF_WITHOUT_DATA_RECOVERY ( MIGRATION_STATE = PAUSED )
          | ( <table_stretch_options> [, ...n] )
        }
          )
    }
<table_stretch_options> ::=
    {
      [ FILTER_PREDICATE = { null | table_predicate_function } , ]
        MIGRATION_STATE = { OUTBOUND | INBOUND | PAUSED }
    }
```

You can specify the following options to enable Stretch DB:

- REMOTE_DATA_ARCHIVE is required and can have these values: ON, OFF_WITHOUT_DATA_RECOVERY or no value.
- MIGRATION_STATE is also mandatory and can have one of the following values: OUTBOUND, INBOUND, or PAUSED.
- FILTER_PREDICATE is optional and is used to define the part of the data that needs to be migrated. If it's not specified, the entire table will be moved.

If your table contains both hot and cold data, you can specify a filter predicate to select the rows that should be migrated. The filter predicate is an inline table-valued function. Its parameters are identifiers for stretch table columns. At least one parameter is required. Here is the function syntax:

```
CREATE FUNCTION dbo.fn_stretchpredicate(@column1 datatype1, @column2 
datatype2 [, ...n])
RETURNS TABLE
WITH SCHEMABINDING
AS
RETURN   SELECT 1 AS is_eligible
         WHERE <predicate>
```

The function returns either a non-empty result or no result set. In the first case, the row is eligible to be migrated, otherwise it remains in the local system.

Note that the function is defined with the SCHEMABINDING option to prevent columns that are used by the filter function from being dropped or altered.

The <predicate> can consist of one condition, or of multiple conditions joined with the AND logical operator:

```
<predicate> ::= <condition> [ AND <condition> ] [ ...n ]
```

Each condition in turn can consist of one primitive condition, or of multiple primitive conditions joined with the OR logical operator. You cannot use subqueries or non-deterministic functions. For a detailed list of limitations, please visit this page in the SQL Server Books Online: https://msdn.microsoft.com/en-us/library/mt613432.aspx.

The following code example shows how to enable the Stretch DB feature for the T1 table in the database Mila:

```
CREATE FUNCTION dbo.StretchFilter(@col DATETIME)
RETURNS TABLE
WITH SCHEMABINDING
AS
      RETURN SELECT 1 AS is_eligible WHERE @col < CONVERT(DATETIME,
'01.02.2018', 104);
GO
ALTER TABLE dbo.T1
  SET (
```

```
        REMOTE_DATA_ARCHIVE = ON (
                                    FILTER_PREDICATE =
dbo.StretchFilter(c2),
                                    MIGRATION_STATE = OUTBOUND
                                  )
        );
```

After executing the preceding commands, Stretch DB is enabled for T1 table. The following screenshot shows the SSMS screen immediately after the execution:

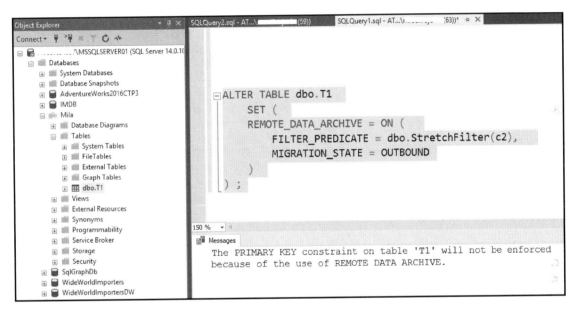

Enabling table for stretch by using Transact-SQL

The Stretch DB feature is enabled, but you can also see a warning message that informs you that although your T1 table has a primary key constraint, it will not be enforced! Thus, you can have multiple rows in your table with the same ID, just because you have enabled the Stretch DB. This schema and integrity change silently implemented as part of Stretch DB enabling can be dangerous; some developers will not be aware of it, since the information is delivered through a message warning.

When you ignore this issue, the rest of the action looks correct. After the table is enabled for stretching, you can expect three rows to remain in the local database (they have a value in the c2 column later than *1st February 2018*). Two rows should be moved to the Azure SQL database. You will confirm this by querying stretch tables, but before that you will learn a tip about the creation of a filter predicate with sliding window.

Filter predicate with sliding window

As mentioned earlier, you cannot call a non-deterministic function in a filter predicate. If you, for instance, want to migrate all rows older than 1 month (where a date column has a value older than 1 month), you cannot simply use the DATEADD function in the filter function because DATEADD is a non-deterministic function.

In the previous example, you created the filter function to migrate all rows older than 1 June 2016. Assume that you want to send all rows older than 1 month to the cloud. Since the function must be deterministic and you cannot alter the existing one because it is defined with SCHEMABINDING attribute, you need to create a new function with the literal date again. For instance, on 1 August, you would need a function that instructs the system to migrate rows older than 1 July:

```
CREATE FUNCTION dbo.StretchFilter20180301(@col DATETIME)
RETURNS TABLE
WITH SCHEMABINDING
AS
        RETURN SELECT 1 AS is_eligible
WHERE @col < CONVERT(DATETIME, '01.03.2018', 104);
```

Now you can assign the newly created function to the T1 table:

```
ALTER TABLE dbo.T1
SET (REMOTE_DATA_ARCHIVE = ON
    (FILTER_PREDICATE = dbo.StretchFilter20180301(c2), MIGRATION_STATE =
OUTBOUND ) );
```

Finally, you should remove the old filter function:

```
DROP FUNCTION IF EXISTS dbo.StretchFilter;
```

Querying stretch databases

When you query a stretch database, the SQL Server Database Engine runs the query against the local or remote database depending on data location. This is completely transparent to the database user. When you run a query that returns both local and remote data, you can see the Remote Query operator in the execution plan. The following query returns all rows from the stretch T1 table:

```
USE Mila;
SELECT * FROM dbo.T1;
```

As expected, it returns five rows:

id	c1	c2
2	Manchester United	2018-02-02 00:00:00.000
4	Juventus Torino	2018-02-25 00:00:00.000
5	Red Star Belgrade	2018-02-25 00:00:00.000
1	Benfica Lisbon	2018-01-15 00:00:00.000
3	Rapid Vienna	2018-01-28 00:00:00.000

You are surely much more interested in how the execution plan looks:

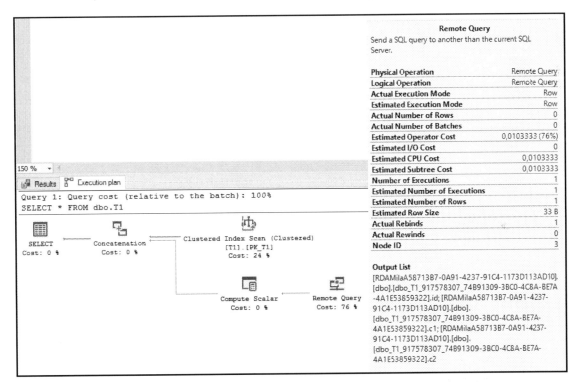

Execution plan for query with stretch tables

You can see that the `Remote Query` operator operates with an Azure database and that its output is concatenated with the output of the Clustered Index Scan that collected data from the local SQL Server instance. Note that the property window for the `Remote Query` operator has been shortened to show only context-relevant information.

What does SQL Server do when only local rows are returned? To check this, run the following code:

```
SELECT * FROM dbo.T1 WHERE c2 >= '20180201';
```

The query returns three rows, as expected:

```
id           c1                      c2
----------   --------------------    -----------------------
2            Manchester United       2018-02-02 00:00:00.000
4            Juventus Torino         2018-02-25 00:00:00.000
5            Red Star Belgrade       2018-02-25 00:00:00.000
```

And the execution plan is shown as follows:

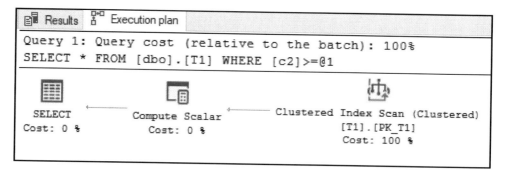

Execution plan for query with stretch tables returning local data only

The plan looks good; it checks only the local database and there is no connection to Azure. Finally, you will check the plan for a query that logically returns remote data only. Here is the query:

```
SELECT * FROM dbo.T1 WHERE c2 < '20180201';
```

You will again get the expected result:

```
id           c1                      c2
----------   --------------------    -----------------------
1            Benfica Lisbon          2018-01-15 00:00:00.000
3            Rapid Vienna            2018-01-28 00:00:00.000
```

Here is the execution plan:

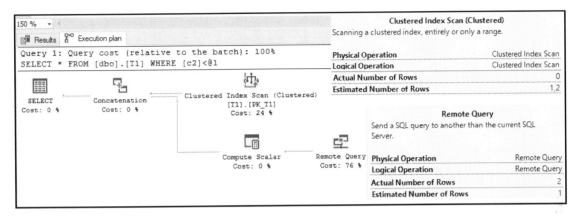

Execution plan for query with stretch tables returning remote data only

You probably did not expect both operators here only `Remote Query` should be shown. However, even if the returned data resides in the Azure SQL database only, both operators should be used since data can be in an eligible state, which means that it has not yet been moved to Azure!

Querying stretch tables is straightforward; you don't need to change anything in your queries. One of the most important things about stretch databases is that the entire execution is transparent to the user and you don't need to change your code when working with stretch tables.

However, you should not forget that enabling `Stretch DB` can suspend primary key constraints in your stretched tables; uniqueness is not enforced for UNIQUE constraints and PRIMARY KEY constraints in the Azure table that contains the migrated data.

Querying and updating remote data

As mentioned earlier, queries with stretch-enabled tables return both local and remote data by default. You can manage the scope of queries by using the system stored procedure `sys.sp_rda_set_query_mode` to specify whether queries against the current Stretch-enabled database and its tables return both local and remote data or local data only. The following modes are available:

- `LOCAL_AND_REMOTE` (queries against Stretch-enabled tables return both local and remote data). This is the default mode.

- LOCAL_ONLY (queries against Stretch-enabled tables return only local data).
- DISABLED (queries against Stretch-enabled tables are not allowed).

When you specify the scope of queries against the Stretch Database, this is applied to all queries for all users. However, there are additional options at the single query level for an administrator (member of the db_owner group). As the administrator, you can add the query hint WITH (REMOTE_DATA_ARCHIVE_OVERRIDE = value) to the SELECT statement to specify data location. The option REMOTE_DATA_ARCHIVE_OVERRIDE can have one of the following values:

- LOCAL_ONLY (query returns only local data)
- REMOTE_ONLY (query returns only remote data)
- STAGE_ONLY (query returns eligible data)

The following code returns eligible data for the T1 table:

```
USE Mila;
SELECT * FROM dbo.T1 WITH (REMOTE_DATA_ARCHIVE_OVERRIDE = STAGE_ONLY);
```

Here is the output:

id	c1	c2	batchID--917578307
1	Benfica Lisbon	2018-01-15 00:00:00.000	1
3	Rapid Vienna	2018-01-28 00:00:00.000	1

Run this code to return data from the T1 table already moved to Azure:

```
SELECT * FROM dbo.T1 WITH (REMOTE_DATA_ARCHIVE_OVERRIDE = REMOTE_ONLY);
```

Here is the output:

id	c1	c2	batchID--917578307
1	Benfica Lisbon	2018-01-15 00:00:00.000	1
3	Rapid Vienna	2018-01-28 00:00:00.000	1

Finally, this code returns data in the T1 table from the local database server:

```
SELECT * FROM dbo.T1 WITH (REMOTE_DATA_ARCHIVE_OVERRIDE = LOCAL_ONLY);
```

As you expected, three rows are returned:

```
id              c1                      c2
----------      --------------------    ----------------------
2               Manchester United       2018-02-02 00:00:00.000
4               Juventus Torino         2018-02-25 00:00:00.000
5               Red Star Belgrade       2018-02-25 00:00:00.000
```

By default, you can't update or delete rows that are eligible for migration or rows that have already been migrated in a Stretch-enabled table. When you have to fix a problem, a member of the db_owner role can run an UPDATE or DELETE operation by adding the preceding hint and will be able to update data in all locations.

SQL Server Stretch Database pricing

You can see price details on the https://azure.microsoft.com/en-us/pricing/details/sql-server-stretch-database/ page. Stretch Database bills compute and storage separately. Compute usage is represented by **Database Stretch Unit (DSU)** and customers can scale up and down the level of performance/DSUs they need at any time. The prices given here were valid on 28th February 2018:

Performance level (DSU)	Price in $ per month
100	1,825
200	3,650
300	5,475
400	7,300
500	9,125
600	10,950
1,000	18,250
1,200	21,900
1,500	27,375
2,000	36,500

Stretch DB price list

Database sizes are limited to 240 TB. Monthly price estimates are based on 730 hours per month at constant DSU levels. `Stretch DB` is generally available in all regions except southern India, Northern China, southern Brazil, north-central America, western India, Australia, Japan, and US Gov.

Data storage is charged based on $0.16/GB/month. Data storage includes the size of your `Stretch DB` and backup snapshots. All Stretch databases have *7 days* of incremental backup snapshots.

You can also use the Azure Pricing calculator to estimate expenses for your planned Azure activities. It is available at `https://azure.microsoft.com/en-us/pricing/calculator/?service=sql-server-stretch-database`. You can choose the Azure region and specify the time period, data storage, and DSU, as shown in the following screenshot:

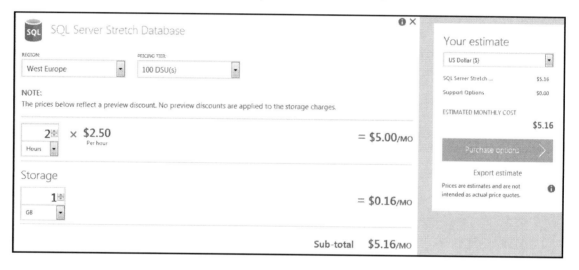

Azure Pricing calculator—Calculating price for Stretch DB

This screen shows the price you would pay when you play with the Stretch DB feature for two hours in a database with less than **1 GB** of data and with **100 DSU(s)** using Azure database in **Western Europe**.

It is also possible to try the feature for free. You can apply for it at `https://azure.` `microsoft.com/en-us/free/`. When you do this, you'll see this screen:

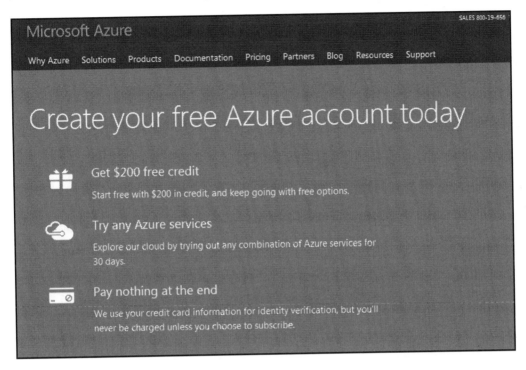

Creating a free Azure account

It is good that you can try the new feature for free, but in this case, you must also give your payment details, which could reduce the number of developers who will try the feature.

Stretch DB management and troubleshooting

To monitor stretch-enabled databases and data migration, you can use the *Stretch Database Monitor* feature, the `sys.remote_data_archive_databases` and `sys.remote_data_archive_tables` catalog views, and the `sys.dm_db_rda_migration_status` dynamic management view.

Monitoring Stretch Databases

To monitor Stretch-enabled databases and data migration, use the *Stretch Database Monitor* feature. It is part of SQL Server Management Studio and you open it when you select your database and then choose **Tasks/Stretch/Monitor**:

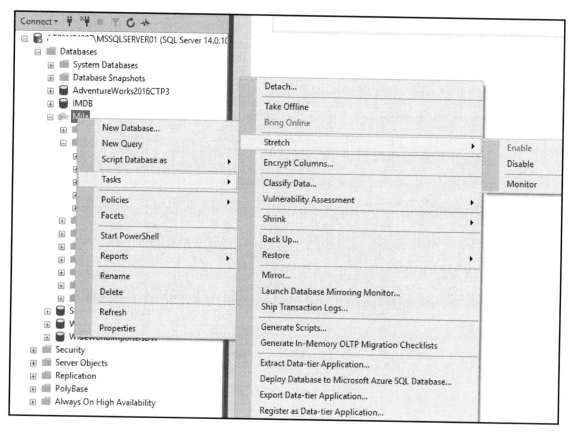

Open Stretch Database Monitor in SSMS

The top portion of the monitor displays general information about both the stretch-enabled SQL Server database and the remote Azure database, while the status of data migration for each stretch-enabled table in the database is shown in the bottom part of the screen:

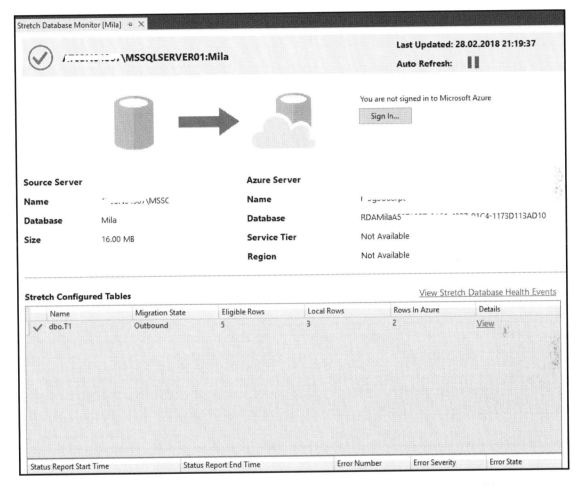

Stretch Database Monitoring

You can also use the dynamic management view `sys.dm_db_rda_migration_status` to check the status of migrated data (how many batches and rows of data have been migrated). It contains one row for each batch of migrated data from each stretch-enabled table on the local instance of SQL Server. Here is the result generated by executing this view:

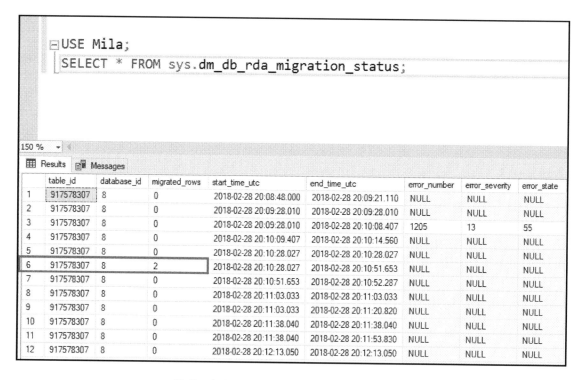

Checking migration status by using DMV sys.dm_db_rda_migration_status

The `sys.remote_data_archive_databases` and `sys.remote_data_archive_tables` catalog views give information about the status of migration at the table and database level.

This query provides archive database information:

```
USE Mila;
SELECT * FROM sys.remote_data_archive_databases;
```

Here is the output:

remote_database_id	remote_database_name	data_source_id	federated_service_account
65536	RDAMilaA58713B7-0A91-4237-91C4-1173D113AD10	65536	0

By using the following command, you can get information about archive tables on the Azure side :

```
USE Mila;
SELECT * FROM sys.remote_data_archive_tables;
```

And here is the output:

object_id	remote_database_id	remote_table_name	filter_predicate
917578307	65536	dbo_T1_917578307_74B91309-3B...	([dbo].[StretchFilter]([c2]))

migration_direction	migration_direction_desc	is_migration_paused	is_reconciled
0	OUTBOUND	0	1

Finally, to see how much space a stretch-enabled table is using in Azure, run the following statement:

```
USE Mila;
EXEC sp_spaceused 'dbo.T1', 'true', 'REMOTE_ONLY';
```

Here is the result of this command:

name	rows	reserved	data	index_size	unused
dbo.T1	2	288 KB	16 KB	48 KB	224 KB

In the next sections, you will see how to pause or disable the Stretch DB feature.

Pause and resume data migration

To pause data migration for a table, choose the table in SSMS and then select the option **Stretch | Pause**. You can achieve the same with the following Transact-SQL command; it temporarily breaks the data migration for the T1 table:

```
USE Mila;
ALTER TABLE dbo.T1 SET (REMOTE_DATA_ARCHIVE (MIGRATION_STATE = PAUSED));
```

To resume data migration for a table, choose the table in SSMS and then select the **Stretch/Resume** option or write the Transact-SQL code, similar to the following one:

```
USE Mila;
ALTER TABLE dbo.T1 SET (REMOTE_DATA_ARCHIVE (MIGRATION_STATE = OUTBOUND));
```

To check whether migration is active or paused, you can open Stretch Database Monitor in SQL Server Management Studio and check the value of the `Migration State` or column check the value of the flag `is_migration_paused` in the system catalog view `sys.remote_data_archive_tables`.

Disabling Stretch Database

Disabling the Stretch DB features for a database and the tables stop data migration immediately and queries don't include remote data anymore. You can copy the already-migrated data back to the local system, or you can leave it in Azure. As with Stretch Database enabling, you can disable it for tables and databases using SSMS and Transact-SQL. In order to disable Stretch DB for a database, you have to disable it for tables involved in stretching. Otherwise, you will get an error that instructs you to disable stretch tables before that action.

Disable Stretch Database for tables by using SSMS

To disable `Stretch DB` for a table, you need to select it in SQL Server Management Studio (SSMS); right-click on it, and select the option **Stretch**. Then, go to one of the following options:

- **Disable | Bring data back from Azure** to copy remote data for the table to the local system and then disable the Stretch DB feature
- **Disable | Leave data in Azure** to disable the Stretch DB feature immediately, without transferring it back to the local system (data remains in Azure)

Be aware that the first option includes data transfer costs! When you choose the second option, you don't have transfer costs, but the data remains in Azure and you still need to pay for storage. You can remove it through the Azure Management portal:

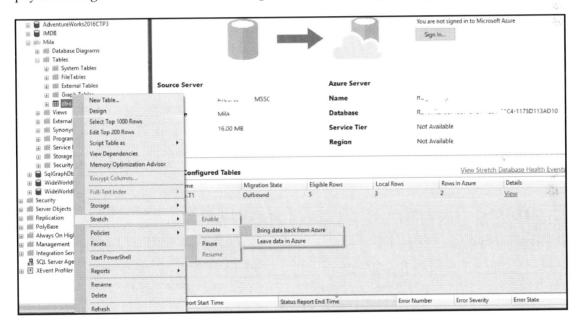

Disable stretching for a table in SSMS

After the `Stretch DB` feature has been disabled for the `T1` table, you can see the following screenshot:

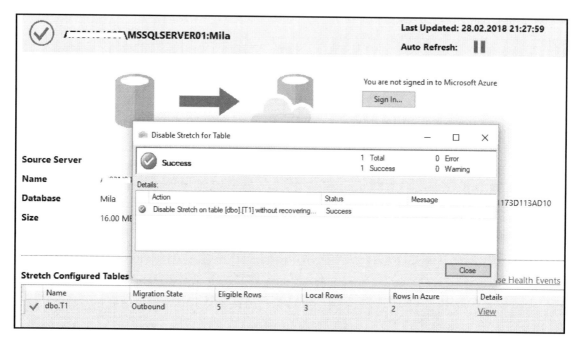

Disable stretching for a table in SSMS

Disabling Stretch Database for tables using Transact-SQL

You can use Transact-SQL to perform the same action. The following code example instructs SQL Server to disable Stretch DB for the stretch table `T1` but to transfer the already-migrated data for the table to the local database first:

```
USE Mila;
ALTER TABLE dbo.T1 SET (REMOTE_DATA_ARCHIVE (MIGRATION_STATE = INBOUND));
```

If you don't need the already-migrated data (or you want to avoid data transfer costs), use the following code:

```
USE Mila;
ALTER TABLE dbo.T1 SET (REMOTE_DATA_ARCHIVE = OFF_WITHOUT_DATA_RECOVERY
(MIGRATION_STATE = PAUSED));
```

Disabling Stretch Database for a database

After you have disabled Stretch DB for all stretch tables in a database, you can disable it for the database. You can do this by selecting the database in SSMS and choosing the **Task/Stretch/Disable** option in the database context menu.

Alternatively, you can use Transact-SQL to achieve the same:

```
ALTER DATABASE Mila SET (REMOTE_DATA_ARCHIVE = OFF_WITHOUT_DATA_RECOVERY
(MIGRATION_STATE = PAUSED));
```

You can check if the action was successful by using this query:

```
SELECT * FROM sys.remote_data_archive_tables;
```

You should get an empty set as the result of this query. As already mentioned for stretch tables, disabling Stretch DB does not drop a database remotely. You need to drop it by using the Azure management portal.

Backing up and restoring Stretch-enabled databases

Since you have delegated a part of your database to the remote Azure instance, when you perform a database backup, only local and eligible data will be backed up; remote data is the responsibility of the Azure service. By default, Azure automatically creates storage snapshots at least every 8 hours and retains them for seven days so that you can restore data to a point in time (by default, 21 points). You can change this behavior and increase the number of hours or backup frequency by using the system stored procedure `sys.sp_rda_set_rpo_duration`. Since the Azure service is not free, this can have additional costs.

As expected, to remotely restore a database you have to log in to the Azure portal. How to restore a live Azure database to an earlier point in time using the Azure portal is shown in the following screenshot:

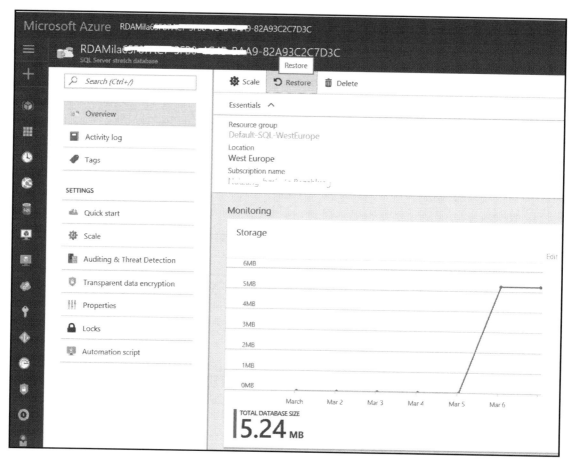

Restore Azure database to an earlier point in time

To restore your Azure database to an earlier point in time, you need to perform the following steps:

1. Log in to the Azure portal.
2. On the left-hand side of the screen, select **BROWSE** and then select **SQL Databases**.
3. Navigate to your database and select it.

4. At the top of the database blade, click on **Restore**.

5. Specify a new **Database name**, select a `Restore Point`, and then click on **Create**.

6. The database restore process will begin and can be monitored using **NOTIFICATIONS**.

After you restore the local SQL Server database, you have to run the `sys.sp_rda_reauthorize_db` stored procedure to re-establish the connection between the stretch-enabled SQL Server database and the remote Azure database. The same action is required if you restore the Azure database with a different name or in a different region. You can also restore a deleted database up to 7 days after dropping it. The *SQL Server Stretch Database service* on Azure takes a database snapshot before a database is dropped and retains it for seven days.

Summary

`Stretch DB` allows the moving of historical or less frequently needed data dynamically and transparently to Microsoft Azure. Data is always available and online, and you don't need to change queries in your solutions; SQL Server takes care of the location of data and combines retrieving data from the local server and remote Azure location. Therefore, you can completely delegate your cold data to Azure and reduce storage, maintenance, and implementation costs of an on-premises solution for cold data storage and availability. However, there are many limitations to using Stretch DB and most OLTP tables cannot be stretched to the cloud—at least not without schema and constraint changes. Stretch Database brings maximum benefits to tables with historical data that is rarely used. You can calculate the price for data storage and querying against the Azure database and decide whether you would benefit from using the `Stretch DB` feature.

In the next chapter, you will learn about temporal data support in SQL Server 2017.

5

Temporal Tables

Databases that serve business applications often need to support temporal data. For example, suppose a contract with a supplier is valid for a limited time only. It could be valid from a specific point in time onward, or it could be valid for a specific time interval—from a starting time point to an ending time point. In addition, often you'll need to audit all changes in one or more tables. You might also need to be able to show the state at a specific point in time, or all changes made to a table in a specific period of time. From a data integrity perspective, you might need to implement many additional temporal-specific constraints.

This chapter introduces temporal problems, deals with manual solutions, and shows you out-of-the-box features in SQL Server 2016 and 2017, including the following:

- Defining temporal data
- Using temporal data in SQL Server before version 2016
- History of temporal data implementation
- System versioned tables in SQL Server 2016 and 2017
- What kind of temporal support is still missing in SQL Server 2017?

What is temporal data?

In a table with temporal support, the header represents a predicate with at least one time parameter that represents when the rest of the predicate is valid; the complete predicate is therefore a **timestamped predicate**. Rows represent timestamped propositions, and the row's valid time period is expressed with one of two attributes: since (for **semi temporal** data) or during (for **fully temporal** data); the latter attribute is usually represented with two values, from and to. The following table shows the original and two additional timestamped versions of an exemplary Suppliers table:

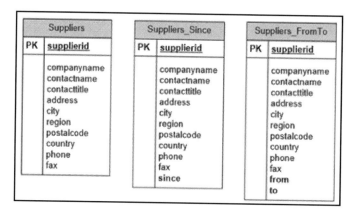

Original Suppliers table and two tables with temporal support

From the original table header, you can read a predicate saying that a supplier with identification supplierid, named companyname, with a contact contactname, and so on is currently our supplier, or is currently under contract. You pretend that this supplier is the supplier forever. The Suppliers_Since table header has this predicate modified with a time parameter; a supplier with the identification supplierid, named companyname, with a contact contactname, and so on has been under contract since some specific point in time. In the Suppliers_FromTo table, the header has this predicate modified with an even more specific time attribute; a supplier with the ID supplierid, named companyname, with a contact contactname, and so on is (or was, or will be, depending on the current time) under contract *from* some specific point in time *to* another point in time.

There is no need to implement semi-temporal tables. You can simply use the maximum possible date and time for the *to* time point. Therefore, the rest of the chapter focuses on fully temporal data only.

In this section, you will learn about:

- Types of temporal tables
- Temporal data algebra
- Temporal constrains
- Temporal data implementation in SQL Server before version 2016
- Optimization of temporal queries

Types of temporal tables

You might have noticed during the introduction part at the beginning of this chapter that there are two kinds of temporal issues. The first one is the **validity time** of the proposition—a time period in which the proposition that a timestamped row in a table represents was actually true. For example, a contract with a supplier was valid only from time point 1 to time point 2. This kind of validity time is meaningful to people and meaningful for the business. The validity time is also called **application time** or **human time**. We can have multiple valid periods for the same entity. For example, the aforementioned contract that was valid from time point 1 to time point 2 might also be valid from time point 7 to time point 9.

The second temporal issue is the **transaction time**. A row for the contract mentioned previously was inserted in time point 1 and was the only version of the truth known to the database until somebody changed it, or even to the end of time. When the row is updated in time point 2, the original row is known as being true to the database from time point 1 to time point 2. A new row for the same proposition is inserted with a time valid for the database from time point 2 to the end of time. The transaction time is also known as **system time** or **database time**.

The **database management systems (DBMSs)** can, and should, maintain the transaction times automatically. The system has to take care to insert a new row for every update and change the transaction validity period in the original row. The system also needs to allow for querying the current and the historical data, and show the state at any specific point in time. There are not many additional issues with the transaction time. The system has to take care that the start time of the database time period is lower than the end time, and that the two periods in two rows for the same entity don't overlap. The database system has to know a single truth at a single point in time. Finally, the database does not care about the future. The end of the database time of the current row is actually the end of time. Database time is about the present and past states only.

Implementing application time might be much more complex. Of course, you might have validity time periods that end or even begin in the future. DBMSs can't take care of future times automatically, and for example check whether they are correct. Therefore, you need to take care of all the constraints you need. The DBMS can only help you by implementing time-aware objects, such as declarative constraints. For example, a foreign key from the products to the suppliers table, which ensures that each product has a supplier, could be extended to check not only whether the supplier for the product exists, but also if the supplier is a valid supplier at the time point when the foreign key is checked.

So far, I've talked about time as though it consists of discrete time points; I used the term *time point* as if it represented a single, indivisible, infinitely small point in time. Of course, time is continuous. Nevertheless, in common language, we talk about time as though it consists of discrete points. We talk in days, hours, and other time units; the granularity we use depends on what we are talking about. The time points we are talking about are actually intervals of time; a day is an interval of 24 hours, an hour is an interval of 60 minutes, and so on.

So what is the granularity level of the time points for the system and application intervals? For the system times, the decision is simple: use the lowest granularity level that a system supports. In SQL Server, with the `datetime2` data type, you can support 100-nanosecond granularity. For application time, the granularity depends on the business problem. For example, for a contract with a supplier, the day level could work well. For measuring the intervals when somebody is using services, such as mobile phone services, the granularity of seconds could be more appropriate. This looks very complex. However, you can make a generalized solution for the application times. You can translate time points to integers, and then use a lookup table that gives you the context—gives the meaning to the integer time points.

Of course, you can also implement both application and system versioned tables. Such tables are called **bitemporal** tables.

Allen's interval algebra

The theory for temporal data in a relational model started to evolve more than thirty years ago. I will define quite a few useful Boolean operators and a couple of operators that work on intervals and return an interval. These operators are known as **Allen's operators**, named after J. F. Allen, who defined a number of them in a 1983 research paper on temporal intervals. All of them are still accepted as valid and needed. A DBMS could help you deal with application times by implementing these operators out of the box.

Let me first introduce the notation I will use. I will work on two intervals, denoted as i_1 and i_2. The beginning time point of the first interval is b_1, and the end is e_1; the beginning time point of the second interval is b_2 and the end is e_2. Allen's **Boolean operators** are defined in the following table:

Name	Notation	Definition
Equals	$(i_1 = i_2)$	$(b_1 = b_2)$ AND $(e_1 = e_2)$
Before	$(i_1 \, before \, i_2)$	$(e_1 < b_2)$
After	$(i_1 \, after \, i_2)$	$(i_2 \, before \, i_1)$
Includes	$(i_1 \sqsupseteq i_2)$	$(b_1 \leq b_2)$ AND $(e_1 \geq e_2)$
Properly includes	$(i_1 \supset i_2)$	$(i_1 \sqsupseteq i_2)$ AND $(i_1 \neq i_2)$
Meets	$(i_1 meets \, i_2)$	$(b2 = e1 + 1)$ OR $(b1 = e2 + 1)$
Overlaps	$(i_1 \, overlaps \, i_2)$	$(b_1 \leq e_2)$ AND $(b_2 \leq e_1)$
Merges	$(i_1 \, merges \, i_2)$	$(i_1 \, overlaps \, i_2)$ OR $(i_1 \, meets \, i_2)$
Begins	$(i_1 \, begins \, i_2)$	$(b_1 = b_2)$ AND $(e_1 \leq e_2)$
Ends	$(i_1 \, ends \, i_2)$	$(e_1 = e_2)$ AND $(b_1 \geq b_2)$

In addition to Boolean operators, three of Allen's operators accept intervals as input parameters and return an interval. These operators constitute simple **interval algebra**. Note that these operators have the same name as relational operators you are probably already familiar with: Union, Intersect, and Minus. However, they don't behave exactly like their relational counterparts.

In general, using any of the three interval operators, if the operation will result in an empty set of time points or in a set that cannot be described by one interval, then the operator should return NULL. A union of two intervals makes sense only if the intervals meet or overlap. An intersection makes sense only if the intervals overlap. The Minus interval operator makes sense only in some cases. For example, (3:10) Minus (5:7) returns NULL because the result cannot be described by one interval.

The following table summarizes the definitions of the operators in interval algebra:

Name	Notation	Definition
Union	$(i_1 \text{ union } i_2)$	$(Min(b_1, b_2) : Max(e_1, e_2))$, when $(i_1 \text{ merges } i_2)$; NULL otherwise
Intersect	$(i_1 \text{ intersect } i_2)$	$(Max(b_1, b_2) : Min(e_1, e_2))$, when $(i_1 \text{ overlaps } i_2)$; NULL otherwise
Minus	$(i_1 \text{ minus } i_2)$	$(b_1 : Min(b_2 - 1, e_1))$, when $(b_1 < b_2)$ AND $(e_1 \leq e_2)$; $(Max(e_2 + 1, b_1) : e_1)$, when $(b_1 \geq b_2)$ AND $(e_1 > e_2)$; NULL otherwise

The following figure shows the interval algebra operators graphically:

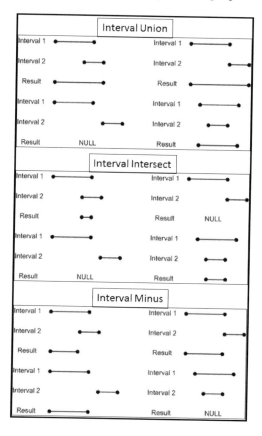

Interval algebra operators

Temporal constraints

Depending on the business problem you are solving, you might need to implement many temporal constraints. Remember that for application time, SQL Server does not help you much. You need to implement the constraints in your code, using SQL Server declarative constraints where possible. However, most of the constraints you need to implement through custom code, either in triggers or in stored procedures, or even in the application code.

Imagine the `Suppliers` table example. One supplier can appear multiple times in the table because the same supplier could be under contract for separate periods of time. For example, you could have two tuples like this in the relation with the shortened header `Suppliers` (`supplierid`, `companyname`, `from`, `to`):

```
{2, Supplier VHQZD, d05, d07}
{2, Supplier VHQZD, d12, d27}
```

Here are some possible constraints you might need to implement:

- *To* should never be less than *from*
- Two contracts for the same supplier should not have overlapping time intervals
- Two contracts for the same supplier should not have abutting time intervals
- No supplier can be under two distinct contracts at the same point in time
- There should be no supplies from a supplier at a point in time when the supplier is not under contract

You might find even more constraints. Anyway, SQL Server 2016 brings support for system versioned tables only. To maintain application validity times, you need to develop the code by yourself.

Temporal data in SQL Server before 2016

As mentioned, in SQL Server versions before 2016, you need to take care of temporal data by yourself. Even in SQL Server 2016, you still need to take care of the human, or application, times. The following code shows an example of how to create a table with validity intervals expressed with the b and e columns, where the beginning and the end of an interval are represented as integers. The table is populated with demo data from the `WideWorldImporters.Sales.OrderLines` table:

```
USE tempdb;
GO
SELECT OrderLineID AS id,
```

```
    StockItemID * (OrderLineID % 5 + 1) AS b,
  LastEditedBy + StockItemID * (OrderLineID % 5 + 1) AS e
INTO dbo.Intervals
FROM WideWorldImporters.Sales.OrderLines;
-- 231412 rows
GO
ALTER TABLE dbo.Intervals ADD CONSTRAINT PK_Intervals PRIMARY KEY(id);
CREATE INDEX idx_b ON dbo.Intervals(b) INCLUDE(e);
CREATE INDEX idx_e ON dbo.Intervals(e) INCLUDE(b);
GO
```

Please note also the indexes created. The two indexes are optimal for searches at the beginning of an interval or on the end of an interval. You can check the minimum beginning and maximum end of all intervals with the following code:

```
SELECT MIN(b), MAX(e)
FROM dbo.Intervals;
```

You can see in the results that the minimum beginning time point is 1 and the maximum end time point is 1155. Now you need to give the intervals some time context. In this case, a single time point represents a day. The following code creates a date lookup table and populates it. Note that the starting date is July 1, 2014:

```
CREATE TABLE dbo.DateNums
  (n INT NOT NULL PRIMARY KEY,
   d DATE NOT NULL);
GO
DECLARE @i AS INT = 1,
 @d AS DATE = '20140701';
WHILE @i <= 1200
BEGIN
INSERT INTO dbo.DateNums
  (n, d)
SELECT @i, @d;
SET @i += 1;
SET @d = DATEADD(day,1,@d);
END;
GO
```

Now you can join the `dbo.Intervals` table to the `dbo.DateNums` table twice, to give context to the integers that represent the beginning and the end of the intervals:

```
SELECT i.id,
  i.b, d1.d AS dateB,
  i.e, d2.d AS dateE
FROM dbo.Intervals AS i
  INNER JOIN dbo.DateNums AS d1
    ON i.b = d1.n
  INNER JOIN dbo.DateNums AS d2
    ON i.e = d2.n
ORDER BY i.id;
```

The abbreviated result from the previous query is:

```
id    b      dateB         e      date
--    ---    ----------    ---    ----------
1     328    2015-05-24    332    2015-05-28
2     201    2015-01-17    204    2015-01-20
3     200    2015-01-16    203    2015-01-19
```

Now you can see which day is represented by which integer.

Optimizing temporal queries

The problem with temporal queries is that when reading from a table, SQL Server can use only one index, successfully eliminate rows that are not candidates for the result from one side only, and then scan the rest of the data. For example, you need to find all intervals in the table that overlap with a given interval. Remember, two intervals overlap when the beginning of the first one is lower than or equal to the end of the second one, and the beginning of the second one is lower than or equal to the end of the first one, or mathematically when $(b_1 \le e_2)$ AND $(b_2 \le e_1)$.

The following query searches for all of the intervals that overlap with the interval $(10, 30)$. Note that the second condition $(b_2 \le e_1)$ is turned around to $(e_1 \ge b_2)$ for simpler reading (the beginning and the end of intervals from the table are always on the left side of the condition). The given or searched interval is at the beginning of the timeline for all intervals in the table:

```
SET STATISTICS IO ON;
DECLARE @b AS INT = 10,
  @e AS INT = 30;
SELECT id, b, e
FROM dbo.Intervals
```

```
WHERE b <= @e
  AND e >= @b
OPTION (RECOMPILE);
GO
```

The query used 36 logical reads. If you check the execution plan, you can see that the query used the index seek in the `idx_b` index with the seek predicate `[tempdb].[dbo].[Intervals].b <= Scalar Operator((30))` and then scanned the rows and selected the resulting rows using the residual predicate `[tempdb].[dbo].[Intervals].[e]>=(10)`. Because the searched interval is at the beginning of the timeline, the seek predicate successfully eliminated a majority of the rows; only a few intervals in the table have a beginning point lower than or equal to 30.

You would get a similarly efficient query if the searched interval was at the end of the timeline; it's just that SQL Server would use the `idx_e` index for the seek. However, what happens if the searched interval is in the middle of the timeline, like the following query shows:

```
DECLARE @b AS INT = 570,
  @e AS INT = 590;
SELECT id, b, e
FROM dbo.Intervals
WHERE b <= @e
  AND e >= @b
OPTION (RECOMPILE);
GO
```

This time, the query used 111 logical reads. With a bigger table, the difference with the first query would be even bigger. If you check the execution plan, you can find out that SQL Server used the `idx_e` index with the `[tempdb].[dbo].[Intervals].e >= Scalar Operator((570))` seek predicate and the `[tempdb].[dbo].[Intervals].[b]<=(590)` residual predicate. The seek predicate excludes approximately half of the rows from one side, while half of the rows from the other side are scanned and the resulting rows extracted with the residual predicate.

There is a solution that uses that index to eliminate rows from both sides of the searched interval by using a single index. The following figure shows this logic:

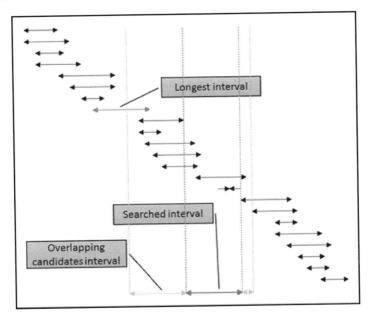

Optimizing a temporal query

The intervals in the figure are sorted by the lower boundary, representing SQL Server's usage of the idx_b index. Eliminating intervals from the right side of the given (searched) interval is simple: just eliminate all intervals where the beginning is at least one unit bigger (more to the right) of the end of the given interval. You can see this boundary in the figure denoted with the rightmost dotted line. However, eliminating from the left is more complex. In order to use the same index, the idx_b index for eliminating from the left, I need to use the beginning of the intervals in the table in the WHERE clause of the query. I have to go to the left side, away from the beginning of the given (searched) interval at least for the length of the longest interval in the table, which is marked with a callout in the figure. The intervals that begin before the left-hand yellow line cannot overlap with the given (blue/dark gray) interval.

Since I already know that the length of the longest interval is 20, I can write an enhanced query in a quite simple way:

```
DECLARE @b AS INT = 570,
  @e AS INT = 590;
DECLARE @max AS INT = 20;
SELECT id, b, e
```

```
FROM dbo.Intervals
WHERE b <= @e AND b >= @b - @max
  AND e >= @b AND e <= @e + @max
OPTION (RECOMPILE);
```

This query retrieves the same rows as the previous one with 20 logical reads only. If you check the execution plan, you can see that the `idx_b` was used, with the seek predicate `Seek Keys[1]: Start: [tempdb].[dbo].[Intervals].b >= Scalar Operator((550)), End: [tempdb].[dbo].[Intervals].b <= Scalar Operator((590))`, which successfully eliminated rows from both sides of the timeline, and then the residual predicate `[tempdb].[dbo].[Intervals].[e]>=(570) AND [tempdb].[dbo].[Intervals].[e]<=(610)` was used to select rows from a very limited partial scan.

Of course, the figure could be turned around to cover cases where the `idx_e` index would be more useful. With this index, elimination from the left is simple—eliminate all of the intervals that end at least one unit before the beginning of the given interval. This time, elimination from the right is more complex—the end of the intervals in the table cannot be more to the right than the end of the given interval plus the maximum length of all intervals in the table.

 Please note that this performance is the consequence of the specific data in the table.

The maximum length of an interval is 20. This way, SQL Server can very efficiently eliminate intervals from both sides. However, if there were to be only one long interval in the table, the code would become much less efficient, because SQL Server would not be able to eliminate a lot of rows from one side, either left or right, depending on which index it would use. Anyway, in real life, interval length often does not vary a lot, so this optimization technique might be very useful, especially because it is simple.

After you finish with the temporal queries in this section, you can clean up your `tempdb` database with the following code:

```
DROP TABLE dbo.DateNums;
DROP TABLE dbo.Intervals;
```

Temporal features in SQL:2011

Temporal data support was introduced in the `SQL:2011`—ANSI standard. There were also attempts to define support in the previous standard versions, but without success (TSQL2 extensions in 1995). They were not widely accepted and vendors did not implement them.

The `SQL:2011` standard proposed that temporal data should be supported in relational database management systems. A very important thing is that SQL:2011 did not introduce a new data type to support temporal data; rather, it introduced the period.

A period is a table attribute and it's defined by two table columns of date type, representing start time and end time, respectively. It is defined as follows:

- A period must have a name.
- The end time must be greater than the start time.
- It is a closed-open period model. The start time is included in the period and the end time is excluded.

The SQL:2011 standard recognizes two dimensions of temporal data support:

- Application time or valid time tables
- System time or transaction time tables

Application time period tables are intended to meet the requirements of applications that capture time periods during which the data is believed to be valid in the real world. A typical example of such an application is an insurance application, where it is necessary to keep track of the specific policy details of a given customer that are in effect at any given point in time.

System-versioned tables are intended to meet the requirements of applications that must maintain an accurate history of data changes either for business reasons, legal reasons, or both. A typical example of such an application is a banking application, where it is necessary to keep previous states of customer account information so that customers can be provided with a detailed history of their accounts. There are also plenty of examples where certain institutions are required by law to preserve historical data for a specified length of time to meet regulatory and compliance requirements.

Bitemporal tables are tables that implement both application time and system-versioned time support.

After the standard was published, many vendors came up with the temporal table implementation:

- **IDM DB2 10** added full support for temporal tables (for both application time and system-versioned).
- **Oracle** implemented a feature called the **Flashback Data Archive** (**FDA**). It automatically tracks all changes made to data in a database and maintains an archive of historical data. Oracle 12c introduced valid time temporal support.
- **PostgreSQL** does not support temporal tables natively, but temporal tables approximate them.
- **Teradata** implements both valid time and transaction time table types based on the TSQL2 specification.

All these implementations most probably affected Microsoft's decision to implement temporal tables in SQL Server 2016.

System-versioned temporal tables in SQL Server 2017

SQL Server 2016 introduces support for system-versioned temporal tables. Unfortunately, application-time tables are not implemented neither in this version, nor in SQL Server 2017. System-versioned temporal tables bring built-in support for providing information about data stored in the table at any point in time rather than only the data that is correct at the current moment in time. They are implemented according to the specifications in the ANSI SQL:2011 standard with a few extensions.

How temporal tables work in SQL Server 2017

A system-versioned temporal table is implemented in SQL Server 2017 as a pair of tables: the current table containing the actual data, and the history table where only historical entries are stored. There are many limitations for both current and history tables. Here are limitations and considerations that you must take into account for the current table of a system-versioned temporal table:

- It must have a primary key defined
- It must have one `PERIOD FOR SYSTEM_TIME` defined with two `DATETIME2` columns

- Cannot be `FILETABLE` and cannot contain `FILESTREAM` data type
- `INSERT`, `UPDATE`, and `MERGE` statements cannot reference and modify period columns; the start column is always set to system time, the end column to max date value
- `INSTEAD OF` triggers are not allowed
- `TRUNCATE TABLE` is not supported

The list of limitations for a history table is significantly longer and brings many additional restrictions. The following applies to the history table of a system-versioned temporal table:

- Cannot have constraints defined (primary or foreign keys, check, table, or column constraints). Only default column constraints are allowed.
- You cannot modify data in the history table.
- You can neither `ALTER` nor `DROP` a history table.
- It must have the same schema as the current table (column names, data types, ordinal position.
- Cannot be defined as the current table.
- Cannot be `FILETABLE` and cannot contain `FILESTREAM` data type.
- No triggers are allowed (neither `INSTEAD OF` nor `AFTER`).
- `Change Data Capture` and `Change Data Tracking` are not supported.

You can read more about considerations and limitations when working with temporal tables at `https://msdn.microsoft.com/en-us/library/mt604468.aspx`.

The list might look long and discouraging, but all these limitations are there to protect data consistency and accuracy in history tables. However, although you cannot change logical attributes, you can still perform actions related to the physical implementations of the history table: you can switch between rowstore and columnstore table storage, you can choose columns for clustered indexes, and you can create additional non-clustered indexes.

Creating temporal tables

To support the creation of temporal tables, the `CREATE TABLE` and `ALTER TABLE` Transact-SQL statements have been extended.

To create a temporal table, you need to perform the following steps:

1. Define a column of DATETIME2 data type for holding the info since when the row has been valid from a system point of view

2. Define a column of DATETIME2 data type for holding the info until the row is valid from the same point of view

3. Define a period for system time by using previously defined and described columns

4. Set the newly added SYSTEM_VERSIONING table attribute to ON

The following code creates a new temporal table named Product in the dbo schema in the WideWorldImporters database:

```
USE WideWorldImporters;
CREATE TABLE dbo.Product
(
    ProductId INT NOT NULL CONSTRAINT PK_Product PRIMARY KEY,
    ProductName NVARCHAR(50) NOT NULL,
    Price MONEY NOT NULL,
    ValidFrom DATETIME2 GENERATED ALWAYS AS ROW START NOT NULL,
    ValidTo DATETIME2 GENERATED ALWAYS AS ROW END NOT NULL,
    PERIOD FOR SYSTEM_TIME (ValidFrom, ValidTo)
)
WITH (SYSTEM_VERSIONING = ON);
```

You can identify all four elements related to temporal table creation from the previous list: *two period columns*, the *period*, and the SYSTEM_VERSIONING attribute. Note that all elements marked bold are predefined and you must write them exactly like this; data type, nullability, and default values for both period columns are also predefined and you can only choose their names and define data type precision. The data type must be DATETIME2; you can only specify its precision. Furthermore, the period definition itself is predefined too; you must use the period column names you have chosen in the previous step.

By defining period columns and the period, you have created the infrastructure required for implementing temporal tables. However, if you create a table with them but without the SYSTEM_VERSIONING attribute, the table will not be temporal. It will contain an additional two columns with values that are maintained by the system, but the table will not be a system-versioned temporal table.

The final, fourth part is to set the `SYSTEM_VERSIONING` attribute to `ON`. When you execute the previous code, you implicitly instruct SQL Server to automatically create a history table for the `dbo.Product` temporal table. The table will be created in the same schema (`dbo`), with a name according to the following naming convention:

`MSSQL_TemporalHistoryFor_<current_temporal_table_object_id>_[suffix]`. The suffix is optional and it will be added only if the first part of the table name is not unique. The following screenshot shows what you will see when you open **SQL Server Management Studio (SSMS)** and find the `dbo.Product` table:

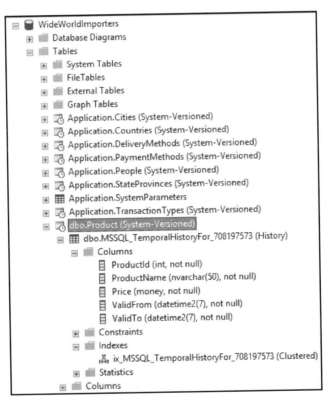

Temporal table in SQL Server Management Studio

You can see that all temporal tables have a small clock icon indicating temporality. Under the table name, you can see its history table. Note that columns in both tables are identical (column names, data types, precision, nullability), but also that the history table does not have constraints (primary key).

Period columns must be of the DATETIME2 data type. If you try to define them with the DATETIME data type, you will get an error. The SQL:2011 standard does not specify data type precision, thus system-versioned temporal tables in SQL Server 2017 are not implemented strictly according to standard. This is very important when you migrate your existing temporal solution to one that uses new temporal tables in SQL Server 2017. Usually, columns that you were using are of the DATETIME data type and you have to extend their data type to DATETIME2.

You can also specify the name of the history table and let SQL Server create it with the same attributes as described earlier. Use the following code to create a temporal table with a user-defined history table name:

```
USE WideWorldImporters;
CREATE TABLE dbo.Product2
(
    ProductId INT NOT NULL CONSTRAINT PK_Product2 PRIMARY KEY,
    ProductName NVARCHAR(50) NOT NULL,
    Price MONEY NOT NULL,
    ValidFrom DATETIME2 GENERATED ALWAYS AS ROW START NOT NULL,
    ValidTo DATETIME2 GENERATED ALWAYS AS ROW END NOT NULL,
    PERIOD FOR SYSTEM_TIME (ValidFrom, ValidTo)
)
WITH (SYSTEM_VERSIONING = ON (HISTORY_TABLE = dbo.ProductHistory2));
```

What storage type is used for the automatically created history table? By default, it is a rowstore table with a clustered index on the period columns. The table is compressed with PAGE compression, if it can be enabled for compression (has no SPARSE or (B)LOB columns). To find out the storage type of the history table, use the following code:

```
SELECT temporal_type_desc, p.data_compression_desc
FROM sys.tables t
INNER JOIN sys.partitions p ON t.object_id = p.object_id
WHERE name = 'ProductHistory2';
```

The result of the preceding query shows that PAGE compression has been applied:

temporal_type_desc	data_compression_desc
HISTORY_TABLE	PAGE

You can also see that the history table has a clustered index. The following code extracts the index name and the columns used in the index:

```
SELECT i.name, i.type_desc, c.name, ic.index_column_id
FROM sys.indexes i
INNER JOIN sys.index_columns ic on ic.object_id = i.object_id
INNER JOIN sys.columns c on c.object_id = i.object_id AND ic.column_id =
c.column_id
WHERE OBJECT_NAME(i.object_id) = 'ProductHistory2';
```

The output of this query shows that the automatically created history table has a clustered index on the period columns and the name in the following ix_<history_tablename> format:

name	type_desc	name	index_column_id
ix_ProductHistory2	CLUSTERED	ValidFrom	1
ix_ProductHistory2	CLUSTERED	ValidTo	2

This index is a good choice, when you want to query the history table only by using dates as criteria. However, when you want to browse through the history of one item, that would be an inappropriate index.

If the predefined implementation of the history table (rowstore and period columns in a clustered index) does not meet your criteria for historical data, you can create your own history table. Of course, you need to respect all constraints and limitations listed at the beginning of the chapter. The following code first creates a history table, then a temporal table, and finally assigns the history table to it. Note that, in order to proceed with the code execution, you need to remove the temporal table created in the first example in this chapter:

```
USE WideWorldImporters;
ALTER TABLE dbo.Product SET (SYSTEM_VERSIONING = OFF);
ALTER TABLE dbo.Product DROP PERIOD FOR SYSTEM_TIME;
DROP TABLE IF EXISTS dbo.Product;
DROP TABLE IF EXISTS dbo.ProductHistory;
GO
CREATE TABLE dbo.ProductHistory
(
    ProductId INT NOT NULL,
    ProductName NVARCHAR(50) NOT NULL,
    Price MONEY NOT NULL,
    ValidFrom DATETIME2 NOT NULL,
    ValidTo DATETIME2 NOT NULL
);
CREATE CLUSTERED COLUMNSTORE INDEX IX_ProductHistory ON dbo.ProductHistory;
```

```
CREATE NONCLUSTERED INDEX IX_ProductHistory_NC ON
dbo.ProductHistory(ProductId, ValidFrom, ValidTo);
GO
CREATE TABLE dbo.Product
(
    ProductId INT NOT NULL CONSTRAINT PK_Product PRIMARY KEY,
    ProductName NVARCHAR(50) NOT NULL,
    Price MONEY NOT NULL,
    ValidFrom DATETIME2 GENERATED ALWAYS AS ROW START NOT NULL,
    ValidTo DATETIME2 GENERATED ALWAYS AS ROW END NOT NULL,
    PERIOD FOR SYSTEM_TIME (ValidFrom, ValidTo)
)
WITH (SYSTEM_VERSIONING = ON (HISTORY_TABLE = dbo.ProductHistory));
```

You will learn how to alter and drop system-versioned tables in more detail later in this chapter. Here, you should focus on the fact that you can create your own history table with a clustered columnstore index on it. The following screenshot shows what you will see when you look at SSMS and find the created temporal table:

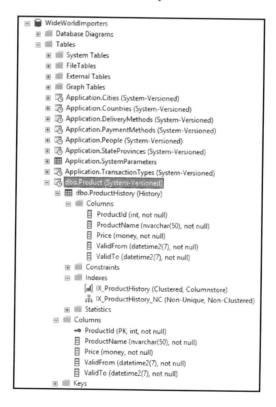

Temporal table in SQL Server Management Studio with user-defined history table

You can see that the table created by you acts as a history table and has a clustered columnstore index.

Period columns as hidden attributes

Period columns are used to support the temporality of data and have no business logic value. By using the HIDDEN clause, you can hide the new PERIOD columns to avoid impacting on existing applications that are not designed to handle new columns. The following code will create two temporal tables, one with default values (visible period column) and the other with hidden period columns:

```
CREATE TABLE dbo.T1(
    Id INT NOT NULL CONSTRAINT PK_T1 PRIMARY KEY,
    Col1 INT NOT NULL,
    ValidFrom DATETIME2 GENERATED ALWAYS AS ROW START NOT NULL,
    ValidTo DATETIME2 GENERATED ALWAYS AS ROW END NOT NULL,
    PERIOD FOR SYSTEM_TIME (ValidFrom, ValidTo)
)
WITH (SYSTEM_VERSIONING = ON (HISTORY_TABLE = dbo.T1_Hist));
GO
INSERT INTO dbo.T1(Id, Col1) VALUES(1, 1);
GO
CREATE TABLE dbo.T2(
    Id INT NOT NULL CONSTRAINT PK_T2 PRIMARY KEY,
    Col1 INT NOT NULL,
    ValidFrom DATETIME2 GENERATED ALWAYS AS ROW START HIDDEN NOT NULL,
    ValidTo DATETIME2 GENERATED ALWAYS AS ROW END HIDDEN NOT NULL,
    PERIOD FOR SYSTEM_TIME (ValidFrom, ValidTo)
)
WITH (SYSTEM_VERSIONING = ON (HISTORY_TABLE = dbo.T2_Hist));
GO
INSERT INTO dbo.T2(Id, Col1) VALUES(1, 1);
GO
```

When you query both tables, you can see that period columns are not listed for the second table:

```
SELECT * FROM dbo.T1;
SELECT * FROM dbo.T2;
```

Here is the result:

```
Id   Col1      ValidFrom                      ValidTo
---  ------    --------------------------     --------------------------
1    1         2017-12-14 23:05:44.2068702    9999-12-31 23:59:59.9999999


Id        Col1
--------  ----------
1         1
```

As you can see, period columns are not shown, even when you use ⋆ in your queries. So, you can implement temporal functionality for a table transparently and you can be sure that your existing code will still work. Of course, if you explicitly specify period columns with their names, they will be shown in the result set.

 I need here to express my concerns about another implementation that takes care of solutions where SELECT ⋆ is implemented. I can understand that the vendor does not want to introduce a feature that can break customers' existing applications, but on the other hand, you cannot expect a developer to stop using SELECT ⋆ when new features and solutions don't sanction bad development habits.

Hidden attributes let you convert normal tables to temporal tables without worrying about breaking changes in your applications.

Converting non-temporal tables to temporal tables

In SQL Server 2017, you can create temporal tables from scratch, but you can also alter an existing table and add attributes to it to convert it to a system-versioned temporal table. All you need to do is to add period columns, define the SYSTEM_TIME period on them, and set the temporal attribute. In this section, for example, you will convert the Department table from the AdventureWorks2017 database into a temporal table. The following screenshot shows the table's content:

DepartmentID	Name	GroupName	ModifiedDate
1	Engineering	Research and Development	2008-04-30 00:00:00.000
2	Tool Design	Research and Development	2008-04-30 00:00:00.000
3	Sales	Sales and Marketing	2008-04-30 00:00:00.000
4	Marketing	Sales and Marketing	2008-04-30 00:00:00.000
5	Purchasing	Inventory Management	2008-04-30 00:00:00.000
6	Research and Development	Research and Development	2008-04-30 00:00:00.000
7	Production	Manufacturing	2008-04-30 00:00:00.000
8	Production Control	Manufacturing	2008-04-30 00:00:00.000
9	Human Resources	Executive General and Administration	2008-04-30 00:00:00.000
10	Finance	Executive General and Administration	2008-04-30 00:00:00.000
11	Information Services	Executive General and Administration	2008-04-30 00:00:00.000
12	Document Control	Quality Assurance	2008-04-30 00:00:00.000
13	Quality Assurance	Quality Assurance	2008-04-30 00:00:00.000
14	Facilities and Maintenance	Executive General and Administration	2008-04-30 00:00:00.000
15	Shipping and Receiving	Inventory Management	2008-04-30 00:00:00.000
16	Executive	Executive General and Administration	2008-04-30 00:00:00.000

Data in the HumanResources.Department table

You can see that the table has one column representing temporality. The `ModifiedDate` column shows the time a table row became valid, that is, when it was recently updated. However, since there is no history table, you don't know previous row versions. By converting the table to a temporal table, you can retain the existing functionality, and add the temporal one. The following code example demonstrates how to convert the `Department` table in the `AdventureWorks2017` database to a temporal table:

```
USE AdventureWorks2017;
--the ModifiedDate column will be replaced by temporal table functionality
ALTER TABLE HumanResources.Department DROP CONSTRAINT
DF_Department_ModifiedDate;
ALTER TABLE HumanResources.Department DROP COLUMN ModifiedDate;
GO
ALTER TABLE HumanResources.Department
ADD ValidFrom DATETIME2 GENERATED ALWAYS AS ROW START HIDDEN NOT NULL
CONSTRAINT DF_Validfrom DEFAULT '20080430 00:00:00.0000000',
    ValidTo DATETIME2 GENERATED ALWAYS AS ROW END HIDDEN NOT NULL CONSTRAINT
DF_ValidTo DEFAULT '99991231 23:59:59.9999999',
    PERIOD FOR SYSTEM_TIME (ValidFrom, ValidTo);
GO
ALTER TABLE HumanResources.Department SET (SYSTEM_VERSIONING = ON
(HISTORY_TABLE = HumanResources.DepartmentHistory));
```

Since the existing temporal data implementation will be replaced by an SQL Server 2017 temporal table, the `ModifiedDate` column is not necessary anymore and can be removed. Furthermore, you have to use two `ALTER` statements; with the first statement, you define the period columns and the period, while the second statement sets the `SYSTEM_VERSIONING` attribute to `ON` and defines the name of the history table that will be created by the system.

You should be aware that you need to provide default constraints for both columns, since they must be non-nullable. You can even use a date value from the past for the default constraint of the first period column (as shown in the preceding code example, where the value is set to the one from the removed column); however, you cannot set values in the future. Finally, period date columns are defined with the `HIDDEN` attribute to ensure that there will be no breaking changes in the existing code.

 Adding a non-nullable column with a default constraint is a metadata operation in Enterprise Edition only; in all other editions that means a physical operation with the allocation space to update all table rows with newly added columns. For large tables, this can take a long time, and be aware that, during this action, the table is locked.

Any further change in the table will be automatically handled by the system and written in the `HumanResources.DepartmentHistory` history table. For instance, you can update the `Name` attribute for the department with the ID of `2` and then check the values in both tables:

```
UPDATE HumanResources.Department SET Name='Political Correctness' WHERE
DepartmentID = 2;
SELECT * FROM HumanResources.Department WHERE DepartmentID = 2;
SELECT * FROM HumanResources.DepartmentHistory;
```

The first table simply shows the new value, while the second shows the previous one, with appropriate validity dates from a system point of view (the time part of the date is shortened for brevity):

DepartmentID	Name	GroupName
2	Political Correctness	Research and Development

DepartmentID	Name	GroupName	ValidFrom	ValidTo
2	Tool Design	Research and Development	2008-04-30	2017-12-15

As you can see, it is very easy and straightforward to add temporal functionality to an existing non-temporal table. It works transparently; all your queries and commands will work without changes.

Migrating an existing temporal solution to system-versioned tables

Most probably, you have had to deal with historical data in the past. Since there was no out-of-the-box feature in previous SQL Server versions, you had to create a custom temporal data solution. Now that the feature is available, you might think to use it for your existing temporal solutions. You saw earlier in this chapter that you can define your own history table. Therefore, you can also use an existing and populated historical table. If you want to convert your existing solution to use system-versioned temporal tables in SQL Server 2017, you have to prepare both tables so that they fill all requirements for temporal tables. To achieve this, you will again use the AdventureWorks2017 database and create both current and history tables by using tables that exist in this database. Use the following code to create and populate the tables:

```
USE WideWorldImporters;
CREATE TABLE dbo.ProductListPrice
(
    ProductID INT NOT NULL CONSTRAINT PK_ProductListPrice PRIMARY KEY,
    ListPrice MONEY NOT NULL,
);
INSERT INTO dbo.ProductListPrice(ProductID, ListPrice)
SELECT ProductID, ListPrice FROM AdventureWorks2017.Production.Product;
GO
CREATE TABLE dbo.ProductListPriceHistory
(
    ProductID INT NOT NULL,
    ListPrice MONEY NOT NULL,
    StartDate DATETIME NOT NULL,
    EndDate DATETIME    NULL,
    CONSTRAINT PK_ProductListPriceHistory PRIMARY KEY CLUSTERED
    (
        ProductID ASC,
        StartDate ASC
    )
);
INSERT INTO
dbo.ProductListPriceHistory(ProductID, ListPrice, StartDate, EndDate)
SELECT ProductID, ListPrice, StartDate, EndDate FROM
AdventureWorks2017.Production.ProductListPriceHistory;
```

Consider the rows for the product with an ID of 707 in both tables:

```
SELECT * FROM dbo.ProductListPrice WHERE ProductID = 707;
SELECT * FROM dbo.ProductListPriceHistory WHERE ProductID = 707;
```

Here are the rows in the current and history tables respectively:

```
ProductID    ListPrice
---------    ---------
707           34.99
ProductID    ListPrice    StartDate               EndDate
---------    ---------    -------------------     -------------------
707           33.6442     2011-05-31 00:00:00.000  2012-05-29 00:00:00.000
707           33.6442     2012-05-30 00:00:00.000  2013-05-29 00:00:00.000
707           34.99       2013-05-30 00:00:00.000  NULL
```

Assume that this data has been produced by your temporal data solution and that you want to use system-versioned temporal tables in SQL Server 2017 instead of it, but also use the same tables. The first thing you have to do is align the columns in both tables. Since the current table has no date columns, you need to add two period columns and define the period. The columns should have the same name as the counterpart columns from the history table. Here is the code that creates the temporal infrastructure in the current table:

```
ALTER TABLE dbo.ProductListPrice
ADD StartDate DATETIME2 GENERATED ALWAYS AS ROW START HIDDEN NOT NULL
CONSTRAINT DF_StartDate1 DEFAULT '20170101 00:00:00.0000000',
    EndDate DATETIME2 GENERATED ALWAYS AS ROW END HIDDEN NOT NULL CONSTRAINT
DF_EndDate1 DEFAULT '99991231 23:59:59.9999999',
    PERIOD FOR SYSTEM_TIME (StartDate, EndDate);
GO
```

The next steps are related to the history table. As you can see from the sample data, your current solution allows gaps in the history table and also contains the current value with the undefined end date. As mentioned earlier in this chapter, the history table only contains historical data and there are no gaps between historical entries (the new start date is equal to the previous end date). Here are the steps you have to implement in order to prepare the dbo.ProductLisPriceHistory table to act as a history table in a system-versioned temporal table in SQL Server 2017:

- Update the non-nullable EndDate column to remove the gap between historical values described earlier and to support the open-closed interval

- Update all rows where the `EndDate` column is null to the `StartDate` of the rows in the current table
- Remove the primary key constraint
- Change the data type for both date columns `StartDate` and `EndDate` to `DATETIME2`

Here is the code that implements all these requests:

```
--remove gaps
UPDATE dbo.ProductListPriceHistory SET EndDate = DATEADD(day,1,EndDate);
--update EndDate to StartDate of the actual record
UPDATE dbo.ProductListPriceHistory SET EndDate = (SELECT MAX(StartDate)
FROM dbo.ProductListPrice) WHERE EndDate IS NULL;
--remove constraints
ALTER TABLE dbo.ProductListPriceHistory DROP CONSTRAINT
PK_ProductListPriceHistory;
--change data type to DATETIME2
ALTER TABLE dbo.ProductListPriceHistory ALTER COLUMN StartDate DATETIME2
NOT NULL;
ALTER TABLE dbo.ProductListPriceHistory ALTER COLUMN EndDate DATETIME2 NOT
NULL;
```

Now, both tables are ready to act as a system-versioned temporal table in SQL Server 2017:

```
ALTER TABLE dbo.ProductListPrice SET (SYSTEM_VERSIONING = ON (HISTORY_TABLE
= dbo.ProductListPriceHistory,  DATA_CONSISTENCY_CHECK = ON));
```

The command has been executed successfully and the `dbo.ProductListPriceHistory` table is now a system-versioned temporal table. Note that the `DATA_CONSISTENCY_CHECK = ON` option is used to check that all rows in the history table are valid from a temporal data point of view (no gaps and the end date is not before the start date). Now, you can check the new functionality by using the `UPDATE` statement. You will update the price for the product by changing the ID of 707 to 50 and then check the rows in both tables:

```
UPDATE dbo.ProductListPrice SET ListPrice = 50 WHERE ProductID = 707;
SELECT * FROM dbo.ProductListPrice WHERE ProductID = 707;
SELECT * FROM dbo.ProductListPriceHistory WHERE ProductID = 707;
```

Here are the rows for this product in both tables:

```
ProductID   ListPrice
---------   ---------
707          50.00
ProductID ListPrice  StartDate                 EndDate
------- -------- ------------------------- -------------------------
  707     33.6442 2011-05-31 00:00:00.0000000 2012-05-30 00:00:00.0000000
  707     33.6442 2012-05-30 00:00:00.0000000 2013-05-30 00:00:00.0000000
  707     34.99   2013-05-30 00:00:00.0000000 2017-12-12 21:21:08.4382496
  707     34.99   2017-12-12 21:21:08.4382496 2017-12-12 21:21:08.4382496
```

You can see another row in the history table (compare with the previous result). Of course, when you try these examples, you will get different values for the columns `StartDate` and `EndDate`, since they are managed by the system.

 `AdventureWorks` has long been one of the most used SQL Server sample databases. After introducing the `WideWorldImporter` database, it was not supported in the SQL Server 2016 RTM, but `AdventureWorks` is back in SQL Server 2017. You can download it at `https://github.com/Microsoft/sql-server-samples/releases/tag/adventureworks`.

As you can see, it is not so complicated to migrate an existing solution to a system-versioned table in SQL Server 2017, but it is not a single step. You should take into account that most probably it will take time to update the data type to `DATETIME2`. However, by using the system-versioned temporal tables feature, your history tables are completely and automatically protected from changes by anyone except the system. This is a great out-of-the-box data consistency improvement.

Altering temporal tables

You can use the `ALTER TABLE` statement to perform schema changes on system-versioned temporal tables. When you use it to add a new data type, change a data type, or remove an existing column, the system will automatically perform the action against both the current and the history table. However, some of these actions will not be metadata operations only; there are changes that will update the entire table.

To check this, run the following code to create (and populate with sample data) the temporal table from the previous section:

```
USE tempdb;
CREATE TABLE dbo.Product
(
    ProductId INT NOT NULL CONSTRAINT PK_Product PRIMARY KEY,
    ProductName NVARCHAR(50) NOT NULL,
    Price MONEY NOT NULL,
    ValidFrom DATETIME2 GENERATED ALWAYS AS ROW START NOT NULL,
    ValidTo DATETIME2 GENERATED ALWAYS AS ROW END NOT NULL,
    PERIOD FOR SYSTEM_TIME (ValidFrom, ValidTo)
)
WITH (SYSTEM_VERSIONING = ON (HISTORY_TABLE = dbo.ProductHistory));
GO
INSERT INTO dbo.Product (ProductId,ProductName,Price)
SELECT message_id,'PROD' + CAST(message_id AS NVARCHAR), severity FROM
sys.messages WHERE language_id = 1033;
```

Now, you will add three new columns into the temporal table:

- A column named `Color`, which allows NULL values
- A column named `Category`, where a non-nullable value is mandatory
- A **Large Object (LOB)** column named `Description`

But before you add them, you will create an **Extended Events (XE)** session to trace what happens under the hood when you add a new column to a temporal table. Use the following code to create and start the XE session:

```
CREATE EVENT SESSION AlteringTemporalTable ON SERVER
ADD EVENT sqlserver.sp_statement_starting(
    WHERE (sqlserver.database_id = 2)),
ADD EVENT sqlserver.sp_statement_completed(
    WHERE (sqlserver.database_id = 2)),
ADD EVENT sqlserver.sql_statement_starting(
    WHERE (sqlserver.database_id = 2)),
ADD EVENT sqlserver.sql_statement_completed(
    WHERE (sqlserver.database_id = 2))
ADD TARGET package0.event_file (SET filename = N'AlteringTemporalTable')
WITH (MAX_DISPATCH_LATENCY = 1 SECONDS)
GO
ALTER EVENT SESSION AlteringTemporalTable ON SERVER STATE = start;
GO
```

Now you can issue the following three `ALTER` statements that correspond to the previously described new columns:

```
ALTER TABLE dbo.Product ADD Color NVARCHAR(15);
ALTER TABLE dbo.Product ADD Category SMALLINT NOT NULL CONSTRAINT
DF_Category DEFAULT 1;
ALTER TABLE dbo.Product ADD Description NVARCHAR(MAX) NOT NULL CONSTRAINT
DF_Description DEFAULT N'N/A';
```

The content collected by the XE session is shown as follows:

name	timestamp	statement
sql_statement_starting	2017-12-17 23:28:28.5382499	SELECT @@SPID
sql_statement_completed	2017-12-17 23:28:28.5382623	SELECT @@SPID
sql_statement_starting	2017-12-17 23:28:28.5418307	ALTER TABLE dbo.Product ADD Color NVARCHAR(15)
sql_statement_completed	2017-12-17 23:28:28.5429845	ALTER TABLE dbo.Product ADD Color NVARCHAR(15)
sql_statement_starting	2017-12-17 23:28:28.5433065	ALTER TABLE dbo.Product ADD Category SMALLINT NOT NULL CONSTRAINT DF_Category DEFAULT 1
sql_statement_completed	2017-12-17 23:28:28.5447483	ALTER TABLE dbo.Product ADD Category SMALLINT NOT NULL CONSTRAINT DF_Category DEFAULT 1
sql_statement_starting	2017-12-17 23:28:28.5447855	ALTER TABLE dbo.Product ADD Description NVARCHAR(MAX) NOT NULL CONSTRAINT DF_Description DEFAULT N'N/A'
sp_statement_starting	2017-12-17 23:28:28.5472037	UPDATE [dbo].[Product] SET [Description] = DEFAULT
sp_statement_completed	2017-12-17 23:28:28.6044360	UPDATE [dbo].[Product] SET [Description] = DEFAULT
sql_statement_completed	2017-12-17 23:28:28.6047962	ALTER TABLE dbo.Product ADD Description NVARCHAR(MAX) NOT NULL CONSTRAINT DF_Description DEFAULT N'N/A'

Displaying 10 Events

Data collected by Extended Event session

It clearly shows that the first two `ALTER` statements have been executed without additional actions. However, adding a LOB column triggers the updating of all rows with the default value as an offline operation.

The first statement adds a column that accepts null values, so the action is done instantly.

When you add a non-nullable column, the situation is different, as illustrated in the second statement. First, you need to provide a default constraint to ensure that all rows will have a value in this column. This action will be online (metadata operation) in the Enterprise and Developer editions only. In all the other editions, all rows in both the current and the history table will be updated to add additional columns with their values.

However, adding LOB or BLOB columns will cause a mass update in both the current and the history table in all SQL Server editions! This action will internally update all rows in both tables. For large tables, this can take a long time and during this time, both tables are locked.

You can also use the `ALTER TABLE` statement to add the `HIDDEN` attribute to period columns or to remove it. This code line adds the `HIDDEN` attribute to the columns `ValidFrom` and `ValidTo`:

```
ALTER TABLE dbo.Product ALTER COLUMN ValidFrom ADD HIDDEN;
ALTER TABLE dbo.Product ALTER COLUMN ValidTo ADD HIDDEN;
```

Clearly, you can also remove the `HIDDEN` attribute:

```
ALTER TABLE dbo.Product ALTER COLUMN ValidFrom DROP HIDDEN;
ALTER TABLE dbo.Product ALTER COLUMN ValidTo DROP HIDDEN;
```

However, there are some changes that are not allowed for temporal tables:

- Adding an `IDENDITY` or computed column
- Adding a `ROWGUIDCOL` column or changing an existing column to it
- Adding a `SPARSE` column or changing an existing column to it, when the history table is compressed

When you try to add a `SPARSE` column, you will get an error, as in the following example:

```
ALTER TABLE dbo.Product ADD Size NVARCHAR(5) SPARSE;
```

The command ends up with the following error message:

```
Msg 11418, Level 16, State 2, Line 20
Cannot alter table 'ProductHistory' because the table either contains
sparse columns or a column set column which are incompatible with
compression.
```

The same happens when you try to add an `IDENTITY` column, as follows:

```
ALTER TABLE dbo.Product ADD ProductNumber INT IDENTITY (1,1);
```

And here is the error message:

```
Msg 13704, Level 16, State 1, Line 26
System-versioned table schema modification failed because history table
'WideWorldImporters.dbo.ProductHistory' has IDENTITY column specification.
Consider dropping all IDENTITY column specifications and trying again.
```

If you need to perform schema changes to a temporal table not supported in the ALTER statement, you have to set its SYSTEM_VERSIONING attribute to false to convert the tables to non-temporal tables, perform the changes, and then convert back to a temporal table. The following code demonstrates how to add the identity column ProductNumber and the sparse column Size into the temporal table dbo.Product:

```
ALTER TABLE dbo.ProductHistory REBUILD PARTITION = ALL WITH
(DATA_COMPRESSION=NONE);
GO
BEGIN TRAN
ALTER TABLE dbo.Product SET (SYSTEM_VERSIONING = OFF);
ALTER TABLE dbo.Product ADD Size NVARCHAR(5) SPARSE;
ALTER TABLE dbo.ProductHistory ADD Size NVARCHAR(5) SPARSE;
ALTER TABLE dbo.Product ADD ProductNumber INT IDENTITY (1,1);
ALTER TABLE dbo.ProductHistory ADD ProductNumber INT NOT NULL DEFAULT 0;
ALTER TABLE dbo.Product SET(SYSTEM_VERSIONING = ON (HISTORY_TABLE = dbo.
ProductHistory));
COMMIT;
```

To perform ALTER TABLE operations, you need to have CONTROL permission on the current and history tables. During the changes, both tables are locked with schema locks.

Dropping temporal tables

You cannot drop a system-versioned temporal table. Both current and history tables are protected until the SYSTEM_VERSIONING attribute of the current table is set to ON. When you set it to OFF, both tables automatically become non-temporal tables and are fully independent of each other. Therefore, you can perform all operations against them that are allowed according to your permissions. You can also drop the period if you definitely want to convert a temporal table to a non-temporal one. The following code converts the Product table into a non-temporal table and removes the defined SYSTEM_TIME period:

```
ALTER TABLE dbo.Product SET (SYSTEM_VERSIONING = OFF);
ALTER TABLE dbo.Product DROP PERIOD FOR SYSTEM_TIME);
```

Note that the period columns ValidFrom and ValidTo remain in the table and will be further updated by the system. However, the history table will not be updated when data in the current table is changed.

Data manipulation in temporal tables

In this section, you will see what happens when data is inserted, updated, or deleted into/in/from a temporal table. Note that all manipulations will be done against the current table. The history table is protected; only the system can write to it.

 Even members of the sysadmin server role cannot insert, update, or delete rows from a history table of a system-versioned temporal table in SQL Server 2017.

As an example, you will use the dbo.Product temporal table created in the previous section. Use this code to recreate the table:

```
USE WideWorldImporters;
--remove existing temporal table if exists
ALTER TABLE dbo.Product SET (SYSTEM_VERSIONING = OFF);
ALTER TABLE dbo.Product DROP PERIOD FOR SYSTEM_TIME;
DROP TABLE IF EXISTS dbo.Product;
DROP TABLE IF EXISTS dbo.ProductHistory;
GO
CREATE TABLE dbo.Product
(
    ProductId INT NOT NULL CONSTRAINT PK_Product PRIMARY KEY,
    ProductName NVARCHAR(50) NOT NULL,
    Price MONEY NOT NULL,
    ValidFrom DATETIME2 GENERATED ALWAYS AS ROW START NOT NULL,
    ValidTo DATETIME2 GENERATED ALWAYS AS ROW END NOT NULL,
    PERIOD FOR SYSTEM_TIME (ValidFrom, ValidTo)
)
WITH (SYSTEM_VERSIONING = ON (HISTORY_TABLE = dbo.ProductHistory));
GO
```

Now, you can insert, update, and delete rows in this table to demonstrate how these actions affect the current and history table.

Inserting data in temporal tables

Assume that the table is empty and you have added the Fog product with a 150 price on 12th November 2017. Here is the code for this action:

```
INSERT INTO dbo.Product(ProductId, ProductName, Price) VALUES(1, N'Fog',
150.00) ;-- on 12th November
```

The state of the current table is as follows:

ProductId	ProductName	Price	ValidFrom	ValidTo
1	Fog	150	12.11.2017	31.12.9999

The state of the history table is as follows:

ProductId	ProductName	Price	ValidFrom	ValidTo

 Note that the dates in the ValidFrom and ValidTo columns are displayed in short format for clarity; their actual value is of DATETIME2 data type.

As you can see, after an INSERT into a temporal table, the following transitions occur:

- **Current table**: A new row has been added with attributes from the INSERT statement, the period start date column is set to the system date and the period end date column is set to the maximum value for the DATETIME2 data type
- **History table**: Not affected at all

Updating data in temporal tables

Now, assume that the price for the product has been changed to 200 and that this change was entered into the database on 28th November 2017. Here is the code for this action:

```
UPDATE dbo.Product SET Price = 200.00 WHERE ProductId = 1;-- on 28th
November
```

The state of the current table is as follows after the preceding statement's execution:

ProductId	ProductName	Price	ValidFrom	ValidTo
1	Fog	200	28.11.2017	31.12.9999

The state of the history table is as follows after the preceding statement's execution:

ProductId	ProductName	Price	ValidFrom	ValidTo
1	Fog	150	12.11.2017	28.11.2017

Note again that values in the `ValidFrom` and `ValidTo` columns are displayed in short format for clarity. The value in the `ValidTo` column in the history table is identical to the `ValidFrom` value in the current table; there are no gaps.

 The start and end time period columns store time in the UTC time zone!

Now, assume that you reduced the price the next day to `180`. Here is the code for this action:

```
UPDATE dbo.Product SET Price = 180.00 WHERE ProductId = 1;-- on 29th
November
```

The state of the current table is as follows after the preceding statement's execution:

ProductId	ProductName	Price	ValidFrom	ValidTo
1	Fog	180	29.11.2017	31.12.9999

The state of the history table is as follows after the preceding statement's execution:

ProductId	ProductName	Price	ValidFrom	ValidTo
1	Fog	150	12.11.2017	28.11.2017
1	Fog	200	28.11.2017	29.11.2017

You can see another entry in the history table indicating that the price `200` was valid for one day. What would happen if you execute the same statement again, say on 30th November? There is no real change; no business logic attributes are changed, but what does it mean for temporal tables? Here is the code for this action:

```
UPDATE dbo.Product SET Price = 180.00 WHERE ProductId = 1;-- on 30th
November
```

The state of the current table is as follows after the preceding statement's execution:

ProductId	ProductName	Price	ValidFrom	ValidTo
1	Fog	180	30.11.2017	31.12.9999

The state of the history table is as follows after the preceding statement's execution:

ProductId	ProductName	Price	ValidFrom	ValidTo
1	Fog	150	12.11.2017	28.11.2017
1	Fog	200	28.11.2017	29.11.2017
1	Fog	180	29.11.2017	30.11.2017

As you can see in the history table, even if there is no real change to the attributes in the current table, an entry in the history table is created and period date columns are updated.

 You can think about this as a bug, but although no attributes have been changed, if you use temporal tables for auditing you probably want to see all attempts at data manipulation in the main table.

Here is how an UPDATE of a single row in a temporal table affects the current and history tables:

- **Current table**: Values in the current table are updated to those provided by the UPDATE statement, the period start date column is set to the system date, and the period end date column is set to the maximum value for the DATETIME2 data type
- **History table**: The row from the current table before updating is copied to the history table, and only the period end date column is set to the system date

You can also see that there are no gaps in the dates in the same row of the history table. Even duplicates are possible; the history table does not have constraints to prevent them! Therefore, it is possible to have multiple records for the same row with the same values in period columns. Moreover, even values in period columns can be identical! The only constraint that is enforced is that the date representing the period end date column cannot be before the date representing the period start date (therefore, it is guaranteed that ValidFrom <= ValidTo).

Deleting data in temporal tables

You will finally remove the row from the current table in order to demonstrate how the DELETE statement affects temporal tables. Here is the code for this action:

```
DELETE FROM dbo.Product WHERE ProductId = 1;-- on 15th December
```

The state of the current table is as follows after the preceding statement's execution:

ProductId	ProductName	Price	ValidFrom	ValidTo

The state of the history table is as follows after the preceding statement's execution:

ProductId	ProductName	Price	ValidFrom	ValidTo
1	Fog	150	12.11.2017	28.11.2017
1	Fog	200	28.11.2017	29.11.2017
1	Fog	180	29.11.2017	30.11.2017
1	Fog	180	30.11.2017	15.12.2017

As you expected, there are no rows the current table, but another row has been added to the history table. After executing the DELETE statement against a single row in a temporal table:

- **Current table**: The row has been removed
- **History table**: The row from the current table before deleting is copied to the history table, and only the period end date column is set to the system date

Use this opportunity to clean up the temporal table created in this section:

```
ALTER TABLE dbo.Product SET (SYSTEM_VERSIONING = OFF);
ALTER TABLE dbo.Product DROP PERIOD FOR SYSTEM_TIME;
DROP TABLE IF EXISTS dbo.Product;
DROP TABLE IF EXISTS dbo.ProductHistory;
```

Querying temporal data in SQL Server 2017

System-versioned tables are primarily intended for tracking historical data changes. Queries on system-versioned tables often tend to be concerned with retrieving table content as of a given point in time, or between any two given points in time.

As you saw, Microsoft has implemented them according to the SQL:2011 standard, which means that two physical tables exist: a table with actual data and a history table. In order to simplify queries against temporal tables, the SQL:2011 standard introduced a new SQL clause, FOR SYSTEM_TIME. In addition to it, some new temporal-specific sub-clauses have been added too. SQL Server 2017 has not only implemented these extensions, but added two more extensions. Here is the complete list of clauses and extensions you can use to query temporal data in SQL Server 2017:

- FOR SYSTEM_TIME AS OF
- FOR SYSTEM_TIME FROM TO
- FOR SYSTEM_TIME BETWEEN AND
- FOR SYSTEM TIME CONTAINED_IN
- FOR SYSTEM_TIME ALL

Retrieving temporal data at a specific point in time

When you want to retrieve temporal data that was valid at a given point in time, the resulting set could contain both actual and historical data. For instance, the following query would return all rows from the People temporal table in the WideWorldImporters sample database that were valid at 20th May 2013 at 8 A.M.:

```
SELECT PersonID, FullName, OtherLanguages, ValidFrom, ValidTo
FROM Application.People WHERE ValidFrom <= '20130520 08:00:00' AND ValidTo
> '20130520 08:00:00'
UNION ALL
SELECT PersonID, FullName, OtherLanguages, ValidFrom, ValidTo
FROM Application.People_Archive WHERE ValidFrom <= '20130520 08:00:00' AND
ValidTo > '20130520 08:00:00';
```

The query returns 1,060 rows. For a single person, only one row is returned: either the actual or a historical row. A row is valid if its start date was before or exactly on the given date and its end date is greater than the given date.

The new FOR SYSTEM_TIME clause with the AS OF sub-clause can be used to simplify the preceding query. Here is the same query with temporal Transact-SQL extensions:

```
SELECT PersonID, FullName, OtherLanguages, ValidFrom, ValidTo
FROM Application.People FOR SYSTEM_TIME AS OF '20130520 08:00:00';
```

Of course, it returns the same result set and the execution plans are identical, as shown in the following screenshot:

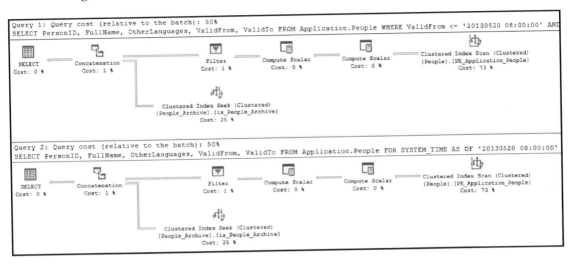

Execution plans for point-in-time queries against temporal tables

Under the hood, the query processor touches both tables and retrieves data, but the query with temporal extensions looks simpler.

The special case of a point-in-time query against a temporal table is a query where you specify the actual date as the point in time. The following query returns actual data from the same temporal table:

```
DECLARE @Now AS DATETIME = SYSUTCDATETIME();
SELECT PersonID, FullName, OtherLanguages, ValidFrom, ValidTo
FROM Application.People FOR SYSTEM_TIME AS OF @Now;
```

The previous query is logically equivalent to this one:

```
SELECT PersonID, FullName, OtherLanguages, ValidFrom, ValidTo FROM
Application.People;
```

However, when you look at the execution plans (see the following screenshot) for the execution of the first query, both tables have been processed, while the non-temporal query had to retrieve data from the current table only:

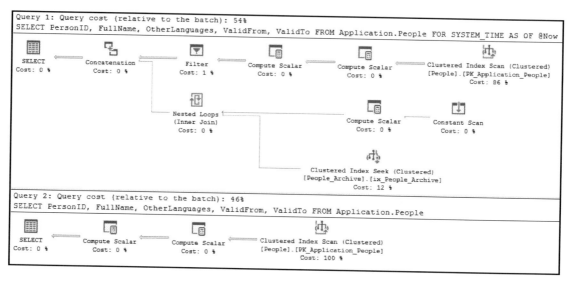

Comparing execution plans for temporal and non-temporal queries that retrieve actual data only

So, you should not use temporal queries with the FOR SYSTEM_TIME AS clause to return data from the current table.

Retrieving temporal data from a specific period

You can use the new FOR SYSTEM_TIME clause to retrieve temporal data that was or is valid between two points in time. These queries are typically used for getting changes to specific rows over time. To achieve this, you could use one of two SQL:2011 standard-specified sub-clauses:

- FROM...TO returns all data that started before or at the beginning of a given period and ended after the end of the period (closed-open interval)
- BETWEEN...AND returns all data that started before or at the beginning of a given period and ended after or at the end of the period (closed-closed interval)

As you can see, the only difference between these two sub-clauses is how data with a starting date to the right side of the given period is interpreted: BETWEEN includes this data, FROM...TO does not.

The following queries demonstrate the usage of these two sub-clauses and the difference between them:

```
--example using FROM/TO
SELECT PersonID, FullName, OtherLanguages, ValidFrom, ValidTo
FROM Application.People FOR SYSTEM_TIME FROM '2016-03-20 08:00:00' TO
'2016-05-31 23:14:00' WHERE PersonID = 7;

--example using BETWEEN
SELECT PersonID, FullName, OtherLanguages, ValidFrom, ValidTo
FROM Application.People FOR SYSTEM_TIME BETWEEN '2016-03-20 08:00:01' AND
'2016-05-31 23:14:00' WHERE PersonID = 7;
```

Here are the result sets generated by the preceding queries:

PersonID	FullName	OtherLanguages	ValidFrom	ValidTo
7	Amy Trefl	NULL	2016-03-20 08:00	2016-05-31 23:13
7	Amy Trefl	["Slovak","Spanish","Polish"]	2016-05-31 23:13	2016-05-31 23:14

PersonID	FullName	OtherLanguages	ValidFrom	ValidTo
7	Amy Trefl	["Slovak","Spanish","Polish"]	2016-05-31 23:14	9999-12-31 23:59
7	Amy Trefl	NULL	2016-03-20 08:00	2016-05-31 23:13
7	Amy Trefl	["Slovak","Spanish","Polish"]	2016-05-31 23:13	2016-05-31 23:14

As you can see, the second query returns three rows, as it includes the row where the start date is equal to the value of the right boundary of the given period.

These two sub-clauses return row versions that overlap with a specified period. If you need to return rows that existed within specified period boundaries, you need to use another extension, CONTAINED IN. This extension (an implementation of one of Allen's operators) is not defined in the SQL:2011 standard; it is implemented in SQL Server 2017.

Rows that either start or end outside a given interval will not be part of a result set when the `CONTAINED IN` sub-clause is used. When you replace the sub-clause `BETWEEN` with it in the previous example, only rows whose whole life belongs to the given interval will survive:

```
SELECT PersonID, FullName, OtherLanguages, ValidFrom, ValidTo
FROM Application.People FOR SYSTEM_TIME CONTAINED IN ('2016-03-20
08:00:01','2016-05-31 23:14:00') WHERE PersonID = 7;
```

Instead of three rows using `BETWEEN`, or two with `FROM...TO` sub-clauses, this time only one row is returned:

PersonID	FullName	OtherLanguages	ValidFrom	ValidTo
7	Amy Trefl	["Slovak","Spanish","Polish"]	2016-05-31 23:13	2016-05-31 23:14

Although this extension is not standard, its implementation in SQL Server 2017 is welcomed; it covers a reasonable and not-so-rare use case, and simplifies the development of database solutions based on temporal tables.

Retrieving all temporal data

Since temporal data is separated into two tables, to get all temporal data you need to combine data from both tables, but there is no sub-clause defined in the SQL:2011 standard for that purpose. However, the SQL Server team has introduced the extension (sub-clause) `ALL` to simplify such queries.

Here is a temporal query that returns both actual and historical data for the person with the ID of 7:

```
SELECT PersonID, FullName, OtherLanguages, ValidFrom, ValidTo FROM
Application.People FOR SYSTEM_TIME ALL WHERE PersonID = 7;
```

The query returns *14 rows*, since there are 13 historical rows and one entry in the actual table. Here is the logically equivalent, standard, but a bit more complex query:

```
SELECT PersonID, FullName, OtherLanguages, ValidFrom, ValidTo FROM
Application.People WHERE PersonID = 7
UNION ALL
SELECT PersonID, FullName, OtherLanguages, ValidFrom, ValidTo FROM
Application.People_Archive WHERE PersonID = 7;
```

The only purpose of this sub-clause is to simplify queries against temporal tables.

Performance and storage considerations with temporal tables

Introducing temporal tables and adding this functionality to existing tables can significantly increase storage used for data in your system. Since there is no out-of-the-box solution for managing the retention of history tables, if you don't do something, data will remain there forever. This can be painful for storage costs, maintenance, and performance of queries on temporal tables, especially if rows in your current tables are heavily updated.

History retention policy in SQL Server 2017

A temporal history retention policy lets you define which rows should stay and which should be cleaned up from the history tables. It can be configured at the individual table level, which allows users to create flexible aging polices. Applying temporal retention is simple; it requires only one parameter to be set during table creation or schema change.

Configuring the retention policy at the database level

The temporal historical retention feature must be enabled at the database level. For new databases, this flag is enabled by default. For databases restored from previous database versions (as with the WideWorldImporters database used in this book), you need to set it manually. The following code enables the temporal historical retention feature for this database:

```
ALTER DATABASE WideWorldImporters SET TEMPORAL_HISTORY_RETENTION ON;
```

Now, you can define the retention policy at the (temporal) table level.

Configuring the retention policy at the table level

To configure the retention policy, you need to specify a value for the HISTORY_RETENTION_PERIOD parameter during table creation or after the table is created. Use the following code to create and populate a sample temporal table:

```
USE WideWorldImporters;
GO
CREATE TABLE dbo.T1(
    Id INT NOT NULL PRIMARY KEY CLUSTERED,
    C1 INT,
    Vf DATETIME2 NOT NULL,
    Vt DATETIME2 NOT NULL
)
```

```
GO
CREATE TABLE dbo.T1_Hist(
    Id INT NOT NULL,
    C1 INT,
    Vf DATETIME2 NOT NULL,
    Vt DATETIME2 NOT NULL
)
GO
--populate tables
INSERT INTO dbo.T1_Hist(Id, C1, Vf, Vt) VALUES
(1,1,'20171201','20171210'),
(1,2,'20171210','20171215');
GO
INSERT INTO dbo.T1(Id, C1, Vf, Vt) VALUES
(1,3,'20171215','99991231 23:59:59.9999999');
GO
```

Here is the content of both tables after the script execution:

Id	C1	Vf	Vt
1	3	2017-12-15 00:00:00.0000000	9999-12-3 23:59:59.9999999

Id	C1	Vf	Vt
1	1	2017-12-01 00:00:00.0000000	2017-12-10 00:00:00.0000000
1	2	2017-12-10 00:00:00.0000000	2017-12-15 00:00:00.0000000

The actual value in the C1 column for the row with the ID of 1 is 3, and there are two historical values. You will now convert the T1 table into a temporal table and so define a retention policy that states historical entries should be retained for one day only. Here is the appropriate code:

```
ALTER TABLE dbo.T1 ADD PERIOD FOR SYSTEM_TIME (Vf, Vt);
GO
ALTER TABLE dbo.T1 SET
  (
    SYSTEM_VERSIONING = ON
    (
      HISTORY_TABLE = dbo.T1_Hist,
      HISTORY_RETENTION_PERIOD = 3 DAYS
    )
  );
```

You had to use two statements to achieve this task: the first one is used for adding a period to the table, and the second converts the table to a temporal table with a retention policy of 3 days. However, when you execute the query, you will see the following message:

```
Msg 13765, Level 16, State 1, Line 31
Setting finite retention period failed on system-versioned temporal table
'WideWorldImporters.dbo.T1' because the history table
'WideWorldImporters.dbo.T1_Hist' does not contain required clustered index.
Consider creating a clustered columnstore or B-tree index starting with the
column that matches end of SYSTEM_TIME period, on the history table.
```

The history table must have a row clustered index on the column representing the end of period; it won't work without it. Use this code to create the index and run the previous code again:

```
CREATE CLUSTERED INDEX IX_CL_T1_Hist ON dbo.T1_Hist(Vt, Vf);
GO
ALTER TABLE dbo.T1 SET
  (
      SYSTEM_VERSIONING = ON
      (
          HISTORY_TABLE = dbo.T1_Hist,
          HISTORY_RETENTION_PERIOD = 3 DAYS
      )
  );
```

The execution was successful. This section is written on 17th December, so the results of the further actions will be shown according to this date. In this example, there are two historical records with the end period dates 10.12. and 15.12. According to the retention policy, only one row should be shown as a history row. To check this, use the following query:

```
SELECT * FROM dbo.T1 FOR SYSTEM_TIME ALL;
```

The query returns the following result:

Id	C1	Vf	Vt
1	3	2017-12-15 00:00:00.0000000	9999-12-31 23:59:59.9999999
1	2	2017-12-10 00:00:00.0000000	2017-12-15 00:00:00.0000000

Rows that do not meet the retention policy have been removed from the result set. The execution plan for the query is shown in the following screenshot:

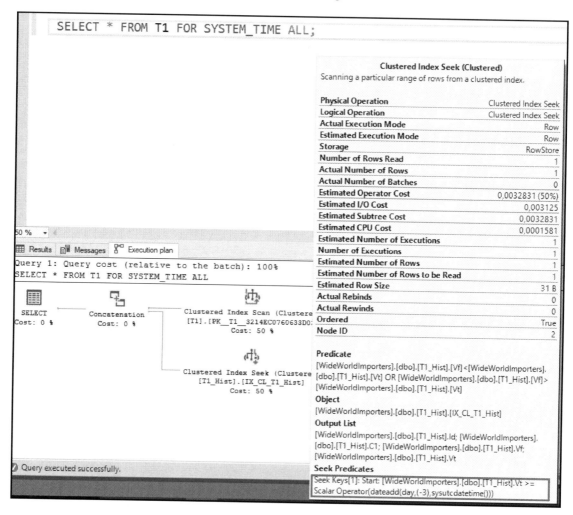

Execution plan for a query with a temporal table with a finite retention period defined

When you look at the execution plan, you can see that the retention policy filter is automatically applied. Therefore, historical rows older than three days are removed from the result set and it contains one actual and one historical row. Rows that meet the following criteria are not shown:

```
Vt < DATEADD (Day, -3, SYSUTCDATETIME ());
```

However, when you query the history table directly, you can still see all rows:

```
SELECT * FROM dbo.T1
UNION ALL
SELECT * FROM dbo.T1_Hist;
```

The query returns the following result:

Id	C1	Vf	Vt
1	3	2017-12-15 00:00:00.0000000	9999-12-31 23:59:59.9999999
1	1	2017-12-01 00:00:00.0000000	2017-12-10 00:00:00.0000000
1	2	2017-12-10 00:00:00.0000000	2017-12-15 00:00:00.0000000

This is not what you expected! How does SQL Server remove the aged rows? Identification of matching rows and their removal from the history table occur transparently, alongside the background tasks that are scheduled and run by the system. Since aged rows can be removed at any point in time and in arbitrary order, you should use Transact-SQL extensions for querying temporal data, as shown in the previous section.

In this example, you have used three days in the retention policy. This information is stored in the sys.tables catalog. Run the following query to check retention policy settings for the T1 table:

```
SELECT temporal_type_desc, history_retention_period,
history_retention_period_unit
FROM sys.tables WHERE name = 'T1';
```

The previous query returns this result set:

temporal_type_desc	history_retention_period	history_retention_period_unit
SYSTEM_VERSIONED_TEMPORAL_TABLE	3	3

The second 3 in the results represents days. If you include the other tables, you can see that all temporal tables in the WideWorldImporters database have a value of -1 in this column, which means that the retention period is not defined for a temporal table, thus the historical rows will be kept forever. Here is the list of possible retention period units you can define in an SQL Server 2017 retention policy:

- **-1**: INFINITE
- **3**: DAY

- **4**: WEEK
- **5**: MONTH
- **6**: YEAR

A history retention policy is good and lets you manage and control data size. However, currently you can use only one criteria to define aged rows: the end of period. If you have a lot of historical entries for some rows and a few for most of the others, this will not help you. It would be nice if you could choose additional criteria such as the number of rows or table size. You also cannot define where aged data will be moved; currently it is simply cleaned up.

Custom history data retention

Unfortunately, you cannot configure a history table to automatically move data to some other table or repository according to a user-defined retention policy. That means that you have to implement this kind of data retention manually. This is not very complicated, but it is not a trivial action. I expected it as a part of the implementation and would be disappointed if this was not delivered in the next SQL Server version. As mentioned, you can use some other SQL Server features to implement data retention for history tables:

- **Stretch databases** allow you to move entire parts of historical data transparently to Azure.
- **Partitioning** history tables allows you to easily truncate the oldest historical data by implementing the sliding window approach.
- **Custom Cleanup** doesn't require any other features. You use Transact-SQL scripts to convert a temporal table to non-temporal, delete old data, and convert the table back to a temporal table.

You can find more details about data retention at Books Online at the following address: `https://docs.microsoft.com/en-us/sql/relational-databases/tables/manage-retention-of-historical-data-in-system-versioned-temporal-tables`.

History table implementation

As mentioned in the *Creating temporal tables* section, you can create the history table in advance, or let SQL Server create it for you. In the former case, the created table is a row stored table with a clustered index on period columns. If the current table does not contain data types that prevent the usage of data compression, the table is created with PAGE compression. This physical implementation is acceptable if you query the history table by using period columns as filter criteria. However, if your temporal queries usually look for historical records for individual rows, this is not a good implementation. To check potential performance issues of an automatic created history table, use the following code to create and populate a sample temporal table:

```
CREATE TABLE dbo.Mila
(
    Id INT NOT NULL IDENTITY (1,1) PRIMARY KEY CLUSTERED,
    C1 INT NOT NULL,
    C2 NVARCHAR(4000) NULL
)
GO
INSERT INTO dbo.Mila(C1, C2)  SELECT message_id, text FROM sys.messages
WHERE language_id = 1033;
GO 50

ALTER TABLE dbo.Mila
ADD ValidFrom DATETIME2 GENERATED ALWAYS AS ROW START NOT NULL CONSTRAINT
DF_Mila_ValidFrom DEFAULT '20170101',
    ValidTo DATETIME2 GENERATED ALWAYS AS ROW END NOT NULL CONSTRAINT
DF_Mila_ValidTo DEFAULT '99991231 23:59:59.9999999',
    PERIOD FOR SYSTEM_TIME (ValidFrom, ValidTo);
GO
ALTER TABLE dbo.Mila SET (SYSTEM_VERSIONING = ON (HISTORY_TABLE =
dbo.Mila_History));
GO
```

As you can see, the INSERT statement is repeated 50 times, so that the sample table has a lot of rows (661,150 rows). At this point, the history table is empty; all rows are in the current table only. To create a history row for each row in the current table, and one additional history row for the row with the ID of 1, use the following command:

```
UPDATE dbo.Mila SET C1 = C1 + 1;
UPDATE dbo.Mila SET C1 = 44 WHERE Id = 1;
```

Now, assume that you want to check the state of the row with the ID of 1 at some time in the past. Ensure also that query statistics parameters are set to on:

```
SET STATISTICS IO ON;
SET STATISTICS TIME ON;
SELECT * FROM dbo.Mila FOR SYSTEM_TIME AS OF '20170505 08:00:00' WHERE Id =
1;
```

This query returns one row:

Id	C1	C2	ValidFrom	ValidTo
1	21	Warning:Fatal error %d occurred	2017-01-01 00:00	2017-12-13 16:57

However, it is most interesting to check the execution parameters. The execution plan for the query is shown as follows:

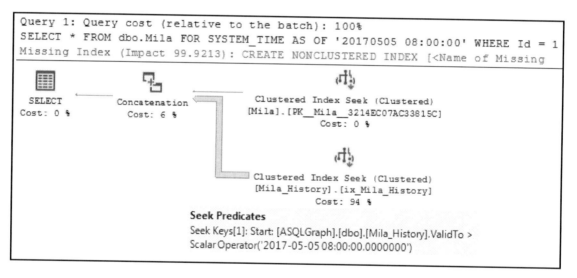

```
Query 1: Query cost (relative to the batch): 100%
SELECT * FROM dbo.Mila FOR SYSTEM_TIME AS OF '20170505 08:00:00' WHERE Id = 1
Missing Index (Impact 99.9213): CREATE NONCLUSTERED INDEX [<Name of Missing
```

SELECT
Cost: 0 %

Concatenation
Cost: 6 %

Clustered Index Seek (Clustered)
[Mila].[PK__Mila__3214EC07AC33815C]
Cost: 0 %

Clustered Index Seek (Clustered)
[Mila_History].[ix_Mila_History]
Cost: 94 %

Seek Predicates

Seek Keys[1]: Start: [ASQLGraph].[dbo].[Mila_History].ValidTo >
Scalar Operator('2017-05-05 08:00:00.0000000')

Execution plan with a default index on the history table

You can see the **Index Seek** operator in the plan, but the plan is not efficient since it uses the `ValidTo` column as filter criteria. Observe the execution parameters:

```
SQL Server Execution Times:
   CPU time = 0 ms,  elapsed time = 0 ms.
SQL Server parse and compile time:
   CPU time = 0 ms, elapsed time = 0 ms.

Table 'Mila_History'. Scan count 1, logical reads 10583, physical reads 0,
```

```
read-ahead reads 0, lob logical reads 0, lob physical reads 0, lob read-
ahead reads 0.
Table 'Mila'. Scan count 0, logical reads 3, physical reads 0, read-ahead
reads 0, lob logical reads 0, lob physical reads 0, lob read-ahead reads 0.

 SQL Server Execution Times:
   CPU time = 188 ms,  elapsed time = 193 ms.
SQL Server parse and compile time:
   CPU time = 0 ms, elapsed time = 0 ms.

 SQL Server Execution Times:
   CPU time = 0 ms,  elapsed time = 0 ms.
```

The query that returns a single row takes almost 200 milliseconds and SQL Server had to read more than 10,000 pages to generate this row! Since you have the `Id` column in the filter, it is clear that you need an index with this column as the leading column:

```
CREATE CLUSTERED INDEX ix_Mila_History ON dbo.Mila_History(Id, ValidTo,
ValidFrom) WITH DROP_EXISTING;
```

When you execute the same query again, you can see the execution plan shown as follows:

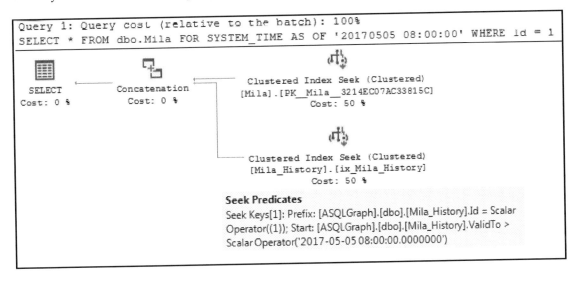

Execution plan with a custom index on the history table

Actually, the plan looks the same, but the `Id` as the leading column in the clustered index on the history table allows SQL Server to search efficiently, as shown in the execution parameters' output:

```
SQL Server Execution Times:
   CPU time = 0 ms,   elapsed time = 0 ms.
SQL Server parse and compile time:
   CPU time = 0 ms, elapsed time = 0 ms.

Table 'Mila_History'. Scan count 1, logical reads 4, physical reads 0,
read-ahead reads 0, lob logical reads 0, lob physical reads 0, lob read-
ahead reads 0.
Table 'Mila'. Scan count 0, logical reads 3, physical reads 0, read-ahead
reads 0, lob logical reads 0, lob physical reads 0, lob read-ahead reads 0.

 SQL Server Execution Times:
   CPU time = 0 ms,   elapsed time = 0 ms.
SQL Server parse and compile time:
   CPU time = 0 ms, elapsed time = 0 ms.

 SQL Server Execution Times:
   CPU time = 0 ms,   elapsed time = 0 ms.
```

It is good when SQL Server can create and configure some objects for you, but you should not forget to check what it means for the performance of your queries.

Finally, if you plan to process a lot of data in temporal queries or to aggregate them, the best approach is to create your own history table with a clustered columnstore index and eventual, additional, non-clustered, normal B-tree indexes.

History table overhead

Converting a non-temporal table into a temporal table is very easy. With two ALTER TABLE statements you get the full temporal table functionality. However, this cannot be completely free. Adding temporal features to a table brings performance overhead in all data modification operations. According to Microsoft, a single update operation against a row in a temporal table is about 30% slower than it would be when the table is non-temporal.

I have performed a simple test where I have updated a different number of rows in a table before it is converted to a temporal table and afterwards. The following graph displays results of this test. For a small amount of rows (<1000), locking, calculating, and inserting data into a history table slows the update down by 50%. Updating 50,000 rows in a temporal table takes about eight times longer than the same operation against the same table when it is implemented as a non-temporal table:

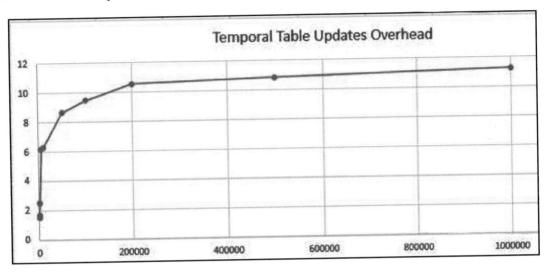

Temporal table updates overhead

Finally, massive updates (>100K rows) are 10 times slower for temporal tables compared to those against their non-temporal counterparts.

Temporal tables with memory-optimized tables

System-versioned temporal tables are also supported for memory-optimized tables. You can assign or let SQL Server create a history table for your memory-optimized table. The history table must be a disk table, but this is exactly what you want; frequently used (hot) data remains in memory, while cold data can reside in disk tables. By taking this approach, you can use all the benefits provided by memory-optimized tables (high transactional throughput, lock-free concurrency), save their historical data on disk-based tables, and leave memory for active datasets only. The following figure shows the architecture of system-versioned memory-optimized tables. It is taken from the Books Online page at https://msdn.microsoft.com/en-us/library/mt590207.aspx:

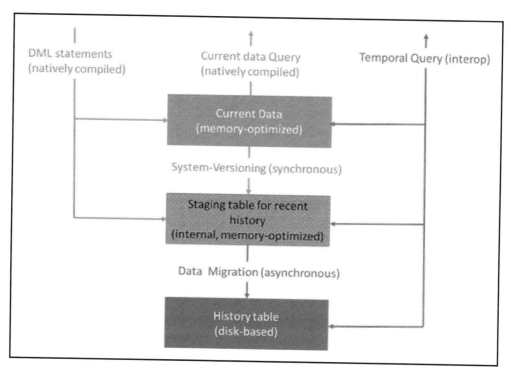

System-versioned temporal tables with memory-optimized table architecture (Source: SQL Server Books Online)

As you can see, system-versioned temporal tables are implemented with three tables:

- **Current table** is a memory-optimized table and all native compiled operations are supported
- **Recent history table** is an internal memory-optimized table that handles changes in the current table synchronously and enables DMLs to be executed from natively compiled code
- **History table** is a disk table that contains changes in the current table and manages them asynchronously

Historical data is a union of data in the recent history and history tables. A history row is either in the staging memory table or in the disk table; it cannot be in both tables. The following code example creates a new memory-optimized temporal table:

```
USE WideWorldImporters;
CREATE TABLE dbo.Product
(
    ProductId INT NOT NULL PRIMARY KEY NONCLUSTERED,
    ProductName NVARCHAR(50) NOT NULL,
    Price MONEY NOT NULL,
    ValidFrom DATETIME2 GENERATED ALWAYS AS ROW START HIDDEN NOT NULL,
    ValidTo DATETIME2 GENERATED ALWAYS AS ROW END HIDDEN NOT NULL,
    PERIOD FOR SYSTEM_TIME (ValidFrom, ValidTo)
)
WITH (MEMORY_OPTIMIZED = ON, DURABILITY = SCHEMA_AND_DATA,
SYSTEM_VERSIONING = ON (HISTORY_TABLE = dbo.ProductHistory));
```

After the execution of this query, you will see that the history table is a memory-optimized table.

```
SELECT CONCAT(SCHEMA_NAME(schema_id),'.', name) AS table_name,
is_memory_optimized, temporal_type_desc FROM sys.tables WHERE name IN
('Product', 'ProductHistory');
```

The result of the preceding query is as follows:

table_name	is_memory_optimized	temporal_type_desc
dbo.Product	1	SYSTEM_VERSIONED_TEMPORAL_TABLE
dbo.ProductHistory	0	HISTORY_TABLE

As mentioned earlier, SQL Server creates a third table automatically: an internal memory-optimized table. Here is the code that you can use to find its name and properties:

```
SELECT CONCAT(SCHEMA_NAME(schema_id),'.', name) AS table_name,
internal_type_desc FROM  sys.internal_tables WHERE name =
CONCAT('memory_optimized_history_table_', OBJECT_ID('dbo.Product'));
```

And here is its output:

table_name	internal_type_desc
sys.memory_optimized_history_table_1575676661	INTERNAL_TEMPORAL_HISTORY_TABLE

Only durable, memory-optimized tables can be system-versioned temporal tables, and history tables must be disk based. Since all current rows are in memory, you can use natively compiled modules to access this data. Use the following code to create a natively compiled stored procedure that handles the inserting and updating of products:

```
CREATE OR ALTER PROCEDURE dbo.SaveProduct
(
@ProductId INT,
@ProductName NVARCHAR(50),
@Price MONEY
)
WITH NATIVE_COMPILATION, SCHEMABINDING, EXECUTE AS OWNER
AS
    BEGIN ATOMIC WITH
    (TRANSACTION ISOLATION LEVEL = SNAPSHOT, LANGUAGE = N'English')
    UPDATE dbo.Product SET ProductName = @ProductName, Price = @Price WHERE
ProductId = @ProductId
    IF @@ROWCOUNT = 0
        INSERT INTO dbo.Product(ProductId,ProductName,Price) VALUES
(@ProductId, @ProductName, @Price);
END
GO
```

Now you can, for instance, add two rows and update one of them by using the previous procedure:

```
EXEC dbo.SaveProduct 1, N'Home Jersey Benfica', 89.95;
EXEC dbo.SaveProduct 2, N'Away Jersey Juventus', 89.95;
EXEC dbo.SaveProduct 1, N'Home Jersey Benfica', 79.95;
```

Under the hood, everything works perfectly; both the current and history tables are updated. Here are the resulting datasets in the current and historical table:

ProductId	ProductName	Price
2	Away Jersey Juventus	89.95
1	Home Jersey Benfica	79.95

ProductId	ProductName	Price	ValidFrom	ValidTo
1	Home Jersey Benfica	89.95	2017-12-17 20:25:50	2017-12-17 20:25:51

The querying of historical data is effectively under the SNAPSHOT isolation level and always returns a union between the in-memory staging buffer and the disk-based table without duplicates. Since temporal queries (queries that use the FOR SYSTEM_TIME clause) touch memory-optimized and disk tables, they can be used only in interop mode; it is not possible to use them in natively compiled procedures.

Data from the internal memory-optimized staging table is regularly moved to the disk-based history table by the asynchronous data flush task. This data flush mechanism has the goal of keeping the internal memory buffers at less than 10% of the memory consumption of their parent objects.

When you add system-versioning to an existing non-temporal table, expect a performance impact on update and delete operations because the history table is updated automatically. Every update and delete is recorded in the internal memory-optimized history table, so you may experience unexpected memory consumption if your workload uses those two operations.

What is missing in SQL Server 2017?

SQL Server 2016 is the first SQL Server version that has some built-in support for temporal data. However, even in SQL Server version 2017, the support is still quite basic. SQL Server 2016 and 2017 support system-versioned tables only. You have seen at the beginning of this chapter that application versioned tables, and of course bitemporal tables, add much more complexity to temporal problems. Unfortunately, in order to deal with application validity times, you need to develop your own solution, including your own implementation of all constraints, on which you need to enforce data integrity. In addition, you need to deal with the optimization of temporal queries by yourself as well.

In SQL Server 2017, you can define the retention period for historical rows. Therefore, you do not have to do the history data cleanup by yourself, like you needed to do in SQL Server 2016. Nevertheless, it would be very useful to also have the ability to define the absolute maximum number of historical rows you want to keep, and the maximum number of versions per row. This way, you could prevent a scenario where frequent updates of some rows occupy the most space in the historical table, overwhelming the history of the rows that are not updated that frequently.

If you are familiar with analytical applications and data warehouses, you might think that system-versioned temporal tables can help you in analytical scenarios. However, as you will learn in the next section, which briefly introduces data warehouses and the slowly changing dimensions problem, analytical applications have typically different granularity requests and system-versioned temporal tables don't help there.

SQL Server 2016 and 2017 temporal tables and data warehouses

For analytical purposes, **data warehouses** have evolved. Data warehouses support historical data. You should not confuse a data warehouse's historical data with temporal data, the subject of this chapter. In a data warehouse, historical data means just archived non-temporal data from the past; a typical data warehouse holds from 5 to 10 years of data for analytical purposes. Data warehouses are not suitable for business applications because a data warehouse typically has no constraints.

Data warehouses have a simplified data model that consists of multiple **star schemas**. You can see a typical star schema in the following figure:

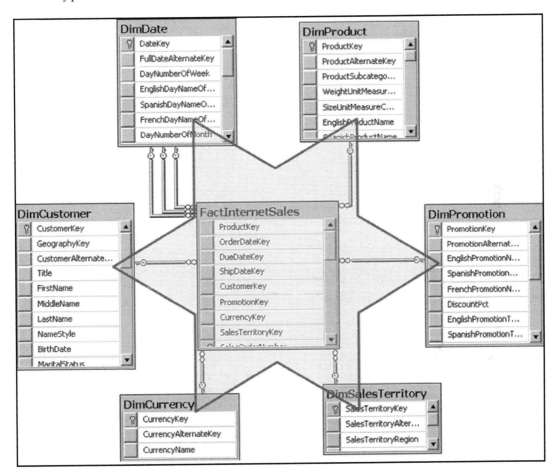

Star schema

One schema covers one business area. It consists of a single central table, called the **fact table**, and multiple surrounding tables, called **dimensions**. The fact table is always on the many side every single relationship, with every single dimension table. Star schema is deliberately denormalized. The fact table includes measures, while dimensions give context to those measures. Shared dimensions connect star schemas in a data warehouse.

Dimensions can change over time. The pace of the changes is usually slow compared to the pace of the changes in fact tables. Transactional systems often show the current state only, and don't preserve the history. In a data warehouse, you might need to preserve the history. This is known as the **slowly changing dimensions (SCD)** problem, which has two common solutions:

- A type 1 solution means not preserving the history in the data warehouse by simply overwriting the values when the values in the sources change
- A type 2 solution means adding a new row for a change, and marking which row is the current one

You can also mix both types; for some attributes, like the city in the example, you use type 2, while for some, like occupation, you use type 1. Note the additional problem: when you update the OCCUPATION attribute, you need to decide whether to update the current row only or also the historical rows that come from the type 2 changes. You can see these possibilities in the following figure:

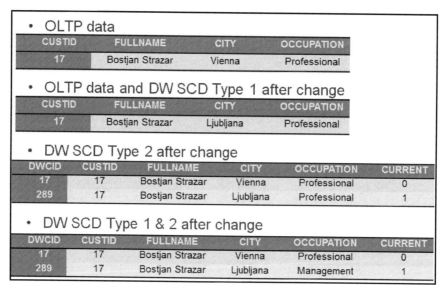

Slowly changing dimensions

On first glance, SQL Server system-versioned tables might be the solution to the SCD problem when using the type 2 implementation. However, this is typically not true. In a data warehouse, most of the time you need to implement a mixed solution: type 1 for some attributes and type 2 for others. The granularity of the time points in system-versioned tables is 100 nanoseconds; in a data warehouse, typical granularity is 1 day. In the source system, the same entity, like customer, can be updated multiple times per day. You can have multiple historical rows for the same entity in a single day. Therefore, when transferring the data from a transactional database to a data warehouse, you need to take care to transfer the last state for each day. The following query illustrates the problem:

```
USE WideWorldImporters;
SELECT PersonID, FullName,
 ValidFrom, ValidTo
FROM Application.People
 FOR SYSTEM_TIME ALL
WHERE IsEmployee = 1
  AND PersonID = 14;
```

In the `WideWorldImporters` database, `Application.People` is a system-versioned table. The previous query returns all rows for an employee called `Lily Code`. Here is the abbreviated result:

PersonID	FullName	ValidFrom	ValidTo
14	Lily Code	2016-05-31 23:14:00.0000000	9999-12-31 23:59:59.9999999
14	Lily Code	2013-01-01 00:00:00.0000000	2013-01-01 08:00:00.0000000
14	Lily Code	2013-01-01 08:00:00.0000000	2013-01-19 08:00:00.0000000
14	Lily Code	2013-01-19 08:00:00.0000000	2013-02-14 08:00:00.0000000

You can see that this person has multiple rows for a single date. For example, there are two rows for `Lily` where the `ValidTo` date (just the date part) equals 2013-01-01. You need to select only the last row per employee per day. This is done with the following query. You can run it and check the results:

```
WITH PersonCTE AS
(
SELECT PersonID, FullName,
 CAST(ValidFrom AS DATE) AS ValidFrom,
 CAST(ValidTo AS DATE) AS ValidTo,
 ROW_NUMBER() OVER(PARTITION BY PersonID, CAST(ValidFrom AS Date)
                   ORDER BY ValidFrom DESC) AS rn
FROM Application.People
 FOR SYSTEM_TIME ALL
```

```
WHERE IsEmployee = 1
)
SELECT PersonID, FullName,
 ValidFrom, ValidTo
FROM PersonCTE
WHERE rn = 1;
```

Summary

SQL Server 2016 and 2017 system-versioned temporal tables are a very nice feature you can start using immediately, without changes to your applications. You can use them for auditing all changes in specific tables. You can retrieve the state of those tables at any point in time in history. You can find all the states and changes in a specific period. SQL Server automatically updates the period in the current row and inserts the old version of the row into the history table as soon as you update the current row.

Nevertheless, there is still a lot to do in future versions of SQL Server. We still need better support for application validity times, including support for constraints and optimization of temporal queries, and more flexibility in the history retention policy.

In the next chapter, you will discover the power of columnstore indexes and memory-optimized objects.

6
Columnstore Indexes

Analytical queries that scan huge amounts of data are always problematic in relational databases. Nonclustered balanced tree indexes are efficient for transactional query seeks; however, they rarely help with analytical queries. A great idea occurred nearly 30 years ago: why do we need to store data physically in the same way we work with it logically, row by row? Why don't we store it column by column and transform columns back into rows when we interact with the data? Microsoft played with this idea for a long time and finally implemented it in SQL Server.

Columnar storage was first added to SQL Server in the 2012 version. It included **nonclustered columnstore indexes** (**NCCI**) only. **Clustered columnstore indexes** (**CCIs**) were added in the 2014 version. In this chapter, readers can revise columnar storage and then explore huge improvements for columnstore indexes in SQL Server 2016 and 2017—updatable nonclustered columnstore indexes, columnstore indexes on in-memory tables, and many other new features for operational analytics.

In the first section, you will learn about SQL Server support for analytical queries without using columnar storage. The next section of this chapter jumps directly to columnar storage and explains the internals, with the main focus on columnar storage compression. In addition, batch execution mode is introduced.

Then it is time to show you columnar storage in action. The chapter starts with a section that introduces nonclustered columnstore indexes. The demo code shows the compression you can get with this storage and also how to create a filtered nonclustered columnstore index.

Clustered columnstore indexes can have even better compression. You will learn how these clustered and nonclustered columnstore indexes compress data and improve the performance of your queries. You can also combine columnar indexes with regular B-tree indexes. In addition, you will learn how to update data in a clustered columnstore index, especially how to insert new data efficiently. Finally, the chapter introduces a method to use columnar indexes, together with regular B-tree indexes, to implement a solution for operational analytics.

This chapter will cover the following points:

- Data compression in SQL Server
- Indexing for analytical queries
- T-SQL support for analytical queries
- Columnar storage basics
- Nonclustered columnstore indexes
- Using clustered columnstore indexes
- Creating regular B-tree indexes for tables with CCI
- Discovering support for primary and foreign keys for tables with CCI
- Discovering additional performance improvements with batch mode
- Columnstore index query performance
- Columnstore for real-time operational analytics
- Data loading for columnstore indexes

Analytical queries in SQL Server

Supporting analytical applications in SQL Server differs quite a lot from supporting transactional applications. The typical schema for reporting queries is the star schema. In a star schema, there is one central table called a **fact table** and multiple surrounding tables called **dimensions**. The fact table is always on the many side of every relationship with every dimension. A database that supports analytical queries and uses the star schema design is called **Data Warehouse (DW)**. Dealing with data warehousing design in detail is beyond the scope of this book. Nevertheless, there is a lot of literature available. For a quick start, you can read the data warehouse concepts MSDN blog at https://blogs.msdn.microsoft.com/syedab/2010/06/01/data-warehouse-concepts/. The WideWorldImportersDW demo database implements multiple star schemas. The following screenshot shows a subset of tables from this database that supports analytical queries for sales:

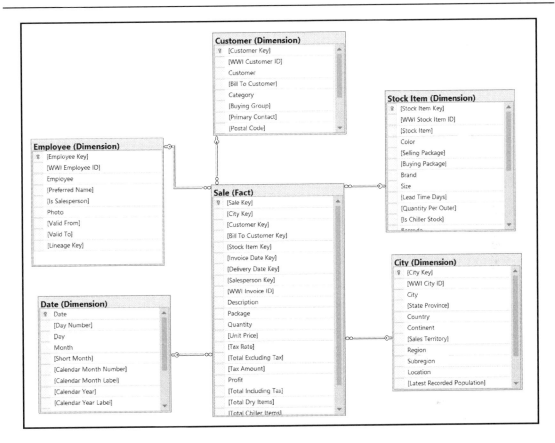

Sales star schema

Typical analytical queries require huge amounts of data, for example, sales data for two years, which is then aggregated. Therefore, index seeks are quite rare. Most of the time, you need to optimize the number of IO reads using different techniques from those you would use in a transactional environment, where you have mostly selective queries that benefit a lot from index seeks. Columnstore indexes are the latest and probably the most important optimization for analytical queries in SQL Server. However, before going into columnar storage, you should be familiar with other techniques and possibilities for optimizing data warehousing scenarios. Everything you will learn about in this and the upcoming section will help you understand the need for, and the implementation of, columnstore indexes. You will learn about the following:

- Join types
- Bitmap filtered hash joins
- B-tree indexes for analytical queries

- Filtered nonclustered indexes
- Table partitioning
- Indexed views
- Row compression
- Page compression
- Appropriate query techniques

Joins and indexes

SQL Server executes a query by a set of physical **operators**. Because these operators iterate through rowsets, they are also called **iterators**. There are different join operators, because when performing joins, SQL Server uses different algorithms. SQL Server supports three basic algorithms: nested loops joins, merge joins, and hash joins.

The nested loops algorithm is a very simple and, in many cases, efficient algorithm. S

QL Server uses one table for the outer loop, typically the table with the fewest rows. For each row in this outer input, SQL Server seeks matching rows in the second table, which is the inner table. SQL Server uses the join condition to find the matching rows. The join can be a **non-equijoin**, meaning that the equality operator does not need to be part of the join predicate. If the inner table has no supporting index to perform seeks, then SQL Server scans the inner input for each row of the outer input. This is not an efficient scenario. A nested loop join is efficient when SQL Server can perform an index seek in the inner input.

Merge join is a very efficient join algorithm. However, it has its own limitations. It needs at least one **equijoin** predicate and sorted inputs from both sides. This means that the merge join should be supported by indexes on both tables involved in the join. In addition, if one input is much smaller than another, then the nested loop join could be more efficient than a merge join.

In a one-to-one or one-to-many scenario, a merge join scans both inputs only once. It starts by finding the first rows on both sides. If the end of the input is not reached, the merge join checks the join predicate to determine whether the rows match. If the rows match, they are added to the output. Then the algorithm checks the next rows from the other side and adds them to the output until they match the predicate. If the rows from the inputs do not match, then the algorithm reads the next row from the side with the lower value from the other side. It reads from this side and compares the row to the row from the other side until the value is bigger than the value from the other side. Then it continues reading from the other side, and so on. In a many-to-many scenario, the merge join algorithm uses a worktable to put the rows from one input side aside for reuse when duplicate matching rows are received from the other input.

If none of the input is supported by an index and an equijoin predicate is used, then the hash join algorithm might be the most efficient one. It uses a searching structure named a hash table. This is not a searching structure you can build, like a balanced tree used for indexes. SQL Server builds the hash table internally. It uses a **hash function** to split the rows from the smaller input into **buckets**. This is the build phase. SQL Server uses the smaller input for building the hash table because SQL Server wants to keep the hash table in memory. If it needs to get spilled out to `tempdb` on disk, then the algorithm might become much slower. The hash function creates buckets of approximately equal size.

After the hash table is built, SQL Server applies the hash function on each of the rows from the other input. It checks to see which bucket the row fits. Then it scans through all rows from the bucket. This phase is called the **probe phase**.

A hash join is a kind of compromise between creating a fully balanced tree index and then using a different join algorithm and performing a full scan of one side of the input for each row of the other input. At least in the first phase, a seek of the appropriate bucket is used. You might think that the hash join algorithm is not efficient. It is true that in single-thread mode, it is usually slower than the merge and nested loop join algorithms, which are supported by existing indexes.

However, SQL Server can split rows from the probe input in advance. It can push the filtering of rows that are candidates for a match with a specific hash bucket down to the storage engine. This kind of optimization of a hash join is called a **bitmap filtered hash join**. It is typically used in a data warehousing scenario, in which you can have large inputs for a query that might not be supported by indexes. In addition, SQL Server can parallelize query execution and perform partial joins in multiple threads. In data warehousing scenarios, it is not uncommon to have only a few concurrent users, so SQL Server can execute a query in parallel. Although a regular hash join can be executed in parallel as well, a bitmap filtered hash join is even more efficient because SQL Server can use bitmaps for early elimination of rows not used in the join from the bigger table involved in the join.

In the bitmap filtered hash join, SQL Server first creates a bitmap representation of a set of values from a dimension table to prefilter rows to join from a fact table. A bitmap filter is a bit array of m bits. Initially, all bits are set to 0. Then SQL Server defines k different hash functions. Each one maps some set elements to one of the m positions with a uniform random distribution. The number of hash functions k must be smaller than the number of bits in array m. SQL Server feeds each of the k hash functions to get k array positions with values from dimension keys. It set the bits at all these positions to 1. Then SQL Server tests the foreign keys from the fact table. To test whether any element is in the set, SQL Server feeds it to each of the k hash functions to get k array positions. If any of the bits at these positions are 0, the element is not in the set. If all are 1, then either the element is in the set, or the bits have been set to 1 during the insertion of other elements. The following figure shows the bitmap filtering process:

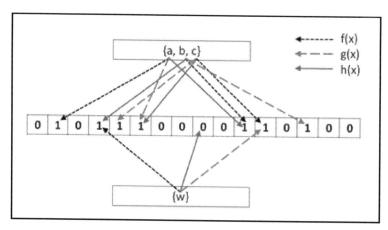

Bitmap filtering

In the preceding figure, the length *m* of the bit array is 16. The number *k* of hash functions is 3. When feeding the hash functions with the values from the set {*a, b, c*}, which represents dimension keys, SQL Server sets bits at positions 2, 4, 5, 6, 11, 12, and 14 to 1 (starting numbering positions at 1). Then SQL Server feeds the same hash functions with the value *w* from the smaller set at the bottom {**w**}, which represents a key from a fact table. The functions set bits at positions 4, 9, and 12 to 1. However, the bit at position 9 is set to 0. Therefore, the value *w* is not in the set {*a, b, c*}.

> If all of the bits for the value *w* were set to 1, this could mean either that the value *w* is in the set {*a, b, v*} or that this is a coincidence.

Bitmap filters return so-called false positives. They never return false negatives. This means that when you declare that a probe value might be in the set, you still need to scan the set and compare it to each value from the set. The more false positive values a bitmap filter returns, the less efficient it is. Note that if the values in the probe side in the fact table are sorted, it will be quite easy to avoid the majority of false positives.

The following query reads the data from the tables introduced earlier in this section and implements star schema-optimized bitmap filtered hash joins:

```
USE WideWorldImportersDW;
SELECT cu.[Customer Key] AS CustomerKey, cu.Customer,
    ci.[City Key] AS CityKey, ci.City,
    ci.[State Province] AS StateProvince, ci.[Sales Territory] AS
SalesTeritory,
    d.Date, d.[Calendar Month Label] AS CalendarMonth,
    d.[Calendar Year] AS CalendarYear,
    s.[Stock Item Key] AS StockItemKey, s.[Stock Item] AS Product, s.Color,
    e.[Employee Key] AS EmployeeKey, e.Employee,
    f.Quantity, f.[Total Excluding Tax] AS TotalAmount, f.Profit
FROM Fact.Sale AS f
    INNER JOIN Dimension.Customer AS cu
        ON f.[Customer Key] = cu.[Customer Key]
    INNER JOIN Dimension.City AS ci
        ON f.[City Key] = ci.[City Key]
    INNER JOIN Dimension.[Stock Item] AS s
        ON f.[Stock Item Key] = s.[Stock Item Key]
    INNER JOIN Dimension.Employee AS e
        ON f.[Salesperson Key] = e.[Employee Key]
    INNER JOIN Dimension.Date AS d
        ON f.[Delivery Date Key] = d.Date;
```

The following figure shows a part of the execution plan. Please note that you can get a different execution plan based on differences in resources available to SQL Server to execute this query. You can see the **Bitmap Create** operator, which is fed with values from the dimension date table. The filtering of the fact table is done in the **Hash Match** operator:

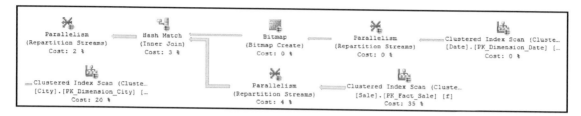

Bitmap Create operator in the execution plan

Benefits of clustered indexes

SQL Server stores a table as a **heap** or as a **balanced tree (B-tree)**. If you create a clustered index, a table is stored as a B-tree. As a general best practice, you should store every table with a clustered index because storing a table as a B-tree has many advantages, as listed here:

- You can control table fragmentation with the ALTER INDEX command using the REBUILD or REORGANIZE option.
- A clustered index is useful for range queries because the data is logically sorted on the key.
- You can move a table to another filegroup by recreating the clustered index on a different filegroup. You do not have to drop the table as you would to move a heap.
- A clustering key is a part of all nonclustered indexes. If a table is stored as a heap, then the row identifier is stored in nonclustered indexes instead. A short integer-clustering key is shorter than a row identifier, thus making nonclustered indexes more efficient.
- You cannot refer to a row identifier in queries, but clustering keys are often part of queries. This raises the probability for covered queries. Covered queries are queries that read all data from one or more nonclustered indexes without going to the base table. This means that there are fewer reads and less disk IO.

Clustered indexes are particularly efficient when the clustering key is short. Creating a clustering index with a long key makes all nonclustered indexes less efficient. In addition, the clustering key should be unique. If it is not unique, SQL Server makes it unique by adding a 4-byte sequential number called a **uniquifier** to duplicate keys. The uniquifier becomes a part of the clustering key, which is duplicated in every nonclustered index. This makes keys longer and all indexes less efficient. Clustering keys can be useful if they are ever-increasing. With ever-increasing keys, minimally logged bulk inserts are possible even if a table already contains data, as long as the table does not have additional nonclustered indexes.

ata warehouse surrogate keys are often ideal for clustered indexes. Because you are the one who defines them, you can define them as efficiently as possible. Use integers with auto-numbering options. The primary key constraint creates a clustered index by default. In addition, clustered indexes can be very useful for **partial scans**. Remember that analytical queries typically involve a lot of data and, therefore, don't use seeks a lot. However, instead of scanning the whole table, you can find the first value with a seek and then perform a partial scan until you reach the last value needed for the query result. Many times, analytical queries use date filters; therefore, a clustering key over a date column might be ideal for such queries.

You need to decide whether to optimize your tables for data load or for querying. However, with partitioning, you can get both—efficient data load without a clustered key on an ever-increasing column, and more efficient queries with partial scans. In order to show the efficiency of partial scans, let's first create a new table organized as a heap with the following query:

```
SELECT 1 * 1000000 + f.[Sale Key] AS SaleKey,
  cu.[Customer Key] AS CustomerKey, cu.Customer,
  ci.[City Key] AS CityKey, ci.City,
  f.[Delivery Date Key] AS DateKey,
  s.[Stock Item Key] AS StockItemKey, s.[Stock Item] AS Product,
  f.Quantity, f.[Total Excluding Tax] AS TotalAmount, f.Profit
INTO dbo.FactTest
FROM Fact.Sale AS f
  INNER JOIN Dimension.Customer AS cu
    ON f.[Customer Key] = cu.[Customer Key]
  INNER JOIN Dimension.City AS ci
    ON f.[City Key] = ci.[City Key]
  INNER JOIN Dimension.[Stock Item] AS s
    ON f.[Stock Item Key] = s.[Stock Item Key]
  INNER JOIN Dimension.Date AS d
    ON f.[Delivery Date Key] = d.Date;
```

Now you can turn STATISTICS IO on to show the number of logical reads in the following two queries:

```
SET STATISTICS IO ON;
-- All rows
SELECT *
FROM dbo.FactTest;
-- Date range
SELECT *
FROM dbo.FactTest
WHERE DateKey BETWEEN '20130201' AND '20130331';
SET STATISTICS IO OFF;
```

SQL Server used a Table Scan operator to execute both queries. For both of them, even though the second one used a filter on the delivery date column, SQL Server performed 5,893 logical IOs.

 Note that your results for the logical IOs might vary slightly for every query in this chapter. However, you should be able to notice which query is more efficient and which is less.

Now let's create a clustered index in the delivery date column:

```
CREATE CLUSTERED INDEX CL_FactTest_DateKey
ON dbo.FactTest(DateKey);
GO
```

If you execute the same two queries, you get around 6,091 reads with the Clustered Index Scan operator for the first query, and 253 logical reads for the second query, with the Clustered Index Seek operator, which finds the first value needed for the query and performs a partial scan afterwards.

Leveraging table partitioning

Loading even very large fact tables is not a problem if you can perform incremental loads. However, this means that data in the source should never be updated or deleted; data should only be inserted. This is rarely the case with LOB applications. In addition, even if you have the possibility of performing an incremental load, you should have a parameterized **Extract- Transform-Load** (**ETL**) procedure in place so you can reload portions of data loaded already in earlier loads. There is always the possibility that something might go wrong in the source system, which means that you will have to reload historical data. This reloading will require you to delete part of the data from your DW.

Deleting large portions of fact tables might consume too much time unless you perform a minimally logged deletion. A minimally logged deletion operation can be done using the `TRUNCATE TABLE` command; however, in previous versions of SQL Server, this command deleted all the data from a table, and deleting all the data is usually not acceptable. More commonly, you need to delete only portions of the data. With SQL Server 2016 and 2017, truncation is somewhat easier, because you can truncate one or more partitions.

Inserting huge amounts of data can consume too much time as well. You can do a minimally logged insert, but as you already know, minimally logged inserts have some limitations. Among other limitations, a table must either be empty, have no indexes, or use a clustered index only on an ever-increasing (or ever-decreasing) key so that all inserts occur on one end of the index.

You can resolve all of these problems by *partitioning a table*. You can achieve even better query performance using a partitioned table because you can create partitions in different filegroups on different drives, thus parallelizing reads. In addition, the SQL Server query optimizer can do early partition elimination, so SQL Server does not even touch a partition with data excluded from the results set of a query. You can also perform maintenance procedures on a subset of filegroups, and thus on a subset of partitions. That way, you can also speed up regular maintenance tasks. Partitions have many benefits.

Although you can partition a table on any attribute, partitioning over dates is most common in data warehousing scenarios. You can use any time interval for a partition. Depending on your needs, the interval could be a day, a month, a year, or any other interval.

In addition to partitioning tables, you can also partition indexes. If indexes are partitioned in the same way as the base tables, they are called **aligned indexes**. Partitioned table and index concepts include the following:

- **Partition function**: This is an object that maps rows to partitions by using values from specific columns. The columns used for the function are called **partitioning columns**. A partition function performs logical mapping.
- **Partition scheme**: A partition scheme maps partitions to filegroups. A partition scheme performs physical mapping.
- **Aligned index**: This is an index built on the same partition scheme as its base table. If all indexes are aligned with their base table, switching a partition is a metadata operation only, so it is very fast. Columnstore indexes have to be aligned with their base tables. Nonaligned indexes are, of course, indexes that are partitioned differently from their base tables.

- **Partition switching**: This is a process that switches a block of data from one table or partition to another table or partition. You switch the data by using the `ALTER TABLE` T-SQL command. You can perform the following types of switching:
  - Reassign all data from a nonpartitioned table to an empty existing partition of a partitioned table
  - Switch a partition of a one-partitioned table to a partition of another partitioned table
  - Reassign all data from a partition of a partitioned table to an existing empty nonpartitioned table

- **Partition elimination**: This is a query optimizer process in which SQL Server accesses only those partitions needed to satisfy query filters.

For more information about table and index partitioning, refer to the MSDN *Partitioned Tables and Indexes* article at `https://msdn.microsoft.com/en-us/library/ms190787.aspx`.

Nonclustered indexes in analytical scenarios

As mentioned, DW queries typically involve large scans of data and aggregation. Very selective seeks are not common for reports from a DW. Therefore, nonclustered indexes generally don't help DW queries much. However, this does not mean that you shouldn't create any nonclustered indexes in your DW.

An attribute of a dimension is not a good candidate for a nonclustered index key. Attributes are used for pivoting and typically contain only a few distinct values. Therefore, queries that filter based on attribute values are usually not very selective. Nonclustered indexes on dimension attributes are not good practice.

DW reports can be parameterized. For example, a DW report could show sales for all customers or for only a single customer, based perhaps on parameter selection by an end user. For a single-customer report, the user would choose the customer by selecting that customer's name. Customer names are selective, meaning that you retrieve only a small number of rows when you filter by customer name. Company names, for example, are typically unique, so by filtering by a company name, you typically retrieve a single row. For reports like these, having a nonclustered index on a name column or columns could lead to better performance.

You can create a filtered nonclustered index. A filtered index spans a subset of column values only and thus applies to a subset of table rows. Filtered nonclustered indexes are useful when some values in a column occur rarely, whereas other values occur frequently. In such cases, you would create a filtered index over the rare values only. SQL Server uses this index for seeks of rare values but performs scans for frequent values. Filtered nonclustered indexes can be useful not only for name columns and member properties but also for attributes of a dimension, and even foreign keys of a fact table. For example, in our demo fact table, the customer with an ID equal to 378 has only 242 rows. You can execute the following code to show that even if you select data for this customer only, SQL Server performs a full scan:

```
SET STATISTICS IO ON;
-- All rows
SELECT *
FROM dbo.FactTest;
-- Customer 378 only
SELECT *
FROM dbo.FactTest
WHERE CustomerKey = 378;
SET STATISTICS IO OFF;
```

Both queries needed 6,091 logical reads. Now you can add a filtered nonclustered index to the table:

```
CREATE INDEX NCLF_FactTest_C378
  ON dbo.FactTest (CustomerKey)
  WHERE CustomerKey = 378;
GO
```

If you execute the same two queries again, you get much less IO for the second query. It needed 752 logical reads in my case and uses the Index Seek and Key Lookup operators.

You can drop the filtered index when you don't need it anymore with the following code:

```
DROP INDEX NCLF_FactTest_C378
  ON dbo.FactTest;
GO
```

Using indexed views

You can optimize queries that aggregate data and perform multiple joins by permanently storing the aggregated and joined data. For example, you could create a new table with joined and aggregated data and then maintain that table during your ETL process.

However, creating additional tables for joined and aggregated data is not best practice because using these tables means you have to change queries used in your reports. Fortunately, there is another option for storing joined and aggregated tables. You can create a view with a query that joins and aggregates data. Then you can create a clustered index on the view to get an **indexed view**. With indexing, you are materializing a view; you are storing, physically, the data the view is returning when you query it. In the Enterprise or Developer Edition of SQL Server, SQL Server Query Optimizer uses an indexed view automatically, without changing the query. SQL Server also maintains indexed views automatically. However, to speed up data loads, you can drop or disable the index before the load and then recreate or rebuild it after the load.

For example, note the following query, which aggregates the data from the test fact table:

```
SET STATISTICS IO ON;
SELECT StockItemKey,
 SUM(TotalAmount) AS Sales,
 COUNT_BIG(*) AS NumberOfRows
FROM dbo.FactTest
GROUP BY StockItemKey;
SET STATISTICS IO OFF;
```

In my case, this query used 6,685 logical IOs. It used the Clustered Index Scan operator on the fact table to retrieve the whole dataset. Now let's create a view with the same query used for the definition:

```
CREATE VIEW dbo.SalesByProduct
WITH SCHEMABINDING AS
SELECT StockItemKey,
 SUM(TotalAmount) AS Sales,
 COUNT_BIG(*) AS NumberOfRows
FROM dbo.FactTest
GROUP BY StockItemKey;
GO
```

Indexed views have many limitations. One of them is that they have to be created with the SCHEMABINDING option if you want to index them, as you can see in the previous code. Now let's index the view:

```
CREATE UNIQUE CLUSTERED INDEX CLU_SalesByProduct
  ON dbo.SalesByProduct (StockItemKey);
GO
```

Try to execute the last query before creating the VIEW again. Make sure you notice that the query refers to the base table and not the view. This time, the query needed only four logical reads. If you check the execution plan, you should see that SQL Server used the Clustered Index Scan operator on the indexed view. If your indexed view was not used automatically, please check which edition of SQL Server you are using. When you finish testing, you can drop the view with the following code:

```
DROP VIEW dbo.SalesByProduct;
GO
```

Data compression and query techniques

SQL Server supports data compression. Data compression reduces the size of the database, which helps improve query performance because queries on compressed data read fewer pages from the disk and thus use less IO. However, data compression requires extra CPU resources for updates, because data must be decompressed before and compressed after the update. Data compression is therefore suitable for data warehousing scenarios in which data is mostly read and only occasionally updated.

SQL Server supports three compression implementations:

- **Row compression**: Row compression reduces metadata overhead by storing fixed data type columns in a variable-length format. This includes strings and numeric data. Row compression has only a small impact on CPU resources and is often appropriate for OLTP applications as well.
- **Page compression**: Page compression includes row compression, but also adds prefix and dictionary compressions. **Prefix compression** stores repeated prefixes of values from a single column in a special compression information structure that immediately follows the page header, replacing the repeated prefix values with a reference to the corresponding prefix. **Dictionary compression** stores repeated values anywhere in a page in the compression information area. Dictionary compression is not restricted to a single column.

- **Unicode compression**: In SQL Server, Unicode characters occupy an average of two bytes. Unicode compression substitutes single-byte storage for Unicode characters that don't truly require two bytes. Depending on collation, Unicode compression can save up to 50 % of the space otherwise required for Unicode strings. Unicode compression is very cheap and is applied automatically when you apply either row or page compression.

You can gain quite a lot from data compression in a data warehouse. Foreign keys are often repeated many times in a fact table. Large dimensions that have Unicode strings in name columns, member properties, and attributes can benefit from Unicode compression.

The following figure explains dictionary compression:

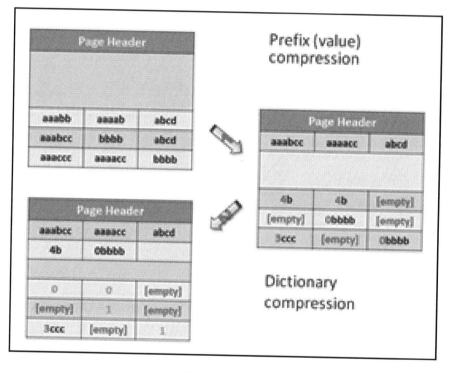

Dictionary compression

As you can see from the figure, dictionary compression (corresponding to the first arrow) starts with prefix compression. In the compression information space on the page right after the page header, you can find stored prefixes for each column. If you look at the top left cell, the value in the first row, and first column, is **aaabb**. The next value in this column is **aaabcc**. A prefix value **aaabcc** is stored for this column in the first column of the row for the prefix compression information. Instead of the original value in the top left cell, the **4b value** is stored. This means use four characters from the prefix for this column and add the letter *b* to get the original value back. The value in the second row for the first column is empty because the prefix for this column is equal to the whole original value in that position. The value in the last row for the first column after the prefix compression is **3ccc**, meaning that in order to get the original value, you need to take the first three characters from the column prefix and add a string **ccc**, thus getting the value **aaaccc**, which is, of course, equal to the original value. Check prefix compression for the other two columns also.

After prefix compression, dictionary compression is applied (corresponding to the second arrow in the *Dictionary compression* figure). It checks all strings across all columns to find common substrings. For example, the value in the first two columns of the first row after the prefix compression was applied is **4b**. SQL Server stores this value in the dictionary compression information area as the first value in this area, with index 0. In the cells, it stores just the index value 0 instead of the value **4b**. The same happens for the **0bbbb** value, which you can find in the second row, second column, and third row, third column, after prefix compression is applied. This value is stored in the dictionary compression information area in the second position with index 1; in the cells, the value 1 is left.

You might wonder why prefix compression is needed. For strings, a prefix is just another substring, so dictionary compression could cover prefixes as well. However, prefix compression can work on nonstring data types as well. For example, instead of storing integers 900, 901, 902, 903, and 904 in the original data, you can store a 900 prefix and leave values 0, 1, 2, 3, and 4 in the original cells.

Now it's time to test SQL Server compression. First of all, let's check the space occupied by the test fact table:

```
EXEC sys.sp_spaceused N'dbo.FactTest', @updateusage = N'TRUE';
GO
```

The result is as follows:

Name	rows	reserved	data	index_size	unused
dbo.FactTest	227981	49672 KB	48528 KB	200 KB	944 KB

The following code enables row compression on the table and checks the space used again:

```
ALTER TABLE dbo.FactTest
 REBUILD WITH (DATA_COMPRESSION = ROW);
EXEC sys.sp_spaceused N'dbo.FactTest', @updateusage = N'TRUE';
```

This time, the result is as follows:

Name	rows	reserved	data	index_size	unused
dbo.FactTest	227981	25864 KB	24944 KB	80 KB	840 KB

You can see that a lot of space was saved. Let's also check the page compression:

```
ALTER TABLE dbo.FactTest
 REBUILD WITH (DATA_COMPRESSION = PAGE);
EXEC sys.sp_spaceused N'dbo.FactTest', @updateusage = N'TRUE';
```

Now the table occupies even less space, as the following result shows:

Name	rows	reserved	data	index_size	unused
dbo.FactTest	227981	18888 KB	18048 KB	80 KB	760 KB

If these space savings are impressive to you, wait for columnstore compression! Anyway, before continuing, you can remove the compression from the test fact table with the following code:

```
ALTER TABLE dbo.FactTest
 REBUILD WITH (DATA_COMPRESSION = NONE);
```

Before continuing with other SQL Server features that support analytics, I want to explain another compression algorithm because this algorithm is also used in columnstore compression. The algorithm is called **LZ77 compression**. It was published by Abraham Lempel and Jacob Ziv in 1977; the name of the algorithm comes from the first letters of the author's last names plus the publishing year. The algorithm uses sliding window dictionary encoding, meaning it encodes chunks of an input stream with dictionary encoding. The following are the steps of the process:

1. Set the coding position to the beginning of the input stream

2. Find the longest match in the window for the look-ahead buffer
3. If a match is found, output the pointer P and move the coding position (and the window) L bytes forward
4. If a match is not found, output a null pointer and the first byte in the look-ahead buffer and move the coding position (and the window) one byte forward
5. If the look-ahead buffer is not empty, return to step 2

The following figure explains this process via an example:

Input stream	Position	1	2	3	4	5	6	7	8	9
	Byte	A	A	B	C	B	B	A	B	C

Step	Position	Match	Byte	Output
1.	1	~	A	(0, 0) A
2.	2	A	~	(1, 1)
3.	3	~	B	(0, 0) B
4.	4	A	C	(0, 0) C
5.	5	B	~	(2, 1)
6.	6	B	~	(1, 1)
7.	7	A B C	~	(5, 3)

LZ77 compression

The input stream chunk that is compressed in the figure is **AABCBBABC**:

- The algorithm starts encoding from the beginning of the window of the input stream. It stores the first byte (the **A** value) in the result, together with the pointer **(0,0)**, meaning this is a new value in this chunk.
- The second byte is equal to the first one. The algorithm stores just the pointer **(1,1)** to the output. This means that in order to recreate this value, you need to move one byte back and read one byte.
- The next two values, **B** and **C**, are new and are stored to the output together with the pointer **(0,0)**.
- Then the **B** value repeats. Therefore, the pointer **(2,1)** is stored, meaning that in order to find this value, you need to move two bytes back and read one byte.

- Then the **B** value repeats again. This time, you need to move one byte back and read one byte to get the value, so the value is replaced with the pointer **(1,1)**. You can see that when you move back and read the value, you get another pointer. You can have a chain of pointers.
- Finally, the substring **ABC** is found in the stream. This substring can be also found in positions 2 to 4. Therefore, in order to recreate the substring, you need to move five bytes back and read 3 bytes, and the pointer **(5,3)** is stored in the compressed output.

Writing efficient queries

Before finishing this section, I also need to mention that no join, compression algorithm, or any other feature that SQL Server offers can help you if you write inefficient queries. A good example of a typical DW query is one that involves running totals. You can use non-equi self joins for such queries, which is a very good example of an inefficient query. The following code calculates the running total for the profit ordered over the sale key with a self join. The code also measures the IO and time needed to execute the query. Note that the query uses a CTE first to select 12,000 rows from the fact table. A non-equi self join is a quadratic algorithm; with double the number of the rows, the time needed increases by a factor of four. You can play with different number of rows to prove that:

```
SET STATISTICS IO ON;
SET STATISTICS TIME ON;
WITH SalesCTE AS
(
SELECT [Sale Key] AS SaleKey, Profit
FROM Fact.Sale
WHERE [Sale Key] <= 12000
)
SELECT S1.SaleKey,
 MIN(S1.Profit) AS CurrentProfit,
 SUM(S2.Profit) AS RunningTotal
FROM SalesCTE AS S1
 INNER JOIN SalesCTE AS S2
  ON S1.SaleKey >= S2.SaleKey
GROUP BY S1.SaleKey
ORDER BY S1.SaleKey;
SET STATISTICS IO OFF;
SET STATISTICS TIME OFF;
```

With 12,000 rows, the query needed 817,584 logical reads in a worktable, which is a temporary representation of the test fact table on the right side of the self join, and on the top of this, more than 3,000 logical reads for the left representation of the fact table. On my computer, it took more than 12 seconds (elapsed time) to execute this query, with more than 72 seconds of CPU time, as the query was executed with a parallel execution plan. With 6,000 rows, the query would need approximately four times less IO and time.

You can calculate running totals very efficiently with window aggregate functions. The following example shows the query rewritten. The new query uses the window aggregate functions:

```
SET STATISTICS IO ON;
SET STATISTICS TIME ON;
WITH SalesCTE AS
(
SELECT [Sale Key] AS SaleKey, Profit
FROM Fact.Sale
WHERE [Sale Key] <= 12000
)
SELECT SaleKey,
 Profit AS CurrentProfit,
 SUM(Profit)
   OVER(ORDER BY SaleKey
        ROWS BETWEEN UNBOUNDED PRECEDING
                AND CURRENT ROW) AS RunningTotal
FROM SalesCTE
ORDER BY SaleKey;
SET STATISTICS IO OFF;
SET STATISTICS TIME OFF;
```

This time, the query used 331 reads in the fact table, 0 (zero) reads in the worktable, 0.15 second elapsed time, and 0.02 second CPU time. SQL Server didn't even bother to find a parallel plan.

Columnar storage and batch processing

Various researchers started to think about **columnar storage** in the 80s. The main idea is that a **relational database management system (RDBMS)** does not need to store the data in exactly the same way we understand it and work with it. In a relational model, a tuple represents an entity and is stored as a row of a table, which is an entity set. Traditionally, database management systems store entities row by row. However, as long as we get rows back to the client application, we do not care how an RDBMS stores the data.

This is actually one of the main premises of the relational model—we work with data on the logical level, which is independent of the physical level of the physical storage. However, it was not until approximately 2000 when the first attempts to create columnar storage came to life. SQL Server added columnar storage first in version 2012.

Columnar storage is highly compressed. Higher compression means more CPU usage because the data must be decompressed when you want to work with it and recompressed when you store it. In addition, SQL Server has to transform columns back to rows when you work with data and vice versa when you store the data. Add to this picture parallelized query execution, and suddenly CPU becomes a bottleneck. CPU is rarely a bottleneck in a transactional application. However, analytical applications have different requests. SQL Server solves the CPU problem by introducing **batch processing**.

In this section, you will learn about SQL Server columnar storage and batch processing, including the following:

- How SQL Server creates columnar storage
- Columnstore compression
- Nonclustered columnstore indexes
- Clustered columnstore indexes
- The limitations of columnar storage in different versions of SQL Server
- Batch processing
- The limitations of batch processing in different versions of SQL Server

Columnar storage and compression

Storing the data column by column instead of row by row gives you the opportunity to store each column in a sorted way. Imagine that you have every column totally sorted. Then for every equijoin, the merge join algorithm could be used, which is, as you already know, a very efficient algorithm. In addition, with sorted data, you get one more type of compression for free—**run-length encoding (RLE)** compression.

The following figure explains the idea graphically:

Row / Col	1	2	3
	Name	Color	City
1	Nut	Red	London
2	Bolt	Green	Paris
3	Screw	Blue	Oslo
4	Screw	Red	London
5	Cam	Blue	Paris
6	Cog	Red	London

Row / Col	1	2	3
	Name	Color	City
1	Bolt [1:1]	Blue [1:2]	London [1:3]
2	Cam [2:2]	Green [3:3]	Oslo [4:4]
3	Cog [3:3]	Red [4:6]	Paris [5:6]
4	Nut [4:4]		
5	Screw [5:6]		
6			

Row / Col	1	2	3
	Name	Color	City
1	Bolt	Blue	London
2	Cam	Blue	London
3	Cog	Green	London
4	Nut	Red	Oslo
5	Screw	Red	Paris
6	Screw	Red	Paris

Sorted columnar storage and RLE

An RDBMS in the first step reorders every single column. Then RLE compression is implemented. For example, if you look at the **Color** column, you don't need to repeat the value **Red** three times; you can store it only once and store either the frequency of the value or the index in the form from position to position, as shown in the figure.

Note that SQL Server does not implement total sorting. Total sorting of every single column would simply be too expensive. Creating such storage would take too much time and too many resources. SQL Server uses its own patented **row-rearranging algorithm**, which rearranges the rows in the most optimal way to order all columns as best as possible, with a single pass through the data. This means that SQL Server does not totally sort any column; however, all columns are at least partially sorted. Therefore, SQL Server does not target the merge join algorithm; the hash join algorithm is preferred. Partial sorts still optimizes the use of bitmap filters because fewer false positives are returned from a bitmap filter when compared to randomly organized values. RLE compression can still reduce the size of the data substantially.

Recreating rows from columnar storage

Of course, there is still the question of how to recreate rows from columnar storage. In 1999, Stephen Tarin patented the Tarin Transform Method, which uses a **row reconstruction table** to regenerate the rows. Mr. Tarin called columnar storage the Trans-Relational Model. This does not mean the model is beyond relational; this was more a marketing term, short for Transform Relational Model.

SQL Server documentation does not publish the row recreation algorithm it uses. I am presenting the Tarin's method here. It should still be good enough to give you a better understanding of the amount of work SQL Server has to do when it recreates rows from columns.

The following figure explains the Tarin Transform Method:

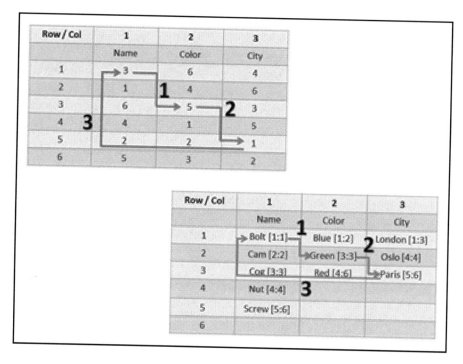

Tarin Transform Method

In the figure, the top table is the row reconstruction table. You start reconstructing the rows in the top left corner. For the first column of the first row value, take the top left value in the columnar storage table at the bottom, in this case the value **Bolt**. In the first cell of the row reconstruction table, there is a pointer to the row number of the second column in this table. In addition, it is an index for the value of the second column in the columnar storage table. In the figure, this value is **3**. This means that you need to find the value in the second column of the columnar storage table with index 3, which is **Green**. In the row reconstruction table, you read the value **5** in the second column, third row. You use this value as an index for the value of the third column in the columnar storage table, which, in the example, is **Paris**. In the row reconstruction table, you read the value **1**. Because this is the last column in the table, this value is used for a cyclic redundancy check, checking whether you can correctly get to the starting point of the row reconstruction process. The row **Bolt**, **Green**, and **Paris**, the second row from the original table from the previous figure, was successfully reconstructed.

As mentioned, how SQL Server reconstructs the rows has not been published. Nevertheless, you can appreciate that this is quite an intensive process. You can also imagine changes in the original data. Just a small update to the original values might cause the complete recreation of the row reconstruction table. This would simply be too expensive. This is why columnar storage, once it is created, is actually read-only. In SQL Server 2014 and 2016, columnstore indexes are updateable; however, SQL Server does not update the columnar storage online. SQL Server uses additional row storage for the updates. You will learn further details later in this chapter.

Columnar storage creation process

SQL Server starts creating the columnar storage by first splitting the data into **rowgroups**. The maximum number of rows per rowgroup is 1,048,576. The idea here is that the time-consuming row rearranging is done on smaller datasets, just like how the hash join algorithm splits the data into buckets and then performs smaller joins on portions of the data. SQL Server performs row rearranging in each of the groups separately. Then SQL Server encodes and compresses each column. Each column's data in each rowgroup is called a **segment**. SQL Server stores segments in blobs in database files. Therefore, SQL Server leverages the existing storage for columnar storage.

The following figure shows the process:

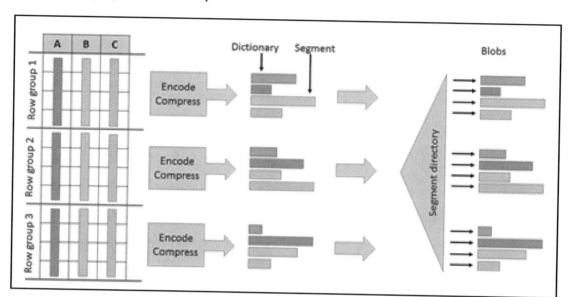

How SQL Server creates columnar storage

SQL Server implements different compressing algorithms:

- SQL Server does bit-packing. Bit-packing is similar to row compression, just pushed one level further. Instead of storing the minimal number of bytes, SQL Server stores the minimal number of bits that can represent the value. For example, with row compression, you would get one byte instead of four bytes for value 5, if this value is an integer. With bit-packing, SQL Server would store this value using three bits only *(101)*.

- Then SQL Server encodes the values to integers with **value encoding** and **dictionary encoding**. Value encoding is similar to prefix encoding in page compression, and dictionary encoding is the same. Therefore, this part of compression uses the ideas of page compression. However, dictionaries for columnar storage are much more efficient because they are built on more values than dictionaries in page compression. With page compression, you get a separate dictionary for each 8 KB page. With columnar storage, you get one dictionary per rowgroup plus one global dictionary over all rowgroups.

- Because of the partial ordering, the run-length encoding algorithm is also used.
- Finally, SQL Server can also use the LZ77 algorithm to compress columnar data.

All of these compression algorithms except the LZ77 one are implemented automatically when you create a columnstore index. This is called COLUMNSTORE compression. You must turn LZ77 compression on manually to get so-called the COLUMNSTORE_ARCHIVE compression.

With all of these compression algorithms implemented, you can count on at least 10 times more compression compared to the original, non-compressed row storage. In reality, you can get much better compression levels, especially when you also implement archive compression with the LZ77 algorithm.

However, compression is not the only advantage of large scans. Because each column is stored separately, SQL Server can retrieve only the columns a query is referring to. This is like having a covering nonclustered index. Each segment also has additional metadata associated with it. This metadata includes the minimal and the maximal value in the segment. SQL Server query optimizer can use this metadata for early segment elimination, just as SQL Server can do early partition elimination if a table is partitioned. Finally, you can combine partitioning with columnstore indexes to maintain even very large tables.

Development of columnar storage in SQL Server

SQL Server introduced columnar storage in version 2012. Only NCCIs were supported. This means that you still need to have the original row storage, either organized as a heap or as a **clustered index (CI)**. There are many other limitations, including the following:

- Nonclustered columnstore index only
- One per table
- Must be partition-aligned
- Table becomes read-only (partition switching allowed)

- Unsupported types
    - Decimals greater than 18 digits
    - Binary, Image, CLR (including Spatial, HierarchyId)
    - (N)varchar(max), XML, Text, Ntext
    - Uniqueidentifier, Rowversion, SQL_Variant
    - Date/time types greater than 8 bytes

SQL Server 2014 introduced **clustered columnstore indexes (CCI)**. This means that the original row storage does not exist anymore; CCI is the only storage you need. Just like in a regular clustered index, SQL Server needs to identify each row in a clustered columnstore index as well. Note that SQL Server 2014 does not support constraints on the columnar storage. Therefore, SQL Server 2014 adds a **bookmark**, which is a unique tuple ID inside a rowgroup, stored as a simple sequence number. SQL Server 2014 has many data types unsupported for columnar storage, including the following:

- Varbinary(MAX), Image, CLR (including Spatial, HierarchyId)
- (N)Varchar(max), XML, Text, Ntext
- Rowversion, SQL_Variant

SQL Server 2014 also optimizes the columnstore index build. For example, SQL Server 2012 used a fixed number of threads to build the index. This number was estimated in advance. If, for some reason, the operating system took some threads away from SQL Server while SQL Server was building a columnstore index, the build might have failed. In SQL Server 2014, the degree of parallelism or the number of threads can be adjusted dynamically while SQL Server builds the columnstore index.

The CCI in SQL 2014 is updateable. However, its columnar storage is immutable. The following figure explains the update process:

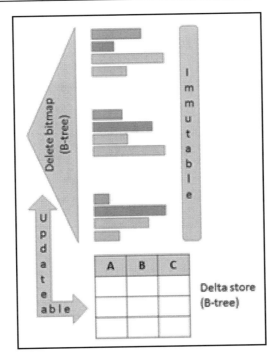

How SQL Server updates columnar storage

Data modification is implemented as follows:

- **Insert**: The new rows are inserted into a delta store
- **Delete**: If the row to be deleted is in a column store row group, a record containing its row ID is inserted into the B-tree storing the delete bitmap; if it is in a delta store, the row is simply deleted
- **Update**: Split into a delete and an insert
- **Merge**: Split into a delete, an insert, and an update

A delta store can be either open or closed. When a new delta store is created, it is open. After you insert the maximum number of rows for a rowgroup in an open delta store, SQL Server changes the status of this delta store to closed. If you remember, this means a bit more than one million rows. Then a background process called tuple-mover converts the closed delta stores to column segments. This process starts by default every five minutes. You can run it manually with the ALTER INDEX ... REORGANIZE or ALTER INDEX ... REBUILD commands.

Non-bulk (trickle) inserts go to an open delta store. Bulk inserts up to 102,400 rows; smaller ones go to an open delta store, and larger ones go directly to column segments. More delta stores mean less compression. Therefore, when using bulk insert, you should try to optimize the batches to contain close to 1,000,000 rows. You can also rebuild the index occasionally.

SQL Server 2016 brings many additional features to the columnstore indexes. The most important features in version 2016 include the following:

- CCI supports additional NCI (B-tree) indexes
- CCI supports through NCI primary and foreign key constraints
- CCI supports snapshot and read-committed snapshot isolation levels
- NCCI on a heap or B-tree updateable and filtered
- Columnstore indices on in-memory tables
- Defined when you create the table in the `CREATE TABLE` statement
- Must include all columns and all rows (not filtered)
- NCI indexes can be filtered

SQL Server 2017 adds only small improvements to columnar storage, compared to version 2016:

- You can build and rebuild NCCIs online
- CCIs now support LOB columns: VARCHAR(MAX), NVARCHAR(MAX), and VARBINARY(MAX)

Batch processing

With columnar storage, the CPU can become a bottleneck. SQL Server solves these problems with **batch mode processing**. In batch mode processing, SQL Server processes data in batches rather than processing one row at a time. A batch represents roughly 900 rows of data. Each column within a batch is stored as a vector in a separate memory area, meaning that batch mode processing is vector-based. Batch mode processing interrupts a processor with metadata only once per batch rather than once per row, as in row mode processing, which lowers the CPU burden substantially. This means that batch mode spreads the metadata access costs over all of the 900 rows in a batch.

Batch mode processing is orthogonal to columnar storage. This means SQL Server can use it with many different operators, no matter whether the data is stored in row or column storage. However, batch mode processing gives the best results when combined with columnar storage. DML operations, such as insert, update, or delete, work in row mode. Of course, SQL Server can mix batch and row mode operators in a single query.

SQL Server introduced batch mode also in version 2012. The batch mode operators in this version include the following:

- Filter
- Project
- Scan
- Local hash (partial) aggregation
- Hash inner join
- Batch hash table build, but only in-memory, no spilling
- Bitmap filters limited to a single column, data types represented with a 64-bit integer

In SQL Server 2014, the following batch mode operators were added:

- All join types
- Union all
- Scalar aggregation
- Spilling support
- Complex bitmap filters, all data types supported

SQL Server 2016 added the following improvements to batch mode processing:

- Single-threaded queries
- Sort operator
- Multiple distinct count operations
- Left anti-semi join operators
- Window aggregate functions
- Window analytical functions
- String predicate and aggregate pushdown to the storage engine
- Row-level locking on index seeks against a nonclustered index and rowgroup-level locking on full table scans against the columnstore

Finally, SQL Server 2017 added two more improvements to batch mode processing:

- Batch mode adaptive joins
- Batch mode memory grant feedback

The following table summarizes the most important features and limitations of columnar storage and batch mode processing in SQL Server versions 2012 to 2106:

Columnstore Index/Batch Mode Feature	SQL 2012	SQL 2014	SQL 2016	SQL 2017
Batch execution for multi-threaded queries	yes	yes	yes	yes
Batch execution for single-threaded queries			yes	yes
Batch mode adaptive joins				yes
Batch mode memory grant feedback				yes
Archival compression		yes	yes	yes
Snapshot isolation and read-committed snapshot isolation			yes	yes
Specify CI when creating a table			yes	yes
AlwaysOn supports CIs	yes	yes	yes	yes
AlwaysOn readable secondary supports read-only NCCI	yes	yes	yes	yes
AlwaysOn readable secondary supports updateable CIs			yes	yes
Read-only NCCI on heap or B-tree	yes	yes	yes	yes
Updateable NCCI on heap or B-tree			yes	yes
NCCI online build and rebuild				yes
B-tree indexes allowed on a table that has a NCCI	yes	yes	yes	yes
Updateable CCI		yes	yes	yes
CCI LOB columns support				yes
B-tree index on a CCI			yes	yes
CCI on a memory-optimized table			yes	yes
Filtered NCCI			yes	yes

You can check whether SQL Server uses row or batch mode for an operator by analyzing the properties of the operator in the execution plan. Before checking the batch mode, the following code adds nine time as many rows to the test fact table:

```
DECLARE @i AS INT = 1;
WHILE @i < 10
BEGIN
SET @i += 1;
INSERT INTO dbo.FactTest
(SaleKey, CustomerKey,
 Customer, CityKey, City,
 DateKey, StockItemKey,
 Product, Quantity,
 TotalAmount, Profit)
SELECT @i * 1000000 + f.[Sale Key] AS SaleKey,
   cu.[Customer Key] AS CustomerKey, cu.Customer,
   ci.[City Key] AS CityKey, ci.City,
   f.[Delivery Date Key] AS DateKey,
   s.[Stock Item Key] AS StockItemKey, s.[Stock Item] AS Product,
   f.Quantity, f.[Total Excluding Tax] AS TotalAmount, f.Profit
FROM Fact.Sale AS f
   INNER JOIN Dimension.Customer AS cu
     ON f.[Customer Key] = cu.[Customer Key]
   INNER JOIN Dimension.City AS ci
     ON f.[City Key] = ci.[City Key]
   INNER JOIN Dimension.[Stock Item] AS s
     ON f.[Stock Item Key] = s.[Stock Item Key]
   INNER JOIN Dimension.Date AS d
     ON f.[Delivery Date Key] = d.Date;
END;
```

Let's check how much space this table uses now:

```
EXEC sys.sp_spaceused N'dbo.FactTest', @updateusage = N'TRUE';
GO
```

The result is as follows:

Name	rows	reserved	data	index_size	unused
dbo.FactTest	2279810	502152 KB	498528 KB	2072 KB	1552 KB

Now let's start querying this table. Before executing the following query, make sure you turn the actual execution plan on:

```
SELECT f.StockItemKey,
  SUM(f.TotalAmount) AS Sales
FROM dbo.FactTest AS f
WHERE f.StockItemKey < 30
GROUP BY f.StockItemKey
ORDER BY f.StockItemKey;
```

You can hover the mouse over any of the operators. For example, the following screenshot shows the details of the Hash Match (Partial Aggregate) operator:

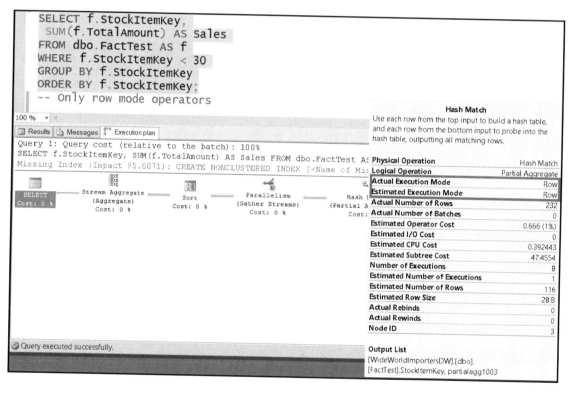

Row mode operators

You can see that SQL Server used row mode processing. As mentioned, batch mode is not strictly bound to columnar storage; however, it is much more likely that SQL Server would use it as you use the columnar storage. The following code creates a filtered nonclustered columnstore index. It is actually empty:

```
CREATE NONCLUSTERED COLUMNSTORE INDEX NCCI_FactTest
ON dbo.FactTest
(SaleKey, CustomerKey,
 Customer, CityKey, City,
 DateKey, StockItemKey,
 Product, Quantity,
 TotalAmount, Profit)
WHERE SaleKey = 0;
GO
```

Now, execute the same query again. As you can see from the following screenshot, this time batch mode is used for the Hash Match (Partial Aggregate) operator:

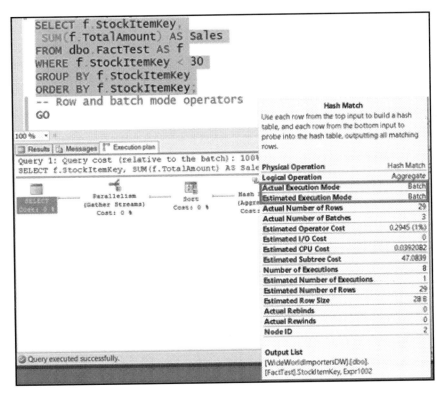

Batch mode operators

Nonclustered columnstore indexes

After a theoretical introduction, it is time to start using columnar storage. You will start by learning how to create and use NCCI. You already know from the previous section that an NCCI can be filtered. Now you will learn how to create, use, and ignore an NCCI. In addition, you will measure the compression rate of the columnar storage.

Because of the different burdens on SQL Server when a transactional application uses it compared to analytical applications usage, traditionally, companies split these applications and created data warehouses. Analytical queries are diverted to the data warehouse database. This means that you have a copy of data in your data warehouse, of course with a different schema. You also need to implement the ETL process for scheduled loading of the data warehouse. This means that the data you analyze is somehow stalled. Frequently, the data is loaded overnight and is thus one day old when you analyze it. For many analytical purposes, this is good enough. However, in some cases, users would like to analyze current data together with archived data. This is called **operational analytics**. SQL Server 2016 with columnar storage and in-memory tables makes operational analytics realistically possible.

In this section, you will learn how to do the following:

- Create nonclustered columnstore indexes
- Ignore an NCCI in a query
- Use NCCI in a query
- Architect an operational analytics solution

Compression and query performance

Without any further hesitation, let's start with the code. The first thing is to drop the filtered (empty) NCCI created in the previous section:

```
DROP INDEX NCCI_FactTest
ON dbo.FactTest;
GO
```

The test fact table is organized as a B-tree with no additional nonclustered index, neither a rowstore nor columnstore one. The clustering key is the date. In order to make a comparison to NCCIs, let's set a baseline. First, recheck the space used by the test fact table:

```
EXEC sys.sp_spaceused N'dbo.FactTest', @updateusage = N'TRUE';
GO
```

The result is as follows:

Name	rows	reserved	data	index_size	unused
dbo.FactTest	2279810	502152 KB	498528 KB	2072 KB	1552 KB

You can measure IO with the SET STATISTICS IO ON command. In addition, you can turn on the actual execution plan. Here is the first sample query; let's call it the *simple* query:

```
SET STATISTICS IO ON;
SELECT f.StockItemKey,
  SUM(f.TotalAmount) AS Sales
FROM dbo.FactTest AS f
WHERE f.StockItemKey < 30
GROUP BY f.StockItemKey
ORDER BY f.StockItemKey;
```

The query did a full clustered index scan, and there were 63,601 logical reads. You may also notice in the execution plan that only row mode operators were used.

> You can get slightly different results for the IO. The exact number of pages used by the table might vary slightly based on your dataset file organization, parallel operations when you load the data or change the table from a heap to a B-tree, and other possibilities. Nevertheless, your numbers should be very similar, and the point is to show how much less space will be used by columnar storage because of the compression.

The next query involves multiple joins; let's call it the *complex* query:

```
SELECT f.SaleKey,
  f.CustomerKey, f.Customer, cu.[Buying Group],
  f.CityKey, f.City, ci.Country,
  f.DateKey, d.[Calendar Year],
  f.StockItemKey, f.Product,
  f.Quantity, f.TotalAmount, f.Profit
FROM dbo.FactTest AS f
  INNER JOIN Dimension.Customer AS cu
    ON f.CustomerKey = cu.[Customer Key]
  INNER JOIN Dimension.City AS ci
    ON f.CityKey = ci.[City Key]
  INNER JOIN Dimension.[Stock Item] AS s
    ON f.StockItemKey = s.[Stock Item Key]
  INNER JOIN Dimension.Date AS d
    ON f.DateKey = d.Date;
```

This time, SQL Server created a much more complex execution plan, yet SQL Server used a full clustered index scan to read the data from the test fact table. SQL Server used 62,575 logical reads in this table.

The third test query is very selective—it selects only the rows for customer 378. If you remember, this customer has only 242 rows in the fact table. Let's call the third query the *point* query:

```
SELECT CustomerKey, Profit
FROM dbo.FactTest
WHERE CustomerKey = 378;
SET STATISTICS IO OFF;
```

The query again did a full clustered index scan, and there were 63,601 logical reads.

Testing the nonclustered columnstore index

The following code creates an NCCI on the fact table, this time without a filter, so all data is included in the NCCI:

```
CREATE NONCLUSTERED COLUMNSTORE INDEX NCCI_FactTest
ON dbo.FactTest
(SaleKey, CustomerKey,
 Customer, CityKey, City,
 DateKey, StockItemKey,
 Product, Quantity,
 TotalAmount, Profit);
GO
```

So how much space is used by the test fact table now? Let's check it again with the following code:

```
EXEC sys.sp_spaceused N'dbo.FactTest', @updateusage = N'TRUE';
GO
```

Name	rows	reserved	data	index_size	unused
dbo.FactTest	2279810	529680 KB	498528 KB	29432 KB	1720 KB

Note the numbers. The index size is about 17 times less than the data size! And remember, in this preceding reported size are also the non-leaf levels of the clustered index, so the actual compression rate was even more than 17 times. This is impressive. So what does this mean for queries? Before measuring the improvements in queries, I want to show how you can ignore the NCCI you just created with a specific option in the OPTION clause of the SELECT statement. So here is a *simple* query that ignores the NCCI:

```
SET STATISTICS IO ON;
SELECT f.StockItemKey,
  SUM(f.TotalAmount) AS Sales
FROM dbo.FactTest AS f
WHERE f.StockItemKey < 30
GROUP BY f.StockItemKey
ORDER BY f.StockItemKey
OPTION (ignore_nonclustered_columnstore_index);
```

Because the NCCI was ignored, the query still did the full-clustered index scan with 63,301 logical reads. However, you can see from the execution plan that this time row mode operators were used, as shown in the following screenshot:

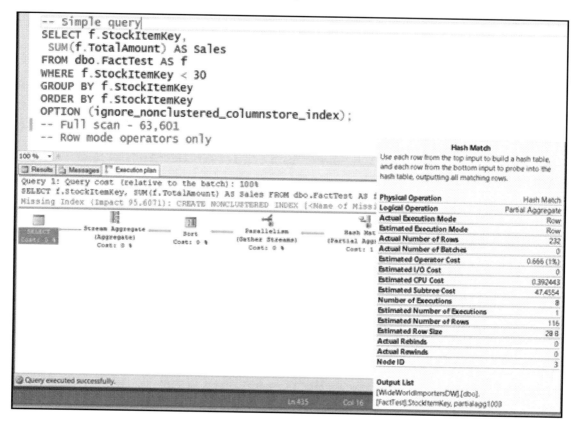

Row mode processing operators

This is different compared to the execution plan SQL Server used for the same query when the NCCI was empty, when SQL Server used batch mode operators. The ignore option really means that SQL Server completely ignores the NCCI. You can check that this is also true for the other two queries, the *complex* and the *point* one. You can also check the execution plans when ignoring the NCCI with the *complex* and *point* queries:

```
-- Complex query
SELECT f.SaleKey,
   f.CustomerKey, f.Customer, cu.[Buying Group],
   f.CityKey, f.City, ci.Country,
   f.DateKey, d.[Calendar Year],
   f.StockItemKey, f.Product,
   f.Quantity, f.TotalAmount, f.Profit
FROM dbo.FactTest AS f
   INNER JOIN Dimension.Customer AS cu
     ON f.CustomerKey = cu.[Customer Key]
   INNER JOIN Dimension.City AS ci
     ON f.CityKey = ci.[City Key]
   INNER JOIN Dimension.[Stock Item] AS s
     ON f.StockItemKey = s.[Stock Item Key]
   INNER JOIN Dimension.Date AS d
     ON f.DateKey = d.Date
OPTION (ignore_nonclustered_columnstore_index);
-- Point query
SELECT CustomerKey, Profit
FROM dbo.FactTest
WHERE CustomerKey = 378
OPTION (ignore_nonclustered_columnstore_index);
SET STATISTICS IO OFF;
```

For both queries, SQL Server did a full table scan on the fact table, with around 63,000 logical reads in this table. Now let's finally see how the queries can benefit from the NCCI. The first query is the *simple* query again:

```
SET STATISTICS IO ON;
SELECT f.StockItemKey,
  SUM(f.TotalAmount) AS Sales
FROM dbo.FactTest AS f
WHERE f.StockItemKey < 30
GROUP BY f.StockItemKey
ORDER BY f.StockItemKey;
```

As you can see from the following screenshot, the columnstore index scan was used, and only four segments were read, with 2,001 LOB reads. Remember that the columnstore indexes are stored in blobs in SQL Server. Compare this to the number of logical reads when the NCCI was ignored. You can also check by yourself that batch mode operators were used:

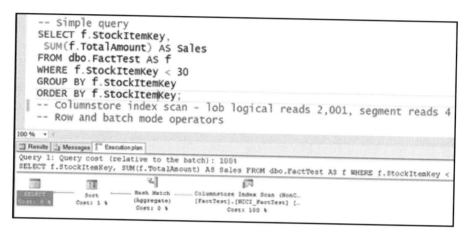

Row mode processing operators

You can check how many segments in total are occupied by the NCCI with the following query using the `sys.column_store_segments` catalog view:

```sql
SELECT ROW_NUMBER()
        OVER (ORDER BY s.column_id, s.segment_id) AS rn,
   COL_NAME(p.object_id, s.column_id) AS column_name,
   S.segment_id, s.row_count,
   s.min_data_id, s.max_data_id,
   s.on_disk_size AS disk_size
FROM sys.column_store_segments AS s
INNER JOIN sys.partitions AS p
    ON s.hobt_id = p.hobt_id
INNER JOIN sys.indexes AS i
    ON p.object_id = i.object_id
WHERE i.name = N'NCCI_FactTest'
ORDER BY s.column_id, s.segment_id;
```

Here is the abbreviated result of this query:

```
rn column_name  segment_id  row_count  min_data_id  max_data_id  disk_size
-- -----------  ----------  ---------  -----------  -----------  ---------
1  SaleKey      0           1048576    1000001      10106307     4194888
2  SaleKey      1           336457     1001951      10185925     1346560
3  SaleKey      2           441851     1106610      10227981     1768336
4  SaleKey      3           452926     1001228      10213964     1812656
5  CustomerKey  0           1048576    0            402          773392
...   ...
44 Profit       3           452926     -64500       920000       25624
45 NULL         0           1048576    0            3539         1678312
...   ...
48 NULL         3           452926     0            3879         725640
```

The total number of segments used is 48. SQL Server created four rowgroups and then one segment per column inside each rowgroup, plus one segment per rowgroup for the rowgroup dictionary. You can also see the number of rows and disk space used per segment. In addition, the `min_data_id` and `max_data_id` columns point to the minimal and the maximal value in each segment. The SQL Server query optimizer uses this information for early segment elimination.

You can also execute the other two queries:

```sql
-- Complex query
SELECT f.SaleKey,
    f.CustomerKey, f.Customer, cu.[Buying Group],
    f.CityKey, f.City, ci.Country,
    f.DateKey, d.[Calendar Year],
    f.StockItemKey, f.Product,
    f.Quantity, f.TotalAmount, f.Profit
FROM dbo.FactTest AS f
    INNER JOIN Dimension.Customer AS cu
        ON f.CustomerKey = cu.[Customer Key]
    INNER JOIN Dimension.City AS ci
        ON f.CityKey = ci.[City Key]
    INNER JOIN Dimension.[Stock Item] AS s
        ON f.StockItemKey = s.[Stock Item Key]
    INNER JOIN Dimension.Date AS d
        ON f.DateKey = d.Date;
-- Point query
SELECT CustomerKey, Profit
FROM dbo.FactTest
WHERE CustomerKey = 378;
SET STATISTICS IO OFF;
```

For the `Complex` query, the number of LOB reads is 7,128. For the `Point` query, the number of LOB reads is 2,351. In both cases, a columnstore index scan was used to read the data from the fact table. The *point* query used fewer LOB reads than the *complex* query because the query refers to fewer columns, and SQL Server retrieves only the columns needed to satisfy the query. Still, the results for the *point* query are not overly exciting. You should be able to get much less IO with a B-tree nonclustered index, especially with a covering one.

In my case, the *complex* query used a serial plan. Note that, depending on the hardware resources and concurrent work, you might get a different execution plan. SQL Server sees eight logical processors in my virtual machine, so you might have expected a parallel plan. SQL Server 2016 is much more conservative about using a parallel plan compared to previous versions. This is better for the majority of queries. If you really need to get a parallel execution plan, you could change the compatibility level to the version 2014, as the following code shows:

```
USE master;
GO
ALTER DATABASE WideWorldImportersDW SET COMPATIBILITY_LEVEL = 120;
GO
```

Now you can try to execute the *complex* query again:

```
USE WideWorldImportersDW;
SET STATISTICS IO ON;
SELECT f.SaleKey,
    f.CustomerKey, f.Customer, cu.[Buying Group],
    f.CityKey, f.City, ci.Country,
    f.DateKey, d.[Calendar Year],
    f.StockItemKey, f.Product,
    f.Quantity, f.TotalAmount, f.Profit
FROM dbo.FactTest AS f
    INNER JOIN Dimension.Customer AS cu
        ON f.CustomerKey = cu.[Customer Key]
    INNER JOIN Dimension.City AS ci
        ON f.CityKey = ci.[City Key]
    INNER JOIN Dimension.[Stock Item] AS s
        ON f.StockItemKey = s.[Stock Item Key]
    INNER JOIN Dimension.Date AS d
        ON f.DateKey = d.Date;
SET STATISTICS IO OFF;
```

This time, SQL Server used a parallel plan on my computer. Before continuing, reset the compatibility level to 2017:

```
USE master;
GO
ALTER DATABASE WideWorldImportersDW SET COMPATIBILITY_LEVEL = 140;
GO
```

Operational analytics

Real-time operational analytics has become a viable option in SQL Server 2016 and 2017, especially if you combine columnar storage together with in-memory tables. Here is just a brief overview of two possible solutions for operational analytics—one with on-disk and another with in-memory storage.

The following figure shows the architecture of an operational analytics solution with on-disk tables:

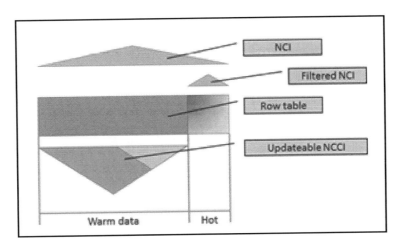

On-disk operational analytics

The majority of the data does not change much (so-called **warm data**), or may even be historical, immutable data (so-called **cold data**). You use a filtered nonclustered columnstore index over this warm or cold data. For **hot data**—data that is changed frequently—you can use a regular filtered nonclustered index. You can also use additional nonclustered indexes over the whole table. The table can be organized as a heap or as B-tree.

For in-memory tables, you can implement a slightly different architecture. You have to take into account that nonclustered columnstore indexes on an in-memory table cannot be filtered. Therefore, they must cover both warm and hot data areas. However, they are updateable, and in-memory updates are much faster than on-disk updates.

You can combine a columnstore index with other in-memory index types, namely with hash indexes and nonclustered indexes.

The in-memory operational analytics solution is shown in the following figure:

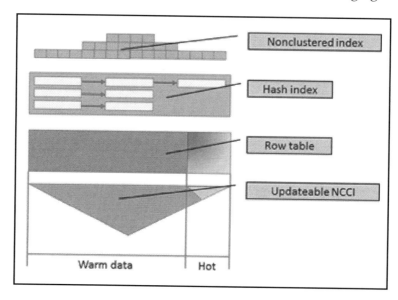

In-memory operational analytics

Clustered columnstore indexes

In the last sections of this chapter, you will learn how to manage a CCI. Besides optimizing query performance, you will also learn how to add a regular B-tree **nonclustered index** (**NCI**) to a CCI and use it instead of the primary key or unique constraints. When creating the NCCI in the previous sections, we didn't use LZ77 or archive compression. You will use it with a CCI in this section. Altogether, you will learn how to do the following:

- Create clustered columnstore indexes
- Use archive compression
- Add B-tree NCI to a CCI

- Use B-tree NCI for a constraint
- Update data in a CCI

Compression and query performance

Let's start by dropping both indexes from the demo fact table, the NCCI and the CI, to make a heap again:

```
USE WideWorldImportersDW;
-- Drop the NCCI
DROP INDEX NCCI_FactTest
   ON dbo.FactTest;
-- Drop the CI
DROP INDEX CL_FactTest_DateKey
   ON dbo.FactTest;
GO
```

Now let's create the CCI:

```
CREATE CLUSTERED COLUMNSTORE INDEX CCI_FactTest
   ON dbo.FactTest;
GO
```

And, of course, the next step is to recheck the space used by the test fact table:

```
EXEC sys.sp_spaceused N'dbo.FactTest', @updateusage = N'TRUE';
GO
```

The result is as follows:

Name	rows	reserved	data	index_size	unused
dbo.FactTest	2279810	23560 KB	23392 KB	0 KB	168 KB

The CCI even uses slightly less space than the NCCI. You can check the number of segments with the following query:

```
SELECT ROW_NUMBER() OVER (ORDER BY s.column_id, s.segment_id) AS rn,
  COL_NAME(p.object_id, s.column_id) AS column_name,
  s.segment_id, s.row_count,
  s.min_data_id, s.max_data_id,
  s.on_disk_size
FROM sys.column_store_segments AS s
INNER JOIN sys.partitions AS p
    ON s.hobt_id = p.hobt_id
INNER JOIN sys.indexes AS i
```

```
    ON p.object_id = i.object_id
WHERE i.name = N'CCI_FactTest'
ORDER BY s.column_id, s.segment_id;
```

This time, the number of segments is 44. The CCI does not show a dictionary segment per row group; it has a global dictionary that apparently covers the whole table. How does that influence the queries?

Testing the clustered columnstore index

Again, the first test is with the *simple* query:

```
SET STATISTICS IO ON;
SELECT f.StockItemKey,
  SUM(f.TotalAmount) AS Sales
FROM dbo.FactTest AS f
WHERE f.StockItemKey < 30
GROUP BY f.StockItemKey
ORDER BY f.StockItemKey;
```

From the IO output, you can see that SQL Server used only 82 logical reads. This time, this is really impressive. Note that the execution plan again used the `Columnstore Index Scan` operator, this time scanning the CCI and selecting only the rowgroups and segments needed to satisfy the query. You can see the execution plan in the following screenshot:

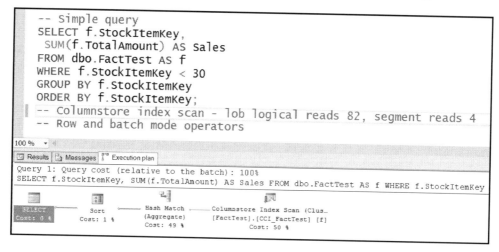

CCI scan execution plan

The next query to test is the *complex* query:

```
SELECT f.SaleKey,
   f.CustomerKey, f.Customer, cu.[Buying Group],
   f.CityKey, f.City, ci.Country,
   f.DateKey, d.[Calendar Year],
   f.StockItemKey, f.Product,
   f.Quantity, f.TotalAmount, f.Profit
FROM dbo.FactTest AS f
   INNER JOIN Dimension.Customer AS cu
     ON f.CustomerKey = cu.[Customer Key]
   INNER JOIN Dimension.City AS ci
     ON f.CityKey = ci.[City Key]
   INNER JOIN Dimension.[Stock Item] AS s
     ON f.StockItemKey = s.[Stock Item Key]
   INNER JOIN Dimension.Date AS d
     ON f.DateKey = d.Date;
```

This time, SQL Server needed 6,101 LOB logical reads. SQL Server used a serial plan on my virtual machine, a mixed batch (for CCI scan and for hash joins), and row mode operators (for other index scans). This is only slightly better than when using an NCCI. How about the *point* query?:

```
SELECT CustomerKey, Profit
FROM dbo.FactTest
WHERE CustomerKey = 378;
SET STATISTICS IO OFF;
```

The *point* query this time used 484 LOB logical reads. Better, but still not the best possible.

Using archive compression

You might remember that there is still one option left for columnar storage compression—archive compression. Let's turn it on with the following code:

```
ALTER INDEX CCI_FactTest
 ON dbo.FactTest
 REBUILD WITH (DATA_COMPRESSION = COLUMNSTORE_ARCHIVE);
GO
```

You can imagine what comes next; recheck the space used by the test fact table:

```
EXEC sys.sp_spaceused N'dbo.FactTest', @updateusage = N'TRUE';
GO
```

The result is as follows:

```
Name            rows      reserved    data       index_size  unused

dbo.FactTest    2279810   19528 KB    19336 KB      0 KB      192 KB
```

The LZ77 algorithm added some additional compression. Compare the data size now with the initial data size when the data size was 498,528 KB; now it is only 19,336 KB. The compression rate is more than 25 times! This is really impressive. Of course, you'd expect test queries to be even more efficient now. For example, here is the *simple* query:

```
SET STATISTICS IO ON;
SELECT f.StockItemKey,
 SUM(f.TotalAmount) AS Sales
FROM dbo.FactTest AS f
WHERE f.StockItemKey < 30
GROUP BY f.StockItemKey
ORDER BY f.StockItemKey;
```

This time, SQL Server needed only 23 LOB logical reads. The next query to test is the *complex* query:

```
SELECT f.SaleKey,
    f.CustomerKey, f.Customer, cu.[Buying Group],
    f.CityKey, f.City, ci.Country,
    f.DateKey, d.[Calendar Year],
    f.StockItemKey, f.Product,
    f.Quantity, f.TotalAmount, f.Profit
FROM dbo.FactTest AS f
  INNER JOIN Dimension.Customer AS cu
    ON f.CustomerKey = cu.[Customer Key]
  INNER JOIN Dimension.City AS ci
    ON f.CityKey = ci.[City Key]
  INNER JOIN Dimension.[Stock Item] AS s
    ON f.StockItemKey = s.[Stock Item Key]
  INNER JOIN Dimension.Date AS d
    ON f.DateKey = d.Date;
```

This time, SQL Server needed 4,820 LOB logical reads in the test fact table. It can't get much better than this for scanning all of the data. And what about the *point* query?:

```
SELECT CustomerKey, Profit
FROM dbo.FactTest
WHERE CustomerKey = 378;
```

This time, it used 410 LOB logical reads. This number can still be improved.

Adding B-tree indexes and constraints

There is still one query, the *point* query, which needs additional optimization. In SQL Server 2016 and 2017, you can create regular, rowstore B-tree nonclustered indexes on a clustered columnstore index, on a table that is organized as columnar storage. The following code adds a nonclustered index with an included column, an index that is going to cover the *point* query:

```
CREATE NONCLUSTERED INDEX NCI_FactTest_CustomerKey
 ON dbo.FactTest(CustomerKey)
 INCLUDE(Profit);
GO
```

Before executing the queries, let's check the space used by the demo fact table:

```
EXEC sys.sp_spaceused N'dbo.FactTest', @updateusage = N'TRUE';
GO
```

The result is as follows:

Name	rows	reserved	data	index_size	unused
dbo.FactTest	2279810	90256 KB	19344 KB	70192 KB	720 KB

You can see that row storage uses much more space than columnar storage. However, a regular NCI is very efficient for seeks. Let's test the queries, starting with the *simple* query:

```
SET STATISTICS IO ON;
SELECT f.StockItemKey,
 SUM(f.TotalAmount) AS Sales
FROM dbo.FactTest AS f
WHERE f.StockItemKey < 30
GROUP BY f.StockItemKey
ORDER BY f.StockItemKey;
```

This query still needed 23 LOB logical reads. If you check the execution plan, you can see that SQL Server is still using the columnstore index scan. Of course, the NCI is not very useful for this query. How about the *complex* query?:

```
SELECT f.SaleKey,
   f.CustomerKey, f.Customer, cu.[Buying Group],
   f.CityKey, f.City, ci.Country,
   f.DateKey, d.[Calendar Year],
   f.StockItemKey, f.Product,
   f.Quantity, f.TotalAmount, f.Profit
FROM dbo.FactTest AS f
   INNER JOIN Dimension.Customer AS cu
```

```
      ON f.CustomerKey = cu.[Customer Key]
   INNER JOIN Dimension.City AS ci
      ON f.CityKey = ci.[City Key]
   INNER JOIN Dimension.[Stock Item] AS s
      ON f.StockItemKey = s.[Stock Item Key]
   INNER JOIN Dimension.Date AS d
      ON f.DateKey = d.Date;
```

Again, SQL Server needed 4,820 LOB logical reads in the test fact table. The NCI didn't improve this query; it is already optimized. Finally, let's check the *point* query:

```
SELECT CustomerKey, Profit
FROM dbo.FactTest
WHERE CustomerKey = 378;
SET STATISTICS IO OFF;
```

This time, the query needed only 13 logical reads. The SQL Server query optimizer decided to use the covering NCI index, as you can see in the following screenshot, showing the execution plan for the *point* query for this execution:

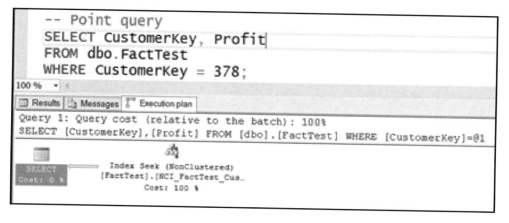

Execution plan for the point query that uses the nonclustered covering index

We don't need the nonclustered index anymore, so let's drop it:

```
DROP INDEX NCI_FactTest_CustomerKey
  ON dbo.FactTest;
GO
```

You can check the physical status of the rowgroups of the CCI using the
`sys.dm_db_column_store_row_group_physical_stats` **Dynamic Management View
(DMV)**, as the following query shows:

```
SELECT OBJECT_NAME(object_id) AS table_name,
  row_group_id, state, state_desc,
  total_rows, deleted_rows
FROM sys.dm_db_column_store_row_group_physical_stats
WHERE object_id = OBJECT_ID(N'dbo.FactTest')
ORDER BY row_group_id;
```

Here is the result:

table_name	row_group_id	state	state_desc	total_rows	deleted_rows
FactTest	0	3	COMPRESSED	1048576	0
FactTest	1	3	COMPRESSED	343592	0
FactTest	2	3	COMPRESSED	444768	0
FactTest	3	3	COMPRESSED	442874	0

You can see that all rowgroups are closed and compressed.

In SQL 2016 and 2017, you can also add a primary key and unique constraints to a CCI
table. The following code adds a unique constraint to the test fact table. Note that you
cannot add a primary key constraint because the `SaleKey` column is nullable:

```
ALTER TABLE dbo.FactTest
  ADD CONSTRAINT U_SaleKey UNIQUE (SaleKey);
GO
```

You can check in the **Object Explorer** that the Unique constraint is enforced with help from the unique rowstore nonclustered index. The following screenshot of the **Object Explorer** window shows that the `SaleKey` column is nullable as well:

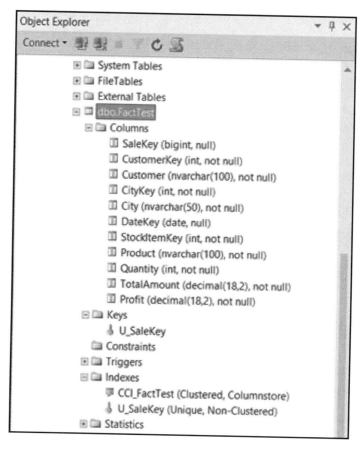

Unique constraint on a CCI table

Let's test the constraint. The following command tries to insert 75,993 rows into the test fact table that already exist in the table:

```
INSERT INTO dbo.FactTest
(SaleKey, CustomerKey,
 Customer, CityKey, City,
 DateKey, StockItemKey,
 Product, Quantity,
 TotalAmount, Profit)
SELECT 10 * 1000000 + f.[Sale Key] AS SaleKey,
  cu.[Customer Key] AS CustomerKey, cu.Customer,
```

```
   ci.[City Key] AS CityKey, ci.City,
   f.[Delivery Date Key] AS DateKey,
   s.[Stock Item Key] AS StockItemKey, s.[Stock Item] AS Product,
   f.Quantity, f.[Total Excluding Tax] AS TotalAmount, f.Profit
FROM Fact.Sale AS f
  INNER JOIN Dimension.Customer AS cu
    ON f.[Customer Key] = cu.[Customer Key]
  INNER JOIN Dimension.City AS ci
    ON f.[City Key] = ci.[City Key]
  INNER JOIN Dimension.[Stock Item] AS s
    ON f.[Stock Item Key] = s.[Stock Item Key]
  INNER JOIN Dimension.Date AS d
    ON f.[Delivery Date Key] = d.Date
WHERE f.[Sale Key] % 3 = 0;
```

If you execute the code, you get error 2627, violating Unique constraint. Let's recheck the status of the rowgroups:

```
SELECT OBJECT_NAME(object_id) AS table_name,
 row_group_id, state, state_desc,
 total_rows, deleted_rows
FROM sys.dm_db_column_store_row_group_physical_stats
WHERE object_id = OBJECT_ID(N'dbo.FactTest')
ORDER BY row_group_id;
```

This time, the result differs slightly:

table_name	row_group_id	state	state_desc	total_rows	deleted_rows
FactTest	0	3	COMPRESSED	1048576	0
FactTest	1	3	COMPRESSED	343592	0
FactTest	2	3	COMPRESSED	444768	0
FactTest	3	3	COMPRESSED	442874	0
FactTest	4	1	OPEN	0	0

Although the insert was rejected, SQL Server did not close or delete the delta storage. Of course, this makes sense since this storage might become useful pretty soon for data updates. You can rebuild the index to get rid of this delta storage. The following command rebuilds the CCI, this time without archive compression:

```
ALTER INDEX CCI_FactTest
  ON dbo.FactTest
  REBUILD WITH (DATA_COMPRESSION = COLUMNSTORE);
GO
```

You can check the rowgroup's status again:

```
SELECT OBJECT_NAME(object_id) AS table_name,
 row_group_id, state, state_desc,
 total_rows, deleted_rows
FROM sys.dm_db_column_store_row_group_physical_stats
WHERE object_id = OBJECT_ID(N'dbo.FactTest')
ORDER BY row_group_id;
```

Here is the result:

table_name	row_group_id	state	state_desc	total_rows	deleted_rows
FactTest	0	3	COMPRESSED	1048576	0
FactTest	1	3	COMPRESSED	343592	0
FactTest	2	3	COMPRESSED	444768	0
FactTest	3	3	COMPRESSED	442874	0

Note that your results for the number of rows in each row group may vary slightly.

Updating a clustered columnstore index

So far, only an unsuccessful insert was tested. Of course, you can also try to insert some valid data. Before that, let's drop the constraint since it is not needed for further explanation:

```
ALTER TABLE dbo.FactTest
 DROP CONSTRAINT U_SaleKey;
GO
```

Next, you can insert some valid rows. The following statement inserts 113,990 rows into the test fact table. Note that this is more than the 102,400 row limit for trickle inserts; therefore, you should expect this to be treated as a bulk insert:

```
INSERT INTO dbo.FactTest
(SaleKey, CustomerKey,
 Customer, CityKey, City,
 DateKey, StockItemKey,
 Product, Quantity,
 TotalAmount, Profit)
SELECT 11 * 1000000 + f.[Sale Key] AS SaleKey,
  cu.[Customer Key] AS CustomerKey, cu.Customer,
  ci.[City Key] AS CityKey, ci.City,
```

```
   f.[Delivery Date Key] AS DateKey,
   s.[Stock Item Key] AS StockItemKey, s.[Stock Item] AS Product,
   f.Quantity, f.[Total Excluding Tax] AS TotalAmount, f.Profit
FROM Fact.Sale AS f
   INNER JOIN Dimension.Customer AS cu
     ON f.[Customer Key] = cu.[Customer Key]
   INNER JOIN Dimension.City AS ci
     ON f.[City Key] = ci.[City Key]
   INNER JOIN Dimension.[Stock Item] AS s
     ON f.[Stock Item Key] = s.[Stock Item Key]
   INNER JOIN Dimension.Date AS d
     ON f.[Delivery Date Key] = d.Date
WHERE f.[Sale Key] % 2 = 0;
```

You can check whether this was a bulk insert by checking the rowgroups again:

```
SELECT OBJECT_NAME(object_id) AS table_name,
 row_group_id, state, state_desc,
 total_rows, deleted_rows
FROM sys.dm_db_column_store_row_group_physical_stats
WHERE object_id = OBJECT_ID(N'dbo.FactTest')
ORDER BY row_group_id;
```

The result shows you that you have only compressed rowgroups:

table_name	row_group_id	state	state_desc	total_rows	deleted_rows
FactTest	0	3	COMPRESSED	1048576	0
FactTest	1	3	COMPRESSED	343592	0
FactTest	2	3	COMPRESSED	444768	0
FactTest	3	3	COMPRESSED	442874	0
FactTest	4	3	COMPRESSED	113990	0

Although all rowgroups are compressed, you will notice that the last rowgroups have fewer rows than the other rowgroups. It would be more efficient if you could use bulk inserts with more rows, closer to 1,000,000 rows. Now let's try to insert a smaller number of rows. This time, you can also turn on the graphical execution plan:

```
INSERT INTO dbo.FactTest
(SaleKey, CustomerKey,
 Customer, CityKey, City,
 DateKey, StockItemKey,
 Product, Quantity,
 TotalAmount, Profit)
SELECT 12 * 1000000 + f.[Sale Key] AS SaleKey,
   cu.[Customer Key] AS CustomerKey, cu.Customer,
   ci.[City Key] AS CityKey, ci.City,
   f.[Delivery Date Key] AS DateKey,
```

```
    s.[Stock Item Key] AS StockItemKey, s.[Stock Item] AS Product,
    f.Quantity, f.[Total Excluding Tax] AS TotalAmount, f.Profit
FROM Fact.Sale AS f
  INNER JOIN Dimension.Customer AS cu
    ON f.[Customer Key] = cu.[Customer Key]
  INNER JOIN Dimension.City AS ci
    ON f.[City Key] = ci.[City Key]
  INNER JOIN Dimension.[Stock Item] AS s
    ON f.[Stock Item Key] = s.[Stock Item Key]
  INNER JOIN Dimension.Date AS d
    ON f.[Delivery Date Key] = d.Date
WHERE f.[Sale Key] % 3 = 0;
```

In the execution, you can see that the insert was a row mode operation. SQL Server does not use batch mode operators for DDL operations. The following screenshot shows a portion of the execution plan, with the `Columnstore Index Insert` operator highlighted to show that row mode processing was used:

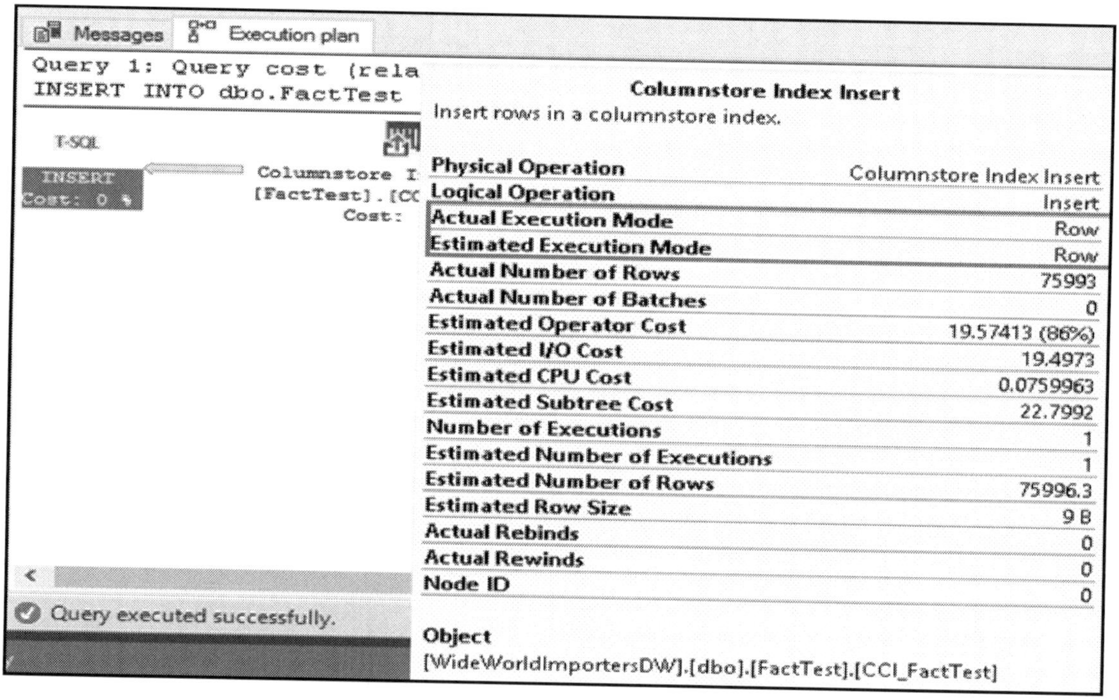

DDL operations are processed in row mode in SQL Server 2016

Note that SSMS in version 17.0 and higher also changed the icons in execution plans. That's why the icons in the previous screenshot are different from those in previous screenshots of execution plans, where I used SSMS version 16.

Anyway, let's recheck the status of the rowgroups:

```
SELECT OBJECT_NAME(object_id) AS table_name,
  row_group_id, state, state_desc,
  total_rows, deleted_rows
FROM sys.dm_db_column_store_row_group_physical_stats
WHERE object_id = OBJECT_ID(N'dbo.FactTest')
ORDER BY row_group_id;
```

This time, another open rowgroup is in the result:

table_name	row_group_id	state	state_desc	total_rows	deleted_rows
FactTest	0	3	COMPRESSED	1048576	0
FactTest	1	3	COMPRESSED	343592	0
FactTest	2	3	COMPRESSED	444768	0
FactTest	3	3	COMPRESSED	442874	0
FactTest	4	3	COMPRESSED	113990	0
FactTest	5	1	OPEN	75993	0

Let's rebuild the index to get only compressed rowgroups again:

```
ALTER INDEX CCI_FactTest
  ON dbo.FactTest REBUILD;
GO
```

After the rebuild, let's see what happened to the rowgroups:

```
SELECT OBJECT_NAME(object_id) AS table_name,
  row_group_id, state, state_desc,
  total_rows, deleted_rows
FROM sys.dm_db_column_store_row_group_physical_stats
WHERE object_id = OBJECT_ID(N'dbo.FactTest')
ORDER BY row_group_id;
```

The result shows you that you have only compressed rowgroups:

table_name	row_group_id	state	state_desc	total_rows	deleted_rows
FactTest	0	3	COMPRESSED	1048576	0
FactTest	1	3	COMPRESSED	428566	0
FactTest	2	3	COMPRESSED	495276	0
FactTest	3	3	COMPRESSED	497375	0

SQL Server has added the rows from the trickle insert to other rowgroups. Let's now select the rows from the last trickle insert:

```
SELECT *
FROM dbo.FactTest
WHERE SaleKey >= 12000000
ORDER BY SaleKey;
```

Deleting from a clustered columnstore index

Let's test what happens when you delete rows from a CCI with the following DELETE command. Before executing the command, you can check the estimated execution plan. Therefore, don't execute the following command yet:

```
DELETE
FROM dbo.FactTest
WHERE SaleKey >= 12000000;
```

The following screenshot shows the actual execution plan. You can see that, for the Columnstore Index Delete operator, row mode was used again:

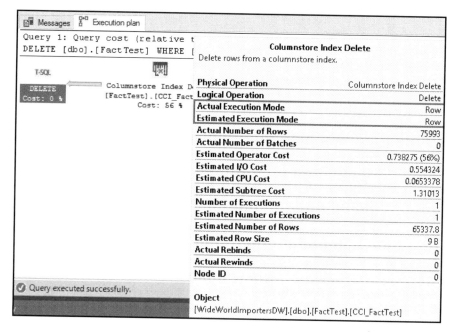

Estimated execution plan for a DELETE

And here is a final check of the state of the rowgroups:

```
SELECT OBJECT_NAME(object_id) AS table_name,
  row_group_id, state, state_desc,
  total_rows, deleted_rows
FROM sys.dm_db_column_store_row_group_physical_stats
WHERE object_id = OBJECT_ID(N'dbo.FactTest')
ORDER BY row_group_id;
```

The result shows you that you have only compressed rowgroups:

table_name	row_group_id	state	state_desc	total_rows	deleted_rows
FactTest	0	3	COMPRESSED	1048576	0
FactTest	1	3	COMPRESSED	428566	0
FactTest	2	3	COMPRESSED	495276	0
FactTest	3	3	COMPRESSED	497375	75993

You can see that one of the rowgroups has deleted rows. Although the total number of rows in this rowgroup did not change, you cannot access the deleted rows; the deleted bitmap B-tree structure for this rowgroup defines which rows are deleted. You can try to retrieve the deleted rows:

```
SELECT *
FROM dbo.FactTest
WHERE SaleKey >= 12000000
ORDER BY SaleKey;
```

This time, no rows are returned.

Finally, let's clean the WideWorldImporters database with the following code:

```
USE WideWorldImportersDW;
GO
DROP TABLE dbo.FactTest;
GO
```

Before finishing this chapter, look at the following table summarizing the space needed for different versions of row and columnar storage:

Storage	Rows	Reserved	Data	Index
CI	227,981	49,672 KB	48,528 KB	200 KB
CI row compression	227,981	25,864 KB	24,944 KB	80 KB
CI page compression	227,981	18,888 KB	18,048 KB	80 KB
CI (10 times more rows)	2,279,810	502,152 KB	498,528 KB	2,072 KB
CI with NCCI	2,279,810	529,680 KB	498,528 KB	29,432 KB
CCI	2,279,810	23,560 KB	23,392 KB	0 KB
CCI archive compression	2,279,810	19,528 KB	19,336 KB	0 KB
CCI archive compression and NCI	2,279,810	90,256 KB	19,344 KB	70,192 KB

Summary

Columnar storage brings a completely new set of possibilities to SQL Server. You can get lightning performance in analytical queries right from your data warehouse, without a special analytical database management system. This chapter started by describing features that support analytical queries in SQL Server other than columnar storage. You can use row or page data compression levels, bitmap filtered hash joins, filtered indexes, indexed views, window analytical and aggregate functions, table partitioning, and more. However, columnar storage adds an additional level of compression and performance boost. You learned about the algorithms behind the fantastic compression delivered by columnar storage. This chapter also included a lot of code, showing you how to create and use the nonclustered and the clustered columnstore indexes, including updating the data, creating constraints, and adding additional B-tree nonclustered indexes.

7
SSIS Setup

In this chapter, we will cover the following recipes:

- SQL Server 2016 download
- Installing JRE for PolyBase
- Installing SQL Server 2016
- SQL Server Management Studio installation
- SQL Server Data Tools installation
- Test SQL Server connectivity

Introduction

This chapter will cover the basics of how to install SQL Server 2016 to properly go through the examples in the rest of this book. The version of SQL Server used in the following chapters is the Developer edition of SQL Server 2016. It's available for free as long as you subscribe to Visual Studio Dev Essentials.

SQL Server 2016 download

Following are the steps to download and install SQL Server 2016.

Getting ready

You need to have access to the internet for this recipe.

How to do it...

1. Open your browser and paste this link: `https://www.visualstudio.com/dev-essentials/`. The following page appears in your browser:

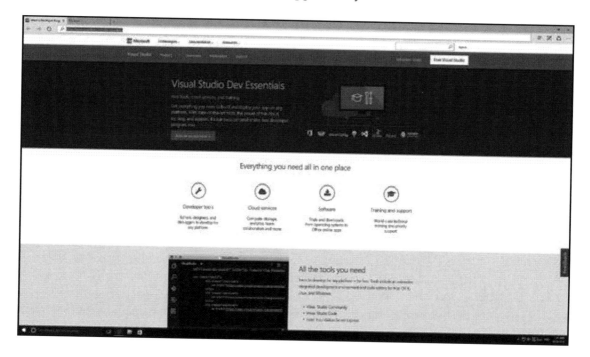

2. Click on **Sign in** visible at the right (top) to log in Visual Studio Dev Essentials. If you don't have an existing subscription, you can create one by clicking on the **Join or access now** button in the middle of the page, as shown in the following screenshot:

3. You are directed to the **My Information** page. Click on **My Benefits** at the top of the page to access the download section as shown in the following screenshot:

4. Click on the **Download** link in the **Microsoft SQL Server Developer Edition** tile as highlighted in the following screenshot:

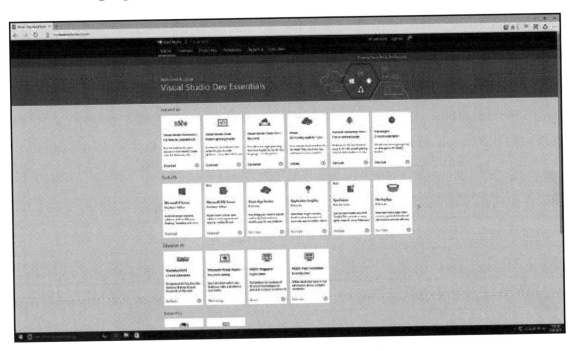

5. This will redirect you to the **SQL Server 2016 Developer Edition** page. Click on the green arrow to start downloading the ISO file as shown in the following screenshot:

6. Don't mount the ISO file for now. We have to install an external component described in the next section before we proceed with the installation of SQL Server.

Installing JRE for PolyBase

Java Runtime Engine (JRE) is required for PolyBase installations. SQL Server PolyBase is the technology that allows data integration from other sources other than SQL Server tables. PolyBase is used to access data stored in **Hadoop File System (HFS)** or **Windows Azure Storage Blob (WASB)**.

As you will see later in this book, SSIS can now interact with these types of storage natively but having PolyBase handy can save us valuable time in our ETL.

Getting ready

For this recipe you will need to have access to the internet and have administrative rights on your PC to install JRE.

How to do it...

1. To download JRE, follow this link:
   `http://www.oracle.com/technetwork/java/javase/downloads/index.html`.
   You will see the screen shown in the following screenshot:

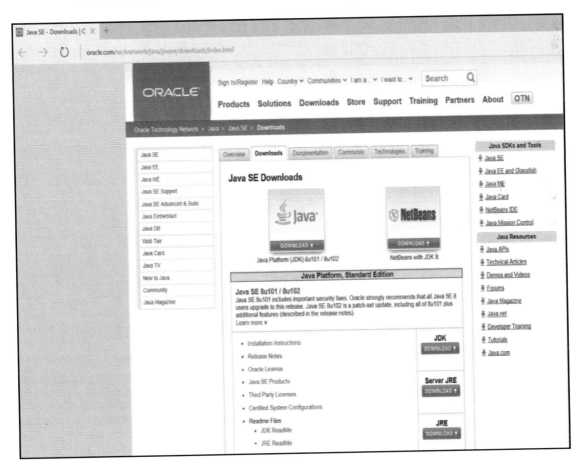

This directs you to the **Java SE Download** at Oracle.

2. Click the download link in the JRE section as shown in the following screenshot:

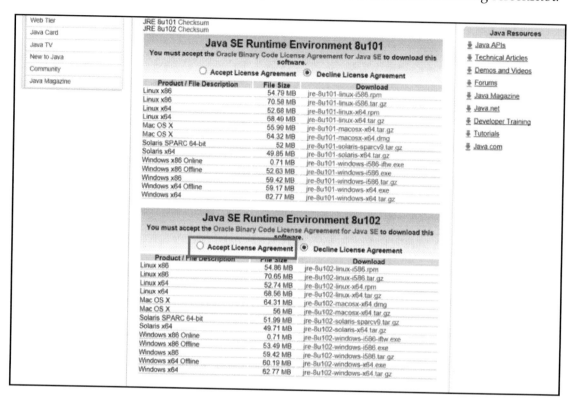

3. You must accept the license agreement to be able to select a file to download. Select **Accept License Agreement** as indicated in the following screenshot:

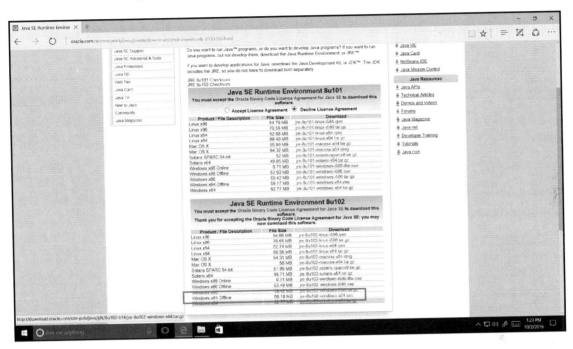

4. Since SQL Server 2016 only exists in a 64-bit version, download the 64-bit JRE. The version of Java SE runtime environment might be different from the one show in the screenshot, which is the one available at the time this book was written:.

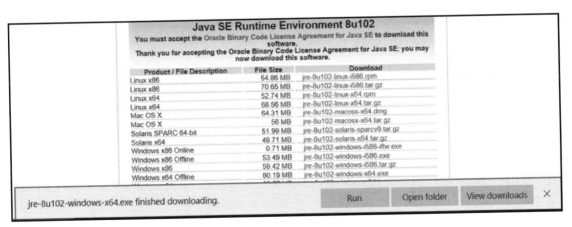

5. Once downloaded, launch the installer. Click on **Run** as shown in Edge browser. Otherwise, go to your Downloads folder and double-click on the file you just downloaded (jre-8U102-windows-x64.exe in our case); you will see the following window:

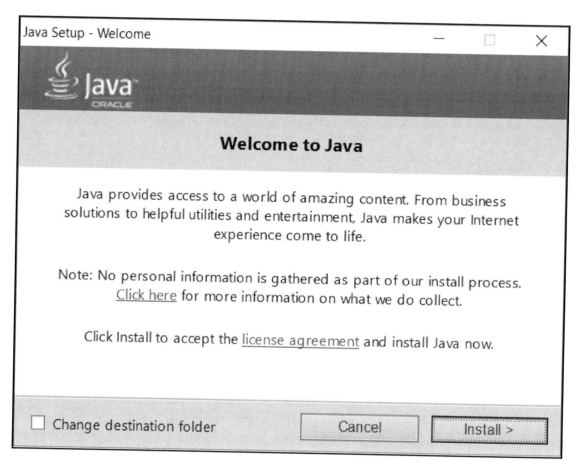

6. The Oracle JRE installation starts. Click on **Install**. The following screen appears. It indicates the progress of the JRE installation.

7. Once the installation is completed, click on **Close** to quit the installer:

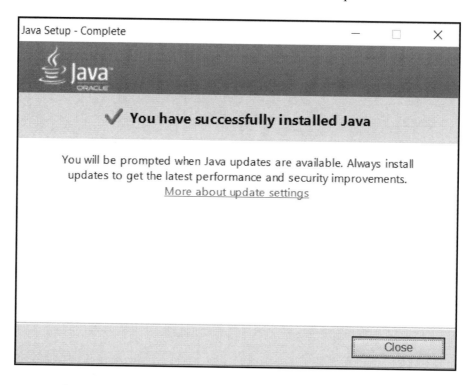

You are now ready to proceed to install SQL Server 2016. We'll do that in the next section.

How it works...

Microsoft integrated PolyBase in SQL Server 2016 to connect almost natively to the Hadoop and NoSQL platforms. Here are the technologies it allows us to connect to:

- HDFS (Hortonworks and Cloudera)
- Azure Blob Storage

Since Hadoop is using Java technology, JRE is used to interact with its functionalities.

Installing SQL Server 2016

This section will go through the installation of SQL Server engine, which will host the database objects used throughout this book.

These are the features available for SQL Server setup:

- **Database engine**: It is the core of SQL Server. It manages the various database objects such as tables, views, stored procedures, and so on.
- **Analysis services**: It allows us to create a data semantic layer that eases data consumption by users.
- **Reporting services (native)**: It allow us to create various reports, paginated, mobile, and KPI's for data consumption.
- **Integration services**: It is the purpose of this book, SQL Server data movement service.
- **Management tools**: We'll talk about these in the next section.
- **SQL Server Data Tools**: We'll talk about these in the next section.

Getting ready

This recipe assumes that you have downloaded SQL Server 2016 Developer Edition and you have installed Oracle JRE.

How to do it...

1. The first step is to open the ISO file that you downloaded from the Microsoft Visual Studio Dev Essentials website as described in the *SQL Server 2016 download* recipe. If you're using Windows 7, you'll need to extract the ISO file into a folder. Third-party file compression utilities such as WinRAR, WinZip, or 7-Zip (and there are many more) can handle ISO file decompression. The setup files will be uncompressed in the folder of your choice. In other versions of Windows such as Windows 8.1, Windows 10, or Windows Server 2012 and beyond, simply double-click on the ISO file that you have downloaded previously and a new drive will appear in Windows Explorer.

2. Double-click on the file named `Setup.exe` to start the SQL Server installation utility. The features we're going to install are as follows:
   - **New SQL Server stand-alone installation or adding features to an existing installation**: This will install a local instance (service) of SQL Server on your PC
   - **SQL Server Management Tools**: The tools used to create, query, and manage SQL Server objects
   - **Install SQL Server Data Tools**: This contains Visual Studio templates to develop and deploy SQL Server databases, integration services packages, analysis service cubes, and reporting services

3. From the installation utility, select the **New SQL Server stand-alone installation...** option as shown in the following screenshot. A new SQL Server setup window opens.

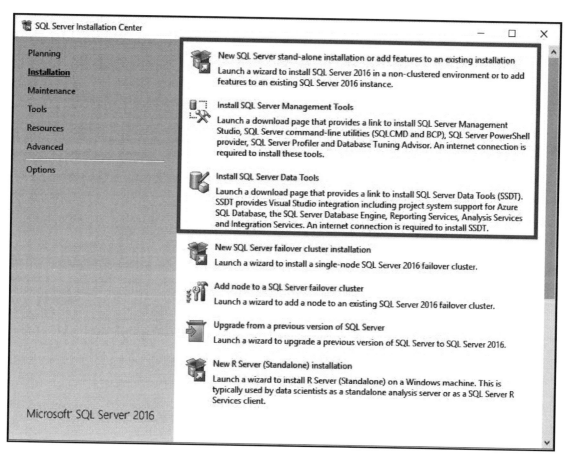

4. The **Product Key** page allows us to specify an edition to install. Since we're going to use the free Developer Edition, click **Next** to go to the next page, as shown in the following screenshot:

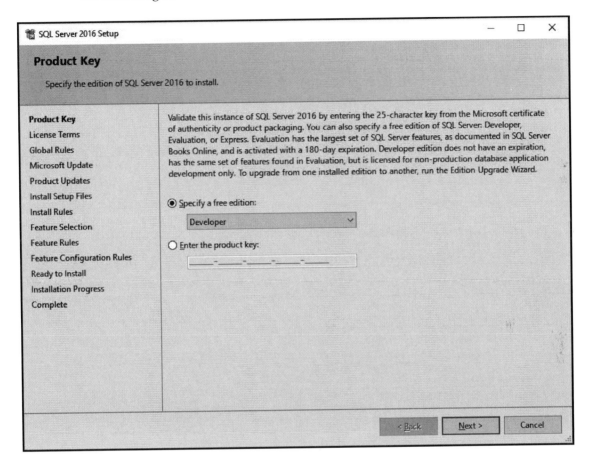

5. Accept the license terms and click **Next** to go to the next page, as shown in the following screenshot:

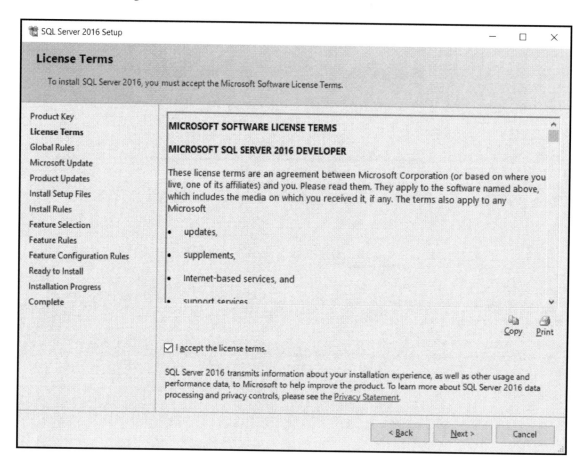

6. In this step, the SQL Server setup will check for product updates and will integrate itself into Windows update checks that are done regularly on your machine. This step is not mandatory but it's better to use the latest code. Check **Use Microsoft Update...** and click **Next**, as shown in the following screenshot:

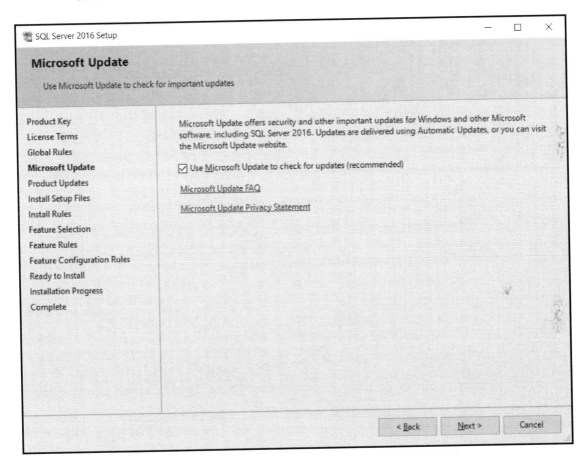

7. Some updates might be found during setup. You can get more information on these updates by clicking the link in the **More Information** column. Click **Next** to install the updates, as shown in the following screenshot:

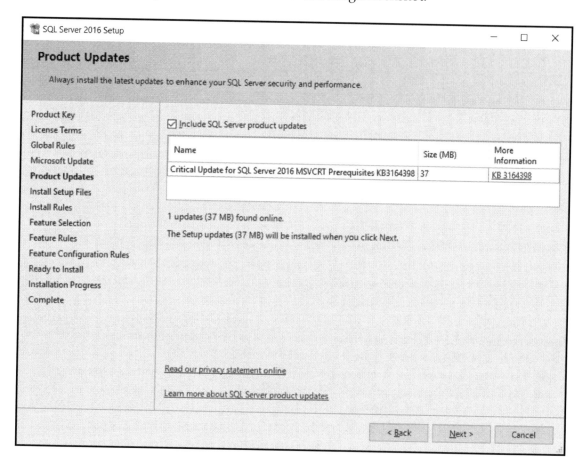

8. This step simply checks to make sure that the latest version of SQL Server is installed. Click **Next** once the setup files are installed, as shown in the following screenshot:

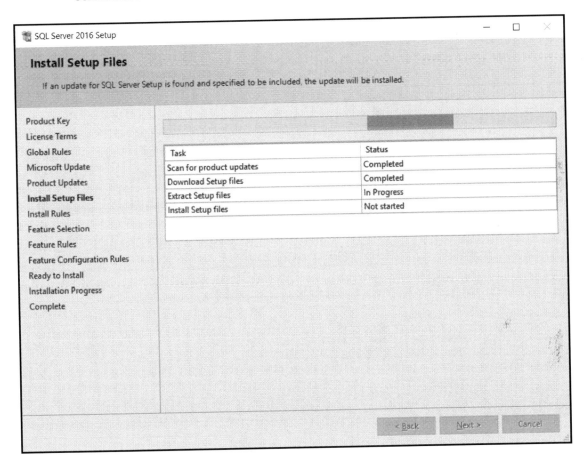

9. SQL Server setup will check several rules to ensure that the computer where we want to install it is setup properly. You might get a warning due to Windows firewall rules. This tells you that the port (1433 by default) is not open and SQL Server won't be available from outside your PC. Don't worry about it. Since we'll be using SQL Server from our PC only, we do not need to open any ports for now. Click **Next** to advance to the feature selection page, as shown in the following screenshot:

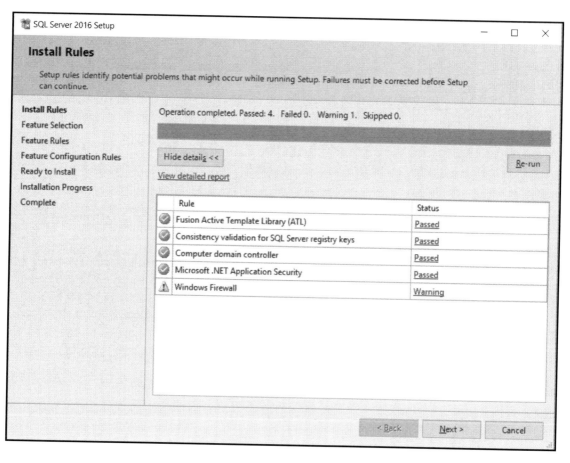

10. Select all features checked in the preceding screenshot and click **Next**, as shown in the following screenshot:

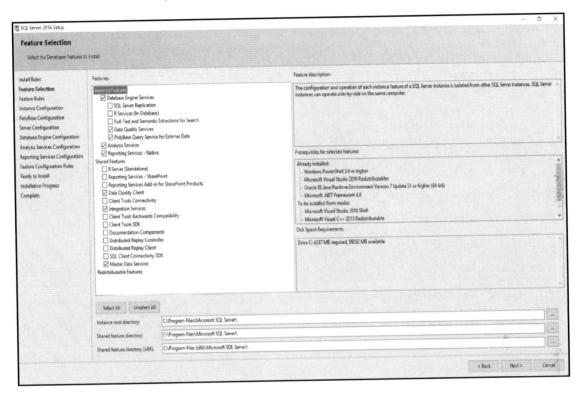

11. Instance configuration allows to specify a name for the SQL Server service. This is done by selecting the **Named instance** radio button. Since we'll only use one SQL Server instance, leave **Default instance** selected and click **Next**, as shown in the following screenshot:

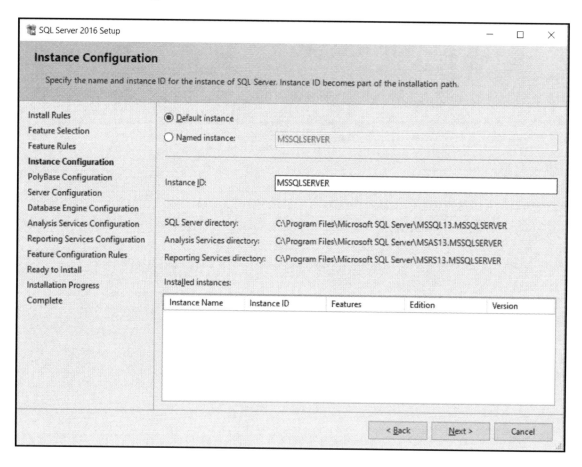

12. This page allows SQL Server to be part of a PolyBase scale out group. Since we're only setting up SQL Server PolyBase to be used by one instance, leave the default **Use this SQL Server as standalone PolyBase-enabled instance** and click **Next**, as shown in the following screenshot:

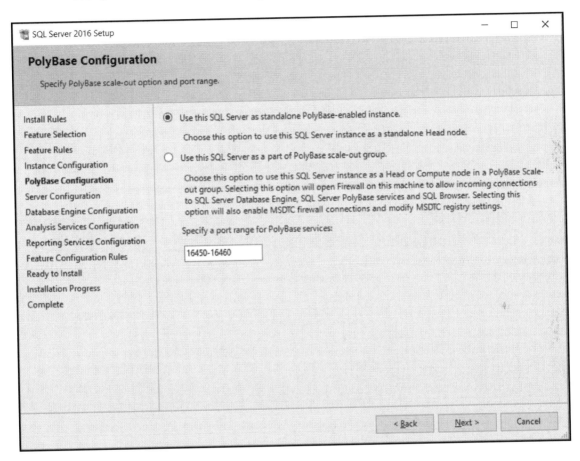

13. Now for server configuration. This step allows us to specify distinct or specific service accounts. Since we're installing SQL Server on a single development machine, we'll use the default accounts, as shown in the following screenshot:

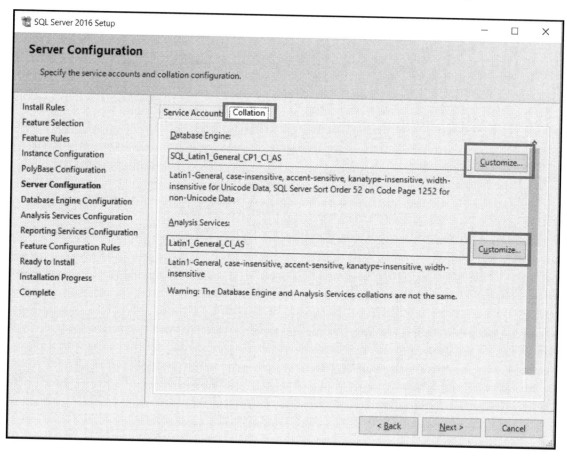

14. Click on the **Collation** tab as highlighted on the preceding screenshot. The default collation used by SQL server is SQL Latin1_General_CP1_CI_AS. This is a legacy collation. The choice of the collation is important for character string columns. The latest (fewer bugs) collation is Latin1_General_100. The last characters CI and AS are for case-insensitive and accent-sensitive, respectively.

15. We'll change the collation defaults. Click **Customize...** at the end of SQL Latin1_General_CP1_CI_AI, as shown in the following screenshot:

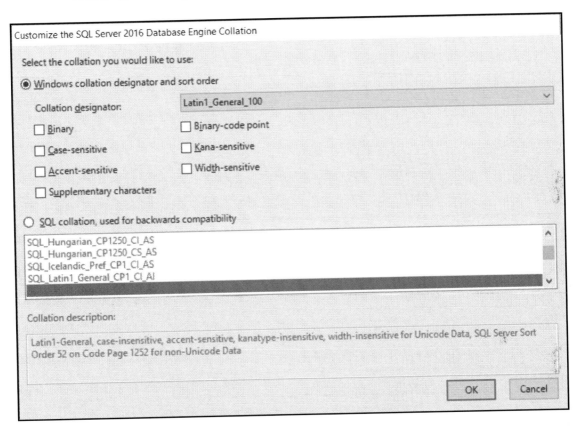

16. As stated previously, we'll use the Windows collation designator Latin1_General_100. Uncheck **Accent-sensitive**. This allows SQL Server to sort character columns without using accentuated characters. For example, suppose that our application has a FirstName column and we have the following first names:
    - Joel
    - Joël

17. If we query SQL Server filtering on `FirstName = 'Joel'` with the **Accent-sensitive** collation option, we end up retrieving the value `Joel` only. If we do not select the **Accent-sensitive** collation option, we will get both values.

18. Click **OK** when done to return to the previous screen. We'll do the same for analysis services; click **Customize...** to customize analysis service collation, as shown in the following screenshot:

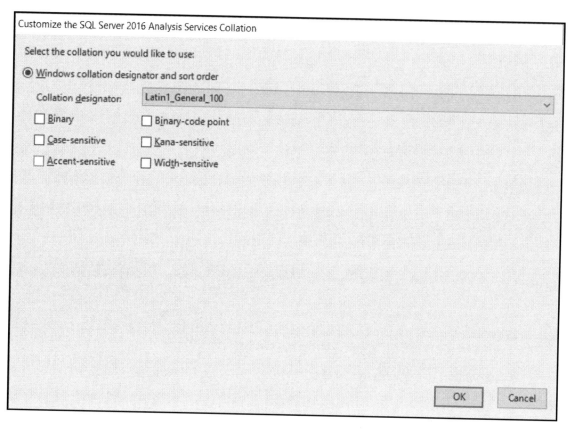

19. Again, choose `Latin1_General_100` in Collation designator and uncheck the **Accent-sensitive** checkbox. Click **OK** to return to the previous screen. Click on **Next**, as shown in the following screenshot:

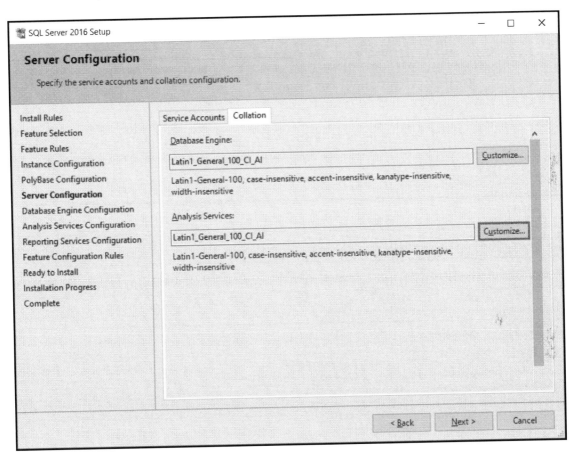

20. This will direct you to the following screen. For the database engine configuration, we'll use **Mixed Mode** to allow us to use SQL Server logins and Windows logins. The default authentication is **Windows authentication mode**, which is more secure than SQL Server authentication because it uses the Kerberos security protocol, password, and account lockout policies, and password expiration. Make sure you use strong passwords for SQL Server logins. By default, password policy, password expiration, and user must change password at next login are turned on also for SQL Server login. You should not disable the password policy and the password expiration. Select the **Mixed Mode** radio box and enter a password for the SA account. Click on **Add Current User** as shown in the screenshot to add your Windows account as an administrator of the instance. You'll have all rights on it. Click **Next**, which will direct you to the **Analysis Services Configuration** window, as shown in the following screenshot:

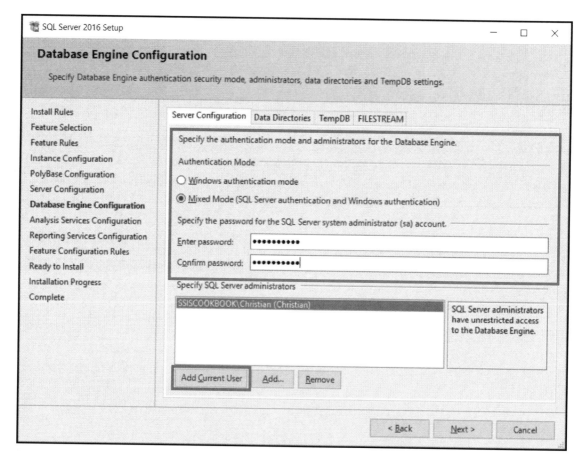

21. For analysis services configuration, the **Server Mode** we'll use is **Tabular Mode** and again click on **Add Current User** as shown in the following screenshot to add your Windows account as an administrator of the service. Click **Next.**

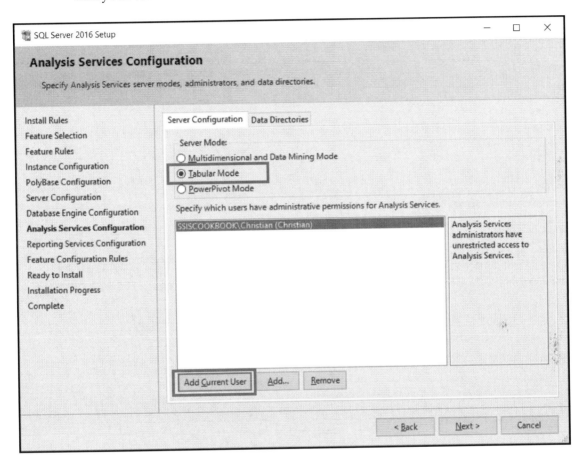

22. For the Reporting services configuration, leave the default values and click **Next**, as shown in the following screenshot:

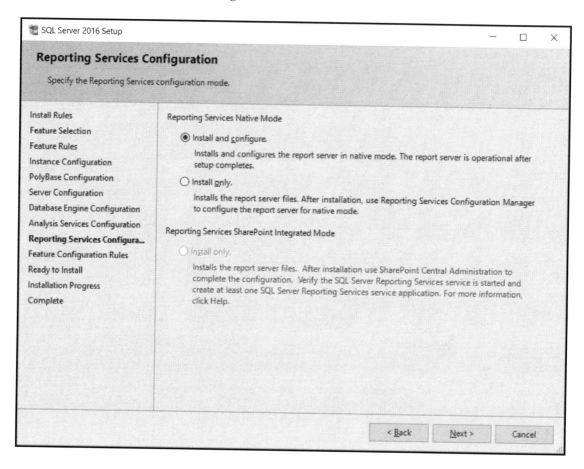

23. We're finally ready to install. Click **Install** to start the installation process, as shown in the following screenshot:

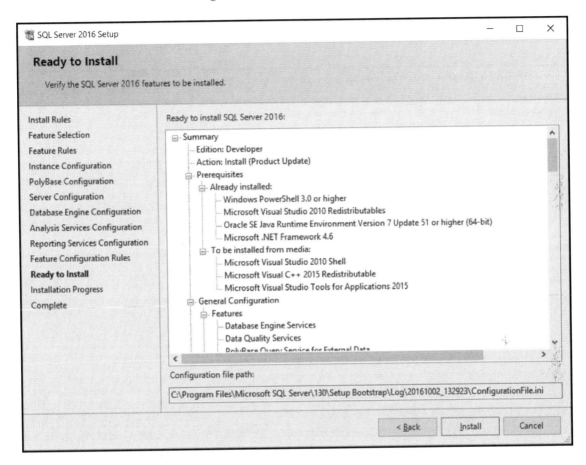

24. The following screenshot shows the installation progress:

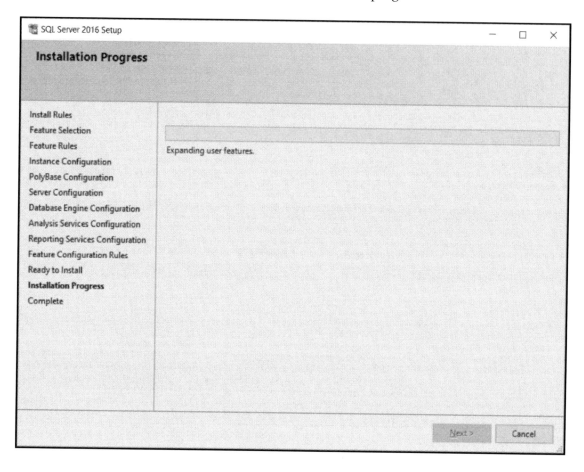

25. Once the installation is complete, you get the following screen:

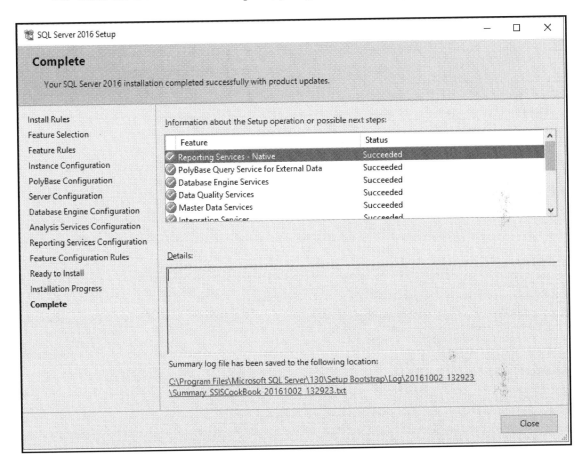

We're done. We just installed SQL Server 2016! In the next section, we'll install SQL Server Management Studio.

 The number, the order, and the appearance of the setup screens change slightly with every version of SQL Server, or even with a service pack. If you encounter a new screen not mentioned here, just use the default settings and proceed with the installation.

SQL Server Management Studio installation

SQL Server Management Studio is a separate download from SQL Server. This program will allow us, among other things, to create database objects and query SQL Server. Without this tool, we wouldn't be able to manage SQL Server databases easily.

Getting ready

This section assumes that you have installed SQL Server 2016.

How to do it...

1. To download and install SQL Server Management Studio, click on Install SQL Server Management Tools, as shown in the following screenshot:

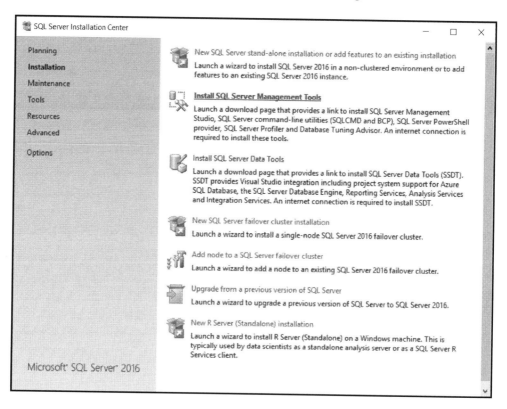

2. The SSMS download page opens in your browser. Click **Download SQL Server Management Studio** (the latest version) to start the download process. Once downloaded, run the installation as shown in the following screenshot:

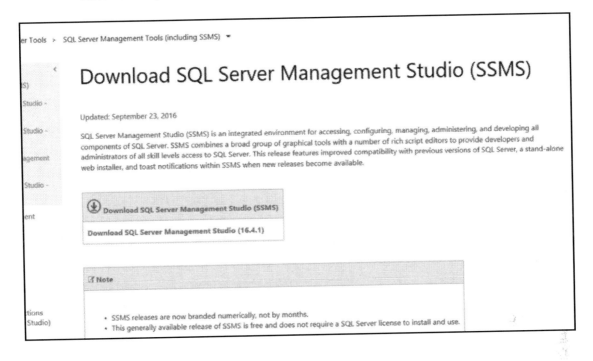

3. Click **Install**, as shown in the following screenshot:

4. This will direct you to the Microsoft SQL Server Management Studio installation screen as follows. The installation is in progress; it may take several minutes to complete.

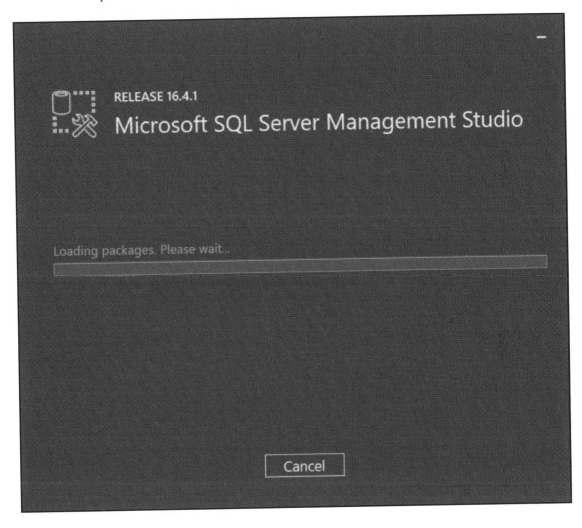

5. Click **Close** to close the installation wizard, as shown in the following screenshot:

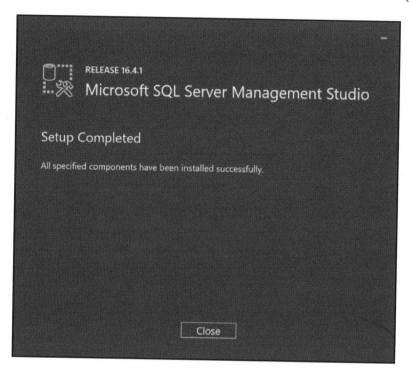

SQL Server Data Tools installation

The last part of our SQL Server 2016 setup is to install SQL Server Data Tools. This will install a Visual Studio Shell that contains BI templates necessary for the following:

- SQL Server integration services
- SQL Server analysis services

- SQL Server reporting services
- Database object management

Getting ready

We'll use SSDT throughout this book to create, deploy, and maintain our SSIS packages and some databases.

SQL Serve 2019 INSTALL From Vstudio Extensions SEARCH for package

How to do it...

1. From the SQL Server 2016 setup utility, click on **SQL Server Data Tools (SSDT)**. This will open the **Download SQL Server Data Tools (SSDT)** download page in your browser as shown in the following screenshot:

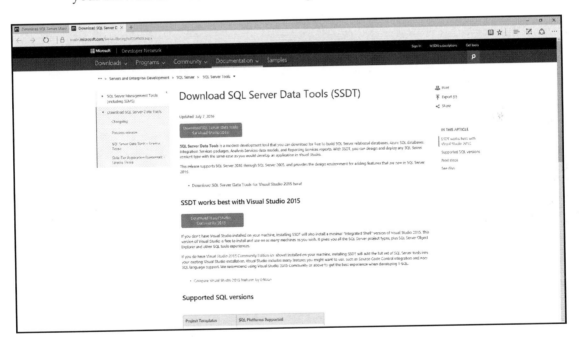

Here, there are two choices:

> **Install SSDT only**: This is the simplest scenario. It only installs SSDT and a development shell.

Install Visual Studio and SSDT: You choose this if you plan to use source control inside Visual Studio or when you want to implement different types of development (.NET, Python, and so on) such as SSIS/SSAS/SSRS development. Since we'll talk about custom components in this book, we'll install Visual Studio Community Edition. This version is free for individuals.

2. Click on the **Download Visual Studio Community 2015** link to download the Visual Studio installer.
3. Once downloaded, click on **Run** to launch the Visual Studio installer.
4. Accept the default installation type and click **Install** to start the installation process. This will give you the following window:

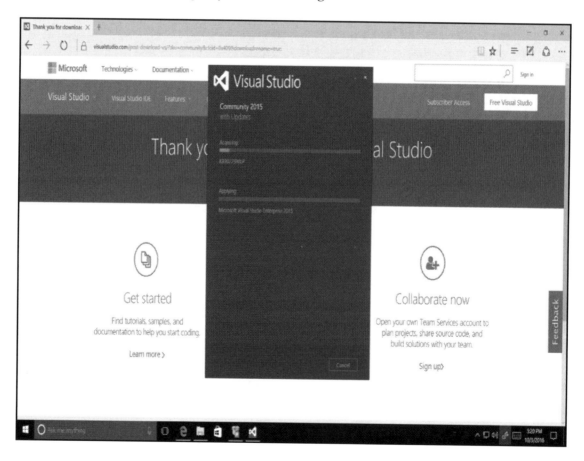

5. Once the installation is completed, since we haven't installed SSDT, don't launch Visual Studio yet. Close this window. We'll install SQL Server Data Tools first. Return to the browser window and click **Download SQL Server Data Tools for Visual Studio 2015** as shown in the following screenshot:

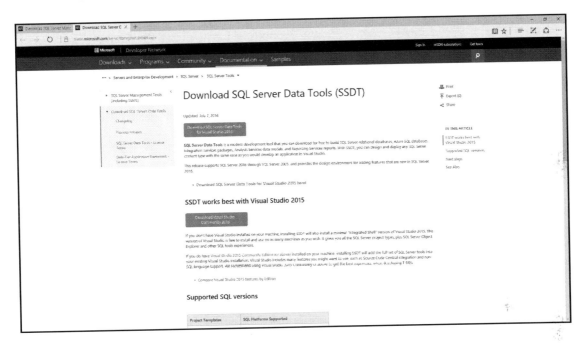

6. This will direct you to the SSDT download screen shown as follows:

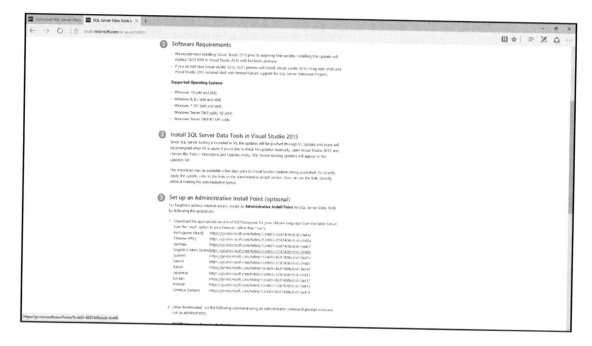

7. From the browser page that opens, choose **English (United States)**. The SSDT setup executable file download starts. Since it's a small file, it takes only a few seconds to download. Once the download completes, click **Run** or double-click on the newly downloaded file to start SSDT installation. Accept the defaults and click **Next** to proceed to the next step, as shown in the following screenshot:

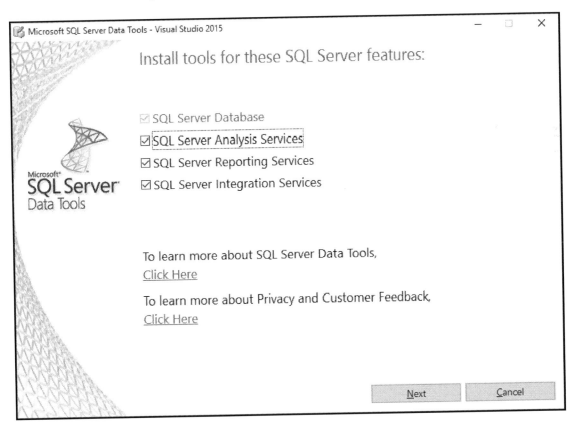

8. Accept the license agreement by checking the **I agree to the license terms and conditions** and click **Install**, as shown in the following screenshot:

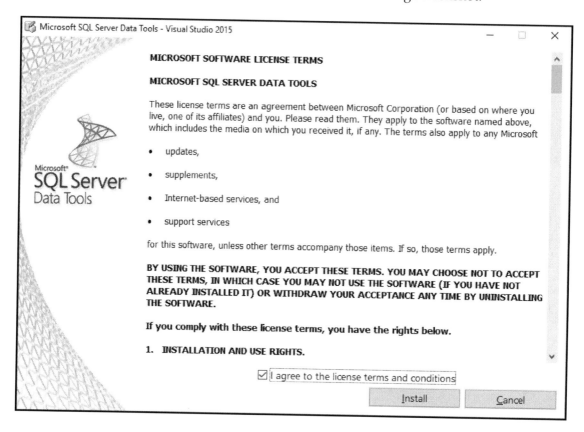

9. The SSDT installer will download the necessary files and proceed to the installation, as shown in the following screenshot:

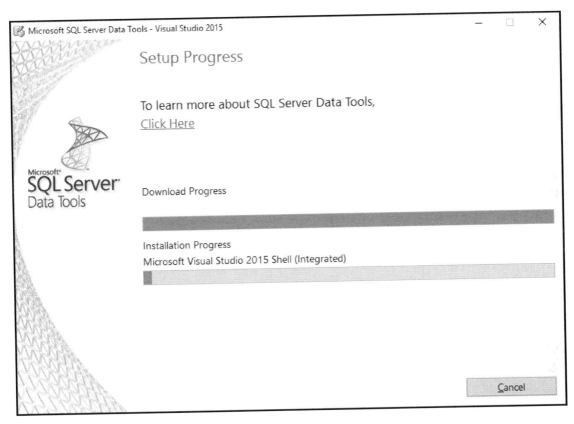

10. Once the installation completes, you might have to restart your computer. If that's the case, restart it, as shown in the following screenshot. Once that's done, look for SQL Server Data Tools in your Start menu and launch it.

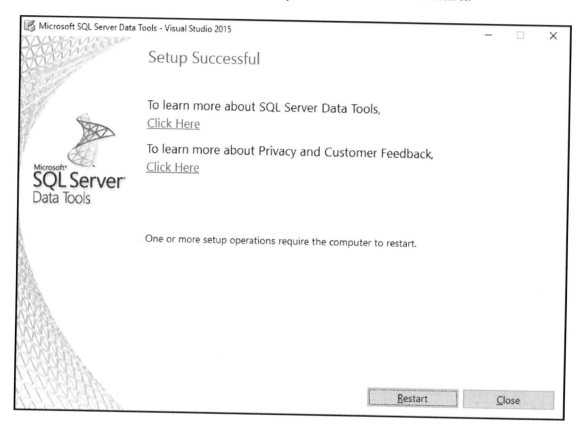

11. From the **File** menu, select **New Project**. Once the **New Project** window appears, you will see **Business Intelligence** in the project templates, as shown in the following screenshot:

12. Close SSDT; we're done with it for now.

Testing SQL Server connectivity

SQL Server Management Studio has been installed in this chapter in the *SQL Server Management Studio installation* recipe. We'll now test whether we're able to connect to our local instance.

Getting ready

This recipe assumes that you have successfully installed SQL Server 2016 Developer Edition as well as SQL Server Management Studio.

How to do it...

1. Look for SQL Server Management Studio in your Start menu and launch it.
2. Once the application opens, you should see your PC's name in the **Server Name** field. Click on **Connect**. SSMS will now connect to your local SQL Server instance, as shown in the following screenshot:

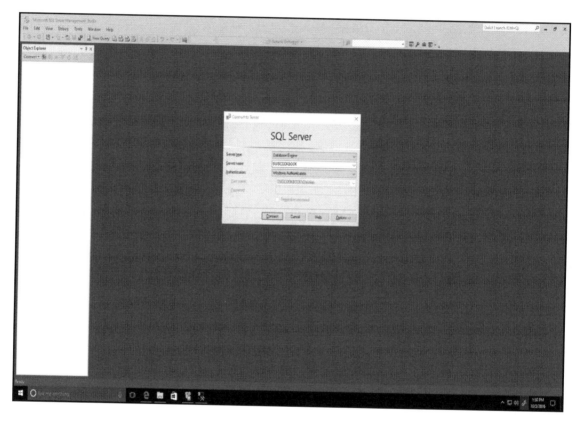

3. You are now able to connect to your local SQL Server instance, and we're now ready to begin work! You will get the following screen:

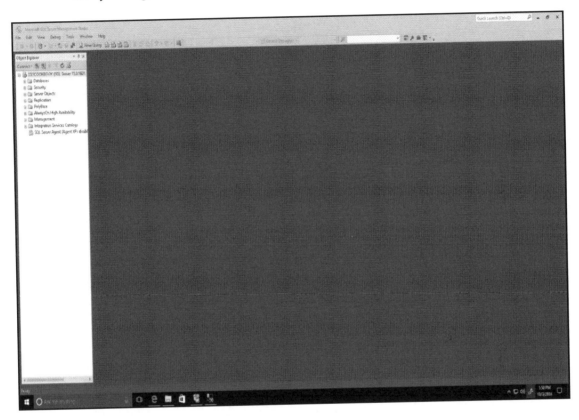

You can now start working!

What Is New in SSIS 2016 **8**

This chapter will cover the following recipes:

- Creating an SSIS Catalog
- Custom logging
- Azure tasks and transforms
- Incremental package deployment
- Multiple version support
- Error column name
- Control flow templates

Introduction

The 2016 release of SQL Server Integration Services is a major revision of the software. But, instead of being a complete re-write of the product, it's more an evolution of the product. Here is the SSIS timeline since its beginning in SQL Server 7.0 (1998):

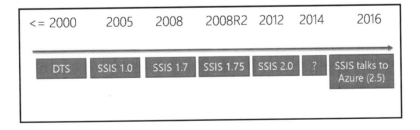

In the early years of SQL Server, Microsoft introduced a tool to help developers and **database administrators (DBA)** to interact with the data: **Data Transformation Services (DTS)**. The tool was very primitive compared to SSIS and it mostly relied on ActiveX and T-SQL to transform the data. SSIS V1.0 (2005) appeared in 2005. The tool was a game changer in the ETL world at the time. It was a professional and (pretty much) reliable tool for 2005. 2008/2008 R2 versions were much the same as 2005 in the sense that they didn't add much functionality, but they made the tool more scalable.

In 2012, Microsoft enhanced SSIS in many ways. They rewrote the package XML to ease source control integration and make the package code easier to read. They also greatly enhanced the way packages are deployed by using an SSIS Catalog in SQL Server. Having the catalog in SQL Server gives us execution reports and many views that allow us access to metadata or metaprocess information in our projects.

Version 2014 didn't have anything for SSIS. Version 2016 brought another set of features, as you will see in the remainder of this chapter. We now also have the ability to integrate with big data, which we'll talk about in some later sections of the book.

Creating SSIS Catalog

This section will walk you through the various steps to create an SSIS Catalog in SSMS. As mentioned before, the SSIS Catalog contains information about the package components and their execution. As we will see later in the book, SSIS projects are deployed into this catalog. It can be easily queried for custom reports as well, allowing us to create SSIS executions using T-SQL. This is very useful for on-demand executions of SSIS packages.

SSIS versions prior to 2012 did not have these capabilities since the catalog appeared with 2012. It is still possible to bypass the deployment to an SSIS Catalog by using a special mode: the *package deployment model*. This is mostly used for backward compatibility with previous SSIS frameworks.

Getting ready

This section assumes you have already installed **SQL Server Management Studio (SSMS)**.

How to do it...

1. We'll first create the SSIS Catalog in SSMS. Open SSMS and connect to your local instance:

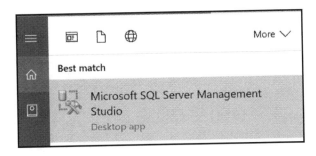

2. Look for the `Integration Services Catalogs` folder in **object explorer**.

3. Right-click on it and select the option **Create Catalog....**

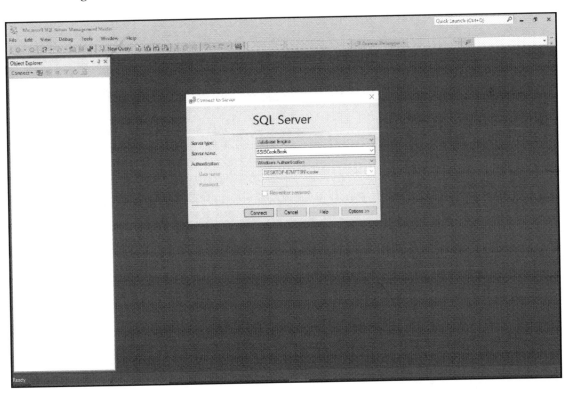

4. If the **Create Catalog...** option is not available (disabled - greyed out), it means that a catalog has already been created. Even if the folder is called Integration Services Catalogs - plural, only one Integration Services Catalog can be created by the SQL Server instance. The **Create Catalog** dialog box appears:

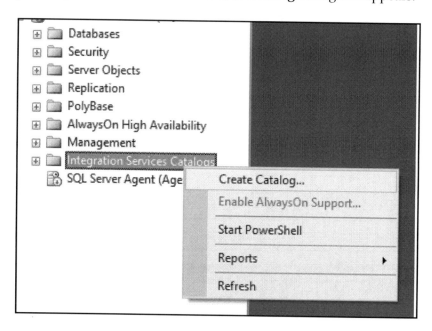

5. SQL Server CLR must be enabled to be able to create a catalog. It's also a good practice to check **Enable automatic execution of Integration Services stored procedures at SQL Server startup**. This creates a job that cleans up the SSIS Calalog tables. To enable the job, the SQL Server Agent must be enabled and started. To enable the SQL Server Agent, right-click on **SQL Server Agent** and select **Start** from the contextual menu that appears.

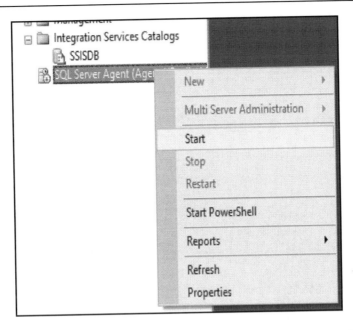

6. A confirmation screen appears to confirm that we want to start the Agent:

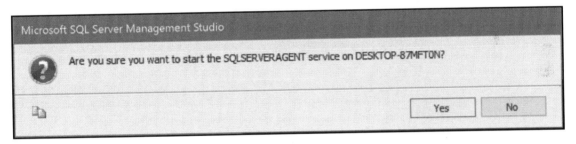

7. Once the Agent has successfully started, we can see in the `Jobs` folder a job called **SSIS Server Maintenance Job**:

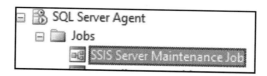

8. Double-clicking on it, you can see that this job is running every day to clean up the SSIS Catalog based on the retention window:

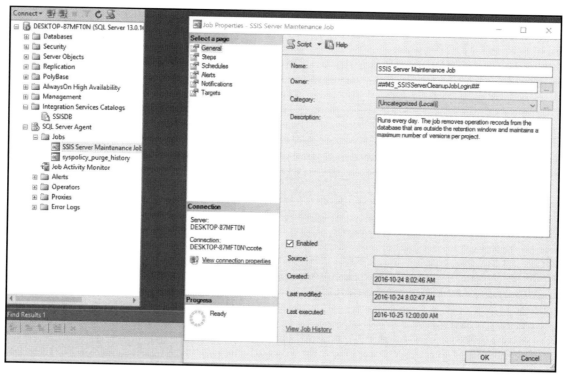

9. By default, the retention window is set to 365 days. We don't have to change it for the recipes we're going to implement from this book. But you should adjust the retention window setting to ensure that the catalog doesn't get filled with too many execution logs.

10. One of the benefits of this job is to execute clean up log entries in the catalog. As all executions are logged (we'll talk about logging in a later section), the catalog tables can fill up fast.

11. To manage the retention window, in SSMS object explorer right-click on the catalog (SSISDB) and select **Properties** from the drop-down menu. The following window appears:

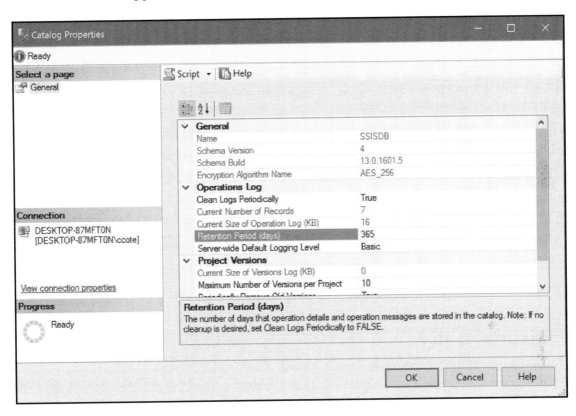

12. You can now modify the **Retention Period (days)** property, as shown in the preceding screenshot. Notice that you also have the ability to stop the clean logs schedule by setting the **Clean Logs Periodically** to **False**.

Custom logging

This section will talk about various loggings and how we can customize logging to suit our needs in terms of logging information. The reason why we need logging is because we want to retrieve some information on our package executions.

Here are some examples of logging info we might be interested in getting:

- How much time it took to execute a specific package
- How many rows have been transferred from one transform to another in our data flows
- What were the warnings or errors that were issued by the package execution
- The new values that have been assigned to a variable in a package, and so on

All the topics listed here will be discussed in the next sections of the book. For now, we'll focus on the customized logging levels.

There are various ways that we can log package execution information in SSIS. In versions prior to 2012 (or if we opt for a **Package Deployment Mode** instead of the default one, the **Project Deployment Mode**), the only way to enable logging was to enable it in each package. If we forgot to enable it in one package, the latter would not log anything. The default Project Deployment Mode can also log using package logging, but it's better to use SSIS Catalog logging, since it's integrated with projects once deployed and SSIS built-in execution reports will use it to display package execution information.

We'll talk about the various deployment models in the next chapter, Chapter 9, *Key Components of a Modern ETL Solution*.

Getting ready

This section requires you to have already installed SSMS and SQL Server Data Tools, and created an SSIS Catalog.

How to do it...

1. We'll start SQL Server Management Studio and connect to our local instance. We'll then expand the Integration Services Catalogs:

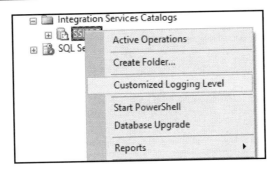

2. The following screen appears. Click on the **Create** button to create a custom logging level:

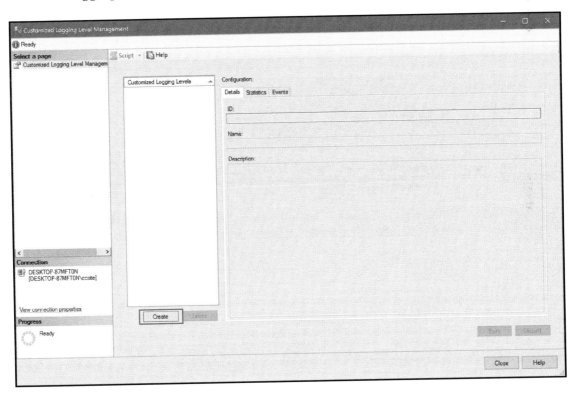

3. The **Create Customized Logging Level** screen appears. Set the various properties as shown in the following screenshot but leave the **Create from existing logging level** unchecked:

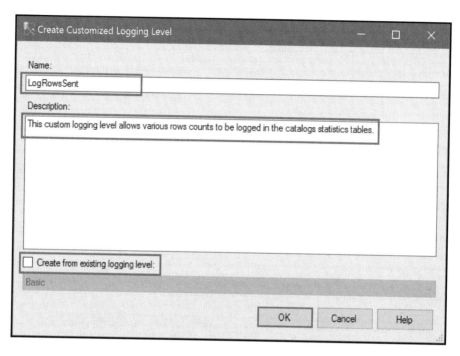

4. In the configuration screen, select **Component Data Volume Statistics**, click **Save,** and then **Close,** as shown in the following screenshot:

That's it for now! We have created our custom logging level.

How it works...

Using logging while executing our SSIS packages creates entries in the SSIS Catalog table called `execution_data_statistics` in the `internal` schema. This table is meant to record data movement statistics in SSIS packages.

We never use tables in the internal schema, as they are seen as system tables. That's the reason we use the view `[catalog].[ execution_data_statistics]` instead.

There's more...

Creating our logging level in SSMS will allow us to use it when our SSIS project will be deployed in the SSIS Catalog. We'll do that in the next recipe, *Azure tasks and transforms*; we'll create a simple SSIS package that will use this logging level when we execute it.

Create a database

This recipe, like many others in this book, requires a database to be created. It can be done by using SQL Server Management Studio. Start SSMS, connect to your local instance and right-click on the database folder. From the contextual menu, choose **New Database....** The following window appears:

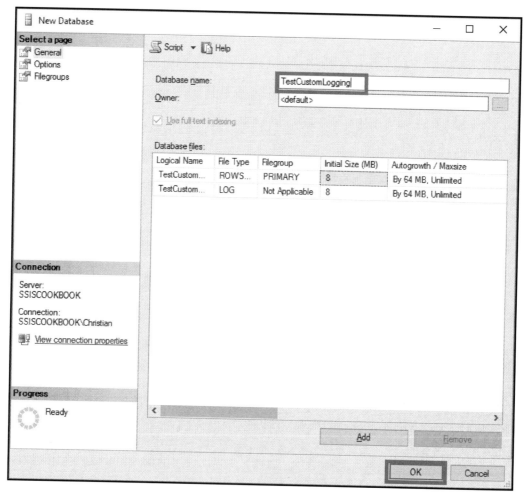

Fill in the **Database name** and click **OK** as we don't need to change the **Owner** and **Database files** information. You should now see the database under the Databases folder in SSMS. We're now ready to create an SSIS package that'll use it.

Create a simple project

This recipe will show you how to create an SSIS project to be able to use the custom logging level that we just created in the previous part of the recipe.

First, start SQL Server Data Tools and create a new Integration Services project: **File | New | Integration Services Project**. The following screenshot suggests how the project can be named:

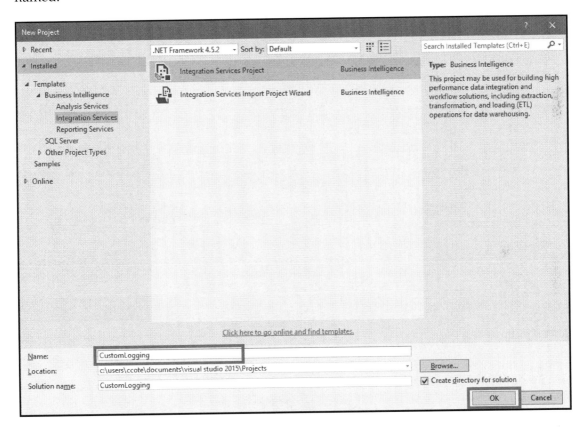

Once the project has been created, we should see a package called `Package.dtsx`. We'll right-click on it and select **Rename,** as shown in the following screenshot:

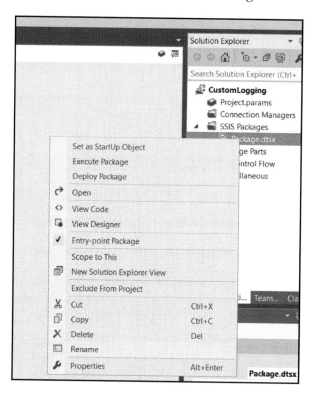

We'll name it `CustomLogging.dtsx`. The solution should now look like the next screenshot:

We will now add a **Data Flow Task** in our package. A **Data FlowTask** is a container that will allow us to do data transformations. Its toolbox has a rich set of data transformation tools.

From the **SSIS Toolbox**, drag a **Data Flow Task** to the package's control flow as shown in the following screenshot:

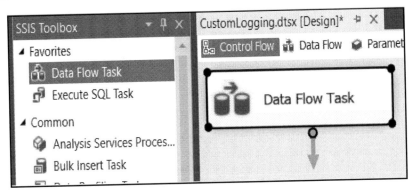

Rename the **Data Flow Task** dft_dbo_CustomLogging, as shown in the following screenshot:

In the next chapter, we'll talk about the way we name our SSIS tasks and transforms.

In the next few steps, we'll start customizing our SSIS toolbox. Double-click on the `dft_dbo_CustomLogging` **Data Flow Task** to go into it.

Throughout the book, we'll often customize the **SSIS Toolbox** to suit our needs. You'll notice that the toolbox has sections such as: **Favorites**, Common, Azure (this will be covered in the next recipe), **Other Sources**, **Other Transforms**, and **Other Destinations**.

For now, we remove the source and destination assistants and add **OLE DB Source** and destination to the favorites transforms:

1. In the **SSIS Toolbox**, scroll down to **Other Sources** and right-click on **OLE DB Source**. From the contextual menu that appears, select **Move to Favorites.**

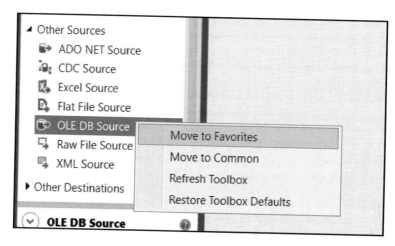

2. Next, scroll down again to **Other Destinations**, right-click on **OLE DB Destination,** and select **Move to Favorites** as shown in the following screenshot:

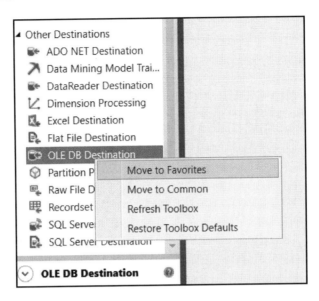

3. Now scroll up to the **Favorites** group at the top. We'll remove the source and destination assistants from the **Favorites**. As the following screenshot demonstrates, right-click on the **Destination Assistant** and select **Move to Other Destinations**. Repeat the same process for the **Source Assistant**:

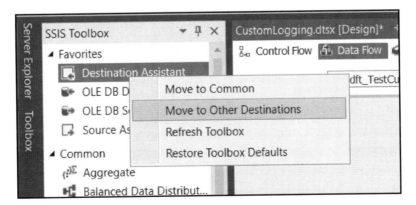

4. Repeat same process for the **Source Assistant**. We'll move it to the **Other Sources** group.

5. Now, we're ready to create a connection manager. We'll use it to read or insert data into the `TestCucstomLogging` database that we created earlier. As shown in the following screenshot, right-click in the **Connection Managers** area and select **New OLE DB Connection** from the menu that appears.

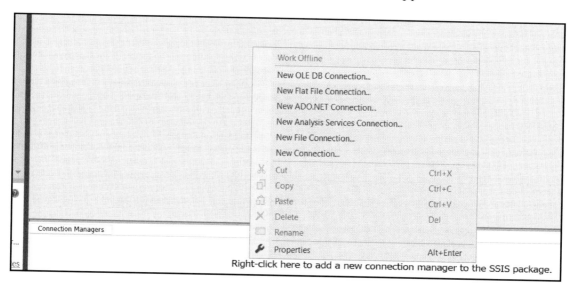

6. Click on **New** in the **Configure OLE DB Connection** window that appears and the following screen will appear. Set the **Server Name** to the name of your machine or the named instance you might have chosen when you set up SQL Server. Select `TestCustomlogging` as the **Database Name**. The following screenshot shows the two properties set up for my PC. Click **OK** once finished.

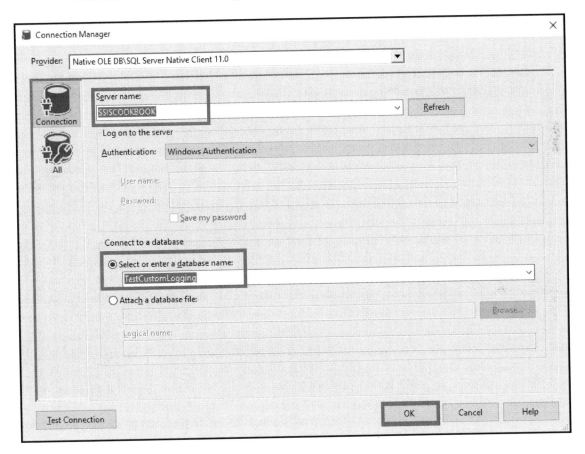

7. You're back on click **OK** in **the Configure OLE DB Connection Manager** window as shown in the following screenshot:

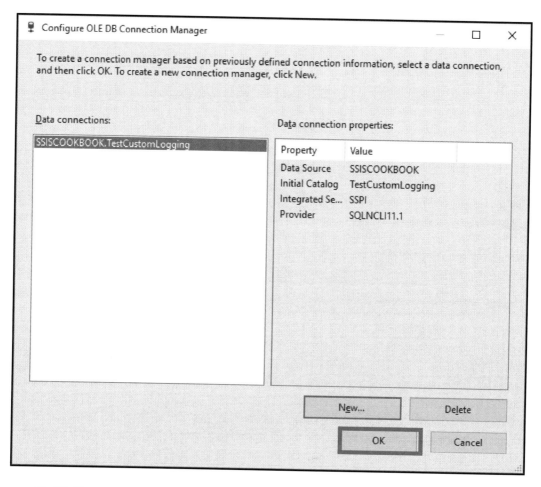

8. We'll now rename our connection manager. Select the newly created connection manager (SSISCOOKBOOK TestCustomLogging) to cmgr_TestCustomLogging as shown in the following screenshot:

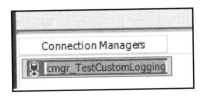

9. Now, from the favorite section of the SSIS toolbox, drag and drop an OLEDB source on the surface of the **Data Flow**. Now, as shown in the following screenshot, rename it to `ole_src_SELECT_1`. Double-click on it to get to the **OLE DB Source Editor** window. Set the **OLE DB connection manager** to `cmgr_TestCustomLogging` as demonstrated in the screenshot. Set the **Data access mode** to **SQL command**.

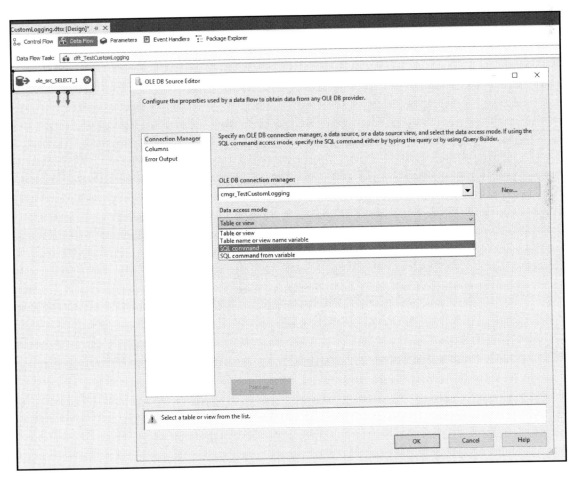

10. Now, enter the following SQL command in the command text and click on **OK**:

```
SELECT 1 AS LogID
UNION ALL
SELECT 2 AS LogID
```

11. Again, from the **Favorites** section of the **SSIS Toolbox**, drag an **OLE DB Destination** in the **Data Flow**. Connect the source to the destination and rename the **OLE_DB Destination** ole_dst_dbo_CustomLogging. Double-click on it, assign the **OLEDB connection manager** property, and click **OK** on the **New** button at the right of the name of the table or the view property. The Create Table window appears. Modify the command as shown in the following screenshot and click on **OK**:

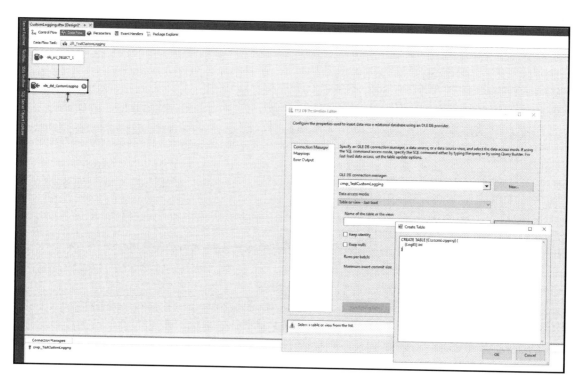

12. Click on **Mappings** in the list at the top left of the **OLE DB Destination Editor**. You should get the same screen as in the following screenshot:

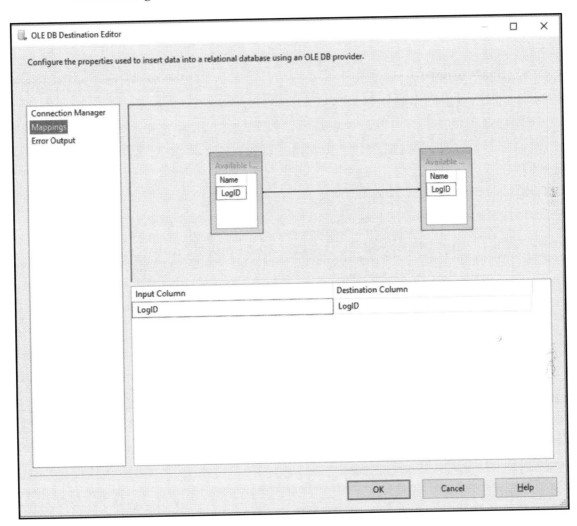

13. Click on **OK** to close the **OLE DB Destination Editor**.

14. Now, we'll bring in the **Layout** toolbar. We'll use it throughout this book to format our package objects properly. Right-click anywhere in an empty section of the quick access toolbar and select **Layout**, as highlighted in the following screenshot:

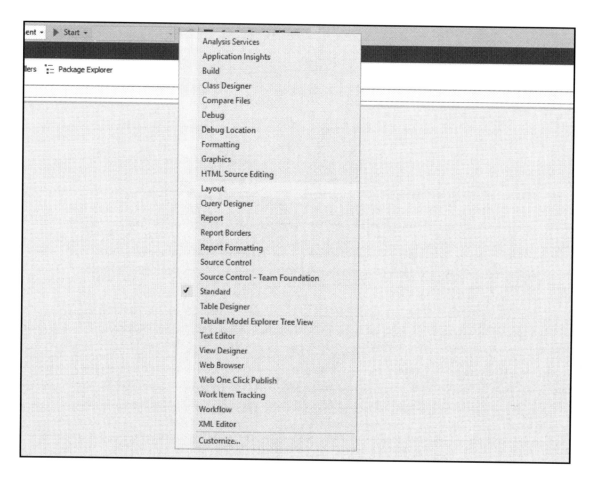

15. Now, from the **Edit** menu, select **Select All** or press *Ctrl + A* to select the entire Data Flow content. In the **Layout** toolbar, click on the *, **Make Same Width** button, as shown in the following screenshot:

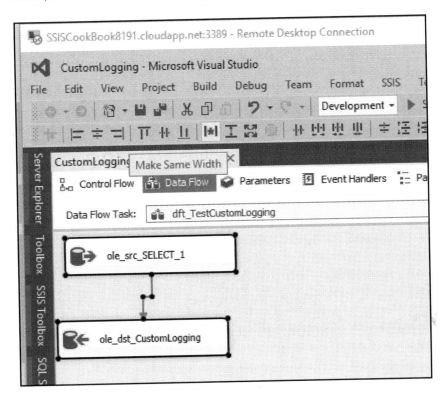

16. From the menu, select **Auto Layout** | **Diagram**. This will format the data flow objects, as shown in the following screenshot:

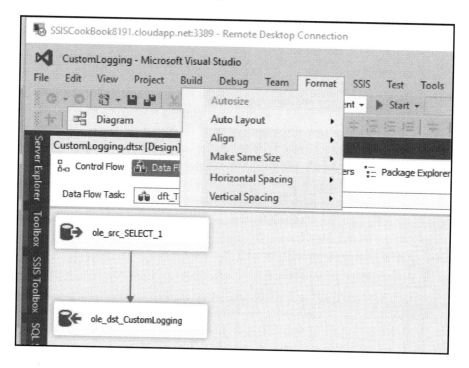

17. Now, right-click anywhere in the data flow task background and select **Execute Task** from the contextual menu that appears. The data flow should execute successfully as follows.

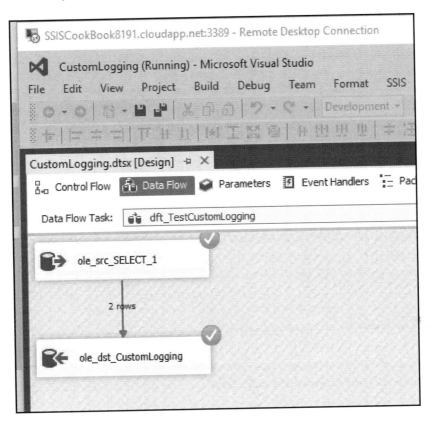

18. Now, we're ready to deploy our project to the SSIS Catalog that we created at the beginning of the chapter, in the recipe *Creating an SSIS Catalog*. Right-click on the `CustomLogging` project in the **Solution Explorer** at the top right of SSDT and hit **Deploy**. The project deployment wizard starts, as shown in the following screenshot:

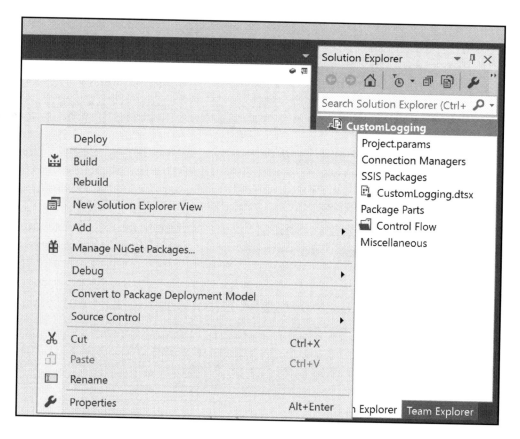

19. The first page explains the step performed by the wizard. Check **Do not show this page again** as in the following screenshot if you want to skip this step in future deployments of the project or individual packages, as we'll see later in this chapter.

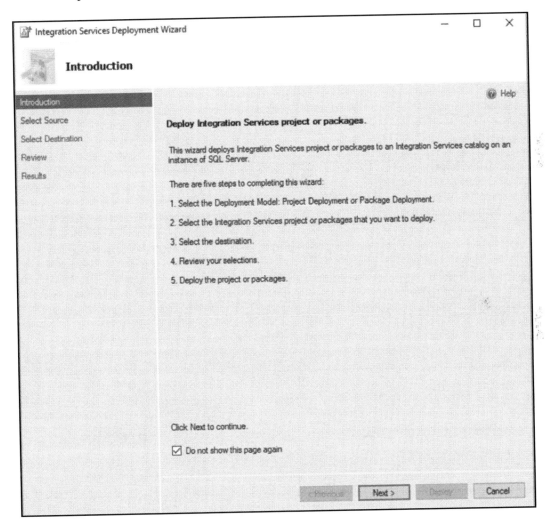

20. The wizard is now asking for an SSIS Catalog and folder. Since we don't have any folder yet in the catalog, we'll create one called CustomLogging, as shown in the following screenshot:
    1. Select the **Server name** by clicking on the **Browse** button. Select your machine name from the list and click on **OK**.

2. The **Path** property specifies where the project will be deployed in the SSIS Catalog. To assign a path to the project deployment, click on **Browse** at the right of it. The **Browse for Folderor Project** window appears. We're going to create a folder for our project. Click on **New folder**. From the **Create New Folder** window that appears, fill the text boxes as shown in the following screenshot. Click **OK** to save and close the window.

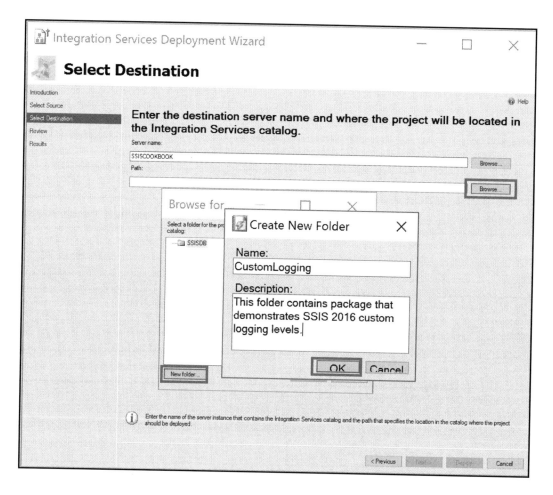

21. Your screen will look like the following screenshot. Click **OK** again to close the **Browse for Folder or Project** window.

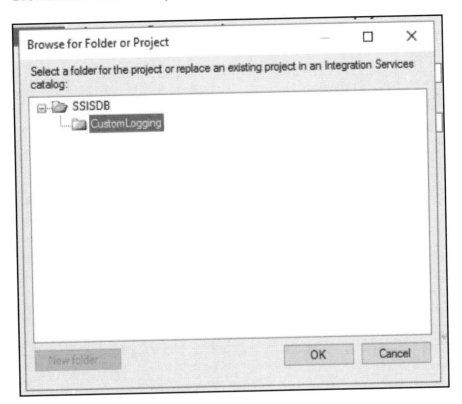

22. Back on the **Integration Services Deployment Wizard**, click on the **Next** button to go to the next deployment step. You should have a window similar to the following screenshot:

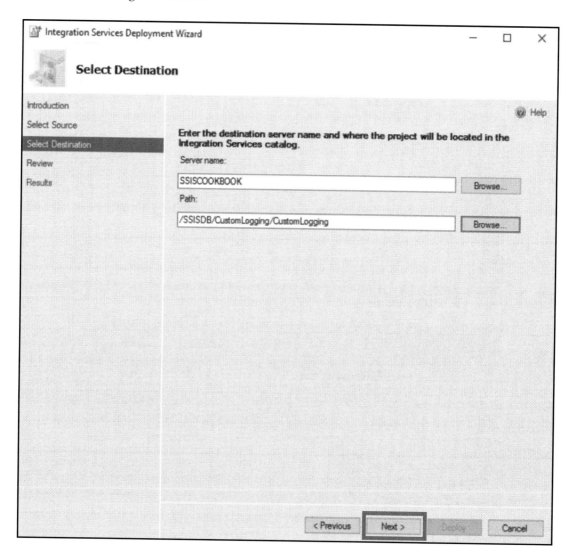

23. Click on **Deploy**, as shown in the following screenshot:

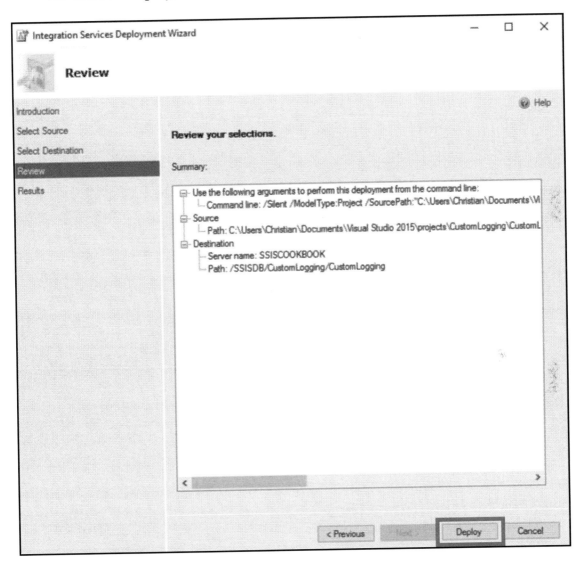

24. As the following screenshot shows, the project is deployed in the SSIS Catalog. If this fails, click on the **Report** button to investigate the error details. Whenever deployment errors occur, you can click on **Previous** to make a correction. Click **Close** to terminate the deployment wizard.

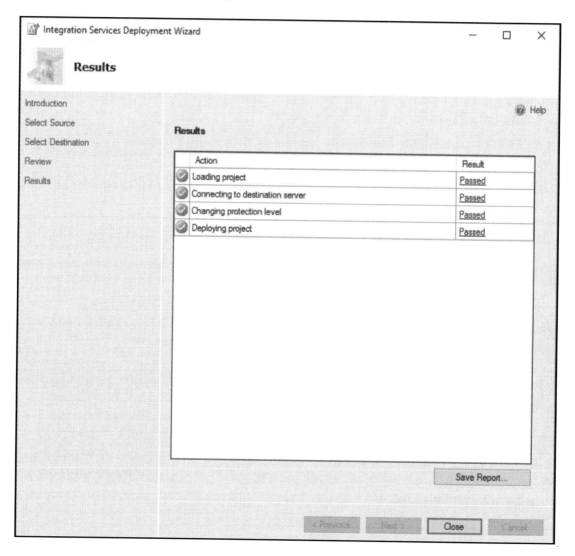

Testing the custom logging level

This part of the recipe will guide you through the steps to execute our sample package on the server (the SSIS Catalog on the local machine). We will use the custom logging level that we created previously in the recipe.

1. Open SSMS and expand the `Integration Services Catalogs` as shown in the following screenshot. Expand the `CustomLogging` folder and navigate to the package as shown in the following screenshot:

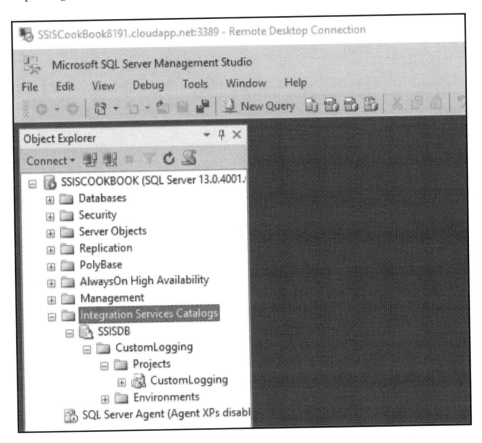

2. When you expand the **SSISDB** catalog, you'll notice that there is a folder called `CustomLogging`; it has been created previously in this recipe when we deployed the SSIS project.

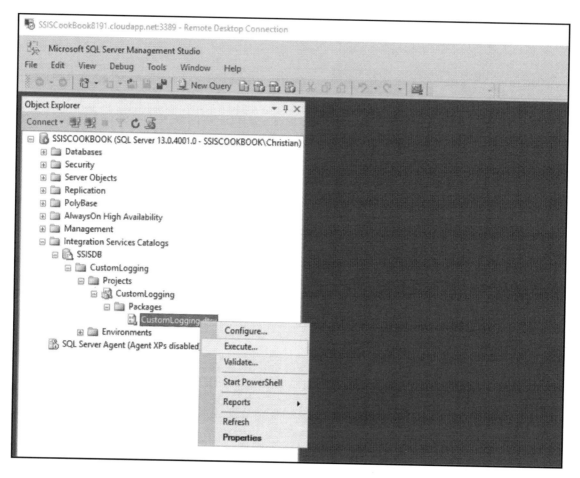

3. Click on the dropdown list near the **Logging level property and select Select customized logging level...** as shown in the following screenshot:

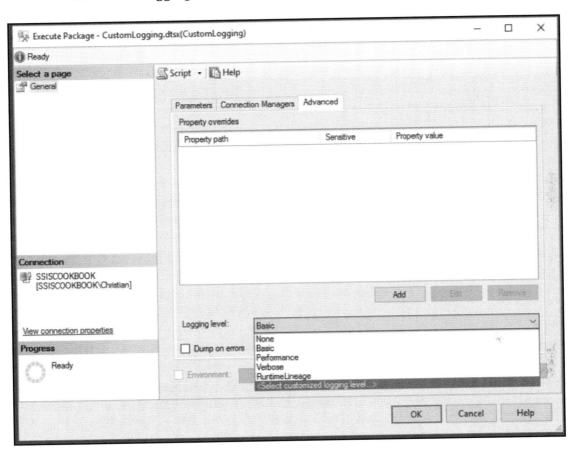

4. Make sure that our custom logging level, **CustomLogging,** is selected and click **OK** as shown in the following screenshot:

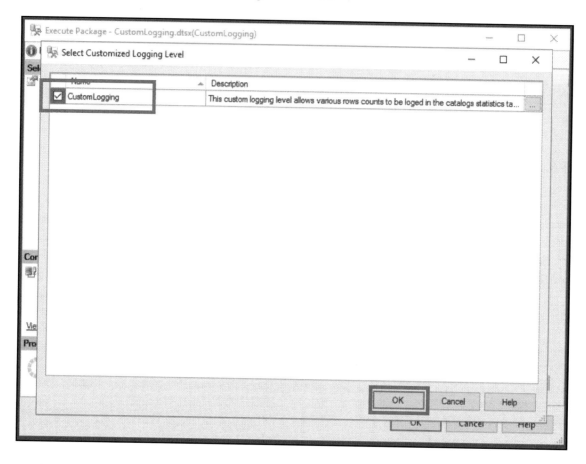

5. Make sure that the **Logging level** property is set to **Customized: CustomLogging** and click on **OK** to close the window and start package execution as in the following screenshot.

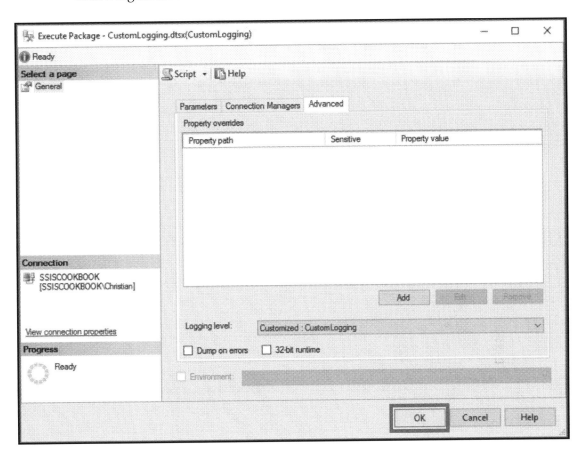

6. The following screen appears. Click on **Yes** to see the execution report.

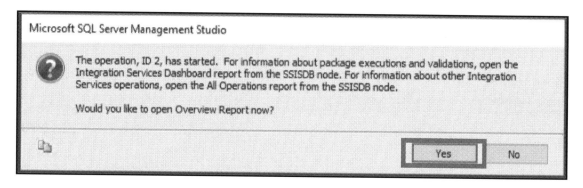

7. The execution report tells us that the package executed properly, as shown in the following screenshot:

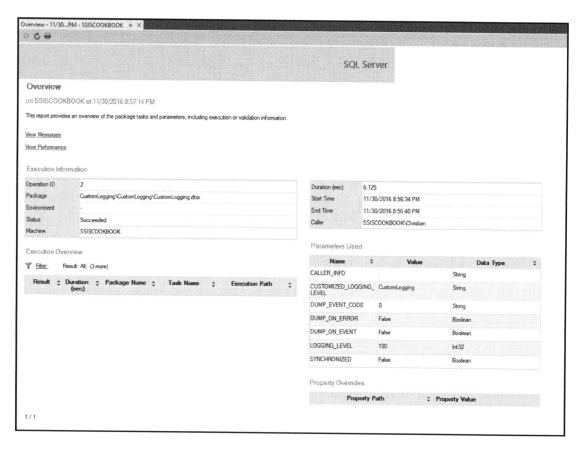

8. Click on **New Query** in SSMS and type the following query. Click on **Execute** or *F5* to execute the query. You should see that the package read and inserted two rows.

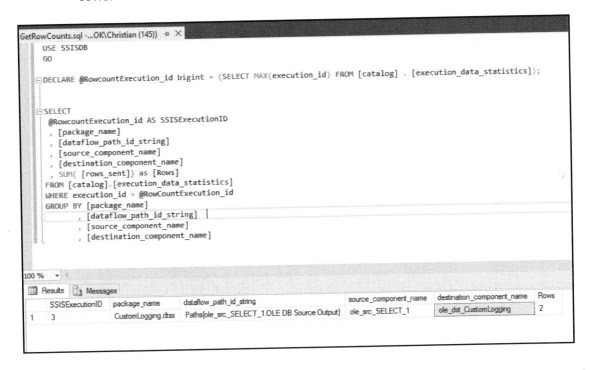

See also

We'll talk more about logging in the next chapter where we'll talk about an SSIS framework. In the meantime, this recipe introduced you to logging in SSIS but there's much more to be covered later in the book.

Azure tasks and transforms

This section will guide you on how to install the Azure Feature Pack that, in turn, will install Azure control flow task and data flow components. The Azure ecosystem is becoming predominant in Microsoft ecosystems and SSIS has not been left over in the past few years.

The Azure Feature Pack is not an SSIS 2016 specific feature. It's also available for SSIS version 2012 and 2014. It's worth mentioning that it appeared in July 2015, a few months before the SSIS 2016 release.

Getting ready

This section assumes that you have installed SQL Server Data Tools 2015.

How to do it...

We'll start SQL Server Data Tools, and open the `CustomLogging` project if not already done:

1. In the SSIS Toolbox, scroll to the **Azure** group. Since the Azure tools are not installed with SSDT, the **Azure** group is disabled in the toolbox. Thee toolss must be downloaded using a separate installer. Click on the **Azure** group to expand it and click on **Download Azure Feature Pack** as shown in the following screenshot:

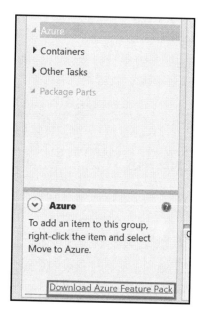

2. Your default browser opens and the **Microsoft SQL Server 2016 Integration Services Feature Pack for Azure** opens. Click on **Download** as shown in the following screenshot:

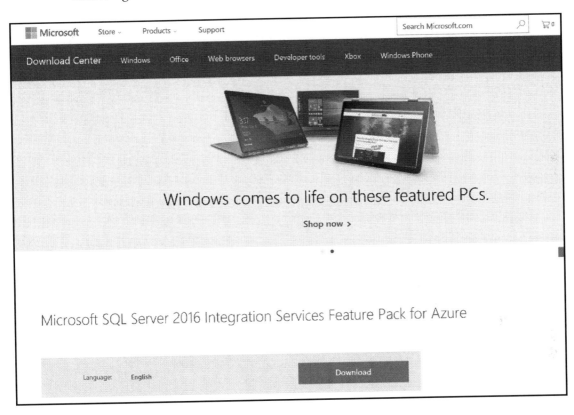

3. From the popup that appears, select both the 32-bit and 64-bit versions. The 32-bit version is necessary for SSIS package development since SSDT is a 32-bit program. Click **Next** as shown in the following screenshot:

4. As shown in the following screenshot, the files are downloaded:

5. Once the download completes, run one the installers downloaded. The following screen appears. In this case, the 32-bit (**x86**) version is being installed. Click **Next** to start the installation process.

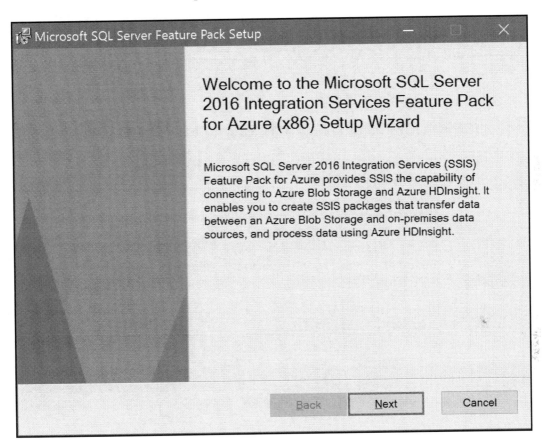

6. As shown in the following screenshot, check the box near **I accept the terms in the License Agreement**and click **Next**. The installation starts.

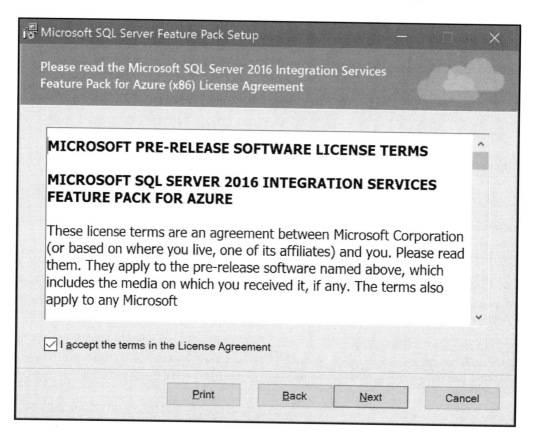

7. The following screen appears once the installation is completed. Click **Finish** to close the screen.

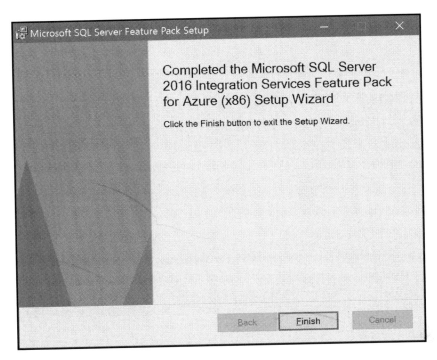

8. Install the other feature pack you downloaded using previous recipe steps in *Custom logging*.

9. If SSDT is opened, close it. Start SSDT again and open the **CustomLogging** project we created in another recipe. In the **Azure** group in the SSIS toolbox, you should now see the Azure tasks as shown in the following screenshot:

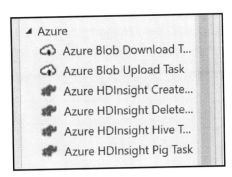

See also

This book contains a dedicated chapter on Azure tasks and transforms in `Chapter 12`, *On-Premises and Azure Big Data Integration*. They will be explained in more detail with useful examples.

Incremental package deployment

Prior to SSIS 2012, packages needed to be deployed one by one. We were usually downloading all packages from the source control software, such as **Team Foundation Server (TFS)**, Visual Source Safe, SVN, and so on. Once downloaded, packages were moved to their destination. At that time, the person who deployed the packages had the choice to overwrite or skip existing packages. Usually, they overwrote all the packages since they were using the source control.

For those who didn't use the source control, they had all the necessary flexibility to deploy what needed to be deployed. Usually, they were keeping a backup somewhere on a file share of all packages. The reason why they chose what to deploy was mainly because they had doubts about the consistency of the packages in the file share. They were simply not sure of the state of the packages because they were using a manual process to maintain their solution. The source control software helps a lot with this. We have the possibility to compare versions between packages committed in the source control, and when and who pushed the package, among other benefits.

Enter SSIS 2012 with Project Deployment. The only way to deploy a package was to deploy the entire project, and thus, all packages in it. If the source control was in place to manage the package code, this was barely an issue. But, not everybody is using the source control and Microsoft recognized it. With SSIS 2016, we can now deploy part of your project packages. You're not forced to deploy the entire project.

Getting ready

This recipe assumes that you have created and deployed the **CustomLogging** recipe.

How to do it...

1. With the **CustomLogging** project opened, right-click on the
   `CustomLogging.dtsx` package and select **Copy** as shown in the following
   screenshot:

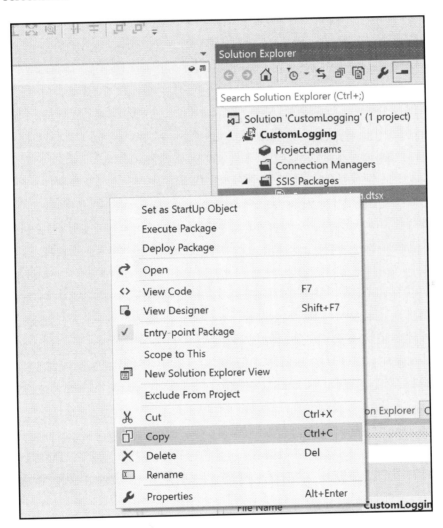

2. Now, right-click on the `SSIS Packages` folder and select **Paste** as shown in the following screenshot:

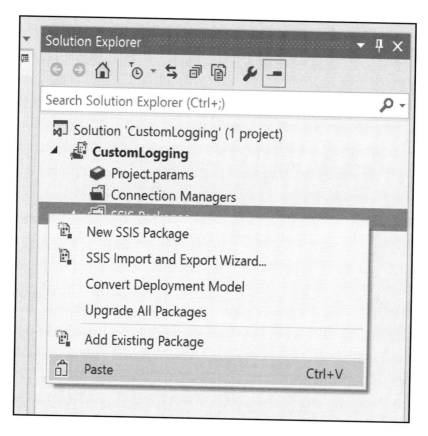

3. A copy of the package is created and named `CustomLogging 1.dtsx` as shown in the following screenshot:

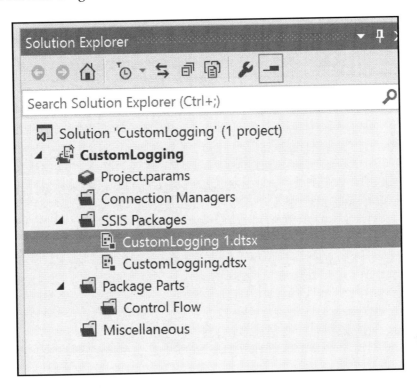

4. Right-click on the newly created package, `CustomLogging 1.dtsx`, and **select Deploy Package** from the menu as shown in the following screenshot:

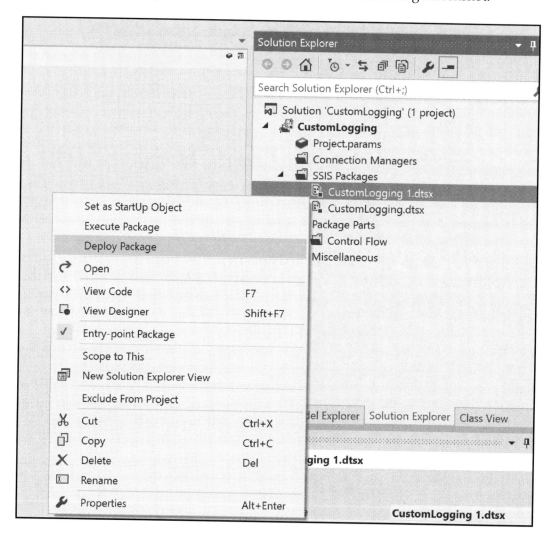

5. As shown in the following screenshot, the **Server name** is already selected since we've deployed the project there before. It can be changed if necessary. The **Path** is where the deployed package will be located; the `SSISDB/CustomLogging/CustomLogging` folder in the SSIS Catalog. Click **Next** to advance to the next step.

6. Now we are at the **Review** screen as shown in the following screenshot.

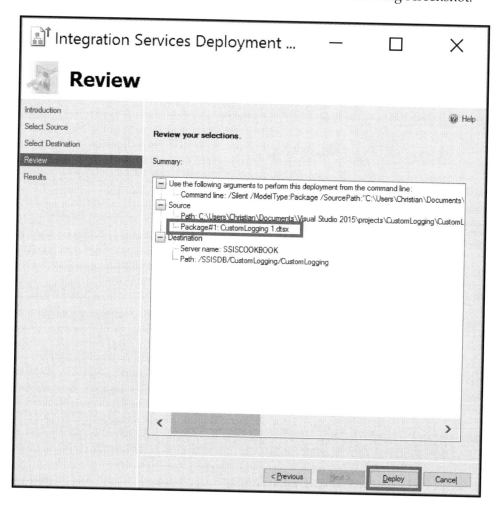

Notice that the package to be deployed is CustomLogging 1.dtsx. It is tagged as **Package#1** since we might have selected multiple packages to deploy. Click **Deploy** to proceed to the deployment.

7. If everything goes well, you should get a screen like the following screenshot meaning that the package has been successfully deployed. Click on **Close** to get rid of it.

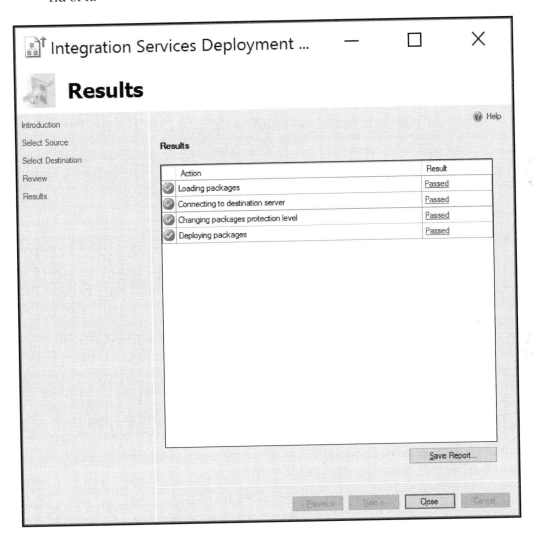

8. Now, go to SSMS and open the SSIS Catalog as shown in the following screenshot. You will see that the package has been deployed. We won't execute it for now as we only wanted to demonstrate how single package deployment works.

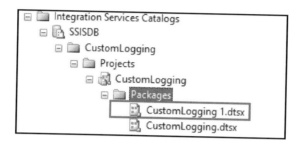

There's more...

The capability to deploy individual packages is possible with SSIS 2016 only. If we have tried to deploy to a SSIS Catalog of a previous version of SSIS (2012-2014), the deployment would have failed. So, to reinforce the point here, SSDT can show you the option that you can deploy individual packages but you'll need SSIS 2016 to be able to use it.

Multiple version support

Since its inception, SSIS designer never supported backward compatibility. For example, if you developed a package in SSIS 2014 and tried to deploy it in a SSIS 2012 catalog, you would not be able to do it. Or worse, if you opened a package developed with SSIS 2012 with a SSDT that was used with SSIS 2014, the package was upgraded. When another developer tried to open it with SSDT used for SSIS 2012, he/she was not able to do it. The package was upgraded, period.

With SSIS 2016, SSDT had the following enhancements:

- Backward compatibility to prior SSIS versions down to SSIS 2012.
- Unified SSDT: as we'll see later in the book, SSDT can be used for BI components development as well as database development. Prior to SSDT for Visual Studio 2015, it was confusing whether we were using SSDT-BI for BI development or SSDT-SQL for database development.

Getting ready

This recipe assumes that you have created an SSIS project in SSDT. We'll be using the CustomLogging SSIS project developed in a previous recipe in this chapter.

How to do it...

1. With SSDT and **CustomLogging** SSIS project opened, right-click on the project and select **Properties** as shown in the following screenshot:

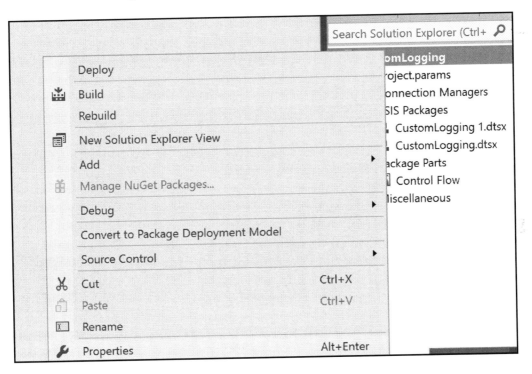

2. The **CustomLogging Property Pages** dialog box opens. Select **Configuration Properties** and you'll notice a drop-down list near the property **TargetServerVersion**. In our case, the selected version is **SQL Server 2016**. You'll notice that you can select prior versions as shown in the following screenshot. Click on **OK** to close this window.

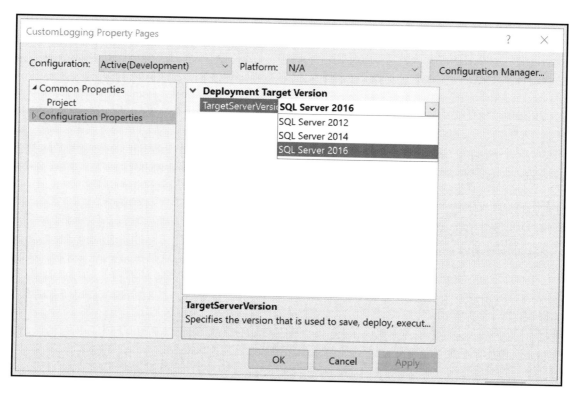

There's more...

This simple recipe shows you how easily we can now use SSDT for Visual Studio 2015 with prior SSIS versions. If you open an existing SSIS project that is developed in the SQL Server 2012 or 2014 SSDT version, the designer (SSDT) will be smart enough to select the right target version (2012 or 2014) without upgrading your project or packages.

The default Target Server version is SQL Server 2016. If you created your SSIS project without setting this property and try to deploy it on a prior version to 2016, the deployment will fail. Also, if you change this property from, for example, SQL Server 2016 down to SQL Server 2014 and your package uses new SSIS functionality, the project won't build and therefore you will not be able to deploy it.

Error column name

This recipe will show you a new neat feature of SSIS, which is the error column name. We could achieve something similar before SSIS 2016 but it involves using a script component and it is difficult to reuse this kind of transform. Although we can copy and paste a script component from one package to another, every time we do so, we must change the input columns and recompile the script. It's not very difficult but it's a tedious task. The error column name native implementation in SSIS 2016 is very welcome.

Getting ready

This recipe assumes that you have created the **CustomLogging** project and package from previous recipe.

How to do it...

1. In the `CustomLogging.dstx` package, navigate to the `dft_dbo_CustomLogging` by double-clicking on the Data Flow task. Click on the path (blue arrow) between the `ole_src_SELECT_1`and the `ole_dst_dbo_CustomLogging` transform to select it. Right-click on it and select **Delete** to delete it.

2. Drag and drop a derived column transform from the SSIS Toolbox onto the data flow. Link it to the `ole_src_SELECT_1` and double-click on it to open the derived column transformation. As shown in the following screenshot, do the following:

   - **Derived Column Name**: **DateToConvert**
   - **Derived Column**: leave it as **<Add as new column>**
   - **Expression**: Type `1600-01-00`. This is not a valid date; it will cause an error and that's precisely what we want.

3. Click on **OK** when finished.

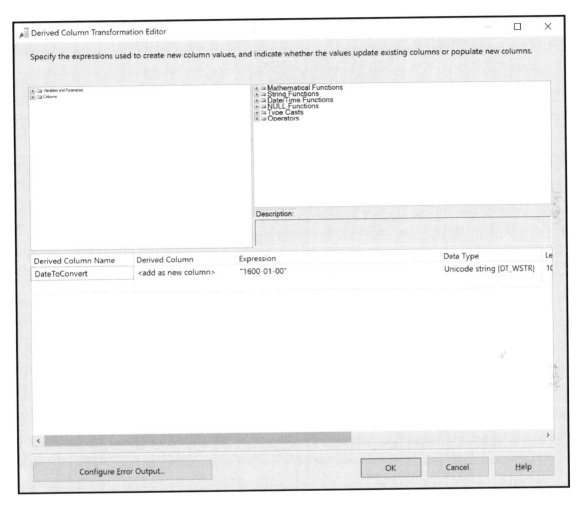

4. Rename the derived column `der_AddDate`.

5. Now, drag and drop a data conversion transform onto the dataflow task. Attach it to the `der_AddDate` derived column created previously and double-click on it to open the **Data Conversion Transformation Editor**. Enter the values as shown in the following screenshot:

- **Input Column**: Check the column **DateToConvert** in the Available Input Columns.
- **Output Alias**: Change it to **DateConverted**.
- **Data Type**: Select **date [DT_DATE]** from the drop-down list.

It is also shown in the following screenshot:

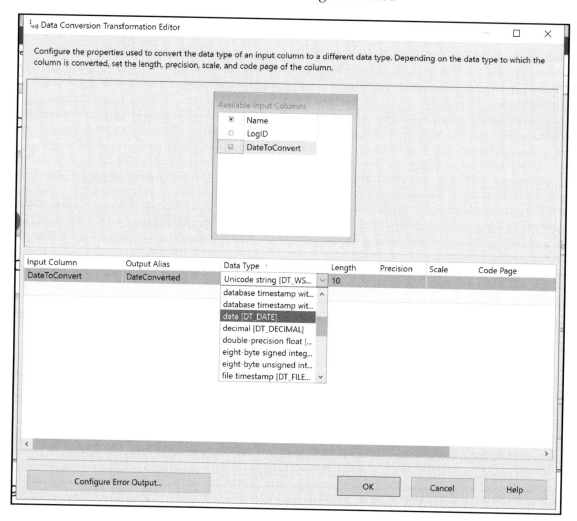

6. The **Data Conversion Transformation Editor** should now look like the following screenshot. Click on the **Configure Error Output...** button.

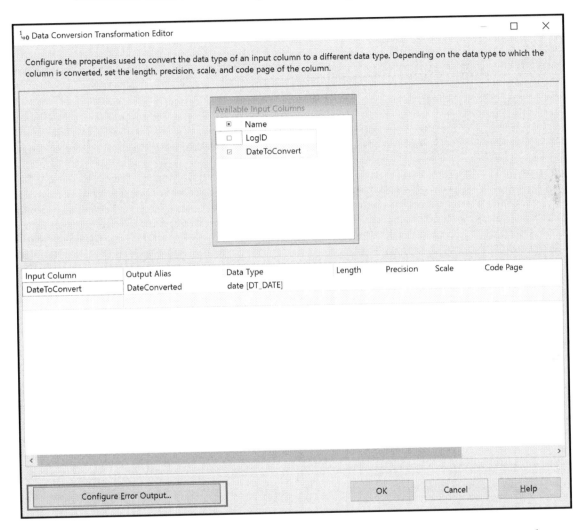

7. You will get a screen like the following screenshot. By default, the **Error** and **Truncation** errors will fail the component.
    1. Select both columns and from the drop-down list near **Set this value to select cells**, select **Redirect row**. Click **Apply**.
    2. You should now see that both column values are now set to **Redirect row**.

3. Click **OK** to close the editor and rename the transform as
   `dcnv_DateConverted`.

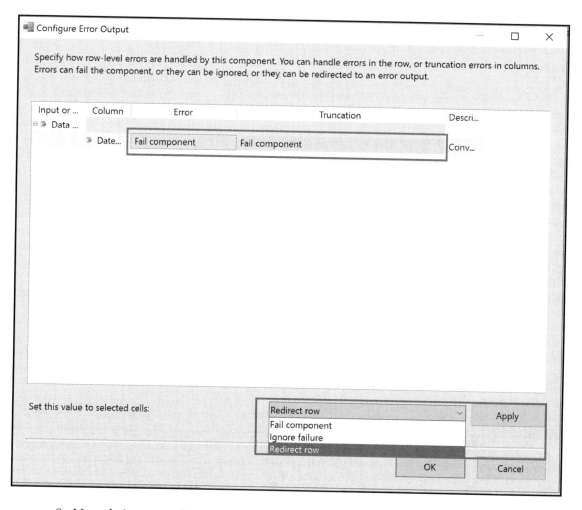

8. Now, bring an audit transform from other transforms onto the dataflow task. The
   following steps detail what's in the following screenshot:
   1. Attach the **Data Conversion Error Output** (red path or arrow) to it.

2. Right-click on the error path and **select Enable Data Viewer** from the menu that appears.

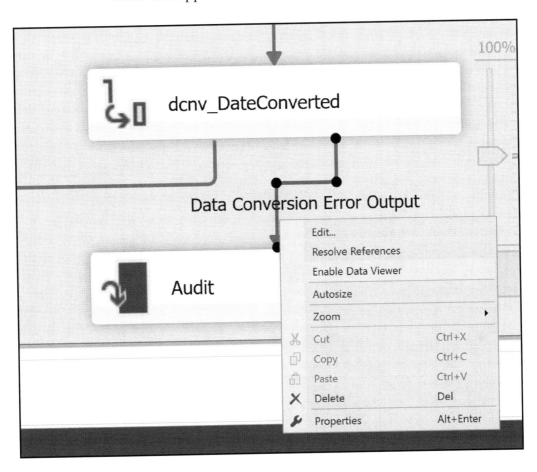

As we did before in the *Customized logging level* recipe, select all the transforms and click on **Make Same Width** from the **Layout** toolbar. From the **Format** menu, select **Format Auto Layout à Diagram** to format the data flow task objects properly.

9. Your data flow task should look like the following screenshot. Now, right-click anywhere in the background of the data flow task and select **Execute Task** from the menu.

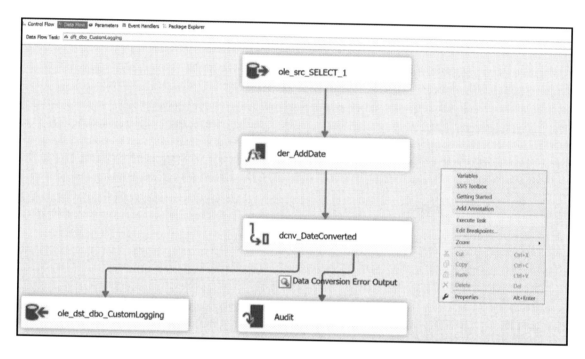

10. You should see a data viewer like the following screenshot:

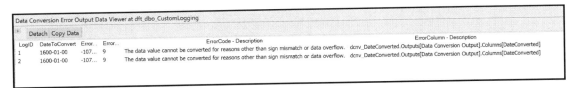

It is explain in as follows:

- The **DateToConvert** is the column we tried to convert.
- The second column is the **ErrorCode**, an internal code to SSIS.
- The third column is the **ErrorColumn** which is a lineage ID that SSIS assigns to all columns in the data flow task.
- **The ErrorCode - Description** column gives us the reason for the error.
- **The ErrorColumn - Description** gives us the column that failed to be converted (**DateConverted**).

Control Flow templates

Control Flow templates are an addition to SSIS 2016 that will surely be promising...in the future. For now, Microsoft put the foundation of something that looks very interesting.

If there's one thing missing with SSIS it is the reusability of custom components without doing .NET code. We'll see how to achieve custom task and transforms later in this book using .NET and you'll see that it's tedious to achieve even for something simple. Let's say that we would like to create a truncated table task; that is, a task that we would use to solely erase a table's content. This task would then appear in the SSIS toolbox and be available to all packages in your projects. This recipe is exactly what we will do using Control Flow templates.

Getting ready

This recipe assumes that you have done all previous recipes in this chapter or you have your own SSIS project open.

How to do it...

1. In SSDT, with your project open, right-click on the `Control Flow` folder in the *Package Parts* section of the solution explorer. As shown in the following screenshot, select **New Control Flow Package Part** from the contextual menu. Rename it `Chapter2Part.dtsxp`.

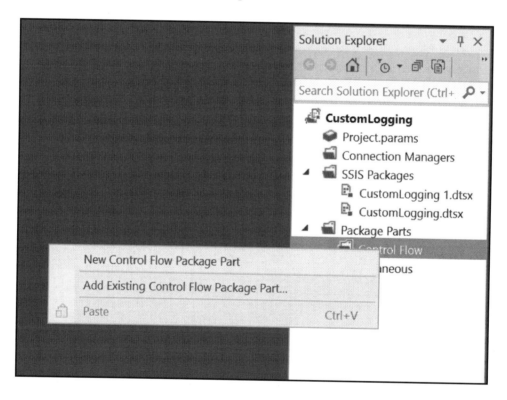

2. Drag and drop an **Execute SQL** task on it:

    1. Rename it `sql_Truncate_dbo_CustomLogging`.

    2. Click anywhere in the **Control Flow**. Set its description property to **This is a simple template that is meant to truncate the table [dbo].[CustomLogging]**.

    3. As shown in the following screenshot, right-click in the Connection Managers area and choose **New OLE DB Connection...** from the menu that appears:

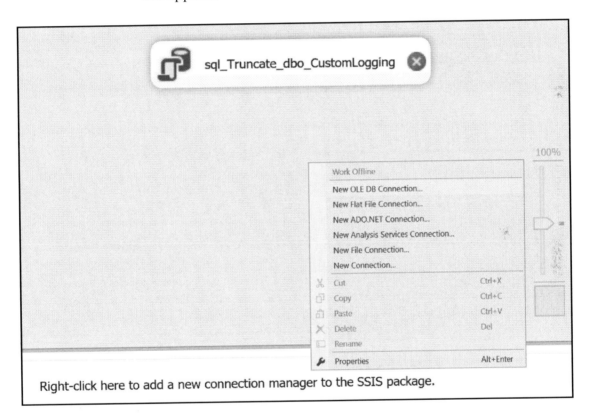

Right-click here to add a new connection manager to the SSIS package.

3. As shown in the following screenshot, select the existing connection (**SSISCOOKBOOK\TestCustomLogging** in this case) in the top left or create a new one by clicking on **NEW....** Click on **OK** when done to close the **Configure OLE DB Connection Manager** window.

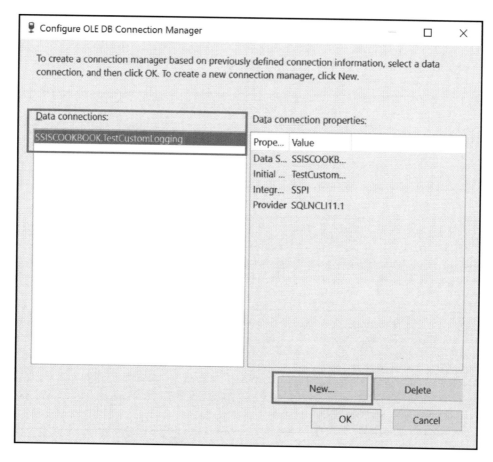

4. Double-click on the `sql_Truncate_dbo_CustomLogging` task to open the **Execute SQL Task Editor**. Set the properties in the **SQL Statement** section as follow:

  - **ConnectionType**: OLE DB, the default value
  - **Connection**: Set it to the connection manager created in the previous step.

- **SQLSourceType**: Leave the default value, **Direct input** type the following SQL DML statement in the **SQL Statement** property:

```
TRUNCATE TABLE [dbo].[CustomLogging];
```

It is also shown in the following screenshot:

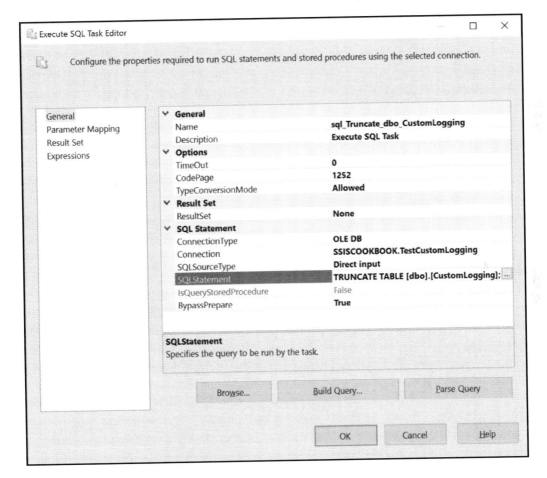

5. Save and close the `Chapter2Part.dtsxp` package part.

6. Now, open the `CustomLogging` package from the solution explorer. As shown in the following screenshot, there is now a new component in the *Package Parts* section of the **SSIS Toolbox**: the **Chapter2Part** created in the previous steps. Also, notice the description below the *Package Parts* section. This is the one that we assigned at the **Control Flow** level of the package part when it was created.

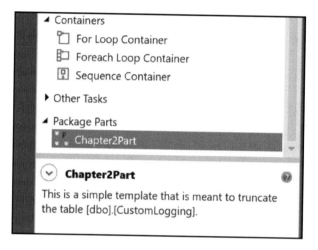

7. Drag and drop a **Chapter2Part** onto the **Control Flow** of the `CustomLogging` package. Now to get the same as in the following screenshot:

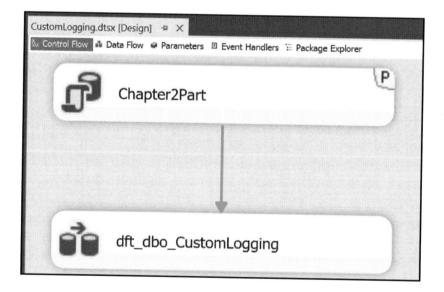

Execute the following steps:

1. Connect it to the **dft_dbo_CustomLogging** data flow task.
2. Select all **Control Flow** components
3. In the **Layout** toolbar, click Make Same Size
4. From the Format menu, select **Auto Layout Diagram** to properly align the tasks
5. Execute the package to make sure that the package part is properly working and stop the package execution when done.
6. Double-click on the **Chapter2Part** to view its properties as shown in the following screenshot. Go to the **Connection Managers** tab. Locate the **ConnectionString** property as highlighted in the screenshot. Notice that it has a fixed value. This is the biggest limitation of these parts; there is no way for now to alter any of the property at runtime. We cannot use package configurations or parameters to alter these values dynamically as we can with regular tasks.

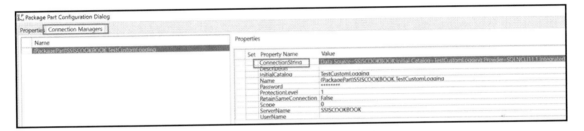

Key Components of a Modern ETL Solution

9

This chapter will cover the following recipes:

- Installing the sample solution
- Deploying the source database with its data
- Deploying the target database
- SSIS projects
- ETL framework

Introduction

Now, let's go for the real stuff! This chapter will cover many topics that will lay out the foundations of a simple and effective ETL solution. Over the years, I have seen many SSIS implementations and one of the goals of this chapter is to give the readers the following:

- A simple but effective SSIS framework
- SSIS development best practices
- New data source integrations

All remaining chapters assume that we want to load a data warehouse that is a star schema with its staging area.

The source (operational) database used is `AdventureWorksLT`, an old well-known database. The following diagram describes the source database that we're going to use:

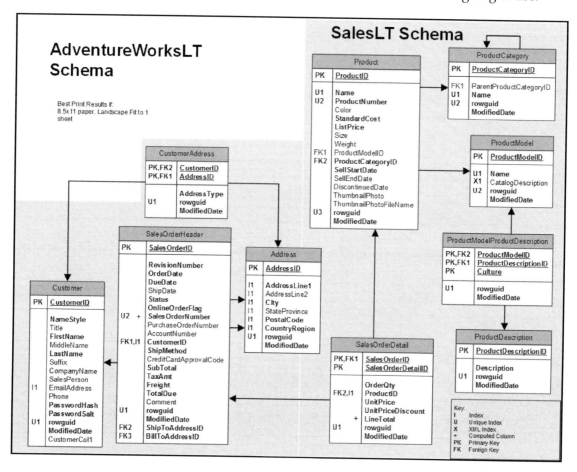

From this database, we'll insert data in a staging area and finally into a data warehouse. The staging area and the data warehouse will be separated in schemas in a database that we'll manage using SSDT.

The following diagram is the representation that describes the staging schema of the `AdventureWorksLTDW` database:

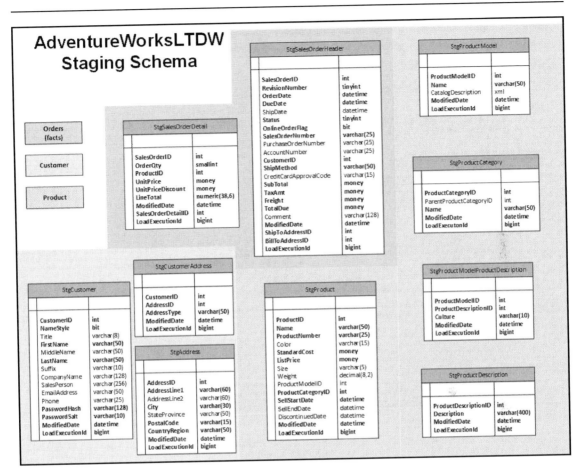

Not all tables are copied in the staging area and three sections have been identified:

- **Orders**: These tables contain order information as well as dates related information. In the data warehouse section, these sections have their own tables.
- **Customer**: These tables contain information related to a customer and their addresses. In the data warehouse, these tables are grouped.
- **Product**: These tables contain the product information such as model, description in multiple languages, and so on. Like customer data, these tables are grouped in the data warehouse.

Once in the staging area, the data will be copied into a star schema database representation. The tables are in the same database, but have a separate schema called DW. The following diagram shows the DW tables:

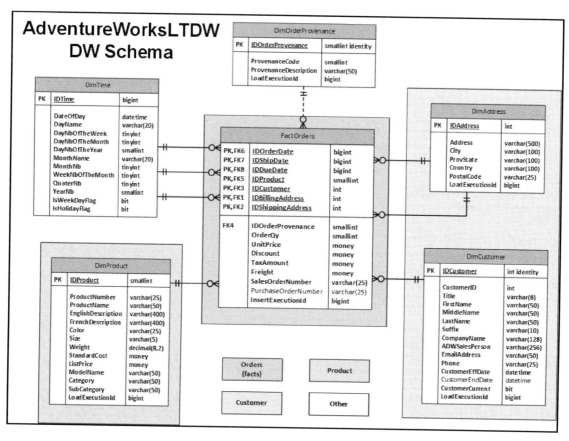

The goal of the data warehouse is to ease data consumptions. It's easy to understand by most users and data is categorized into areas (tables) that represent the subjects that the end users will base their analysis on.

The customer information has been regrouped into two tables, `DimCustomer` and `DimAddress`. The `DimAddress` table has two links to the fact table. These relationships represent the multiple addresses, two in our case: the billing and shipping address of the customer.

The product information has been flattened into one dimension: `DimProduct`. Although the base model allowed for more than one language when it comes to the product descriptions, only two are retained in the dimension: French and English - `EnglishDesctiption` and `FrenchDescription`.

The orders tables have been merged into one fact table: `FactOrders`. The `DimTime` dimension has been added to allow better querying of the orders using various dates: order, shipped, and due dates. The `SalesOrderNumber` and `PurchaseOrderNumber` are considered derived dimensions and stay in the fact table. We don't have enough information that can be derived from these columns and they are strongly tied to the facts.

The remaining dimension, `DimOrderProvenance`, has no source in the `AdventureWorksLT` operational database. It has been added and is managed by Master Data Services, another service that comes with SQL Server 2016 Developer Edition. We'll talk about this service and this dimension later in this book.

In the next few recipes, we'll deploy these databases and the ETL's (SSIS packages) that load these tables.

Installing the sample solution

This section will walk you through the deployment of the databases contained in the sample solution.

Getting ready

This section assumes that you have downloaded the solution files.

How to do it...

1. We'll first create a folder that will hold the solution files. In our case, we created a folder called `C:\Projects\SSISCookbook` and we uncompressed the solution file in it, as shown in the following screenshot:

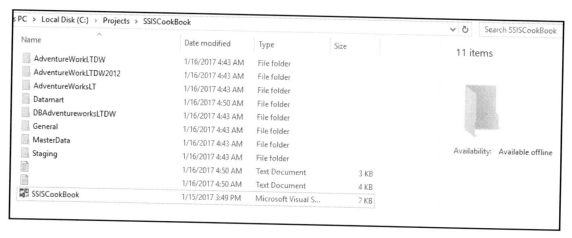

2. Now, we open the solution in Visual Studio by double-clicking on the `SSISCookBook` solution file, as highlighted in the preceding screenshot.

3. The solution opens and you will see its projects, as shown in the following screenshot:

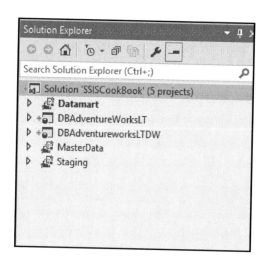

The following point will describe the projects that are shown in the **Solution Explorer** in SQL Server Data Tools (Visual Studio):

- `DB.AdventureWorksLT`: This is an SQL Server database project that contains the `AdventureWorksLT` database objects.
- `DB.AdventureWorksLTDW`: This is the SQL Server database project that contains the staging, DW, the framework database objects. We'll talk about the framework in a subsequent recipe.
- `ETL.DW`: This is an SSIS project that fills the tables in the DW schema.
- `ETL.MasterData`: This is an SSIS project that connects to Master Data Services and loads the `DW.DimOrderProvenance` table in the `AdventureWorksDW` database.
- `ETL.Staging`: This is an SSIS project that loads the tables in the staging schema in the `AdventureWorksDW` database.

There's more...

The solution is not completed yet. We'll add new projects as we move forward in the chapter's recipes.

Deploying the source database with its data

The first thing we have to do now is to deploy the SQL Server database, which are `AdventureWorksLT` and `AdventureWorksLTDW`.

Getting ready

This section requires you to have copied the sample solution on your PC and opened the `SSISCookBook.sln` solution file.

How to do it...

1. In SQL Server Data Tools (Visual Studio), right-click on the
   DB.AdventureWorksLT project and select **Publish...**, as shown in the following
   screenshot:

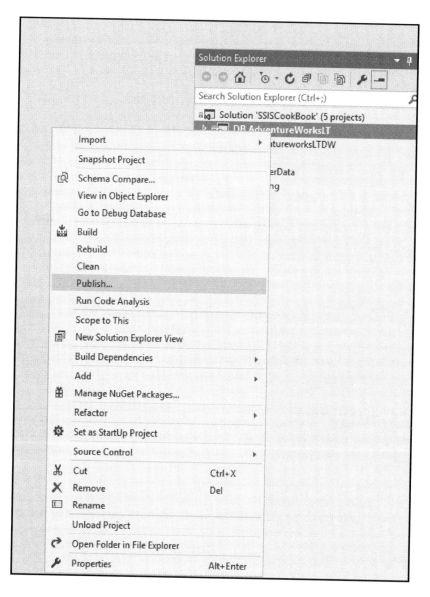

2. The following screen appears; click on the **Edit...** button to create a connection string to our local SQL Server instance:

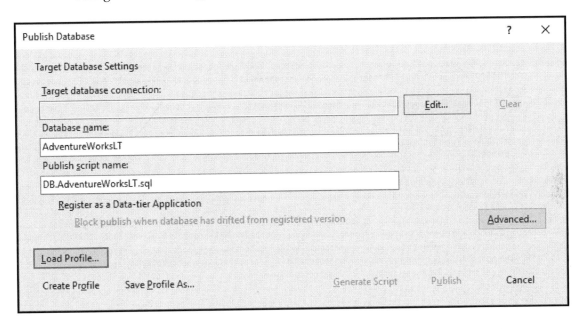

3. As shown in the following screenshot, clicking on the **Browse** tab brings up a screen where we can choose the SQL Server instance location. In our case, we'll choose `Local`. Expand the `Local` label and choose your SQL Server instance, in our case `SSISCOOKBOOK`. The **Server Name** textbox will display the server you chose. Click **OK** to return to the previous screen.

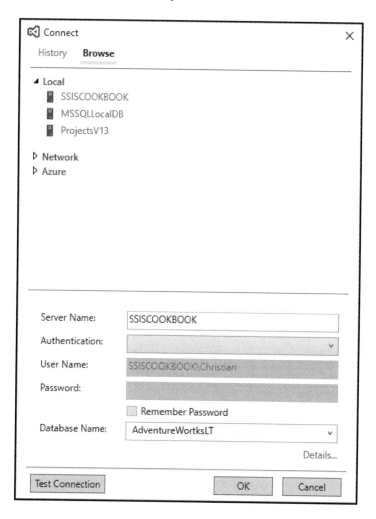

4. Back in the **Publish Database** screen, click on the **Advanced...** button, and the following screen appears. This screen allows us to manage many options when we deploy a database. Check the **Always re-create database** option and click on **OK** to close the screen.

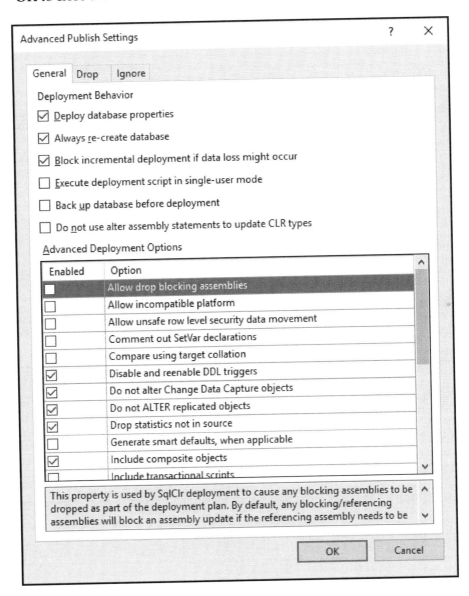

5. Back in the **Publish Database** screen, fill the textboxes as follows:
   - **Database name**: AdventureWorksLT
   - **Publish script name**: DB.AdventureWorksLT.sql

   It is also shown in the following screenshot:

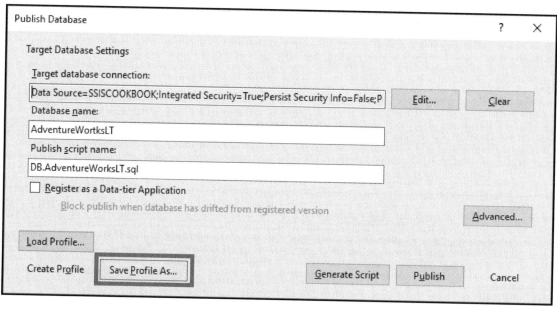

6. Click on the **Save Profile As...** button.
7. We're going to save these settings as a publish profile for this database project. That will allow us to reuse it in the future without having to repeat the preceding steps. Fill in the filename as shown in the following screenshot. It will create a publish profile in the project. As shown in the following screenshot, name the publish profile DB.AdventureWorksLT and click on **Save**.

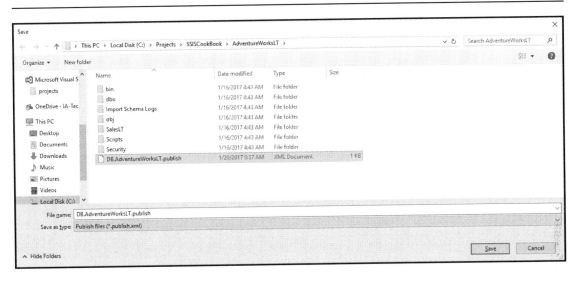

8. Back in the **Publish Database** window, click the **Publish** button as shown in the following screenshot. The **Generate Script** option is used when we want to only create a deployment script without deploying the database immediately. A good example of this is when we create a script to handle it to a DBA that will be responsible for the database deployment.

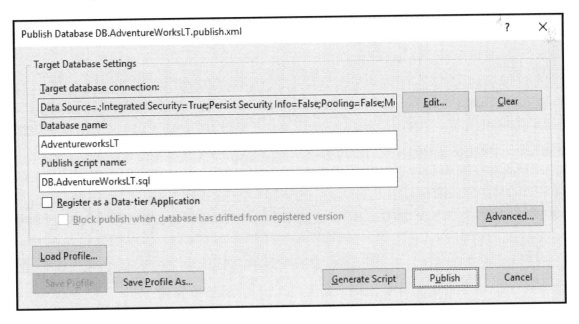

9. The **Data Tools Operations** window opens and displays the steps required that are executed to deploy the database. You should get something very similar to the following screenshot:

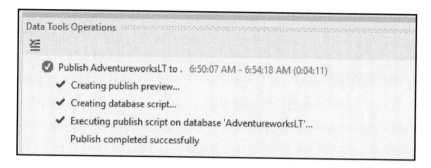

10. Start **SQL Server Management Studio (SSMS)** and look for the AdventureWorksLT database in the object explorer, as shown in the following screenshot:

11. Right-click on any table and choose **Select Top 1000 Rows**, as shown in the following screenshot:

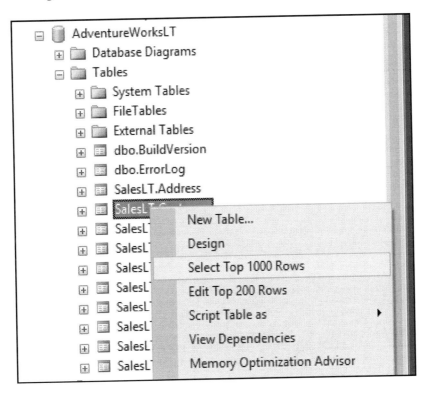

12. This command will generate an SQL statement and execute it. The right pane will show that the table has data, as shown in the following screenshot:

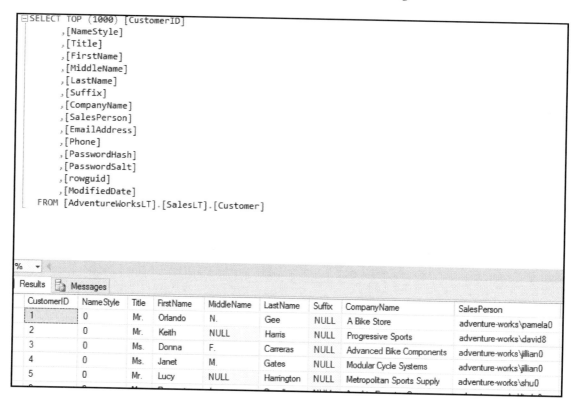

There's more...

Usually, SSDT database projects only create empty database shells when we select the option that always recreates the database. The reason why we have data in the newly deployed database is because we added a script to the database project, as shown in the following screenshot (AdventureWorksLTData.sql):

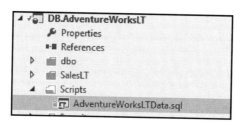

This file contains `INSERT` statements that load the different tables. You can glimpse its content in the following screenshot:

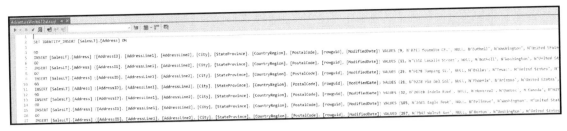

This SQL file is called via a special script in SSDT: a post deployment script. To create it, we simply need to add a script in the project, as shown in the following screenshot. This dialog box appears when we right-click on a folder and select **Add | New | Script**.

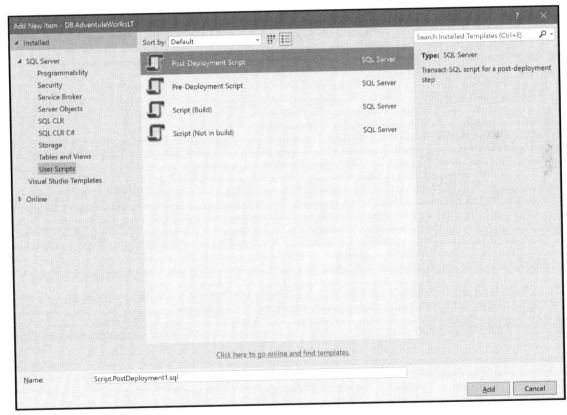

Several scripts are available. The following list describes them and how they can be used:

- **Post-deployment script**: This script is executed after all the database objects have been deployed. This is what we've used to load the `AdventureWorksLT` database tables.
- **Pre-deployment script**: This script is executed before the database objects are created. It might be used to back up certain data from tables or views before altering a table structure.
- **Script (build)**: These scripts are SQLCMD scripts that are parsed for errors by SSDT when it builds the database project.
- **Script (not in build)**: These scripts are not included in the build, meaning that their content is not validated by SSDT when the project is built, only their existence will be checked, that is, that the scripts really exist. There can be any SQL in these scripts. It's the developer's responsibility to make sure that the SQL is valid inside the scripts. Otherwise, the script will throw an error at deployment. An example of a script not in build is `ADVentureWorksLTData.sql`.

The following screenshot shows the post deployment script used in the `DB.AdventureWorksLT` project:

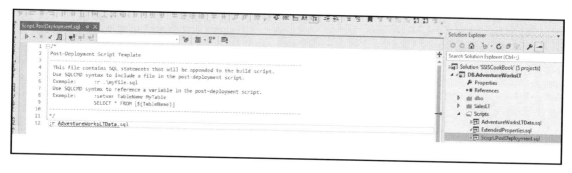

The command starts with `:r`, which is an SQL command that tells SQL Server to simply run the file following command, in our case, `AdventureWorksLTData.sql`.

Deploying the target database

We'll now deploy the data warehouse database that is called `AdventureWorksLTDW2016`.

Getting ready

This recipe assumes that you have access to the sample solution that is available for this book and you have read and executed all the steps to deploy the source database.

How to do it...

The steps will be essentially similar to the ones used to deploy the source database. Since we explained most of the steps previously, this recipe will be more concise:

1. The `DB.AdventureworksLTDW` project contains the following schemas:
   - `Cube`: This contains specific database objects, mainly views that can be used by an SSAS cube.
   - `dbo`: This the default schema.
   - `DW`: This folder contains database objects that belong to the `DW` schema, that is, the data warehouse star schema objects.
   - `Scripts`: This is a folder that holds pre or post-deployment scripts, as well as utility scripts.
   - `Staging`: This folder contains database objects used by the `Staging` schema.
   - `SystemLog`: This folder contains database objects used by the SSIS framework. We'll talk about it in a section later in this book.

   It is also shown in the following screenshot:

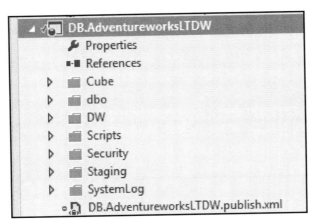

2. Right-click on the `DB.AdventureWorksLTDW` project in the solution and select **Publish...** as shown in the following screenshot:

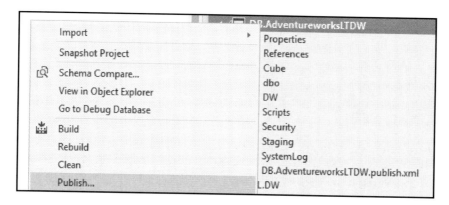

3. The **Publish Database** window appears. Click on **Load Profile...** and select the `DB.AdventureWorks2016.publish.publish` profile from the **Publish Settings** window that appears. Click on **Open,** as shown in the following screenshot:

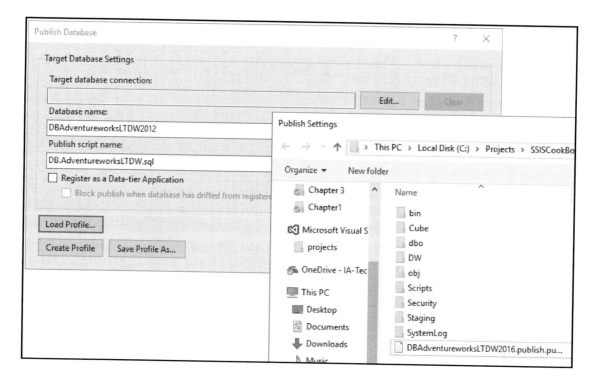

4. Back in the **Publish Database** window, click on **Publish** to deploy the database, as shown in the following screenshot:

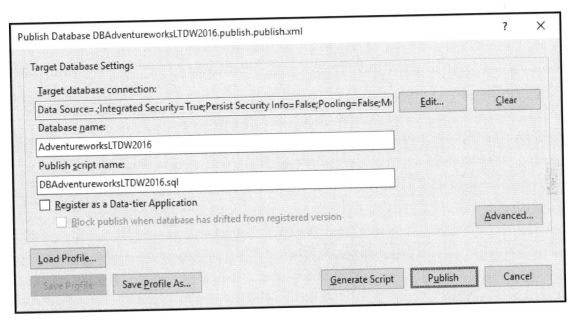

5. The database starts deploying. You can see its progress in the **Data Tools Operations** window, located at the bottom of the screen. It should look like the following screenshot:

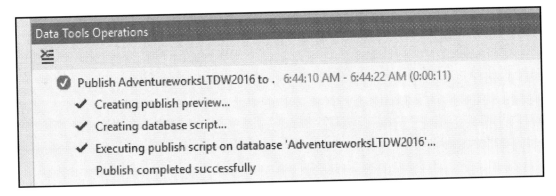

6. Once the deployment has completed, open SSMS and verify that
   `AdventureWorksLTDW2016` is in the object explorer, as shown in the following
   screenshot:

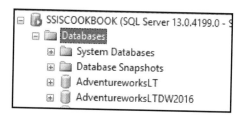

7. Expand the database by clicking on the + sign. You will see that all database
   objects are published successfully, as shown in the following screenshot:

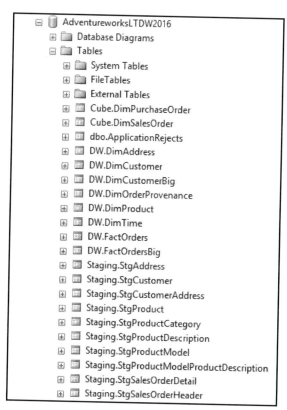

8. As with the `AdventureWorksLT` database, there are some tables that contain data: the dimensions. There's a post-deployment script that calls another not in build script: `DimensionsUnknownMembers.sql`. This script contains SQL `INSERT` statements, one for each table. These SQL statements insert one entry in the dimensions with a `-1` value for the primary key column, `N/A` for the codes, and `Not available` for longer text entries. They are referred to as unknown members and we'll talk about them in a later chapter of this book covering data warehouse loads.

9. If you right-click on a dimension table -- they're all prefixed with `Dim`.

SSIS projects

This section will now focus on the SSIS projects that move the data from various locations. There are several SSIS projects in the solution:

- `ETL.Staging`: This contains SSIS packages that transfer data from `AdventreWorksLT` to the `Staging` schema in `AdventureWorksLTDW2016`
- `ETL.DW`: This contains packages that transfer and transform data from the `Staging` schema to the `DW` schema in `AdventureWorksLTDW2016`

We'll have recipes in this section that will explain how the packages are structured and how we'll deploy and run them to load data from the source database to the data warehouse.

There are two types of SSIS packages in the projects:

- Entry-point packages: These packages orchestrate the **Extract, Transform, and Load (ETL)** flow of the solution. It's in these packages that other packages call and in what order they are called. In the solution, there's only one entry-point package per project.

- Regular (child) packages: These packages are doing the ETL work, that is, extracting the data from the source system and loading it in the destination tables. There is one child package for each destination table. For example, the `StgAddress.dtsx` package will only load the `AdventureWorksLTDW2016.Staging.StgAddress` table. Doing so gives better flexibility in terms of orchestration of packages in the entry-point packages. As we will see later, we can make good use of parallelism since our child package does only one task. It also makes the naming of the packages more straightforward: we give them the same name as the destination table that they load.

This project contains packages that load the `Staging` schema of the `AdventreWorksLTDW2016` database. The following screenshot shows the structure of the project:

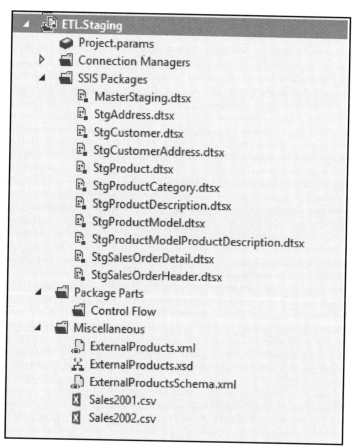

In project deployment mode, the following sections are present in the project:

- `Project.params`: This project artifact contains parameters that are passed by the calling program or job of any of the packages in the project. Most of the time, a project's connection manager's connection strings are part of it. The following screenshot shows a glimpse of the `ETL.Staging` project parameters:

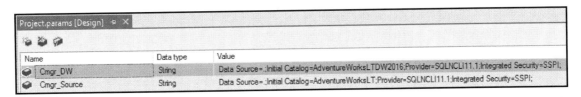

- `Connection Managers`: The project's level connection managers are available to all packages in the project. In `ETL.Staging`, the following project's connection managers have been created:
  - cmgr_DW: Connection to the `AdventureWorksLTDW2016` database
  - cmgr_MDS_DB: Connection to the Master Data Services database
  - cmgr_Source: Connection to the source database `AdventureWorksLT`

  It is also shown in the following screenshot:

- `SSIS Packages`: This folder contains all the packages necessary to load the `Staging` schema of the `ADVentureWorksLTDW2016` database. As stated previously, there's one package per table loaded, as shown in the following screenshot:

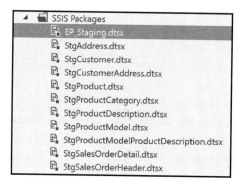

- As shown in the following screenshot, the package called `EP_Staging.dtsx` is the main package of the project. It is tagged as **Entry-point Package**. We'll see later what it does when the project will be deployed. So `EP` stands for entry-point in that case. There's usually one entry-point package per project.

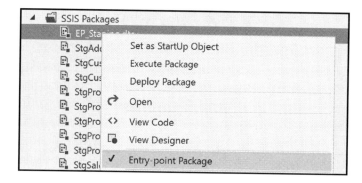

We'll now deploy the project and load the staging tables from the sources.

Getting ready

This recipe assumes that you have access to the companion solution and have the `ETL.Staging` SSIS project handy.

How to do it...

1. From SSDT, right-click on the ETL.Staging project and choose **Deploy** from the contextual menu, as shown in the following screenshot:

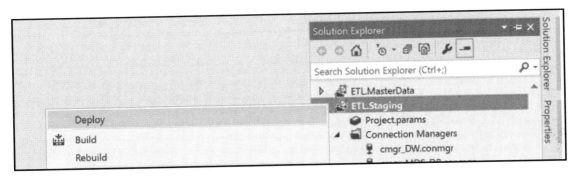

2. From the **Integration Services Deployment Wizard**, create SSISCookBookSolution, as shown in the following screenshot:

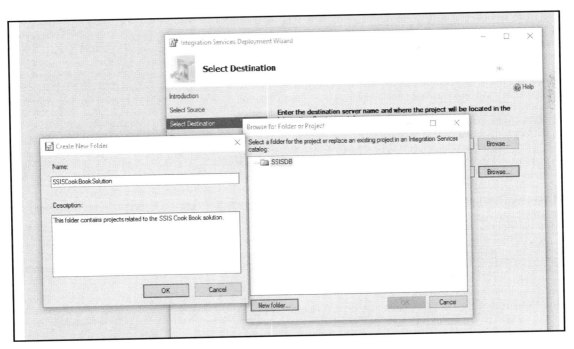

3. Click on **OK** twice to dismiss both the **Create New Folder** and the **Browse for Folder in Project** windows. Make sure that the path is named `/SSISDB/SSISCookBookSolution/ETL.Staging` and click on **Next** and then **Deploy** to deploy the project.

4. Once deployed, go back to SSMS; we're going to configure the project. Navigate to the project and right-click on it. As shown in the following screenshot, select **Configure**:

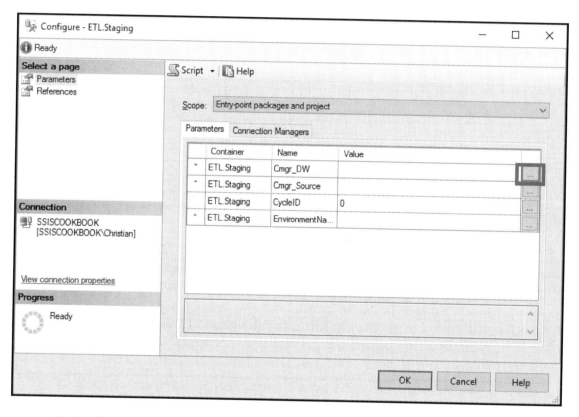

5. As shown in the preceding screenshot, click on the ellipsis (**...**) button for each parameter and set the property as follows:

   - Cmgr_DW: `Data Source=.;Initial Catalog=AdventureWorksLTDW2016;Provider=SQLNCLI11.1;Integrated Security=SSPI`

   - Cmgr_Source: `Data Source=.;Initial Catalog=AdventureWorksLT;Provider=SQLNCLI11.1;Integrated Security=SSPI`

- `CycleID`: No need to change it
- `EnvironmentName`: Staging

6. Once set, you should have something like the following screenshot. Configuring the project parameters stores the values in the project's catalog view `[SSISDB].[catalog].[object_parameters]`. Click on **OK** to close the window and go back to SSMS.

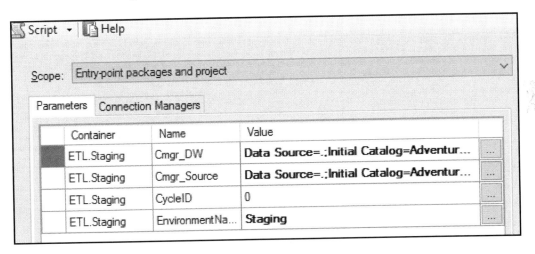

7. Still in SSMS object explorer, navigate to the `EP_Staging.dtsx` package. Right-click on it and select **Execute...** from the contextual menu that appears, as shown in the following screenshot:

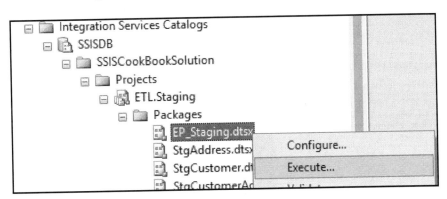

8. Click on **Yes** when asked to view the execution report. Your screen should look like the following screenshot:

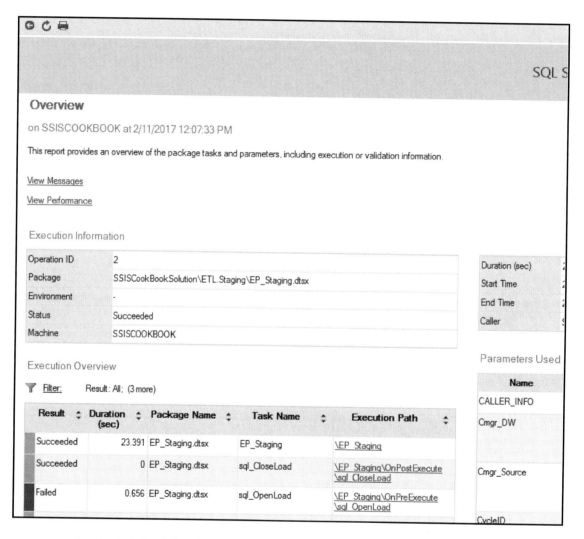

9. Still in SSMS, right-click on any table in the Staging schema to view its data. The Staging schema is now loaded.

Framework calls in EP_Staging.dtsx

This section of the book introduces an ETL framework. The purposes of such a framework are the following:

- Store execution statistics outside the SSIS catalog: although the Microsoft SSIS team always enhances catalog performance, keeping all execution data in the catalog will degrade catalog performance.
- Align the data in such a way to be able to do some analytics on the execution data. In that case, think of the framework as an SSIS package execution data warehouse.

The following diagram is the ER diagram of the framework tables. These tables are stored in the SystemLog schema:

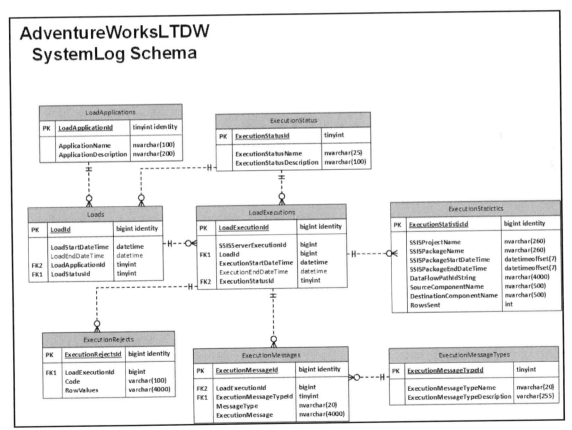

Here's the table list and their purposes:

- LoadApplications: This table contains one value: SSISCookBook sample solution. The purpose of this table, coupled with the Loads table that we'll describe next, is to group many SSIS executions together into a common solution. For example, in this book, we'll have an entry-point package that will call the execution of the entry-point packages of both ETL.Staging and ETL.DW projects.

- Loads: Using this table is not mandatory. The purpose of this table is to group many SSIS executions together to know how much time it took to execute all related projects. It can also be used to determine if all related projects finished successfully or not.

- LoadExecutions: This table contains information related to a specific SSIS execution. The execution start and end time allow us to calculate the execution time, while the execution status will tell us what happened for this execution.

- ExecutionStatistics: Now we're as detailed as possible in SSIS package components. This table contains various row counts and/or execution times for each component in the SSIS package.

- ExecutionStatus: This table shows SSIS execution statuses according to the product's documentation:

    - Execution created
    - Running
    - Cancelled
    - Failed
    - Pending
    - Ended unexpectedly
    - Succeeded
    - Stopping
    - Completed

- ExecutionRejects: This table will hold rows that have failed to load properly in a target table. The Code column can contain error code as well as business keys. The rows values hold the column values for a specific row from the source. We'll talk about this table's usage later in the book.

- ExecutionMessages: This table is mainly used to hold various warnings and errors that occur during packages execution.

- `ExecutionMessageTypes`: This table contains the possible message types used by the framework:
    - Errors
    - Warnings
    - Information

These tables have been deployed as part of the `ADVentureWorks2016` database. They are used with stored procedures called **Execute SQL Tasks** from the entry-point packages.

These stored procedures are in the `SystemLog` schema. The following list describes the various stored procedures used to load these tables:

- `OpenLoad`: This procedure inserts a row in the `Systemlog.Loads` table and it returns the `LoadId` column value to the calling program; in our case, an entry-point package. The newly created row status is set to `Running` and the `LoadStartDateTime` is set to the system date and time of the machine where the code is executed.
- `CloseLoad`: This procedure takes a `LoadId` parameter and does the following updates on the table `SystemLog.Loads` table:
    - Check if all related `LoadExecutions` entries have run successfully. If that's the case, the status will change from `Running` to `Success`. Otherwise, the status will be set to `Failed`.
    - In any case, set the `LoadEndDateTime` value to the system date and time of the machine where the code is executed.

- `OpenLoadExecution`: This procedure has the following parameters:
    - `@ServerExecutionId`: The SSIS execution ID that is sent from the calling SSIS package.
    - `@LoadId`: The `SystemLog.Loads` table's `LoadId` value. Since this value is optional, the parameter has a default value of -1.

    It then inserts a row in the `SystemLog.LoadExecutions` table with parameters values and system date and time. It also returns the `LoadExecutionId` column value that has been assigned by the insertion of the row to the calling program (SSIS entry-point package).

- CloseLoadExecution: This is one of the most complex procedures. It receives a single parameter, @LoadExecutionId and does the following:
    - It retrieves the status for the SSISExecutionId column value for the @LoadExecutionId value
    - It retrieves the row counts of various packages components for the SSISExecutionId and inserts them into the ExecutionStatistics table
    - It assigns the @ExecutionEndDatetime column to system date and time

- LogExecutionMessage: This procedure receives three parameters: @LoadExecutionId, @ExecutionMessageType, and @ExecutionMessage. It simply inserts a row into the SystemLog.ExecutionMessages table.
- LogExecutionRejects: This procedure is used to log rows that have been rejected by the package executions. It has three parameters: @LoadExecutionId, @RejectCode, and @RowValues.

This constitutes the basics of an ETL framework. As well see in future recipes, we'll use the preceding procedures in the entry-point packages.

The Loads, ExecutionStatus, and ExecutionMessageTypes tables have some predefined data inserted via a ScriptPostDeployment.

Now we're going to insert the framework procedure calls into the EP_Staging package.

Getting ready

This recipe assumes that you have access to this book's companion solution.

How to do it...

1. With the solution opened, expand the ETL.Staging SSIS project. Select the EP_Staging.dtsx package and open it. Navigate to the **Event Handler** tab and select the OnPreExecute event handler from the drop-down list, as shown in the following screenshot:

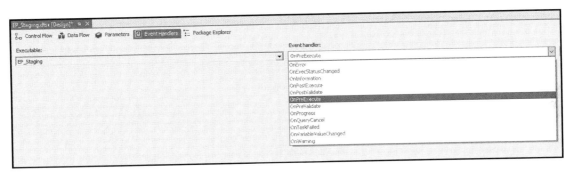

2. As shown in the following screenshot, click the hyperlink to create the OnPreExecute event handler:

Click here to create an 'OnPreExecute' event handler for executable 'EP_Staging'

3. If you look at the **Variable** pane, you'll notice that there are is a variable in that package that is called LoadExecutionId. This variable will hold the value returned by the OPenLoadExecution stored procedure call. From the SSIS toolbox, drag and drop an **Execute SQL Task** onto the designer surface and name it sql_OpenLoadExecution.

4. Double-click on the SQL task (or right-click on it and select **Edit**) and set the following properties on the **General** tab:
   - **ResultSet**: Choose **None** from the drop-down list. This is the default value.
   - **Connection**: From the drop-down list, choose cmgr_DW.
   - **SQLStatement**: Enter EXECUTE [SystemLog].[OpenLoadExecution] ?,?,? OUTPUT.The ? marks correspond to parameters. We'll set them up next in this recipe.

5. Now, click on the **Parameter Mapping** tab in the list at the left of the **Execute SQL Task Editor** and add the following parameters:
    - First parameter:
        - **Variable Name**: System::ServerExecutionID
        - **Direction**: Inpu
        - **Data Type**: Long
        - **Parameter Name**: 0
        - **Parameter Size**: -1

    - Second parameter:
        - **Variable Name**: $Project::LoadId
        - **Direction**: Input
        - **Data Type**: Long
        - **Parameter Name**: 1
        - **Parameter Size**: -1

    - Third parameter:
        - **Variable Name**: SystemLog::LoadExecutionId
        - **Direction**: Output
        - **Data Type**: Long
        - **Parameter Name**: 2
        - **Parameter Size**: -1

6. Now, right-click on the task and select **Execute Task** from the contextual menu that appears. The task should execute successfully.
7. In SSMS, right-click on the SystemLog.LoadExecutions table and click on the **Select Top 1000 Row** to see the data. You should have one row in the table.
8. Now, let's move to the OnPostExecute event handler. Click the hyperlink to create an OnPostExecute event handler and drag an SQL task onto its surface. Assign the following properties on the **General** tab:
    - **ResultSet**: Choose **None** from the drop-down list. This is the default value.
    - **Connection**: From the drop-down list, choose cmgr_DW.
    - **SQLStatement**: Enter EXECUTE [SystemLog].[CloseLoadExecution] ? Again. The ? marks correspond to parameters. In this case, we have only one.

9. Now, click on the **Parameter Mapping** tab in the list at the left of the **Execute SQL Task Editor** and add the following parameters:
   - First parameter:
     - **Variable Name**: SystemLog::LoadExecutionId
     - **Direction**: Output
     - **Data Type**: Long
     - **Parameter Name**: 0
     - **Parameter Size**: -1

10. That's it! All framework objects are set up for the ETL.Staging SSIS project!

There's more...

The issue faced many times with SSIS load applications is that collecting execution statistics and messages are not built upfront. In the past, before the SSIS catalog facilities, developers needed to add substantial elements, such as **Execute SQL Tasks** in the various event handlers or add row counts and variables in every child package. This was most of the time accomplished by using template packages, packages that contained all the necessary plumbing. They were then adapted to the load tasks necessary to load data. When these templates were not used up front, developers needed to open all developed packages and modify them. With medium to large sized project's that had 50+ packages, this task was tedious and most of the time not done.

Creating framework calls in SSIS entry-point packages is the simplest way to collect row counts and execution messages while the package is executing. The framework shown here is both simple and efficient at doing it. Nothing special must be set in the called (child) package to record execution information.

10
Dealing with Data Quality

In this chapter, we will cover the following recipes:

- Profiling data with SSIS
- Creating a DQS knowledge base
- Data cleansing with DQS
- Creating a MDS model
- Matching with DQS
- Using SSIS fuzzy components

Introduction

Business intelligence projects often reveal previously unseen issues with the quality of the source data. Dealing with data quality includes data quality assessment, or data profiling, data cleansing, and maintaining high quality over time.

In SSIS, the data profiling task helps you find unclean data. The data profiling task is not like the other tasks in SSIS because it is not intended to be run over and over again through a scheduled operation. Think about SSIS as being the wrapper for this tool. You use the SSIS framework to configure and run the data profiling task, and then you observe the results through the separate data profile viewer. The output of the data profiling task will be used to help you in your development and design of the ETL and dimensional structures in your solution. Periodically, you may want to rerun the data profile task to see how the data has changed, but the package you develop will not include the task in the overall recurring ETL process.

SQL Server **Data Quality Services** (**DQS**) is a knowledge-driven data-quality solution. This means that it requires you to maintain one or more **knowledge bases** (**KB**). In a KB, you maintain all knowledge related to a specific portion of data—for example, customer data. In DQS projects, you perform cleansing, profiling, and matching activities. You can also use an intermediate staging database to which you copy your source data and export DQS project results. DQS includes server and client components. Before you can use DQS, you must start by installing the DQS components.

The following diagram shows the DQS architecture:

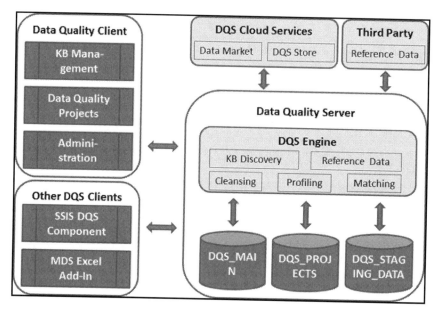

The **Data Quality Server** component includes three databases:

- DQS_MAIN: This includes DQS stored procedures. The DQS stored procedures make up the actual DQS engine. In addition, DQS_MAIN database includes published KBs. A published KB is a KB that has been prepared for use in cleansing projects.
- DQS_PROJECTS: This includes data for KB management and data needed during cleansing and matching projects.
- DQS_STAGING_DATA: This provides an intermediate storage area where you can copy source data for cleansing and where you can export cleansing results.

You can prepare your own knowledge bases locally, including reference data. However, you can also use reference data from the cloud. You can use Windows Azure Marketplace data market to connect to reference data providers. You can also use a direct connection to a third-party reference data provider through a predefined interface.

With the data quality client application, you can manage knowledge bases; execute cleansing, profiling, and matching projects; and administer DQS. SQL Server includes two tools to assist with these tasks. You can use the SSIS DQS cleansing transformation to perform cleansing inside a data flow of your SSIS package. This allows you to perform batch cleansing without the need for interactivity required by the data quality Client. With the free **master data services (MDS)** add-in for Microsoft Excel, you can perform master data matching in an Excel worksheet. The DQS components must be installed together with MDS in order to enable DQS/MDS integration.

Many companies or organizations do regular data cleansing. When you cleanse the data, the data quality goes up to some higher level. The data quality level is determined by the amount of work invested in the cleansing. As time passes, the data quality deteriorates, and you need to repeat the cleansing process. If you spend an equal amount of effort as you did with the previous cleansing, you can expect the same level of data quality as you had after the previous cleansing. Then the data quality deteriorates over time again, and the cleansing process starts over and over again.

The idea of data quality Services is to mitigate the cleansing process. While the amount of time you need to spend on cleansing decreases, you will achieve higher and higher levels of data quality. While cleansing, you learn what types of errors to expect, discover error patterns, find domains of correct values, and so on. You don't throw away this knowledge. You store it, and use it to find and correct the same issues automatically during your next cleansing process.

The idea of master data management, which you can perform with MDS, is to prevent data quality from deteriorating. Once you reach a particular quality level, the MDS application—together with the defined policies, people, and master data management processes—allows you to maintain this level permanently.

There are four main parts of the MDS application. In the MDS database, the master data is stored along with MDS system objects. MDS system objects include system tables and many programmatic objects such as system stored procedures and functions. The MDS service performs the business logic and data access for the MDS solution. Master data manager is a web application for MDS users and administrators. In addition, advanced users can use the master data services add-in for Microsoft Excel.

The following diagram shows the MDS architecture:

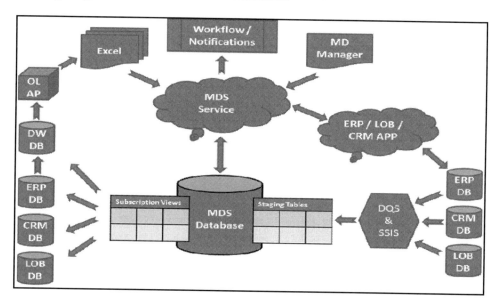

Profiling data with SSIS

The objective of this task is to work with SSIS to profile the data to find the potentially wrong values. In this exercise, you will create an SSIS package with a single task, the data profiling task. Then you will execute the package to profile a set of data. Finally, you will check the results with the data profile viewer application.

Getting ready

You need to have installed the AdventureWorkDW2014 demo database for this exercise.

You can download the full database backup ZIP file `Adventure Works DW 2014 Full Database Backup.zip` from this link: `https://msftdbprodsamples.codeplex.com/releases`. In addition, the backup file is provided with the source code for this book. Assuming that you copied the `AdventureWorksDW2014.bak` file to the `C:\SSIS2016Cookbook` folder, you can use **SQL Server Management Studio (SSMS)** to execute the following command to restore the database:

```
USE master;
RESTORE DATABASE AdventureWorksDW2014
  FROM  DISK = N'C:\SSIS2016Cookbook\AdventureWorksDW2014.bak'
  WITH  FILE = 1,
  MOVE N'AdventureWorksDW2014_Data'
    TO N'C:\SSIS2016Cookbook\AdventureWorksDW2014_Data.mdf',
  MOVE N'AdventureWorksDW2014_Log'
    TO N'C:\SSIS2016Cookbook\AdventureWorksDW2014_Log.ldf',
  STATS = 5;
GO
```

Then you need to prepare the table you are going to profile. In SSMS, execute the following code:

```
USE AdventureWorksDW2014;
SELECT CustomerKey, FirstName,
MiddleName, LastName,
EmailAddress, MaritalStatus,
Gender, TotalChildren, NumberChildrenAtHome,
EnglishEducation AS Education,
EnglishOccupation AS Occupation,
HouseOwnerFlag, NumberCarsOwned,
CommuteDistance, Region,
BikeBuyer, YearlyIncome,
Age - 10 AS Age
INTO dbo.Chapter05Profiling
FROM dbo.vTargetMail;
GO
```

For your convenience, the T-SQL code needed for this chapter is provided in the `Chapter05.sql` file.

How to do it...

1. Open **SQL Server Data Tools** (**SSDT**) and create a new project using the Integration Services Project template. Place the solution in the `C:\SSIS2016Cookbook` folder and name the project `Chapter10`.

2. Rename the default package to `DataProfiling.dtsx`.

3. From the SSIS toolbox, drag the data profiling task onto the control flow work area.

4. Double-click the task to open the **Data Profiling Task Editor**.

5. On the **General** page of the **Data Profiling Task Editor**, select **FileConnection** in the drop-down list for the **DestinationType** property. Select **New File Connection** from the **Destination** property drop-down list. In the File Connection Manager Editor that appears, select **Create File** and enter `C:\SSIS2016Cookbook\DataProfiling.xml`. Click **Open**, and then click **OK**.

6. Back in the **Data Profiling Task Editor** set the **OverwriteDestination** property to **True**. Your **Data Profiling Task Editor** should look like the following screenshot:

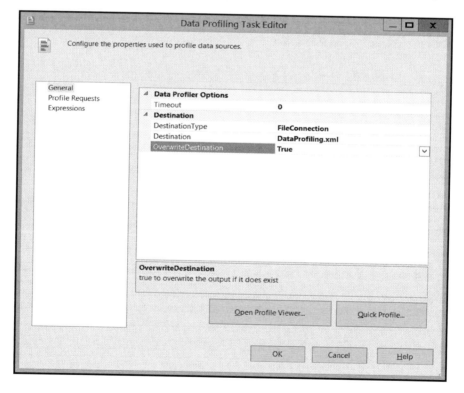

7. Go to **Profile Requests** page. Click somewhere in the first row of the **Profile Type** column and select the **Column Length Distribution Profile Request**. Click the **Request ID** column to finish creating this request.

8. Fill in the **Request Properties** section in the lower half of the window. For the **ConnectionManager** property, create a new ADO.NET connection to connect to the AdventureWorksDW2014 database on the local SQL Server instance. Select the dbo.Chapter05Profiling table for the **TableOrView** property. Select the **MiddleName** column.

9. Add another profile request, but this time create a **Functional Dependency Profile Request**. Use the same ADO.NET connection manager and the same table. Use Education, HouseOwnerFlag, MaritalStatus, and NumberCarsOwned for the **DeterminantColumns** property. Use Occupation for the **DependentColumn** property. Lower the **FDStrengthThreshold** property to 0.3 so that slightly lower strength dependencies are included.

10. Add a **Candidate Key Profile Request**. For the **KeyColumns** property, select all the columns from the dbo.Chapter05Profiling table.

11. Add a **Column Null Ratio Profile Request**. Select the MiddleName column.

12. Add a **Column Pattern Profile Request**. Select the EmailAddress column.

13. Add a **Column Statistics Profile Request**. Select the Age column.

14. Add a **Column Value Distribution Profile Request**. Select the NumberCarsOwned column.

15. Your **Data Profiling Task Editor** window should resemble the one shown in the following screenshot. Click **OK** to close the **Data Profiling Task Editor**:

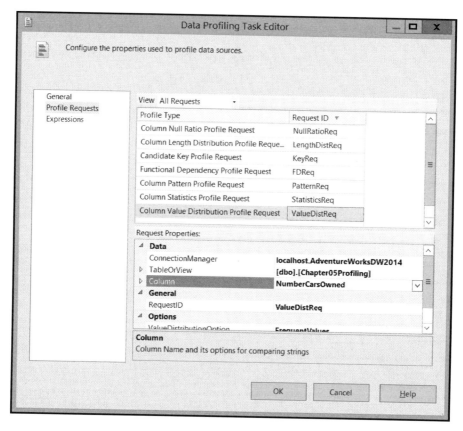

16. Save the package and execute it in debug mode. When the execution is finished, exit the debugging mode. Review the XML file that was created during execution with Visual Studio, Notepad, or Internet Explorer. Close SSDT.

17. Start the **Data Profile Viewer**.

18. In the **Data Profile Viewer** window, click the **Open** button in the upper-left corner.

19. Navigate to the `C:\SSIS2016Cookbook` folder and open the `DataProfiling.xml` file.

20. Click the **Candidate Key Profiles** option in the left-hand pane. Check which columns are suitable to be used as keys (these are the columns that have more unique values than the threshold **Percentage** property for the profile).

21. Click the **Column Length Distribution Profiles** option in the left-hand pane. Check the `MiddleName` distribution. In the middle area of the right-hand pane, click the row that shows the distribution for length `10`. In the right-hand corner of this middle area, click the drill down button to show the source row, as shown in the following screenshot:

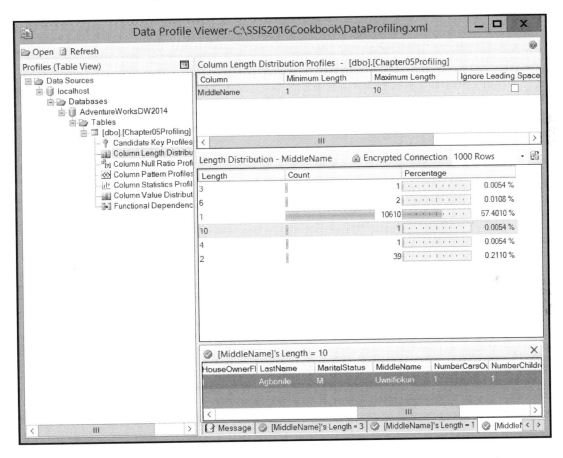

22. Check the **Column Pattern Profiles**. Note the patterns extracted from the `EmailAddress` column. The patterns are expressed as regular expressions. You can use these regular expressions in a rule for the column in a DQS knowledge base domain.

23. Check the other profiles. After you have finished, close the **Data Profile Viewer**. If it is still open, close SSDT as well.

Creating a DQS knowledge base

A DQS KB is the place where you store the knowledge about the data and the cleansing in order to speed up the regular cleansing process. In a real-life scenario, you constantly add knowledge to the KB, and thus improve the cleansing process over time. In this recipe, you will create a basic DQS KB.

Getting ready

For this recipe, you will need DQS and Data Quality Client installed. Please refer to the following link to learn how to install the DQS components:
https://docs.microsoft.com/en-us/sql/data-quality-services/install-windows/install-data-quality-services.

You also need to prepare the data you will use to create a DQS KB. In SSMS, execute the following code:

```
USE AdventureWorksDW2014;
SELECT DISTINCT
City, StateProvinceName AS StateProvince,
EnglishCountryRegionName AS CountryRegion
INTO dbo.AWCitiesStatesCountries
FROM dbo.DimGeography;
GO
```

How to do it...

1. Open the Data Quality Client application and connect to your DQS instance.
2. In the **Knowledge Base Management** group, click the **New KnowledgeBase** button.
3. Name the database AWCustomers. If you want, add a description. Make sure that the **None** option is selected in the **Create Knowledge Base from** drop-down list. Select the **Knowledge Discovery** option in the **Select Activity** list in the lower-right corner of the screen. Click **Next**.
4. On the **Map** tab of the **Knowledge Base Management** screen, select **SQL Server** as your data source. Select the AdventureWorksDW2014 database and the dbo.AWCitiesStatesCountries table.

5. In the **Mappings** section, click the **Create a domain** button (the third button from the left in the group of buttons above the **Mappings** grid, marked with a circle with a yellow star) to create a domain.

6. In the dialog box that appears, enter `City` as the **Domain Name**, and use **String** as the **Data Type**. Make sure that the **Use Leading Values**, **Normalize String**, and **Disable Syntax Error Algorithms** options are checked, and that the **Enable Speller** option is not checked. Make sure that the **Format Output to** option is set to **None** and that the **Language** selected is **English**, as shown in the following screenshot. Click **OK**:

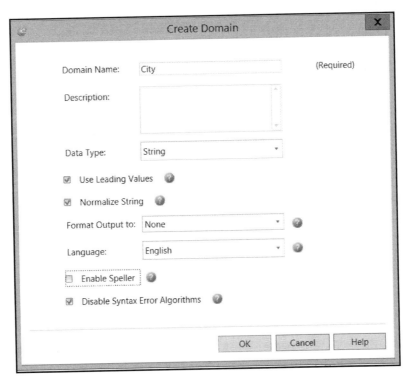

7. Create two additional domains, named `State` and `Country`, with the same settings you used for the `City` domain in step 6.

8. In the **Mappings** grid, select the `City` column from the source in the left-hand column of the first row and map it to the `City` domain in the right-hand column of the first row in the grid.

9. Repeat step 8 twice to add a mapping from the `StateProvince` source column to the `State` domain, and from the `CountryRegion` source column to the `Country` domain. Click Next.

10. On the **Discover** tab, click the **Start** button to start the knowledge discovery. Wait until the process is finished, then review all of the information in the **Profiler** section. This section gives you a quick profile of your data. When you are finished reviewing the profiler information, clickan class="packt_screen">Next.

11. On the **Manage Domain Values** tab, make sure that the `City` domain is selected in the left-hand pane. Then click the **Add new domain value** button (the button with a small green plus sign on a grid) in the right-hand pane above the grid listing the extracted domain values.

12. In the `Value` cell, enter `Munich`. Change the type to **Error** (a red cross). Enter München in the `Correct to` cell. Press the *Enter* key and note that the data is rearranged alphabetically.

 To write ü, hold the *Alt* key and type *0252* or *129* on the numeric keyboard.

13. Click the other two domains in the left-hand pane to check the extracted values. Then click **Finish**. Select **No** in the pop-up window because you are not ready to publish the KB yet. You will edit the domains.

14. Click the **Open Knowledge Base** button in the **Knowledge Base Management** group on the Data Quality Client main screen.

15. In the grid in the left-hand pane, select the `AWCustomers` KB. Make sure that the **Domain Management** activity is selected. Click **Next**.

16. In the **Domain Management** window, make sure that the `City` domain is selected in the left-hand pane. Click the **Domain Values** tab in the right-hand pane. Then click the **Add new domain value** button in the right-hand pane above the grid with the extracted domain values.

17. In the `Value` cell, enter `Muenchen`. Change the type to **Error** (a red cross). Enter München in the `Correct to` cell. Press the *Enter* key and note that the data is rearranged alphabetically.

18. Find the **München** value in the grid. Note that this is now the leading value for two additional synonyms, `Munich` and `Muenchen`.

19. In the left-hand pane, click the **Create a domain** button. Name the domain `StreetAddress` and use **String** as the data type. Make sure that the **Use Leading Values**, **Normalize String**, and **Disable Syntax Error Algorithms** options are checked, and that the **Enable Speller** option is not checked. Also make sure that the **Format Output to** option is set to **None** and that the language selected is **English**. Click **OK**.

20. Click the **Term-Based Relations** tab for the `StreetAddress` domain. You will add a term-based relation to correct all occurrences of a term in the domain values.

21. Click the **Add new relation** button. Enter `Ct.` in the `Value` cell and `Court` in the `Correct to` cell. Press *Enter*. The **Apply Changes** button should be unavailable because you do not have any domain values yet.

22. Add a new domain called `BirthDate`. Select **Date** as the data type. Use the leading values and do not format the output. Click **OK**.

23. Click the **Domain Rules** tab for the `BirthDate` domain. In the right-hand pane, click the **Add a new domain rule** button.

24. In the rules grid, enter `MinBirthDate` in the `Name` cell.

25. In the **Build a Rule: MinBirthDate** section, make sure that the **Value is greater than** option is selected in the drop-down condition list. Then enter `1/1/1900` in the textbox and press *Enter*. Check whether this was successfully changed to `Monday, January 01, 1900`.

26. Add a new domain, `Occupation`. Use **String** as the data type. Make sure that the **Use Leading Values** and **Normalize String** options are checked. However, this time **Enable Speller** should be checked and uncheck **Disable Syntax Error Algorithms**. Do not format the output, and use the English language. Click **OK**.

27. Add a new domain, `EmailAddress`. Use **String** as the data type. Make sure that the **Use Leading Values**, **Normalize String**, and **Disable Syntax Error Algorithms** options are checked, and that the **Enable Speller** option is not checked. Do not format the output, and use the English language. Click **OK**.

28. Click the **Domain Rules** tab for the `EmailAddress` domain. Add a new rule called `EmailRegEx`.

29. Select the **Value matches regular expression** option in the **Build a Rule: EmailRegEx Conditions** drop-down list. Then enter `\p{L}+\d\d@ADVENTURE-WORKS\.COM` as the expression. Click outside the textbox.

30. Click the **Add a new condition to the selected clause** button (the leftmost button in the upper-right part of the **Build a Rule area**).

31. Select the **OR** operator to connect the conditions. Select the **Value matches regular expression** option for the second condition from the drop-down list in the **Build a Rule: EmailRegEx Conditions** drop-down list. Then enter `\p{L}+\d@ADVENTURE-WORKS\.COM` as the expression. Click outside the textbox.

The regular expressions needed for this exercise were extracted with the data profiling task in the previous recipe.

32. Click **Finish** to complete domain management. Then click the **Publish** button in the pop-up window. Finally, click **OK** in the next pop-up window. Your knowledge base is now prepared for use.

Data cleansing with DQS

In this recipe, you will create a view with some dirty data and use a DQS cleansing project to cleanse it. You will use the DQS knowledge base prepared in the previous exercise.

Getting ready

This recipe assumes that you have built the DQS knowledge base from the previous recipe. In addition, you need to prepare some demo data in advance. In SSMS, use the following query to prepare the data:

```
USE DQS_STAGING_DATA;
SELECT C.CustomerKey,
C.FirstName + ' ' + c.LastName AS FullName,
C.AddressLine1 AS StreetAddress,
G.City, G.StateProvinceName AS StateProvince,
G.EnglishCountryRegionName AS CountryRegion,
C.EmailAddress, C.BirthDate,
C.EnglishOccupation AS Occupation
INTO dbo.CustomersCh05
FROM AdventureWorksDW2014.dbo.DimCustomer AS C
INNER JOIN AdventureWorksDW2014.dbo.DimGeography AS G
ON C.GeographyKey = G.GeographyKey
WHERE C.CustomerKey % 10 = 0;
GO
```

How to do it...

1. The data prepared in the previous section is clean. For the DQS cleansing project, use the following code to add two rows with incorrect data:

```
USE DQS_STAGING_DATA;
```

```
SELECT CustomerKey, FullName,
 StreetAddress, City,
 StateProvince, CountryRegion,
 EmailAddress, BirthDate,
 Occupation
INTO dbo.CustomersCh05DQS
FROM dbo.CustomersCh05
UNION
SELECT -11000,
 N'Jon Yang',
 N'3761 N. 14th St',
 N'Munich',                               -- incorrect city
 N'Kingsland',                            -- incorrect state
 N'Austria',                              -- incorrect country
 N'jon24#adventure-works.com',            -- incorrect email
 '18900224',                              -- incorrect birth date
 'Profesional'                            -- incorrect occupation
UNION
SELECT -11100,
 N'Jacquelyn Suarez',
 N'7800 Corrinne Ct.',                    -- incorrect term
 N'Muenchen',                             -- another incorrect city
 N'Queensland',
 N'Australia',
 N'jacquelyn20@adventure-works.com',
 '19680206',
 'Professional';
GO
```

2. Open the Data Quality Client application if necessary, and connect to your DQS instance.

3. In the **Data Quality Projects** group, click the **New Data Quality Project** button.

4. Name the project `AWCustomersCleansing`. Use the `AWCustomers` knowledge base you created in the previous exercise. Make sure that the **Cleansing** activity is selected. Click **Next**.

5. The **Data Quality Project** window will open with the **Map** tab as the active tab. Select **SQL Server** as the data source, choose the `DQS_STAGING_DATA` database, and select the `dbo.CustomersCh05DQS` table in the **Table/View** drop-down list.

6. In the **Mappings** area, click the button with the small green plus sign above the **Mappings** grid twice to add two rows to the **Mappings** grid. (Five mappings are provided by default, but you need seven.)

7. Use the drop-down lists in the **Source Column** and **Domain** cells to map the following columns and domains:

Column	Domain
BirthDate	BirthDate
StreetAddress	StreetAddress
City	City
StateProvince	State
CountryRegion	Country
EmailAddress	EmailAddress
Occupation	Occupation

8. The following screenshot shows the correct mappings of columns to domains. When your mappings are correct, click **Next**:

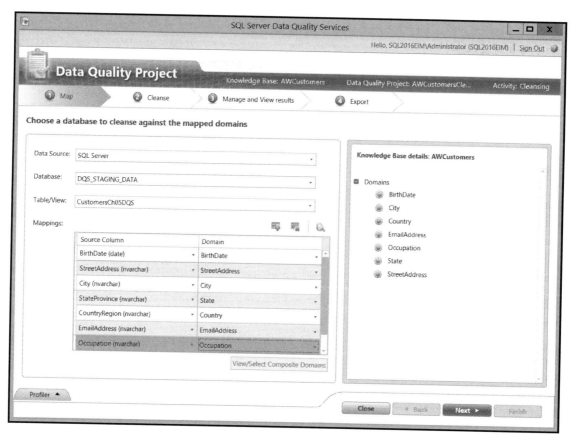

9. On the **Cleanse** tab, click **Start**. Wait until the computer-assisted cleansing is finished, then review the results of the profiling. Click **Next**.

10. On the **Manage and View results** tab, check the results, one domain at a time. Start with the BirthDate domain. There should be one invalid value. Make sure that the BirthDate domain is selected in the left-hand pane, and click the **Invalid** tab in the right-hand pane. Note the invalid value that was detected. You could write a correct value now in the **Correct to** cell of the grid with invalid values, but this action is not needed for this exercise. Note that all correct values were suggested as new.

11. Select the StreetAddress domain in the left-hand pane. One value should be corrected. However, because only the term-based relation (and not the whole value) was corrected, it does not appear among the corrected values. It should appear among the new values. Click the **New** tab in the right-hand pane. Search for the value 7800 Corrinne Ct. and note that it was corrected with 100 percent confidence to 7800 Corrinne Court.

12. Clear the **Search Value** textbox. Select the State domain in the left-hand pane. Click the **New tab** in the right-hand pane. Note that one value (Kingsland) was found as new. The similarity threshold to the original value (Queensland) was too low for DQS to automatically correct or even suggest the value. You could correct this value manually, but this is not needed in this exercise.

13. Select the City domain in the left-hand pane. Two values should be corrected. Click the **Corrected** tab in the right-hand pane. Note the corrections of the synonyms for München (Munich and Muenchen) to the leading value (München). Note also that the confidence for these two corrections is 100 percent. All other values already existed in the KB, and therefore DQS marked them as correct.

14. Select the Country domain in the left-hand pane. One value should be suggested. Click the **Suggested** tab in the right-hand pane. Note that DQS suggests replacing Austria with Australia with 70 percent confidence. You can approve a single value by checking the **Approve** option in the grid. However, don't approve it, because, of course, this is a wrong suggestion. Note that DQS identified all other countries as correct.

15. Select the EmailAddress domain in the left-hand pane. One value should be invalid. Click the **Invalid** tab in the right-hand pane. DQS tells you that the jon24#adventure-works.com email address does not comply with the EmailRegEx rule. Note that all other values are marked as new.

16. Select the `Occupation` domain in the left-hand pane. Note that all values are new. Click the **New** tab in the right-hand pane. Note that the value `Profesional` is underlined with a red squiggly line. This is because you enabled the spelling checker for the `Occupation` domain. Enter `Professional` in the `Correct to` field for the incorrect row. Note that, because you corrected the value manually, the confidence is set to `100` percent. Select the **Approve** checkbox for this row. The row should disappear and appear among the corrected values. Click the **Corrected** tab. Observe the corrected value along with the reason. Click **Next**.

17. On the **Export** tab, look at the output data preview on the left-hand side of the window. You could export the results to a SQL Server table and then correct the original data. However, you don't need to export the results in this lab. Just click **Finish**.

18. Close SSMS and the Data Quality Client application.

Creating a MDS model

In this recipe, you are going to create an MDS model with the entities, attributes, and hierarchies needed for a customer's entity set. Then you will populate the entities and check your business rules.

Getting ready

In order to test this recipe, you need to have MDS installed. Please refer to the following link to learn how to install the MDS components:
`https://docs.microsoft.com/en-us/sql/master-data-services/install-windows/insta ll-master-data-services`.

How to do it...

1. You need to open the Master Data Manager application. Open your web browser, navigate to your Master Data Manager site, and log in. Navigate to the home page.
2. Click the **System Administration** link.
3. In the **Manage Models** page, click **Add**.

4. Name the model `AWCustomer`. Make sure that the option **Create entity with the same name as model** is checked. Leave the **Description** textbox empty, and **Log Retention** drop-down list to the default, **System Setting**, as the shown in the following screenshot. Click the **Save** button:

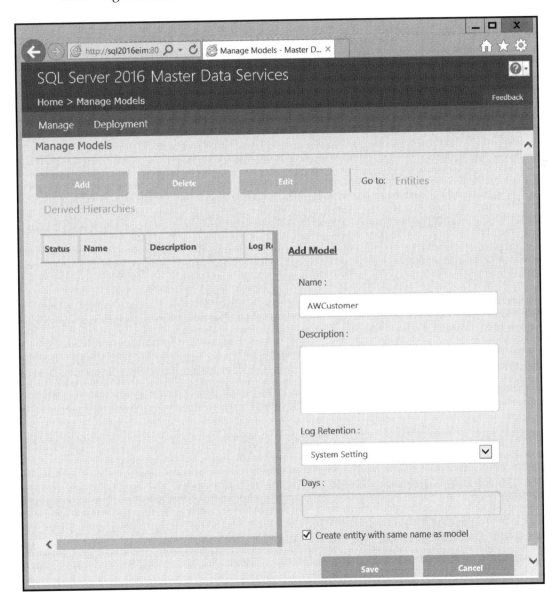

5. On the **Manage Models** page, click the **Entities** link in the **Go to** section.

6. On the **Manage Entities** page, click the **Add** button. Name the entity StateProvince. Check the **Create code values automatically** option. Write 1 in the **Start with** text box. Make sure that the **Enable data compression** checkbox is checked and the **Approval Required** is not checked. Click the **Save** button.

7. Click the **Manage Entities** link at the top left of the page. Create another entity, CountryRegion, with the same settings as the StateProvince created in the previous step. Save it.

8. Click the **Manage Entities** link at the top left of the page. Click the StateProvince entity in the list of entities to highlight it. Click the **Attributes** link in the **Go to** section.

9. Note that there are already two attributes created, the Name and the Code attributes.

10. Click the **Add** button. Name the new attribute CountryRegion. Make the new attribute domain-based and use the CountryRegion entity for the domain values. Do not change the display pixel width and do not enable change tracking. Save the attribute.

11. Start editing the AWCustomer entity. Select it in the **Entity** drop-down list. Add a domain-based leaf member attribute, StateProvince. Use the StateProvince entity for the domain of possible values. Do not enable change tracking. Save the attribute.

12. Add a free-form leaf member attribute, StreetAddress. Use the **Text** data type. Change the Display Width (Pixel) to 200. Do not enable change tracking. Save the attribute.

13. Add a free-form leaf member attribute, City. Use the **Text** data type. Leave the default length of 100 and the default pixel width of 100. Do not enable change tracking. Save the attribute.

14. Add a free-form leaf member attribute, EmailAddress. Use the **Text** data type. Leave the default length of 100 and the default pixel width of 100. Do not enable change tracking. Save the attribute.

15. Add a free-form leaf member attribute, MaritalStatus. Use the **Text** data type. Change the length to 1. Change the display pixel width to 20. Do not enable change tracking. Save the attribute.

16. Add a free-form leaf member attribute, BirthDate. Use the **DateTime** data type. Use the default pixel width of 100. Use the yyyy/MM/dd input mask. Do not enable change tracking. Save the attribute.

17. Add a free-form leaf member attribute, `YearlyIncome`. Use the **Number** data type with two decimals. Use the default pixel width of `100`. Use the `-####` input mask. Do not enable change tracking. Save the attribute.

18. Navigate to the **Manage Entities** page (**Home** | **AWCustomer Model** | **Manage Entities**). Select the `AWCustomer` entity.

19. Click the **Attribute Groups** link. Click **Add**. Name the group `Demography`.

20. In the **Attributes** section, add the `MaritalStatus`, `BirthDate`, and `YearlyIncome` attributes to this attribute group, as shown in the following screenshot, and then save the attribute group:

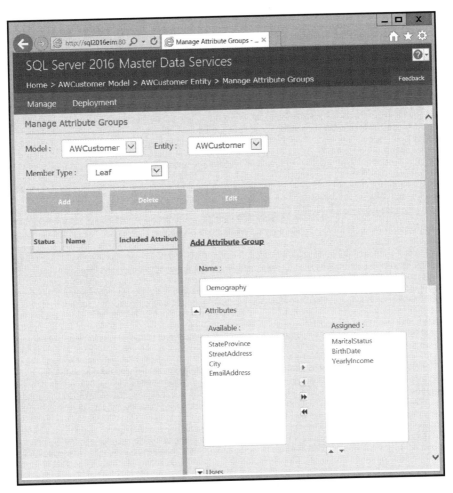

21. Navigate to the **Manage Entities** page (**Home | AWCustomer Model | Manage Entities**). Select the `AWCustomer` entity.

22. Click the **Business Rules** link. Click **Add**. Name the rule `EmailAt`.

23. In the **Add Business Rule** pop-up window, click the **Add** link in the **Then** section.

24. In the **Create Action** pop-up window, select the `EmailAddress` attribute in the **Attribute** drop-down list.

25. In the **Operator** drop-down list, select the **must contain the pattern** operator.

26. In the **Must contain the pattern** drop-down list, select **Attribute value**.

27. In the **Attribute value** textbox, write the @ sign. Make sure that your **Create Action** pop-up window looks like the one in the following screenshot, then click **Save**:

28. In the **Add Business Rule** window, click **Save**.

29. In the **Business Rules** window, click the **Publish All** button to activate all business rules.

30. Navigate to the home page. Make sure that the AWCustomer model is selected in the **Model** drop-down list. Then click **Explorer**.

31. Click the **Entities** button at the top-left of the screen, and select the CountryRegion entity. In the editor, click the **Add Member** button.

32. In the **Details** pane on the right, enter Australia as the value of the Name field. Note that the value for the Code field is assigned automatically. Click **OK**.

33. Add another member with the value United States as the Name field.

34. Using the **Entities** button, select the StateProvince entity. In the editor, click the **Add Member** button.

35. In the **Details** pane, enter Queensland as the value of the Name field. Note that the value for the Code field is assigned automatically. In the CountryRegion drop-down list, select 1 {Australia}. Click **OK**.

36. Add another member with the value Washington for the Name field. Click the button to the right of the CountryRegion drop-down list to open another window with a list of members of the CountryRegion entity. Check the code for the United States member. Go back to the window where you are editing the StateProvince entity and insert the appropriate CountryRegion code. Click **OK**.

37. Using the **Entities** button, select the AWCustomer entity. Note that there are two views: one with the attributes from the Demography attribute group only and another one with all the attributes. Click the **[All Attributes]** tab to see all of the attributes. You are going to add two members with data based on two customers from the dbo.DimCustomer table in the AdventureWorksDW2014 sample database. In the editor, click the **Add Member** button.

38. Insert the following information and then click **OK**:

Parameters	Values
Name	Jon Yang
Code	1
StateProvince	1 {Queensland}
StreetAddress	3761 N. 14th St
City	Rockhampton
EmailAddress	jon24@adventure-works.com
MaritalStatus	M
BirthDate	1970/04/08
YearlyIncome	90000

39. Add another customer with the following information:

Parameters	Values
Name	Lauren Walker
Code	2
StateProvince	2 {Washington}
StreetAddress	4785 Scott Street
City	Bremerton
EmailAddress	lauren41#adventure-works.com
MaritalStatus	M
BirthDate	1970/01/18
YearlyIncome	100,000.00

40. Before clicking **OK** to save the member, try to change the value of the MaritalStatus field to UNKNOWN. You should get an error immediately notifying you that the length of this field cannot be greater than one. Correct the value back to M.

41. Try to insert the birth date in a different format.

42. Note that the EmailAddress field contains the # character instead of the @ character. Click **OK** to save the member anyway.

43. Note that in the grid showing all customers, there is a red exclamation point near the `Lauren Walker` entry. Point to it and read the message. Note also the message about validation errors in the **Details** pane on the right, as shown in the following screenshot:

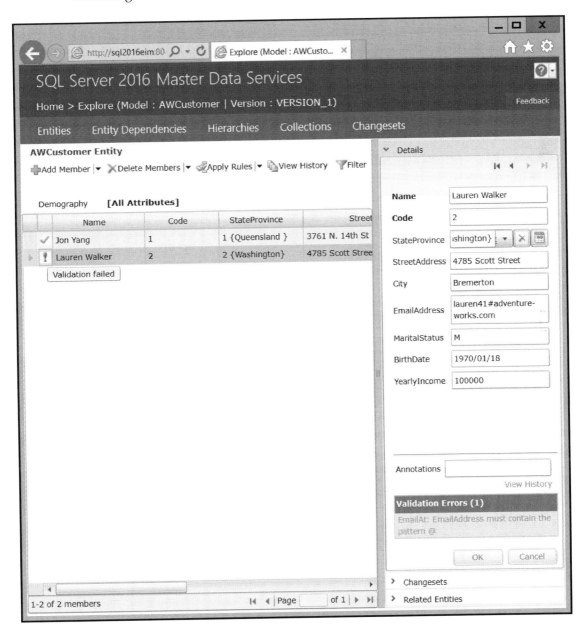

44. In the **Details** pane, correct the value in the `EmailAddress` field and click **OK**. Now the validation should succeed.

Matching with DQS

Often, you need to match entities without having a common identification. For example, you might get data about customers from two different sources. Then you need to do the matching based on similarity of attributes, for example, names and addresses. Matching is a very complex task. In SQL Server, DQS is one of the tools that can help you with this task.

Getting ready

In order to test the DQS matching, you need to prepare some data. The following section contains a lot of code; therefore, you might want to use the code provided in the book's companion content.

First, you need to prepare a table with clean data. In SSMS, execute the following code:

```
-- Preparing the clean data table
USE DQS_STAGING_DATA;
CREATE TABLE dbo.CustomersClean
(
CustomerKey INT NOT NULL PRIMARY KEY,\
FullName NVARCHAR(200) NULL,
StreetAddress NVARCHAR(200) NULL
);
GO
-- Populating the clean data table
INSERT INTO dbo.CustomersClean
(CustomerKey, FullName, StreetAddress)
SELECT CustomerKey,
FirstName + ' ' + LastName AS FullName,
AddressLine1 AS StreetAddress
FROM AdventureWorksDW2014.dbo.DimCustomer
WHERE CustomerKey % 10 = 0;
GO
```

Then you create a similar table for the dirty data, and also initially populate it with clean data:

```
-- Creating and populating the table for dirty data
CREATE TABLE dbo.CustomersDirty
(
```

```
CustomerKey INT NOT NULL PRIMARY KEY,
FullName NVARCHAR(200) NULL,
StreetAddress NVARCHAR(200) NULL,
Updated INT NULL,
CleanCustomerKey INT NULL
);
GO
INSERT INTO dbo.CustomersDirty
(CustomerKey, FullName, StreetAddress, Updated)
SELECT CustomerKey * (-1) AS CustomerKey,
FirstName + ' ' + LastName AS FullName,
AddressLine1 AS StreetAddress,
0 AS Updated
FROM AdventureWorksDW2014.dbo.DimCustomer
WHERE CustomerKey % 10 = 0;
GO
```

The next step is the most complex one. You need to make random changes in the dirty data table. Note that in this table, the original `CustomerKey` column is multiplied by –1, and that there is a space for the clean `CustomerKey`. This way, you will be able to check the quality of the matches. Nevertheless, the following code makes somehow random changes in the table, mimicking human errors:

```
-- Making random changes in the dirty table
DECLARE @i AS INT = 0, @j AS INT = 0;
WHILE (@i < 3) -- loop more times for more changes
BEGIN
SET @i += 1;
SET @j = @i - 2; -- control here in which step you want to update
-- only already updated rows
WITH RandomNumbersCTE AS
(
SELECT CustomerKey
,RAND(CHECKSUM(NEWID()) % 1000000000 + CustomerKey) AS RandomNumber1
,RAND(CHECKSUM(NEWID()) % 1000000000 + CustomerKey) AS RandomNumber2
,RAND(CHECKSUM(NEWID()) % 1000000000 + CustomerKey) AS RandomNumber3
,FullName, StreetAddress, Updated
FROM dbo.CustomersDirty
)
UPDATE RandomNumbersCTE SET
FullName = STUFF(FullName,
CAST(CEILING(RandomNumber1 * LEN(FullName)) AS INT), 1,
CHAR(CEILING(RandomNumber2 * 26) + 96))
,StreetAddress = STUFF(StreetAddress,
CAST(CEILING(RandomNumber1 * LEN(StreetAddress)) AS INT), 2, '')
,Updated = Updated + 1
WHERE RAND(CHECKSUM(NEWID()) % 1000000000 - CustomerKey) < 0.17
```

```
AND Updated > @j;
WITH RandomNumbersCTE AS
(
SELECT CustomerKey
,RAND(CHECKSUM(NEWID()) % 1000000000 + CustomerKey) AS RandomNumber1
,RAND(CHECKSUM(NEWID()) % 1000000000 + CustomerKey) AS RandomNumber2
,RAND(CHECKSUM(NEWID()) % 1000000000 + CustomerKey) AS RandomNumber3
,FullName, StreetAddress, Updated
FROM dbo.CustomersDirty
)
UPDATE RandomNumbersCTE SET
FullName = STUFF(FullName,
CAST(CEILING(RandomNumber1 * LEN(FullName)) AS INT), 0,
CHAR(CEILING(RandomNumber2 * 26) + 96))
,StreetAddress = STUFF(StreetAddress,
CAST(CEILING(RandomNumber1 * LEN(StreetAddress)) AS INT), 2,
CHAR(CEILING(RandomNumber2 * 26) + 96) +
CHAR(CEILING(RandomNumber3 * 26) + 96)) ,Updated = Updated + 1
WHERE RAND(CHECKSUM(NEWID()) % 1000000000 - CustomerKey) < 0.17
AND Updated > @j;
WITH RandomNumbersCTE AS
(
SELECT CustomerKey
,RAND(CHECKSUM(NEWID()) % 1000000000 + CustomerKey) AS RandomNumber1
,RAND(CHECKSUM(NEWID()) % 1000000000 + CustomerKey) AS RandomNumber2
,RAND(CHECKSUM(NEWID()) % 1000000000 + CustomerKey) AS RandomNumber3
,FullName, StreetAddress, Updated
FROM dbo.CustomersDirty
)
UPDATE RandomNumbersCTE SET
FullName = STUFF(FullName,
CAST(CEILING(RandomNumber1 * LEN(FullName)) AS INT), 1, '')
,StreetAddress = STUFF(StreetAddress,
CAST(CEILING(RandomNumber1 * LEN(StreetAddress)) AS INT), 0,
CHAR(CEILING(RandomNumber2 * 26) + 96) +
CHAR(CEILING(RandomNumber3 * 26) + 96))
,Updated = Updated + 1
WHERE RAND(CHECKSUM(NEWID()) % 1000000000 - CustomerKey) < 0.16
AND Updated > @j;
END;
GO
```

You can compare the data after the changes with the original data using the following query:

```
SELECT C.FullNameD.FullNameC.StreetAddressD.StreetAddress, D.Updated
FROM dbo.CustomersClean AS C
INNER JOIN dbo.CustomersDirty AS D
ON C.CustomerKey = D.CustomerKey * (-1)
WHERE C.FullName <> D.FullName
OR C.StreetAddress <> D.StreetAddress
ORDER BY D.Updated DESC;
GO
```

There should be more than 700 rows updated. The exact number changes with every execution. When executing the code as an example for this chapter, I got 756 rows updated. This means 756 customers that need to be matched with the clean data table.

How to do it...

1. In SSDT, open the `Chapter10` solution from the first recipe of this chapter.
2. Add a new package to the solution and rename it to `DataMatching.dtsx`.
3. Create a new package OLE DB connection manager to your local SQL Server instance, the `DQS_STAGING_DATA` database.
4. In the control flow of the package, add a data flow task. Open the data flow editor for this task.
5. Add an OLE DB source. Rename it to `CustomersDirty`. Open the **OLE DB Source Editor** and select the `dbo.CustomersDirty` table as the source table. Click the **Columns** tab to check the columns. Click **OK** to close the editor.
6. The next step in the preparation for identity mapping (or matching) is to perform the exact matches. Drag the lookup transformation to the working area and connect it with the blue data flow path using the OLE DB source. Name it `Exact Matches` and double-click it to open its editor.

7. In the **Lookup Transformation Editor**, select the **Connection** tab in the left-hand pane. Use the connection manager for the DQS_STAGING_DATA database. Select the dbo.CustomersClean table. Click the **Columns** tab.

8. Drag the FullName and StreetAddress columns from the **Available Input Columns** onto the columns with the same name in the **Available Lookup Columns** table. Select the checkbox next to the CustomerKey column in the **Available Lookup Columns** table. In the **Lookup Operation** field in the grid in the bottom part of the editor, select the Replace 'CleanCustomerKey' option. Rename the output alias CleanCustomerKey, as shown in the following screenshot:

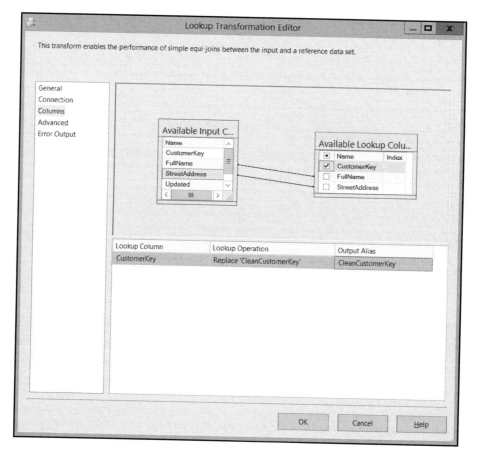

9. Click the **General** tab. In the **Specify how to handle rows with no matching entries** drop-down list, select the **Redirect rows to no match output** option. Click **OK** to close the **Lookup Transformation Editor**.

10. Drag two multicast transformations to the working area. Rename the first one `Match` and the second one `NoMatch`. Connect the lookup transformation with them, the first by using the lookup match output and the second by using the lookup no match output. You do not need to multicast the data for this recipe. However, you are going to expand the package in the next recipe.

11. In SSMS, create a new table in the `DQS_STAGING_DATA` database in the `dbo` schema and name it `CustomersDirtyMatch`. Use the following code:

```
CREATE TABLE dbo.CustomersDirtyMatch
(
    CustomerKey INT NOT NULL PRIMARY KEY,
    FullName NVARCHAR(200) NULL,
    StreetAddress NVARCHAR(200) NULL,
    Updated INT NULL,
    CleanCustomerKey INT NULL
);
```

12. Add another new table in the `dbo` schema and name it `CustomersDirtyNoMatch`. Use the following code, which uses the same schema as the previous table:

```
CREATE TABLE dbo.CustomersDirtyNoMatch
(
    CustomerKey INT NOT NULL PRIMARY KEY,
    FullName NVARCHAR(200) NULL,
    StreetAddress NVARCHAR(200) NULL,
    Updated INT NULL,
    CleanCustomerKey INT NULL
);
```

13. In the data flow in SSDT, add a new OLE DB destination and rename it `CustomersDirtyMatch`. Connect it to the match multicast transformation. Double-click it to open the editor. Select the `dbo.CustomersDirtyMatch` table. Click the **Mappings** tab to check the mappings. Click **OK**.

14. Add a new OLE DB destination and rename it `CustomersDirtyNoMatch`. Connect it to the no match multicast transformation. Double-click it to open the editor. Select the `dbo.CustomersDirtyNoMatch` table. Click the **Mappings** tab to check the mappings. Click **OK**.

15. Save the project. Execute the package in debug mode. After the execution has completed, review the contents of the dbo.CustomersDirtyMatch and dbo.CustomersDirtyNoMatch tables.

16. Stop debugging. Do not exit SSDT.

17. In the DQS_STAGING_DATA database in SSMS, create a table that unions clean and dirty customer data by using the following code:

```
SELECT CustomerKey, FullName, StreetAddress
INTO dbo.CustomersDQSMatch
FROM dbo.CustomersClean
UNION
SELECT CustomerKey, FullName, StreetAddress
FROM dbo.CustomersDirtyNoMatch;
```

18. Start the Data Quality Client and connect to your DQS server.

19. Create a new knowledge base. Name it AWCustomersMatching. Make sure that the **Matching Policy** activity is selected. Click **Next**.

20. In the **Knowledge Base Management** window, on the **Map** tab (the first one), select **SQL Server** as the data source. Select the DQS_STAGING_DATA database and the CustomersDQSMatch table.

21. Create a domain named FullName. Use the data type **String**, and select the **Use Leading Values**, **Normalize String**, and **Disable Syntax Error Algorithms** checkboxes. Clear the **Enable Speller** checkbox. Set the **Format Output to** option to **None** and select **English** as the language. Click **OK**.

22. Create another domain named StreetAddress with the same settings as for the FullName domain.

23. Map the FullName column to the FullName domain, and map the StreetAddress column to the StreetAddress domain.

24. Create a new composite domain (click the second icon from the right, above the column/domain mappings grid in the left-hand pane). For matching, you typically use a composite domain, which encompasses all columns involved in an approximate match. Name the domain `NameAddress` and add the `FullName` and `StreetAddress` columns from the **Domain List** listbox to the **Domains in Composite Domains** listbox. Click **OK**. Your screen should resemble the one shown in the following screenshot. After you have made sure that you have the correct domains and mappings, click **Next**.

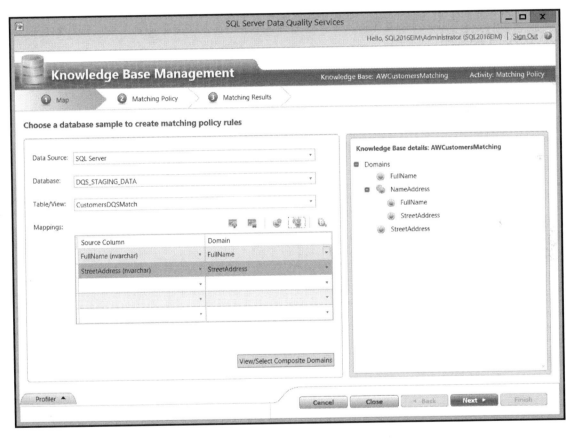

25. On the **Matching Policy** tab, click the **Create a matching rule** button in the left-hand pane. In the **Rule Details** pane on the right-hand side, change the name of the rule to `Composite100`.

26. In the **Rule Editor** area on the right, click the **Add a new domain element** button in the upper-right corner. The `NameAddress` domain should appear. Scroll to the right of the `Similarity` column (leave the value `Similar` in it) to show the `Weight` column. Change the weight to `100%` for the `NameAddress` composite domain. You could also start matching with exact matches for one domain by requesting this domain as a prerequisite—for example, by selecting the checkbox in the `Prerequisite` column for the `FullName` domain to lower the number of rows for matching in one pass. However, the number of customers to match is not too high for this recipe, so you do not need to additionally reduce the matching search space. When you are done defining the rule, click **Start** in the **Matching Results** section of the screen to run the matching policy.

27. When the matching policy run has finished, review the results. Filter on matched or unmatched records by selecting the appropriate option in the **Filter** drop-down list.

28. You should test multiple rules. Therefore, create a new rule. Name it `Name60Address40`. In the **Rule Editor** section, click the **Add a new domain element** button. Scroll to the right of the `Similarity` column (leave the value `Similar` in it) to show the `Weight` column. Change the weight to `60%` for the `FullName` domain and `40%` for the `StreetAddress` domain. Click `Start` to test this rule.

29. When the rule testing has finished, review the results. Double-click a few of the matched records to get the **Matching Score Details** window for the records. Check how much the name and how much the address contributed to the score. Then close the window. When you are done with your review, click **Next**.

30. In the **Matching Results** window, you can check all the relevant rules at once. Make sure that the **Execute on previous data** option (which is below the **Start** button) is selected. Click the **Start** button. Wait until DQS finishes the process, then check the **Profiler**, **Matching Rules**, and **Matching Results**. In **Matching Results**, double-click a few of the matched records to show the **Matching Score Details** window, and check which rule was used. The composite domain should be used more often than the single domains.

31. When you are done with your review and have closed the **Matching Score Details** window, click **Finish**. Then click **Publish** in the pop-up window to publish the KB. When it is published, click **OK** in the next pop-up window.

32. The next step is to create a DQS matching project. Click the **New Data Quality Project** button in the Data Quality Client main screen.

33. Name the project `AWCustomersMatchingProject`. Select the `AWCustomersMatching` KB. Make sure that the **Matching** activity is selected. Click **Next**.

34. On the **Map** tab (the first one) in the **Knowledge Base Management** window, select **SQL Server** as the data source. Select the `DQS_STAGING_DATA` database and the `CustomersDQSMatch` table. Note that in a real project, you would have a separate table with sample data for learning during the KB creation and another table for the actual matching.

35. Map the `FullName` column to the `FullName` domain and the `StreetAddress` column to the `StreetAddress` domain, unless they have already been mapped automatically. Click **Next**.

36. On the **Matching** tab, click **Start**. Wait until the matching process finishes, then review the results. When you are finished, click **Next**.

37. On the **Export** page, choose **SQL Server** as the destination type and choose the `DQS_STAGING_DATA` database. Select both the **Matching Results** and **Survivorship Results** checkboxes. Export the matching results to a table named `DQSMatchingResults` and the survivorship results to a table named `DQSSurvivorshipResults`. Do not add schema names to table names; the tables will be created in the `dbo` schema. Select the **Most complete and longest record** survivorship rule. Click the **Export** button.

38. When the export is finished, click **Close** in the **Matching Export** pop-up window and then click **Finish**.

39. In SSMS, review the exported results. You can quickly see that the survivorship policy is not sophisticated enough because many customers with negative `CustomerKey` values are selected as survivors. You should use the matching results and define your own survivorship rules, or select the survivors manually.

40. Close the Data Quality Client.

Using SSIS fuzzy components

SSIS includes two really sophisticated matching transformations in the data flow. The fuzzy lookup transformation is used for mapping the identities. The fuzzy grouping transformation is used for de-duplicating. Both of them use the same algorithm for comparing the strings and other data.

Identity mapping and de-duplication are actually the same problem. For example, instead for mapping the identities of entities in two tables, you can union all of the data in a single table and then do the de-duplication. Or vice versa, you can join a table to itself and then do identity mapping instead of de-duplication. This recipe shows how to use the fuzzy lookup transformation for identity mapping.

Getting ready

This recipe assumes that you have successfully finished the previous recipe.

How to do it...

1. In SSMS, create a new table in the DQS_STAGING_DATA database in the dbo schema and name it dbo.FuzzyMatchingResults. Use the following code:

```
CREATE TABLE dbo.FuzzyMatchingResults
(
  CustomerKey INT NOT NULL PRIMARY KEY,
  FullName NVARCHAR(200) NULL,
  StreetAddress NVARCHAR(200) NULL,
  Updated INT NULL,
  CleanCustomerKey INT NULL
);
```

2. Switch to SSDT. Continue editing the **DataMatching** package.
3. Add a fuzzy lookup transformation below the no match multicast transformation. Rename it FuzzyMatches and connect it to the no match multicast transformation with the regular data flow path. Double-click the transformation to open its editor.
4. On the **Reference Table** tab, select the connection manager you want to use to connect to your DQS_STAGING_DATA database and select the dbo.CustomersClean table. Do not store a new index or use an existing index.

When the package executes the transformation for the first time, it copies the reference table, adds a key with an integer data type to the new table, and builds an index on the key column. Next, the transformation builds an index, called a match index, on the copy of the reference table. The match index stores the results of tokenizing the values in the transformation input columns. The transformation then uses these tokens in the lookup operation. The match index is a table in a SQL Server database. When the package runs again, the transformation can either use an existing match index or create a new index. If the reference table is static, the package can avoid the potentially expensive process of rebuilding the index for repeat sessions of data cleansing.

5. Click the **Columns** tab. Delete the mapping between the two `CustomerKey` columns. Clear the checkbox next to the `CleanCustomerKey` input column. Select the checkbox next to the `CustomerKey` lookup column. Rename the output alias for this column to `CleanCustomerKey`. You are replacing the original column with the one retrieved during the lookup. Your mappings should resemble those shown in the following screenshot:

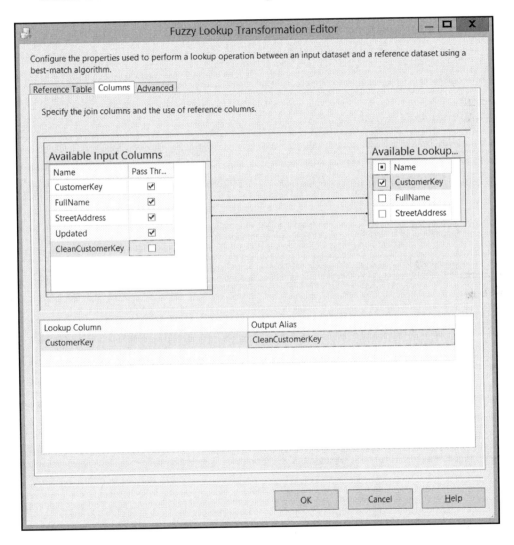

6. Click the **Advanced** tab. Raise the **Similarity threshold** to 0.50 to reduce the matching search space. With similarity threshold of 0.00, you would get a full cross join. Click **OK**.

7. Drag the union all transformation below the fuzzy lookup transformation. Connect it to an output of the matchmulticast transformation and an output of the FuzzyMatches fuzzy lookup transformation. You will combine the exact and approximate matches in a single row set.

8. Drag an OLE DB destination below the union all transformation. Rename it FuzzyMatchingResults and connect it with the union all transformation. Double-click it to open the editor.

9. Connect to your DQS_STAGING_DATA database and select the dbo.FuzzyMatchingResults table. Click the **Mappings** tab. Click **OK**. The completed data flow is shown in the following screenshot:

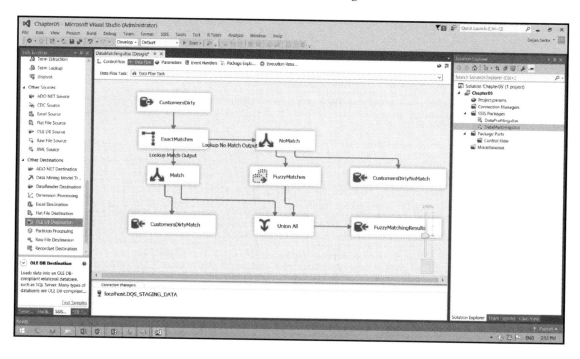

10. You need to add restart ability to your package. You will truncate all destination tables. Click the **Control Flow** tab. Drag the execute T-SQL statement task above the data flow task. Connect the tasks with the green precedence constraint from the execute T-SQL statement task to the data flow task. The execute T-SQL statement task must finish successfully before the data flow task starts.

11. Double-click the execute T-SQL statement task. Use the connection manager to your DQS_STAGING_DATA database. Enter the following code in the T-SQL statement textbox, and then click **OK**:

```
TRUNCATE TABLE dbo.CustomersDirtyMatch;
TRUNCATE TABLE dbo.CustomersDirtyNoMatch;
TRUNCATE TABLE dbo.FuzzyMatchingResults;
```

12. Save the solution. Execute your package in debug mode to test it. Review the results of the fuzzy lookup transformation in SSMS. Look for rows for which the transformation did not find a match, and for any incorrect matches. Use the following code:

```
-- Not matched
SELECT * FROM FuzzyMatchingResults
WHERE CleanCustomerKey IS NULL;
-- Incorrect matches
SELECT * FROM FuzzyMatchingResults
WHERE CleanCustomerKey <> CustomerKey * (-1);
```

13. You can use the following code to clean up the AdventureWorksDW2014 and DQS_STAGING_DATA databases:

```
USE AdventureWorksDW2014;
DROP TABLE IF EXISTS dbo.Chapter05Profiling;
DROP TABLE IF EXISTS dbo.AWCitiesStatesCountries;
USE DQS_STAGING_DATA;
DROP TABLE IF EXISTS dbo.CustomersCh05;
DROP TABLE IF EXISTS dbo.CustomersCh05DQS;
DROP TABLE IF EXISTS dbo.CustomersClean;
DROP TABLE IF EXISTS dbo.CustomersDirty;
DROP TABLE IF EXISTS dbo.CustomersDirtyMatch;
DROP TABLE IF EXISTS dbo.CustomersDirtyNoMatch;
DROP TABLE IF EXISTS dbo.CustomersDQSMatch;
DROP TABLE IF EXISTS dbo.DQSMatchingResults;
DROP TABLE IF EXISTS dbo.DQSSurvivorshipResults;
DROP TABLE IF EXISTS dbo.FuzzyMatchingResults;
```

14. When you are done, close SSMS and SSDT.

11
Unleash the Power of SSIS Script Task and Component

In this chapter, we will cover the following recipes:

- Using variables in SSIS Script tasks
- Execute complex filesystem operations with the Script task
- Reading data profiling XML results with the Script task
- Correcting data with the Script component
- Validating data using regular expressions in a Script component
- Using the Script component as a source
- Using the Script component as a destination

Introduction

The **Script task** and **Script component** allow you to execute custom Visual Basic or Visual C# code inside your SSIS package control flow or data flow. This way, you can perform complex operations beyond the capabilities of other built-in tasks and transformations. The Script task works like any other task in the control flow. You can use the Script component in the data flow as the **source**, **transformation**, or **destination**.

Both the Script task and the Script component have two design-time modes: you begin editing by specifying properties using the common editors for tasks and components that you are already familiar with, and then switch to a development environment to write the .NET code. The second environment is the **Microsoft Visual Studio Tools for Applications (VSTA)** environment.

The Script task provides the entire infrastructure for the custom code for you, letting you focus exclusively on the code. You can use any .NET class library and namespace in your code. In addition, from your code, you can interact with the containing SSIS package through the global **Dts object**. For example, the Dts object exposes package variables, and you can read and modify them in your custom code.

When you add the Script component to your data flow, you have to make the first decision immediately. You can use the Script component as a custom data source, a destination, or a transformation. When you add it to the data flow, you will be asked which Script component type you are creating.

The next step to designing a Script component, after you have determined its type, is to configure its metadata. In the metadata configuration part, you use the Script Component Editor to define the component's properties, such as the name and the language you will use. You also have to enlist the SSIS package variables you are going to use in the script in the `ReadOnlyVariables` and `ReadWriteVariables` properties. Note that, as always, variable names are case sensitive.

The Script component metadata configuration is slightly more complex than the Script task configuration. You need to define the input and output columns of the data flow buffers for the component as well. If you use the Script component as a data source, then you define the output columns only. The Script component is then responsible for creating the data flow buffers. If you use the component for a transformation, then you have to configure input and outputs. If you use it for a data destination, you configure the input only. You have to select which columns from the input buffers you are going to use in the script, and which columns you are going to send to the output buffers or to the data destination.

An output of an SSIS component can be **synchronous** or **asynchronous**, and thus the component can be non-blocking or blocking. Each output of the component has the `SynchronousInputID` property. If the value of this property is None, then the output is asynchronous, and you can completely redefine it. In addition, you can also define whether the output is sorted. If the value of the `SynchronousInputID` property is the component's input ID, then the output is synchronous. You process input row by row, and you cannot change the sort order of the input rows for the output. If you use synchronous outputs, then you can also configure the `ExclusionGroup` property to identify redirections of rows to different outputs. For example, you could redirect some of the rows to the regular output and some to the error output.

Using variables in SSIS Script task

The objective of this task is to teach you how to work with SSIS variables in a Script task. You will learn two ways, a more complex one and a simpler one. You will typically use the latter in your packages.

Getting ready

There are no special prerequisites for this recipe, except, of course, SSIS 2016. In addition, you can use either your own text files for testing, or the three text files provided with the code for this chapter (Ch11_03.txt, Ch11_08.txt, and Ch11_10.txt).

 For your convenience, the VB and C# code snippets needed for this chapter are provided in the Chapter11.txt file.

How to do it...

1. Open SQL Server Data Tools (SSDT) and create a new project using the Integration Services Project template. Place the solution in the C:\SSIS2016Cookbook\Chapter11\Solution folder and name the project AdventureWorksETL.
2. Rename the default package UsingVariables.dtsx.
3. Create a intCounter variable with data type Int32 and a default value of 0.
4. Create a strFile variable of type String with the default value blank. Your **Variables** window should look like the following screenshot:

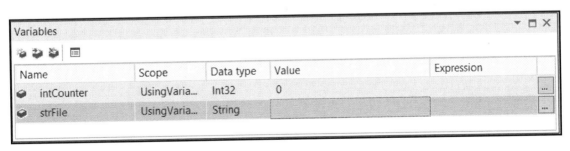

5. Add a For Loop container to the control flow. Rename it LoopThreeTimes.

6. Add a `Foreach Loop` container to the control flow. Rename it `GetFileNames`.

7. Connect the `GetFileNames` container with the `LoopThreeTimes` container with the **green (on success) arrow** from the LoopThreeTimes container. The `For Loop` container should finish with success before the Foreach Loop container starts executing.

8. Start editing the `LoopThreeTimes` container. Set the following properties:
   - **InitExpression** to @intCounter = 0
   - **EvalExpression** to @intCounter < 3
   - **AssignExpression** to @intCounter = @intCounter + 1

9. When you have finished setting the expressions, click on **OK**.

10. Add a Script task to the `LoopThreeTimes` container. Rename it `VariableDispenser`. You will use the `VariableDispenser` class from the `Microsoft.SqlServer.Dts.Runtime` namespace to handle a variable in the script. With this class, you have a detailed control over locking and unlocking variables during the script. You need to lock the variables inside the script either for reading or for writing before you use them, because the SSIS execution is parallelized, and some other thread might want to use the same variables at the same time.

11. Double-click the `VariableDispenser` task to open the Script Task editor. Change the default script language to Microsoft Visual Basic 2015. Leave the `ReadOnlyVariables` and `ReadWriteVariables` properties empty. Click the Edit Script button.

12. Expand the **Imports** region. Note that the `Microsoft.SqlServer.Dts.Runtime` namespace is already imported for you.

13. Locate the `Main()` method. Place the following script between the `Add your code here` comment and the `Dts.TaskResult = ScriptResults.Success` line:

```
Dim vars As Variables = Nothing
Dts.VariableDispenser.LockForRead("intCounter")
Dts.VariableDispenser.GetVariables(vars)
MsgBox("Iteration: " & CStr(vars(0).Value))
```

14. Save the script and close the VSTA environment. Click on **OK** in the Script task editor to close it.

15. Double-click the `GetFileNames` container to open the editor. Click the **Collection** tab.

16. Specify the **Foreach File Enumerator** in the **Enumerator** property.

17. Use the `C:\SSIS2016Cookbook\Chapter07\Files` folder (or any other folder you wish if you have put the text files provided in some other folder). Three text files, `Ch11_03.txt`, `Ch11_08.txt`, and `Ch11_10.txt` are provided with the code download for this book.
18. Specify the `Ch11*.txt` file pattern in the **Files** textbox. Retrieve the name and extension only.
19. Do not check the **Traverse subfolders** checkbox. The following screenshot shows what your settings should look like:

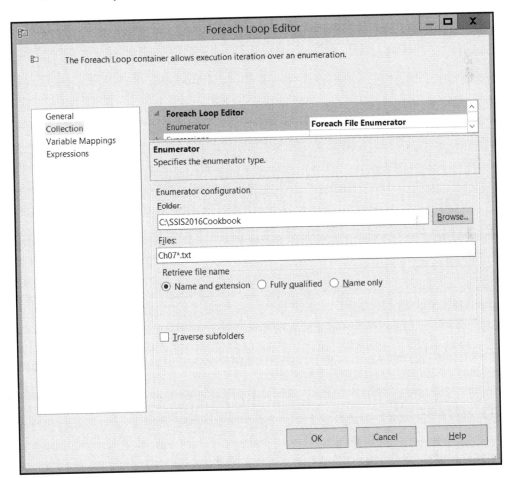

20. Click the **Variable Mappings** tab.
21. Map the `User::strFile` variable to Index 0. Click on **OK**.

22. Drag the **Script task** to the container. Rename it `ReadOnlyVariables`. Open the task editor.

23. In the **Script** tab, select **Microsoft Visual Basic 2015** as the scripting language.

24. Select the **User::strFile** variable in the **ReadOnlyVariables** property. When you define variables here, they are locked for the whole script. Lock and unlock happen automatically. This is a much simpler way to do the locking than with the VariableDispenser class, although you have more control, or control on a finer grain, with the VariableDispenser class.

25. Click the **Edit Script** button.

26. Locate the `Main()` method. Place the following script between the `Add your code here` comment and the `Dts.TaskResult = ScriptResults.Success` line:

```
MsgBox("File name: " & CStr(Dts.Variables("strFile").Value))
```

27. Save the script and close the VSTA environment. Click on **OK** in the Script task editor to close it.

28. Execute the package. Note how you see three iterations and three files. Save the solution, but don't exit SSDT if you want to continue with the next recipe.

Execute complex filesystem operations with the Script task

In the previous recipe, you retrieved filenames filtered by name and extension using the Foreach File enumerator of the Foreach Loop container. Sometimes you need more precise filters. For example, you might need to retrieve files with a larger size than a predefined value. You can get the collection of the filenames that satisfy your custom criteria with the Script task.

Getting ready

There are no special prerequisites for this recipe, except, of course, SSIS 2016. In addition, you can use either your own text files for testing, or the three text files provided with the code for this chapter (`Ch11_03.txt`, `Ch11_08.txt`, and `Ch11_10.txt`). Note that the length of the `Ch11_03.txt` file is 3 bytes, the `Ch11_08.txt` file is 8 bytes, and the `Ch11_10.txt` file is 10 bytes.

How to do it...

1. In **File Explorer**, right-click the `Ch11_08.txt` file and select **Properties**, as shown in the following screenshot:

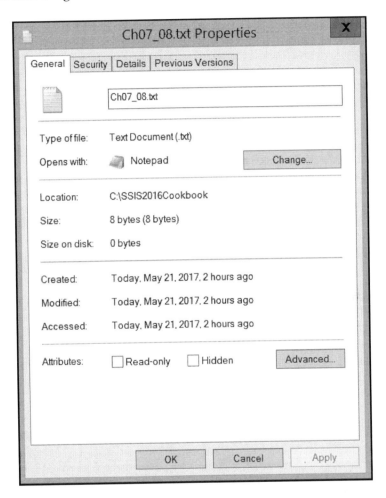

2. Note the file size, 8 bytes. Click **OK**.
3. In SSDT, add a new package to the `Chapter11` project. Rename it `FileSizes.dtsx`.

4. Add two variables to the package:
    - intSize, with data type Int64, and default value 5
    - objList, with data type Object, default System.Object

5. Add a new **Script task** to the control flow. Rename it FilesBySize.

6. Open the task editor. This time, use the Microsoft Visual C# 2015 language. Add the User::intSize variable to the ReadOnlyVariables and the User::objList variable to the ReadWriteVariables collection.

7. Click on **Edit Script**.

8. Expand the **Namespaces** region and add the following two lines:

```
using System.IO;
using System.Collections;
```

9. Just before the Main method, add the following declarations of the constants and variables:

```
private const string FILE_PATH = "C:\\SSIS2016Cookbook";
private const string FILE_FILTER = "Ch07*.txt";
long fileSizeLimit;
private ArrayList listForEnumerator;
```

10. Please note that you might need to change the FILE_PATH and FILE_FILTER constants appropriately.

11. In the Main method, add the following code, that reads the file size limit from the package variable intSize, declares an array to store the names of the local files, a variable to store the file size, and an ArrayList, which will hold the filenames that will satisfy your custom criteria. The Directory.GetFiles method returns an array of the full names (including paths) for the files in the specified directory:

```
fileSizeLimit = (long)(Dts.Variables["intSize"].Value);
string[] localFiles;
long fileSize;
ArrayList listForEnumerator = new ArrayList();
localFiles = Directory.GetFiles(FILE_PATH, FILE_FILTER);
```

12. Add the following code to populate the **ArrayList** with the qualifying filenames:

```
foreach (string localFile in localFiles)
{
  FileInfo fi = new FileInfo(localFile);
  fileSize = fi.Length;
  if (fileSize >= fileSizeLimit)
  {
    listForEnumerator.Add(localFile);
  }
}
```

13. Finally, just before the `Dts.TaskResult = (int)ScriptResults.Success;` line, add the following code to show the number of matching files and to populate the `objList` package variable:

```
MessageBox.Show("Matching files: " + listForEnumerator.Count, "Results",
    MessageBoxButtons.OK, MessageBoxIcon.Information);
    Dts.Variables["objList"].Value = listForEnumerator;
```

14. Save the code and exit the VSTA environment. Also exit the Script task editor.

15. Add a `Foreach` container to the control flow. Connect it with the FilesBySize Script task with the green arrow from the Script task. Rename the container `GetFileNameBySize`. Open the container editor.

16. In the **Collection** tab, specify the **Foreach From Variable Enumerator**. Use the `User::objList` variable.

17. In the **Variable Mappings** tab, map the `User::objList` variable to index 0. Click on **OK** to close the editor.

18. Add a **Script task** inside the container. Rename it `ShowFileNames`. Open the Script task editor.

19. Use the Microsoft Visual C# 2015 language. Define the `User::objList` variable as a read only variable. Click on **Edit Script**.

20. Add the following line of code to the `Main` method to show the names of the qualifying files:

```
MessageBox.Show(Dts.Variables["objList"].Value.ToString());.
```

21. Save the script and exit the task editor.

22. Run the package and observe the results.

Reading data profiling XML results with the Script task

This recipe assumes that you have finished the first recipe of Chapter 10, *Dealing with Data Quality,* and have the results of the Data Profiling task at your hand.

In this recipe, you will read the XML file produced by the Data Profiling task and use the Script task to read the regular expressions extracted and store them in package variables.

Getting ready

This recipe assumes that you have the results of the Data Profiling task at your hand.

 For your convenience, the results of the Data Profiling task needed for this recipe are provided in the DataProfiling.xml file.

How to do it...

1. Add a new package to the AdventureWorksETL project. Rename the default package RegExValidation.dtsx.
2. Create two package variables. Name them EmailRegEx1 and EmailRegEx2. Use the **String** data type for both variables.
3. Drag the Script task to your control flow. Rename it ReadPatterns.
4. Open the editor for this task. On the Script page of the Script Task Editor, make sure that the Visual C# language is selected. Add the User::EmailRegEx1 and User::EmailRegEx2 variables to the ReadOnlyVariables property, as shown in the following screenshot:

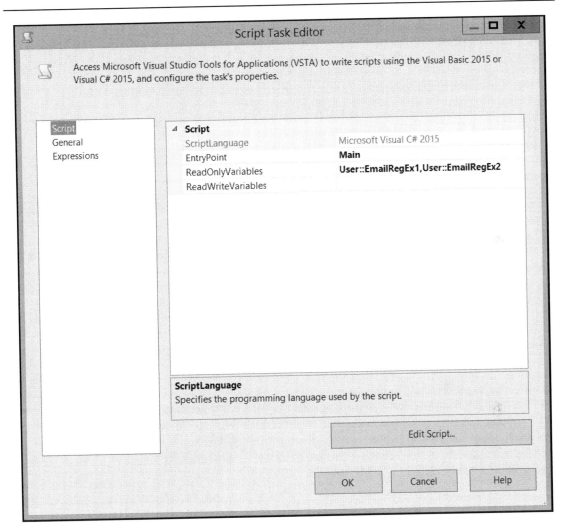

5. Click the **Edit Script** button. Expand the **Namespaces** region. Add the `System.Xml` namespace with the following code: `using System.Xml;`.

6. Declare private variables for the `ScriptMain` class. These private variables will point to the Data Profiling task result XML file, to the XML namespace URI for the Data Profiling task results, and to the two nodes in the XML file with the extracted regular expressions. Enter the following code right after the `ScriptMain` class definition and before the first help region in the class:

```
private string fileName =
@" C:\SSIS2016Cookbook\Chapter07\Files \DataProfiling.xml";
private string profileNamespaceUri =
```

```
        "http://schemas.microsoft.com/sqlserver/2008/DataDebugger/";
        private string erx1Path =
        "/default:DataProfile/default:DataProfileOutput/default:Profiles" +
    "/default:ColumnPatternProfile[default:Column[@Name='EmailAddress']]" +
        "/default:TopRegexPatterns/default:PatternDistributionItem[1]
        /default:RegexText/text()";
        private string erx2Path =
        "/default:DataProfile/default:DataProfileOutput/default:Profiles" +
    "/default:ColumnPatternProfile[default:Column[@Name='EmailAddress']]" +
        "/default:TopRegexPatterns/default:PatternDistributionItem[2]
        /default:RegexText/text()";
```

7. The previous part of the code looks ugly. This is due to the fact that XML is ugly.

8. Modify the `Main` method of the class. Add the following code after the // TODO:... comment and before the last command of the method, the Dts.TaskResult =... command.

```
        // Local variables
        string profilePath;
        XmlDocument profileOutput = new XmlDocument();
        XmlNamespaceManager profileNSM;
        XmlNode regExNode1;
        XmlNode regExNode2;
        // Open output file
        profilePath = fileName;
        profileOutput.Load(profilePath);
        profileNSM = new XmlNamespaceManager(profileOutput.NameTable);
        profileNSM.AddNamespace("default", profileNamespaceUri);
        // Get regExNodes
        regExNode1 = profileOutput.SelectSingleNode(erx1Path, profileNSM);
        regExNode2 = profileOutput.SelectSingleNode(erx2Path, profileNSM);
        // Assign variable values
        Dts.Variables["User::EmailRegEx1"].Value = regExNode1.Value;
        Dts.Variables["User::EmailRegEx2"].Value = regExNode2.Value;
        // Show variable values
MessageBox.Show(Dts.Variables["User::EmailRegEx1"].Value.ToString());
MessageBox.Show(Dts.Variables["User::EmailRegEx2"].Value.ToString());
```

9. Note that this code reads the data profiling results, loads the XML file, and then assigns the extracted regular expression patterns to the values of the two SSIS package variables you just created. Finally, the code shows the variable values in two message boxes.

10. Save the script and close the VSTA environment. In the Script Task Editor, click on the **OK** button to close the editor.

11. Right-click the **ReadPatterns** task and execute it. Check the two message boxes with the two regular expressions extracted by the Data Profiling task. Click on **OK** in each of the boxes to close them. Stop debugging the package.

Correcting data with the Script component

In this recipe, you will use the Script Component in the data flow as a transformation for advanced data cleansing. You will read an Excel file and do a custom transformation in order to make the output ready for further processing in the data flow.

Getting ready

In order to test this recipe, you need to have an Excel file prepared. In the file, there should be a single sheet with the following content:

OrderId	Date	Product	Quantity
1	20160915	ABC	1
		DEF	5
		GHI	3
2	20160916	GHI	2
		ABC	4

 For your convenience, an Excel file with the content needed is provided in the `Ch07_Orders.xls` file.

Note that the table represents simple orders with order details. However, the order info is added to the first order details line only. Your task is to add the appropriate order info to every single line.

How to do it...

1. Add a new package to the `AdventureWorksETL` project. Rename it
   `ProcessingExcel.dtsx`.

2. Add a new package-level Excel connection manager. Rename it
   `Excel_Ch11_Orders`. Point to your Excel file path and define your Excel version
   appropriately, as shown in the following screenshot:

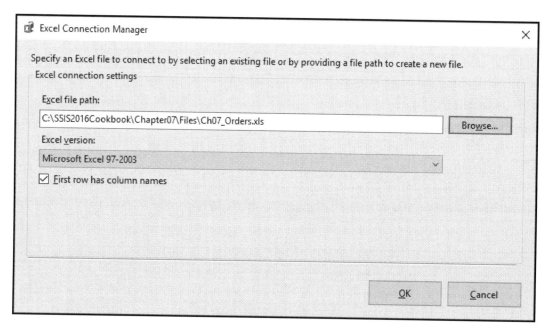

3. Add a **Data Flow task** to the control flow. Rename it to `ProcessExcelOrders`.
   Open the Data Flow tab.

4. Add an **Excel source**. Double-click it to open the editor.

5. Using the **Connection Manager** tab, define the **Excel connection manager**. Point
   to the `Excel_Ch11_Orders` connection manager you just created. Use the **Table
   or view data access** mode. Select `Sheet1$` in the name of the Excel sheer drop-
   down list. Click on the **Preview** button to preview the content of the file, as
   shown in the following screenshot:

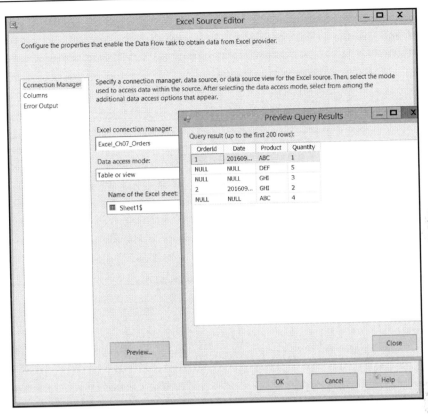

6. You can note in the data preview pop-up window that order info columns are NULL except for the first order detail of an order. When finished with the preview, click the Close button.

7. Click the **Columns** tab to check the columns mapping. Then click on **OK** to close the data source editor.

8. Add a **Script Component** to the data flow. In the **Select Script Component Type** pop-up window, make sure that **Transformation** option button is selected. Then click on **OK**.

9. Connect the Script component with the blue arrow (regular data flow) from the data source.

10. Double-click the Script component to open the editor. Note that the **Script** tab is more complex than the Script tab of the Script task. Nevertheless, you can easily find the `ScriptLanguage`, `ReadOnlyVariables`, and `ReadWriteVariables` properties. Leave all of them with their defaults, meaning you will use the Microsoft Visual C# 2015 language and that you don't need any variables in the script.

11. Click the **Input Columns** tab. In the `Available Input Columns` table, select all columns. In the lower part of the window, check the mappings between input columns and output aliases. Don't change any of the output aliases. However, change the usage type for the `OrderId` and `Date` columns to `ReadWrite`, as shown in the following screenshot:

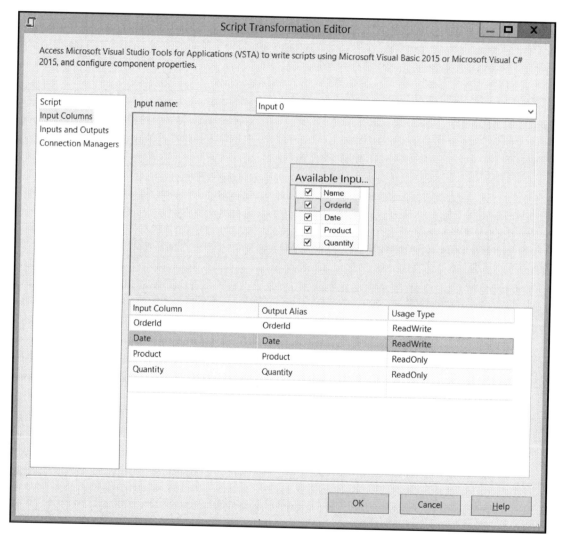

12. When setting up the columns correctly, click the **Script** tab and then the **Edit Script** button to open the VSTA environment.

13. In the script, find the `Input0_ProcessInputRow` method. Add the following two variables just before the method definition and after the comments, with the summary and parameters description of this method:

```
Double MyDate;
Double MyOrderId;
Add the following code to the method:
// Check if OrderId column is null
if (Row.OrderId_IsNull)
{
    // if null then replace value with variable value
    Row.OrderId = MyOrderId;
}
else
{
   // if not null then replace variable value with column value
   MyOrderId = Row.OrderId;
}
// Check if Date column is null
if (Row.Date_IsNull)
{
    // if null then replace value with variable value
    Row.Date = MyDate;
}
else
{
    // if not null then replace variable value with column value
    MyDate = Row.Date;
}
```

14. Save the code end exit the VSTA environment. In the Script Transformation Editor, click on **OK**.

15. Add a **Multicast** transformation to the data flow and connect it with the blue arrow from the Script component. This transformation serves as a placeholder only, in order to enable a Data Viewer after the Script transformation does its job.

16. Enable two **Data Viewers**, one on the path from the source to the Script component, and one from the **Script** component to the Multicast transformation. Your data flow should look as shown in the following screenshot:

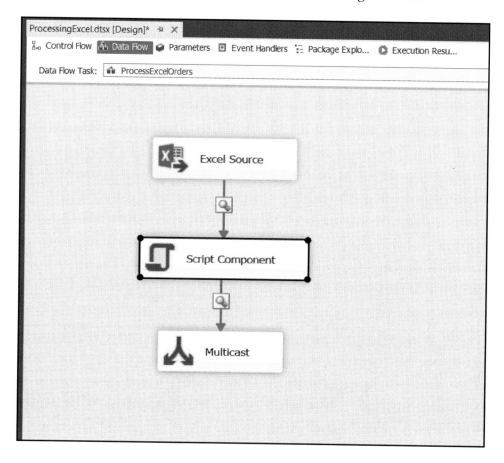

17. Note that, depending on the Excel version you are using, you might need to change the `Run64BitRuntime` property of your project to False before running the package, as shown in the following screenshot:

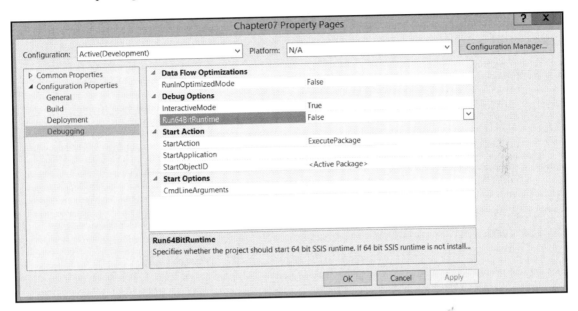

18. Save the package and run it. Observe the data before correction with the Script component and after it. When finished, stop debugging.

Validating data using regular expressions in a Script component

In this recipe, you will create a Script Component that will use the regular expressions in the `DataProfiling.xml` file to validate the emails of the personal data extracted from a flat file.

Getting ready

This recipe assumes that you successfully completed the *Reading data profiling XML results with Script task* recipe earlier in this chapter. If you did not complete that recipe, you can prepare an appropriate SSIS package simply by completing step 1 of that recipe.

How to do it...

1. Make sure that the `RegExValidation.dtsx` package is active in the control flow designer.
2. Right-click in the empty canvas of the **Connection Managers** pane at the bottom of the SSDT window and select **New Flat File Connection...** from the shortcut menu.
3. Use the **Flat File Connection Manager Editor** to create a new connection manager, and on the **General** page enter `PersonData` into the Connection manager name textbox.
4. To determine the **File name** property, click **Browse...**, and then select the `Ch11_PersonData.csv` file in the `C:\SSIS2016Cookbook\Chapter11\Files\` folder.

   The file should be recognized as a Unicode file automatically; otherwise, check the **Unicode** option below the **Browse...** button.

5. Leave the rest of the properties unchanged, as shown in the following screenshot:

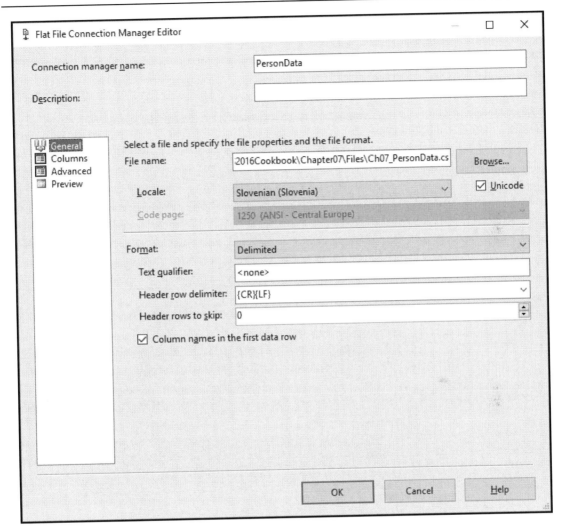

6. On the **Columns** page, verify that all the source columns have been recognized: Title, FirstName, MiddleName, LastName, Suffix, and EmailAddress.

   If any of the columns are missing, click **Reset Columns** below the columns list.

7. Click on **OK** to complete the configuration.

8. Add a new package parameter by using the following settings:

Property	Value
Name	DataProfileName
Data type	String
Value	C:\SSIS2016Cookbook\Chapter11\Files\DataProfiling.xml

9. Save the package.
10. From the SSIS Toolbox, drag a Data Flow task to the control flow designer, change its name to Validate Person Data, and—as long as you have completed the *Reading data profiling XML results with Script task*—connect the precedence constraint from the **ReadPatterns** task to the newly added data flow task.
11. Open the **Validate Person Data** task in the data flow designer.
12. For the SSIS Toolbox, drag a **Flat File Source** component to the data flow, and change its name to Person Data.
13. Configure the **Person Data** source to connect to the **PersonData** flat file connection manager, and make sure that all the source columns are extracted.
14. From the SSIS Toolbox, drag a **Script Component** to the data flow designer. When prompted about its type, select **Transformation**, as shown in the following screenshot:

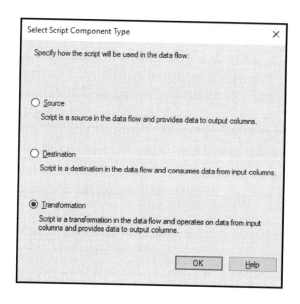

15. Click **OK** to confirm the component type, and then change its name to Validate Email.

16. Connect the regular data path from the **Person Data** source to the **Validate Email** transformation.

17. Double-click the **Validate Email** transformation to open the Script Task Editor.

18. On the Script page, add the **$Package::DataProfileName** package parameter to the **ReadOnlyVariables** collection, and make sure that Microsoft Visual C# 2015 is selected as the **ScriptLanguage** property, as shown in the following screenshot:

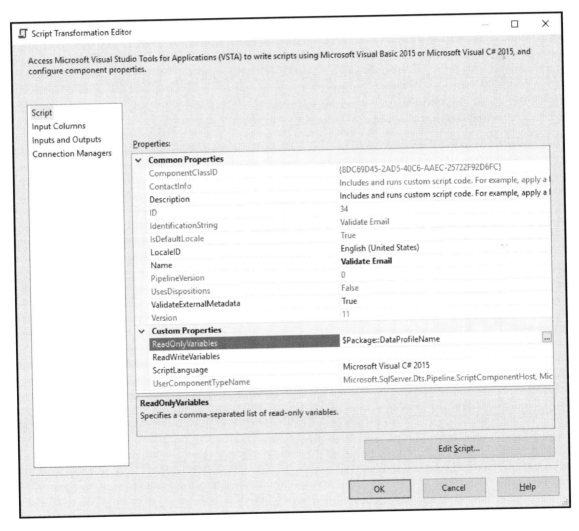

19. On the **Input Columns** page, make sure that all the input columns are selected; their usage type should be **ReadOnly**.

20. On the **Inputs and Outputs** page, in the **Inputs and outputs** list, select the **Input 0** input, and in the properties pane on the right-hand side of the editor, change its **Name** property to `PersonDataInput`.

21. Select the **Output 0** output, and change its name to `PersonDataOutput`.

22. In the `PersonDataOutput` properties, locate the `SyncronousInputID` property and make sure it references the `Validate Email.Inputs[PersonDataInput]` input.

> This means that the component's output is synchronous.

23. Expand the `PersonDataOutput` in the **Inputs and outputs** list and select the Output Columns node.

24. Click on **Add Column** to create a column in the output; use the following settings to configure it:

```
Property Value
Name IsValidEmail
DataType Boolean [DT_BOOL]
```

25. Click on **OK** to confirm the component's configuration so far.

It is recommended to save all Script component settings, such as variables, inputs, outputs, and additional connection managers, before creating the script.

This way, if there are problems with the script that you cannot resolve during editing, the rest of the settings do not need to be set again.

26. Open the **Validate Email** transformation editor again, and on the Script page click **Edit Script...** to start **Visual Studio for Applications** (**VSTA**) IDE.

27. Locate the `Namespaces` region at the beginning of the component definition and add the following references to the region:

```
using System.Collections.Generic;
using System.Text.RegularExpressions;
using System.Xml;
```

28. In the `ScriptMain` class definition, add the following constant and private variable declarations:

```
private const String DATA_PROFILE_NAMESPACE =
"http://schemas.microsoft.com/sqlserver/2008/DataDebugger/";
private const String DATA_PROFILE_NAMESPACE_ALIAS = "dp";

private String _regexElementXPath =
"/dp:DataProfile/dp:DataProfileOutput/dp:Profiles" +
"/dp:ColumnPatternProfile[dp:Column[@Name='EmailAddress']]" +
"/dp:TopRegexPatterns/dp:PatternDistributionItem/dp:RegexText/text()";

private List<String> _regexPatterns = new List<String>();
```

Typically, variable definitions are placed at the beginning of the class definition, right after the three `Help` regions.

29. At the end of the `ScriptMain` class definition (before the last closing brace) place the following function definition:

```
private List<String> LoadRegularExpressions(String dataProfileName)
{
  List<String> result = new List<String>();
  XmlDocument dataProfile = new XmlDocument();
  dataProfile.Load(dataProfileName);
  XmlNamespaceManager dataProfileNSM = new
  XmlNamespaceManager(dataProfile.NameTable);
  dataProfileNSM.AddNamespace(DATA_PROFILE_NAMESPACE_ALIAS,
  DATA_PROFILE_NAMESPACE);

  foreach (XmlNode regexPatternElement in
  dataProfile.SelectNodes(_regexElementXPath, dataProfileNSM))
  {
    String regexPattern = regexPatternElement.Value;
    if (!result.Contains(regexPattern))
    {
      result.Add(regexPattern);
    }
  }

  return result;
}
```

This function extracts all relevant regular expression patterns from the data profiling result and loads them into a variable.

30. Right after the `LoadRegularExpressions()` function, add another function:

```
private Boolean IsValidEmail(String emailAddress)
{
  Boolean result = false;
  if (!String.IsNullOrEmpty(emailAddress))
  {
    foreach (String regexPattern in _regexPatterns)
    {
      if (Regex.IsMatch(emailAddress, regexPattern,
      RegexOptions.IgnoreCase))
      {
        result = true;
        break;
      }
    }
  }
  return result;
}
```

This function tests the supplied email address against all available regular expressions, and returns `true` as soon as one of the patterns is matched; otherwise, it returns `false`.

31. Locate the `PreExecute()` method add the following command to its definition:

```
_regexPatterns.AddRange(this.LoadRegularExpressions(Variables.DataProfileNa
me));
```

The `PreExecute()` data flow component method is called at the beginning of the data flow execution, before the rows are acquired from the upstream pipeline. As the same set of regular expressions is going to be used throughout the data flow execution, it only needs to be loaded once, not for every row.

32. Locate the `PersonDataInput_ProcessInputRow()` method, and add the following command to its definition:

    ```
    Row.IsValidEmail = this.IsValidEmail(Row.EmailAddress);
    ```

    The `IsValidEmail()` function needs to be called for each row as it needs to validate each e-mail address extracted from the source.

33. Save the VSTA project and build it by selecting the **Build** command from the **Build** menu.

    If you entered all the code correctly, the build should succeed; otherwise, you need to follow the error messages in the Error pane to resolve the errors.

34. After the successful build, close the VSTA window, and return to SSDT.

35. In the Script Transformation Editor, click on **OK**, to confirm and save the component script, and then save the package.

36. From the SSIS Toolbox, drag a **Conditional Split** transformation to the data flow designer, and change its name to `Valid or Invalid Email`.

37. Connect the regular data path from the **Validate Email** transformation to the **Conditional Split** transformation.

38. Double-click the newly added transformation to open the **Conditional Split Transformation Editor**.

39. Create a new output using the following settings:
    - **Property**: `Value`
    - **Output name**: `Valid Email`
    - **Condition**: `IsValidEmail`

    Alternatively, to reduce typing, you can drag the `IsValidEmail` column from the **Columns** list in the top-left part of the **Conditional Split Transformation Editor**.

40. Change the **Default output name** to `Invalid Email`.

Refer to the following screenshot to verify your settings:

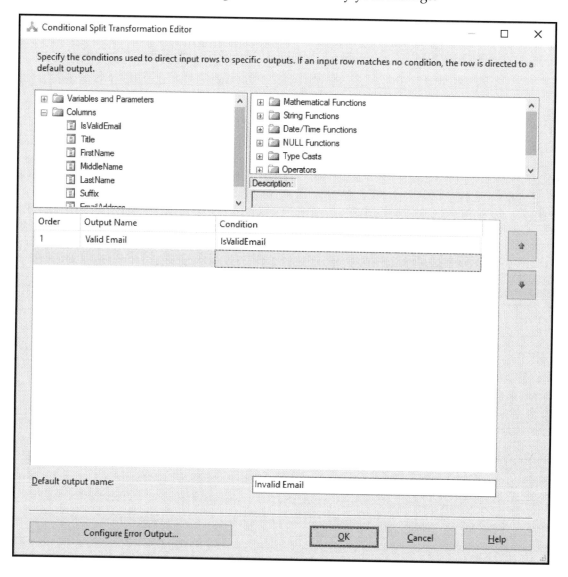

41. Click on **OK** to complete the configuration.
42. From the SSIS Toolbox, drag a **Multicast** transformation to the data flow designer and connect the regular data path from the **Valid** or **Invalid Email** transformation to it.
43. When prompted by the **Input Output Selection** dialog, select the **Invalid Email** in the **Output** selection box, as shown in the following screenshot:

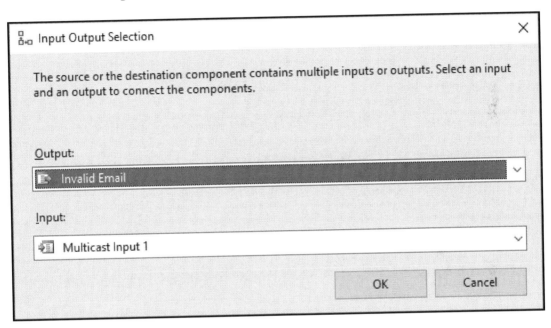

44. Click on **OK** to confirm the selection.
45. Enable the **Data Viewer** on the **Invalid Email** data path.
46. Save the package and execute it in debug mode. Observe the execution and inspect the rows placed in the **Invalid Email** data path.
47. Stop the debug mode execution; leave the solution open, as you will need it for the next recipe.

Using the Script component as a source

In this recipe, you will create a custom source by using the Script Component as a data flow source.

You will connect to a web service and retrieve the data from it, which you will then place into the data flow pipeline.

How to do it...

1. Add a new SSIS package to the **AdventureWorksETL** project you created at the beginning of this chapter.
2. Change the name of the newly created package to CustomWebServiceSource.dtsx and save it.
3. Make sure the **CustomWebServiceSource.dtsx** package is active, and then create a new package parameter using the following settings:
   - **Property**: Value
   - **Name**: CountryName
   - **Data type**: String
   - **Value**: France
4. Drag a **Data Flow** task to the control flow designer and change its name to Airport Information.
5. Open the **Airport Information** task in the data flow designer and drag a **Script Component** to the data flow designer.
6. In the **Select Script Component Type** dialog, select **Source**, as shown in the following screenshot:

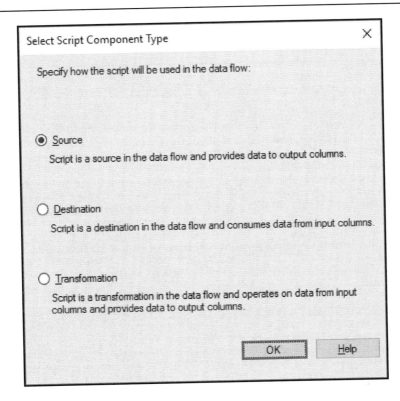

7. Click on **OK** to confirm the selection.
8. Change the name of the Script component to Airport Info by Country.
9. Double-click on the **Airport Info by Country** source to open the Script Transformation Editor.
10. On the **Script** page, add the $Package::CountryName parameter to the ReadOnlyVariables collection, and make sure that Microsoft Visual C# 2015 is selected as the **ScriptLanguage** property.
11. On the **Inputs and Outputs** page, select **Output 0** and change its name to AirportInfoOutput.
12. Add columns to the output's Column Collection using the following settings:

```
Name DataType Length
Country Unicode string [DT_WSTR] 50
AiportName Unicode string [DT_WSTR] 50
AirportCode Unicode string [DT_WSTR] 3
RunwayLengthFeet four-byte signed integer [DT_I4] /
```

Refer to the following screenshot to verify your settings:

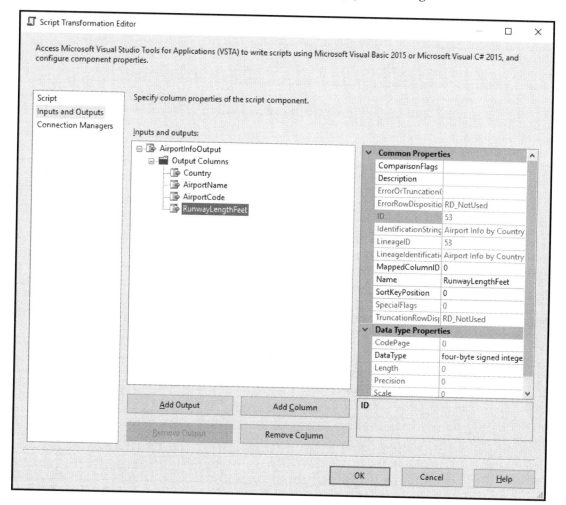

 To ensure that each new column is added to the end of the list, click on the **Output Columns** node before adding the next column.

13. Click **OK** to confirm the configuration.
14. Open the **Airport Info by Country** transformation editor again, and this time click **Edit Script...** to start VSTA.

15. In the **Solution Explorer**, right-click the **References** node and select **Add Service Reference...** from the shortcut menu, as shown in the following screenshot:

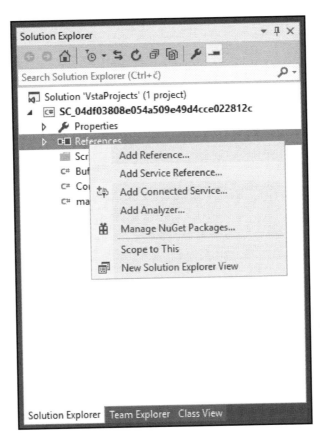

16. In the **Add Service Reference** dialog, click on **Advanced...** on the bottom-left of the dialog.
17. In the **Service Reference Settings** dialog, click on **Add Web Reference...** to open the **Add Web Reference** dialog.
18. Enter the following URL in the **URL** textbox:

```
http://www.webservicex.net/airport.asmx?WSDL
```

19. Click the arrow pointing to the right, on the right-hand side of the textbox, to load the information from the web service.

20. Enter `AirportInfo` into the **Web reference name** textbox.

Refer to the following screenshot to verify your settings:

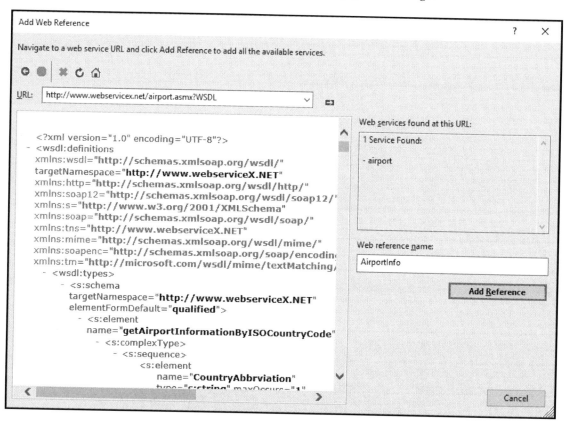

21. Click **Add Reference** to confirm the settings and create the reference.
22. Save the project.
23. In the component definition, at the beginning of the code, locate the `Namespaces` region and expand it to list the existing references.
24. Add another `using` command after the last one, and start typing the name of the project (it should be similar to `SC_04df03808e054a509e49d4cce022812c`); allow the Visual Studio *intellisense* to suggest the complete namespace, and then complete the reference to the `AirportInfo` namespace:

```
using SC_04df03808e054a509e49d4cce022812c.AirportInfo;
```

25. The `SC_04df03808e054a509e49d4cce022812c` value in this example is used for the name of the VSTA project and for its default namespace. When you add a web reference to the project, proxy classes, and functions are created automatically and placed in the project's default namespace.

26. Add the following reference as it will be needed later:

```
using System.Xml;
```

27. From the **Build** menu, select **Build**, to save and build the project.

28. If you followed the preceding steps correctly, the project should build successfully; otherwise, inspect the errors reported in the Error pane and make the necessary corrections.

    1. If errors are returned from the automatically generated code, remove the web reference by right-clicking it in the **Solution Explorer** and selecting **Delete** from the shortcut menu, then rebuild the project and repeat steps 14 through 21.

29. Add the following variable declarations to the `ScriptMain` class of the component definition:

```
private String _countryName;
private String _airportXPath = @"/NewDataSet/Table";
private XmlNodeList _airportXmlNodes;
```

30. Add the following commands to the `PreExecute()` method:

```
airport airportInfo = new airport();
String airportInfoByCountry =
airportInfo.GetAirportInformationByCountry(_countryName);
XmlDocument airportInfoByCountryXml = new XmlDocument();
airportInfoByCountryXml.LoadXml(airportInfoByCountry);
_airportXmlNodes = airportInfoByCountryXml.SelectNodes(_airportXPath);
```

31. The `GetAirportInformationByCountry` function of the given web service returns a list of airports and their properties for the supplied country name. This function only needs to be invoked once per data flow execution; therefore, you should place it in the `PreExecute()` method, which is invoked once, at the beginning of the data flow execution.

32. Add the following commands to the `CreateNewOutputRows()` method:

```
foreach (XmlNode airportXmlNode in _airportXmlNodes)
{
    AirportInfoOutputBuffer.AddRow();

    AirportInfoOutputBuffer.Country = _countryName;
    AirportInfoOutputBuffer.AirportName =
airportXmlNode.SelectSingleNode("CityOrAirportName").InnerText;
    AirportInfoOutputBuffer.AirportCode =
airportXmlNode.SelectSingleNode("AirportCode").InnerText;
    AirportInfoOutputBuffer.RunwayLengthFeet =
Int32.Parse(airportXmlNode.SelectSingleNode("RunwayLengthFeet").InnerText);
}
```

This code will read all the items retrieved from the web service `GetAirportInformationByCountry()` function and place each one of them in the component's output.

33. Use the **Build** command from the **Build** menu to save and build the component project. In case of any errors, inspect the **Error** pane and resolve the problems.

34. After the project is built successfully, close the VSTA window and return to SSDT.

35. In the **Script Transformation Editor**, click **OK** to complete the configuration of the **Airport Info by Country** source component.

36. Save the package.

37. From the SSIS Toolbox, drag a **Multicast** transformation to the data flow designer.

38. Connect the regular data path from the **Airport Info by Country** source component to the **Multicast** transformation and activate the **Data Viewer** on this data path.

39. Save, and execute the package in debug mode. Observe the rows in the **Data Viewer**.

40. Stop the debug mode execution; leave the solution and the package open, as you will need them in the following recipe.

How it works...

The **Airport Info by Country** source component connects to a publicly available web service that provides information about airports in various countries. It retrieves the list of airports for the country specified by the **CountryName** package parameter.

Alternatively, the country name could also be supplied via a variable populated in a **Foreach Loop** container, so that the same data flow is executed multiple times for multiple countries.

After the data is retrieved from the web service, it is placed into a variable. When the component starts to generate rows, specific properties of each item retrieved from the web service are placed into the downstream pipeline. Each row in the components output represents one entity retrieved from the web service.

Using the Script component as a destination

In this recipe, you will design a custom data flow destination by using the Script Component.

You will use the data retrieved by using the source component created in the *Using the Script component as a source* recipe and export it in JSON format to one or more files.

The acronym JSON stands for JavaScript Object Notation, an open-source format for representing data in human-readable form that can also be consumed by automated processes.

Getting ready

Before you can complete this recipe, you need to complete the *Using the Script component as a source* recipe.

How to do it...

1. Make sure that the `CustomWebServiceSource.dtsx` package of the `AdventureWorksETL` solution from the `C:\SSIS2016Cookbook\Chapter11\Solution\` folder is active in the control flow editor.

2. Add a package parameter using the following settings:
   - **Property**: Value
   - **Name**: JSONFilePath
   - **Data type**: String
   - **Value**: C:\SSIS2016Cookbook\Chapter11\Files

3. Add another package parameter using the following settings:
   - **Property**: Value
   - **Name**: JSONFileNameFormat
   - **Data type**: String
   - **Value**: AirportInfo_{0:D3}.JSON

4. Open the **Airport Information** data flow in the data flow designer.
5. Form the SSIS Toolbox, drag a Script Component to the data flow designer.
6. In the **Select Script Component Type** dialog, select **Destination**, as shown in the following screenshot:

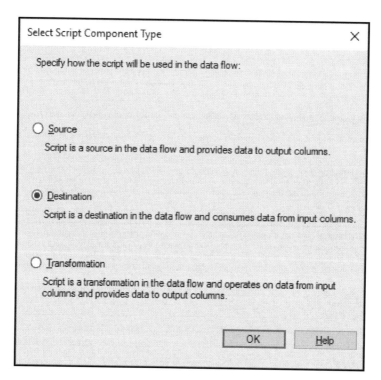

7. Click on **OK** to confirm the selection.

8. Change the name of the destination component to JSON File.

9. Connect the regular data path from the Multicast transformation to the **JSON File** destination.

10. Double-click the **JSON File** destination to open its editor, and on the **Script** page, add the `$Package::JSONFilePath` and `$Package::JSONFileNameFormat` parameters to the `ReadOnlyVariables` collection.

11. On the **Input Columns** page, make sure that all the input columns are selected. The usage type for all the columns can remain **ReadOnly**.

12. On the Inputs and Outputs page, rename the **Input 0** input to `JSONFileInput`.

13. Click **OK** to confirm the configuration.

14. Open the **JSON File** destination again, and on the **Script** page click **Edit Script...** to open the component's project in VSTA.

15. In the Solution Explorer, right-click **References** and select **Add Reference...** from the shortcut menu.

16. In the **Reference Manager**, in the navigator on the left, make sure that the **Assemblies / Framework** node is selected, and then in the list in the middle of the dialog, locate the **System.Web.Extensions** assembly and check it, as shown in the following screenshot:

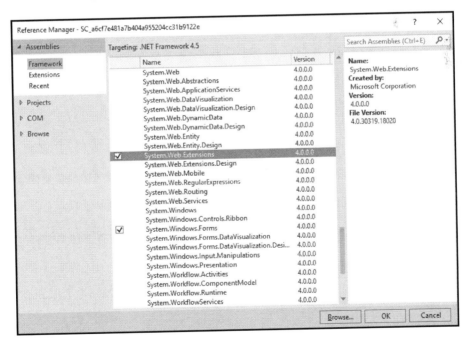

17. Click **OK** to confirm the selection.

18. At the beginning of the component definition, locate the `Namespaces` region and expand it to inspect the existing namespace references.

19. Add the following references below the existing ones:

```
using System.Web.Script.Serialization;
using System.Collections.Generic;
using System.IO;
```

The `System.Web.Script.Serialization` namespace contains the functionalities needed to create and consume JSON data. The `System.IO` namespace provides access to the functionalities needed to work with the Windows operating system filesystem.

20. In the `ScriptMain` class, add the following constant and variable declarations:

```
private const Int32 JSON_MAX_ITEM_COUNT = 50;

private String _jsonFilePath;
private String _jsonFileNameFormat;
private Int32 _fileCounter = 0;

private JavaScriptSerializer _jsonSerializer =
new JavaScriptSerializer();
```

21. Also inside the `ScriptMain` class, at the end of the existing code (before the last closing brace), add the following class definition:

```
public class AirportInfo
{
  public String CountryName { get; set; }
  public String AirportName { get; set; }
  public String AirportCode { get; set; }
  public Int32 RunwayLengthFeet { get; set; }

  public AirportInfo()
  {
  }

  public AirportInfo(String countryName, String airportName,
  String airportCode, Int32 runwayLengthFeet)
  {
    this.CountryName = countryName;
    this.AirportName = airportName;
    this.AirportCode = airportCode;
    this.RunwayLengthFeet = runwayLengthFeet;
```

```
        }
    }
```

This class allows you to store the pipeline data during processing, and it provides the metadata to the `JavaScriptSerializer.Serialize()` method that creates the JSON documents.

Unless explicitly marked **public**, class members are, by default, marked **private**, and thus *inaccessible* to the caller. If the metadata for the JSON document cannot be determined, the serialization will *not* fail, but the resulting document will also not contain any data for which the metadata was not available during serialization.

22. Before the `AirportInfo` class definition, place the definition of the function that will be used to write the data to the file:

```
private void WriteJSONFile(List<AirportInfo> airportInfo,
Int32 fileCount)
{
   String airportInfoJSON = _jsonSerializer.Serialize(airportInfo);

   String jsonFileName = Path.Combine(_jsonFilePath,
   String.Format(_jsonFileNameFormat, fileCount));

   using (StreamWriter jsonStreamWriter = new
StreamWriter(jsonFileName))
   {
      jsonStreamWriter.Write(airportInfoJSON);
      jsonStreamWriter.Flush();
   }
}
```

23. Add the following variable assignments to the `PreExecute()` method:

```
_jsonFilePath = Variables.JSONFilePath;
_jsonFileNameFormat = Variables.JSONFileNameFormat;
```

24. Remove the `JSONFileInput_ProcessInputRows` method, as this component will not process individual rows in the traditional way.

25. Instead, just after the `PostExecute()` method definition, enter a new line, and start typing the `override` directive. Visual Studio will list the overridable methods of the component; select the `JSONFileInput_ProcessInput` method to override, and add the following code to its definition:

```
List<AirportInfo> airportInfo = new List<AirportInfo>();

Int32 index = 0;
while (Buffer.NextRow())
{
  airportInfo.Add
  (
    new AirportInfo
    (
      Buffer.Country,
      Buffer.AirportName,
      Buffer.AirportCode,
      Buffer.RunwayLengthFeet
    )
  );
  index++;
  if (index % JSON_MAX_ITEM_COUNT == 0)
  {
    _fileCounter++;
    this.WriteJSONFile(airportInfo, _fileCounter);
    airportInfo.Clear();
  }
}
if (airportInfo.Count > 0)
{
  _fileCounter++;
  this.WriteJSONFile(airportInfo, _fileCounter);
  airportInfo.Clear();
}
```

26. Build the project by selecting the **Build** command from the **Build** menu.
27. Close VSTA and return to SSDT.
28. In the Script Transformation Editor, click OK to complete the configuration of the **JSON File** destination.
29. Save the package and execute it in debug mode. The **JSON File** destination loads the rows from the pipeline into files, 50 rows at a time.
30. In Windows Explorer, navigate to the **C:\SSIS2016Cookbook\Chapter07\Files** folder; it should contain six additional files, named **AirportInfo_001.JSON** through **AirportInfo_006.JSON**.

31. Right-click one of the files and use the **Open With** command to open the file in Notepad. Inspect the file; it should contain the JSON representation of the information about the airports.

32. Return to SSDT, stop the debug mode execution, and close SSDT.

How it works...

The **JSON File** destination receives the rows from the upstream component, stores them in a variable (50 rows at a time), and converts the row set into a JSON document, which it then loads into a file in the file system.

The `JSONFileInput_ProcessInput` method contains all the logic needed to process the incoming pipeline data; it creates batches of up to 50 rows so that no resulting JSON document contains more than 50 items.

The `WriteJSONFile` function uses the `Serialize()` method of the `JavaScriptSerializer` class to create a JSON document from the row set, and the metadata needed to create the document's structure is provided by the `AirportInfo` class.

12
On-Premises and Azure Big Data Integration

This chapter will cover the following recipes:

- Azure Blob storage data management
- Installing a Hortonworks cluster
- Copying data to an on-premises cluster
- Using Hive - creating a database
- Transforming the data with Hive
- Transferring data between Hadoop and Azure
- Leveraging a HDInsight big data cluster
- Managing data with Pig Latin
- Importing Azure Blob storage data

Introduction

Data warehouse architects are facing the need to integrate many types of data. Cloud data integration can be a real challenge for on-premises data warehouses for the following reasons:

- The data sources are obviously not stored on-premises and the data stores differ a lot from what ETL tools such as SSIS are usually made for. As we saw earlier, the out-of-the-box SSIS toolbox has sources, destinations, and transformation tools that deal with on-premises data only.

- The data transformation toolset is quite different to the cloud one. In the cloud, we don't necessarily use SSIS to transform data. There are specific data transformation languages such as Hive and Pig that are used by the cloud developers. The reason for this is that the volume of data may be huge and these languages are running on clusters. as opposed to SSIS, which is running on a single machine.

While there are many cloud-based solutions on the market, the recipes in this chapter will talk about the Microsoft Azure ecosystem.

Azure Blob storage data management

This recipe will cover the following topics:

- Creating a Blob storage in Azure
- Using SSIS to connect to a Blob storage in Azure
- Using SSIS to upload and download files
- Using SSIS to loop through the file using a for each loop task

Getting ready

This recipe assumes that you have a Microsoft Azure account. You can always create a trial account by registering at `https://azure.microsoft.com`.

How to do it...

1. In the Azure portal, create a new storage account and name it `ssiscookbook`.
2. Add a new package in the `ETL.Staging` project and call it `AggregatedSalesFromCloudDW`.
3. Right-click in the **Connection Manager** pane and select **New file connection** from the contextual menu that appears.
4. The **Add SSIS Connection Manager** window appears. Select **Azure Srorage** and click on the **Add...** button.

5. Fill the **Storage account name** textbox, as shown the following screenshot:

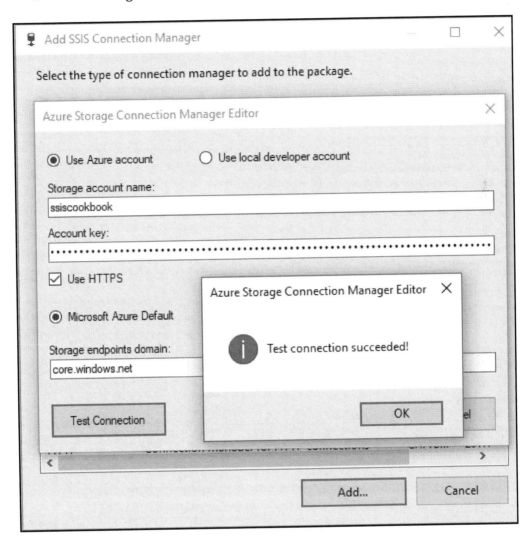

6. Rename the connection manager `cmgr_AzureStorage_ssiscookbook`.

7. Right-click on the newly created connection manager and select **Convert to Project Connection**, as shown in the following screenshot:

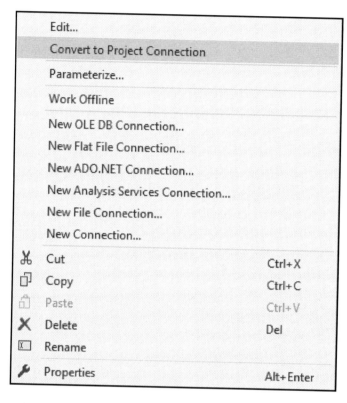

8. Parameterize the `AccountKey`, as shown in the following screenshot:

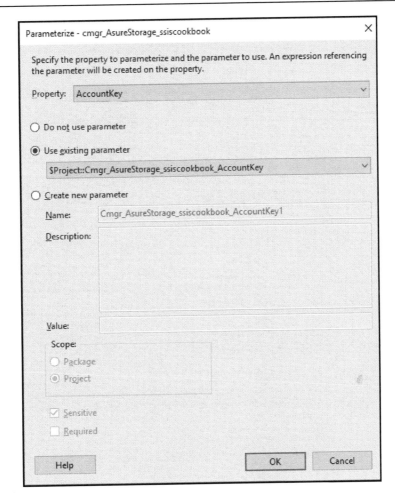

9. Copy and paste the Azure Blob storage key in the `Cmgr_AzureStorage_ssiscookbook_AccountKey` parameter.

10. From the SSIS toolbox-Azure section, drag and drop an Azure Blob upload task to the control flow. Set its properties as shown here:

   - Rename the task `abut_test`
   - Assign the **Connection** property to the `cmgr_AzureStorage_ssiscookbook` connection manager we created earlier.
   - Create a folder on your C drive and name it `test`.
   - Copy any file; in our case, we used a file called `ExtendedProperties.sql`.

- Set the **BlobContainer** property to `test`.
- Set the optional property **BlobDirectory** to `uploadfiletest/`.
- Set the **LocalDirectory** to `C:\test`.
- Leave the other properties as they are.

See also shown in the following screenshot:

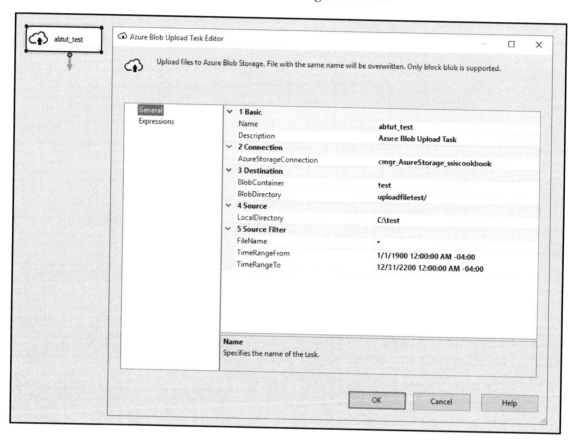

11. Now, right-click on the package to execute it.

12. After the execution has completed, go to your Azure storage account and you should see the file uploaded there, as shown in the following screenshot:

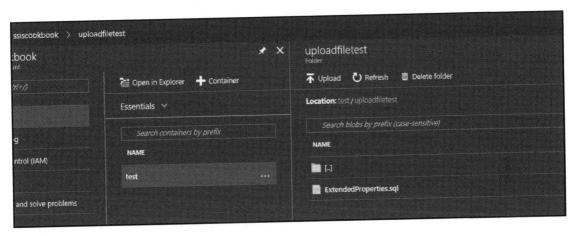

That's it. We have successfully uploaded a file to a Blob storage with SSIS. We just did a `Hello world` test. The next recipes with Azure will fill out this storage account with more useful files.

Installing a Hortonworks cluster

In the previous recipe, we created and managed files using an Azure Blob storage. This recipe will do similar actions but this time using an on-premises Hadoop cluster.

Getting ready

This recipe assumes that you can download and install a virtual machine on your PC.

How to do it...

1. You will need to download and install a Hortonworks sandbox for this recipe. Go to `https://hortonworks.com/downloads/` to download a Docker version of the sandbox. You can choose the sandbox you want, as shown in the following screenshot:

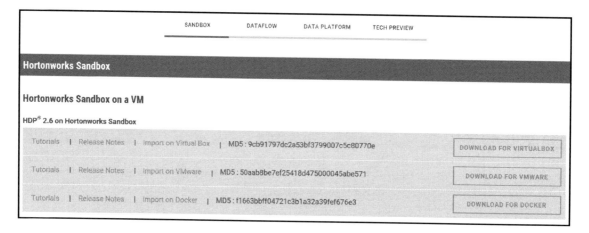

2. Download the VM you want; in our case, we used the last one, **DOWNLOAD FOR DOCKER**. Once done, follow the instructions to configure it and make sure you have added the following entry to the `%systemroot%\system32\drivers\etc\hosts` file:

   `127.0.0.1 sandbox.hortonworks.com`

   This is shown in the following screenshot:

   ```
   # Additionally, comments (such as these) may be inserted on individual
   # lines or following the machine name denoted by a '#' symbol.
   #
   # For example:
   #
   #      102.54.94.97     rhino.acme.com          # source server
   #       38.25.63.10     x.acme.com              # x client host

   # localhost name resolution is handled within DNS itself.
   #       127.0.0.1       localhost
   #       ::1             localhost
   127.0.0.1 sandbox.hortonworks.com
   ```

3. Open your browser and navigate to
   `http://sandbox.hortonworks.com:8888`. Your browser screen should look
   like the following screenshot:

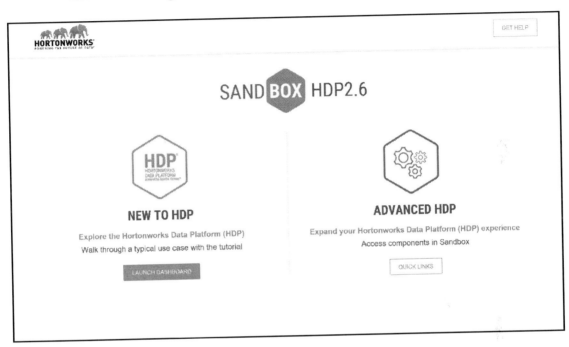

4. Click on **NEW TO HDP**. The **Ambari** screen will appear. Now, click the more
   icon, as shown in the following screenshot, and select **Files View**:

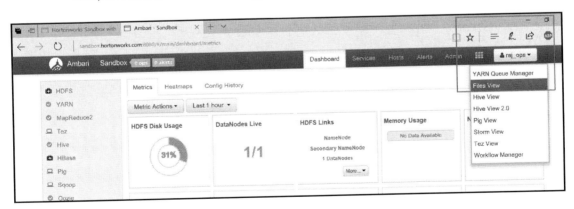

5. The following screen appears. Click on **New Folder** and type `SSISCookBook` as shown in the following screenshot. Click on the **+Add** button to add the folder:

That's it! We're now ready to interact with our local cluster using SSIS.

Copying data to an on-premises cluster

In this recipe, we'll add a package that will copy local data to the local cluster.

Getting ready

This recipe assumes that you have access to an on-premises cluster and have created a folder to hold the files in it from the previous recipe.

How to do it...

1. In the solution explorer, open (expand) the `ETL.DW` project and right-click on it to add a new package. Name it `FactOrdersToHDPCuster.dtsx`.

2. Go to the **Parameters** tab and add a new parameter:
     - **Name**: LoadExecutionId
     - **Data type**: Int64
     - **Value**: Leave the default value 0
     - **Sensitive**: Leave the default value False
     - **Required**: True

3. Add a data flow task on the control flow and name it dft_FactOrders.
4. In the data flow task, drag and drop an OLE DB source. Name it ole_src_DW_vwFactOrders.
5. Double-click on it to open the OLE DB source editor.
6. Set the OLE DB connection manager to cmgr_DW.
7. For data access mode, use the SQL command.
8. Set the SQL command text to the following:

```
SELECT          OrderDate, FirstName, LastName, CompanyName,
Category, ProductName, ProvenanceCode, ProvenanceDescription,
EnglishDescription, OrderQy, UnitPrice, Discount, TaxAmount,
Freight, SalesOrderNumber, PurchareOrderNumber
FROM            DW.vwFactOrders
```

9. Click on **OK** to close the **OLE DB Source Editor**.
10. Drag and drop a **Derived Column** transform from the SSIS toolbox.
11. Name it der_LoadExecutionId and tie it to the ole_src_DW_vwFactOrders.
12. Open it and assign the following properties:
     - **Derived Column Name**: LoadExecutionId
     - **Derived Colum**: Leave the default (add as new column)
     - **Expression**: @[$Package::LoadExecutionId]

13. Click on **OK** to close the derived column editor.
14. Right-click on the **Connection Manager** pane and select **New Connection...** from the contextual menu that appears. The **ADD SSIS Connection Manager** window opens.

15. Select **Hadoop** from the **Type** column as shown in the following screenshot and click on **Add...**:

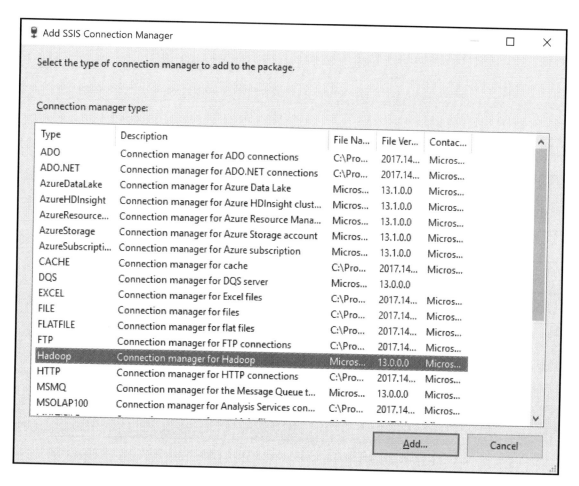

16. The Hadoop connection manager editor opens. Set the properties as shown in the following screenshot. Make sure the connection works and click on **OK** to close the window.

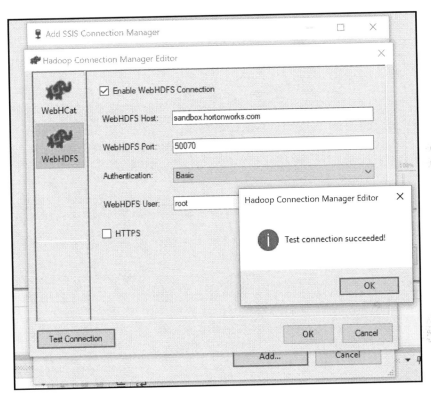

17. Drag and drop a **HDFS File Destination** from the SSIS toolbox onto the data flow task. Tie it to the der_LoadExecutionId derived column. Name it hdfs_dst_FactOrders. Double-click on **OK** and set the properties as follows:
    - In the **Hadoop Connection Manager** select cmgr_Hadoop_Sandbox
    - Set the **File path** to /SSISCookBook/Import/FactOrders.txt
    - Select mappings from the left-hand pane to set the mapping between the source and destination columns

18. Click on **OK** to close the **HDFS File Destination Editor**.

19. Now, as usual, make sure that the transforms are the same size and aligned properly. Your data flow task should look like the following screenshot:

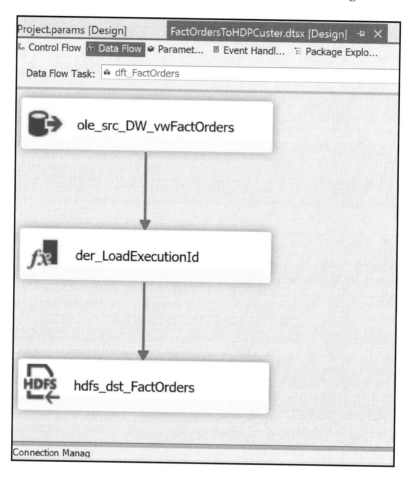

20. Now we can run the package. Once done, we can see that a file has been created in the cluster in the `/SSISCookBook/Import/` folder, as shown in the following screenshot. Go to **Ambari** | **Files View** and browse to the `SSISCookBook/Import` folder. You can open the file as shown in the following screenshot:

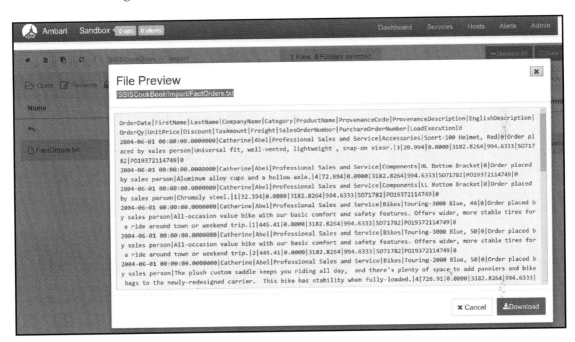

That's it! We have successfully transferred data from SQL Server to our Hortonworks sandbox cluster on HDFS, a totally different OS and filesystem than Windows. We'll continue working with the file in the following recipes.

Using Hive – creating a database

Hive is one of the languages used in Hadoop to interact with large volumes of data. It is very easy to learn since it uses SQL commands. This recipe will show you how we can use Hive to transform data from our source. Although we have only 542 lines of data in our file, we can still use it to learn Hadoop services calls.

In this recipe, we're going to create a database in Hive.

Getting ready

This recipe assumes that you have access to a Hortonworks sandbox on-premises or in Azure. It is also assumed that you have executed the previous recipe.

How to do it...

1. Open Ambari and navigate to `http://Sandbox.Hortonworks.com:8080`. Use `raj_ops` for both the username and password to log in.

2. Click on the more icon (nine-squares button near `raj_ops`) in the toolbar and select **Hive View 2.0**, as shown in the following screenshot:

3. Type `create database SSISCookBook` in **Worksheet1** and click on **Execute**, as shown in the following screenshot:

4. Refresh your browser and click on **Browse**, as shown in the following screenshot. The database has been created.

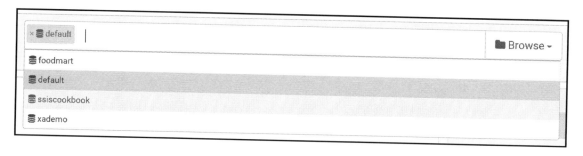

There's more...

The first step is done; we have created the database. We'll interact with the data in the following recipe.

Transforming the data with Hive

The data is now in the cluster in HDFS. We'll now transform it using a SQL script. The program we're using is Hive. This program interacts with the data using SQL statements.

With most Hadoop programs (Hive, Pig, Sparks, and so on), source is read-only. It means that we cannot modify the data in the file that we transferred in the previous recipe. Some languages such as HBase allow us to modify the source data though. But for our purpose, we'll use Hive, a well-known program in the Hadoop ecosystem.

Getting ready

This recipe assumes that you have access to a Hortonworks cluster and that you have transferred data to it following the previous recipe.

How to do it...

1. If not already done, open the package created in the previous recipe, `FactOrdersToHDPCuster.dtsx`.
2. Add a Hadoop Hive task and rename it `hht_HDPDWHiveTable`.

3. Double-click on it to open the **Hadoop Hive Task Editor**, as shown in the following screenshot:

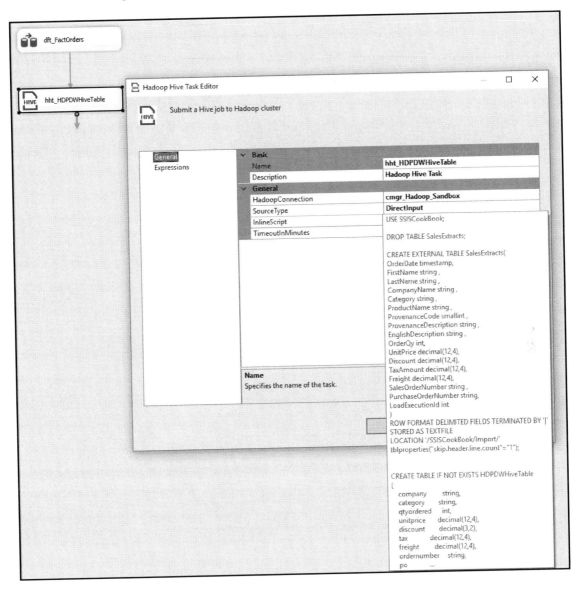

Update the following parameters:

HadoopConnection: cmgr_Hadoop_Sandbox

SourceType: DirectInput

InlineScript: Use the following script:

```
USE SSISCookBook;

DROP TABLE SalesExtracts;

CREATE EXTERNAL TABLE SalesExtracts(
OrderDate timestamp,
FirstName string ,
LastName string ,
CompanyName string ,
Category string ,
ProductName string ,
ProvenanceCode smallint ,
ProvenanceDescription string ,
EnglishDescription string ,
OrderQy int,
UnitPrice decimal(12,4),
Discount decimal(12,4),
TaxAmount decimal(12,4),
Freight decimal(12,4),
SalesOrderNumber string ,
PurchaseOrderNumber string,
LoadExecutionId int
)
ROW FORMAT DELIMITED FIELDS TERMINATED BY '|'
STORED AS TEXTFILE
LOCATION '/SSISCookBook/Import/'
tblproperties("skip.header.line.count"="1");


CREATE TABLE IF NOT EXISTS HDPDWHiveTable
(
    company        string,
    category       string,
    qtyordered     int,
    unitprice      decimal(12,4),
    discount       decimal(3,2),
    tax            decimal(12,4),
    freight        decimal(12,4),
    ordernumber    string,
    po             string
```

```
)
ROW FORMAT DELIMITED FIELDS TERMINATED BY ',' LINES TERMINATED
BY '10' STORED AS TEXTFILE
LOCATION '/SSISCookBook/Export/';


INSERT OVERWRITE TABLE HDPDWHiveTable
SELECT CompanyName, Category ,    SUM(OrderQy) AS OrderQy,
AVG(UnitPrice) AS UnitPrice, SUM(Discount) AS Discount,
SUM(TaxAmount) AS TaxAmount, SUM(Freight) AS Freight,
            SalesOrderNumber, PurchaseOrderNumber
FROM   SalesExtracts
GROUP BY CompanyName, Category, SalesOrderNumber,
PurchaseOrderNumber;
```

The preceding script does the following:

- Switches context to the SSISCookBook database we created in a preceding recipe.
- Creates an external table, that is, a table stored outside Hive. These tables have the characteristic that, whether we drop the table in Hive, the data file will not be dropped. Regular (internal) tables will drop the files underneath when dropped.
- The external table created has the same structure as the data we copied over in a preceding recipe. The command skip.header.line.count skips one line, the header line of the file.
- Then, another external table is created but this time in another folder: Export. It will create a file called 000000_0. The trailing 0 is the reducer number that created the file. If we had a large volume of data and were using a real cluster that would create the result in parallel we would have many files (000000_1, 000000_2, and so on). You will notice that a comma is now used as the column delimiter.
- Lastly, we insert into the table previously created. The overwrite clause will overwrite the table content as opposed to appending it, like a regular INSERT command would have done.

There's more...

The recipe, as simplistic as it is, was a quick introduction to Hive in Hadoop. This language mainly transforms the data by creating structures on top of others. In a further recipe later in this chapter, we'll use another program to transform the data: Pig Latin. But now, we'll leave the on-premises big data world to go into Azure.

Transferring data between Hadoop and Azure

Now that we have some data created by Hadoop Hive on-premises, we're going to transfer this data to a cloud storage on Azure. Then, we'll do several transformations to it using Hadoop Pig Latin. Once done, we'll transfer the data to an on-premises table in the staging schema of our `AdventureWorksLTDW2016` database.

In this recipe, we're going to copy the data processed by the local Hortonworks cluster to an Azure Blob storage. Once the data is copied over, we can transform it using Azure compute resources, as we'll see in the following recipes.

Getting ready

This recipe assumes that you have created a storage space in Azure as described in the previous recipe.

How to do it...

1. Open the `ETL.Staging SSIS` project and add a new package to it. Rename it `StgAggregateSalesFromCloud.dtsx`.
2. Add a Hadoop connection manager called `cmgr_Hadoop_Sandbox` like we did in the previous recipe.
3. Add another connection manager, which will connect to the Azure storage like the `cmgr_AsureStorage_ssiscookbook` we did in a previous recipe in this chapter.
4. Add a **Foreach Loop** container to the control flow and rename it `felc_HDP_Export`.

5. Double-click on it to open the **Foreach Loop** editor. Set the **Collection** properties, as shown in the following screenshot:

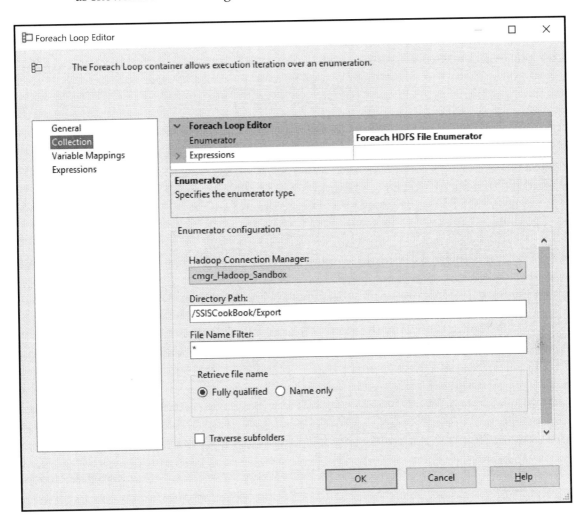

6. Click on the **Variable Mappings**, create a new variable at the package level, and name it `HDPFileNamePath`, as shown in the following screenshot:

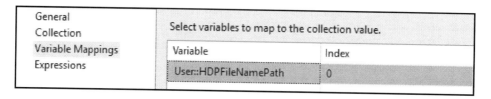

7. Click **OK** to close the **Foreach Loop** editor.
8. Go to the **Variables** pane and set the value of the `HDPFileNamePath` to `/SSISCookBook/Export/000000_0`.
9. From the SSIS toolbox, drag and drop a HDFS file source into the `felc_HDP_Export` Foreach Loop container. Rename it `hfs_src_SSISCookBook_Export`.
10. Click anywhere in the data flow task background and go to the **Properties** pane (or press F4 to display it). Scroll down to **Expressions** and click on the ellipsis (...) button.
11. From the drop-down list, click on the ellipsis button to the right of the `hfs_src_SSISCookBook_Export.FilePath` expression. Fill the **Expression Builder**, as shown in the following screenshot. Click on **OK** to close the **Expression Builder**:

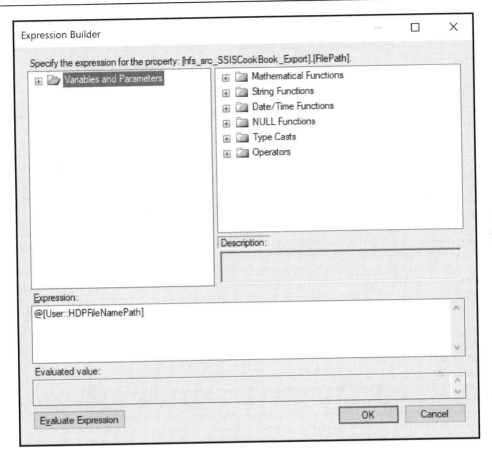

12. Close and reopen the package to force the expression to be considered.

13. Double-click on it to open the **HDF File Source** editor and assign the following:

- **Hadoop Connection Manager**: Select the `cmgr_Hadoop_Sandbox` from the drop-down list.
- **File Path**: It should be `/SSISCookBook/Export/000000_0`. This is the value of the variable expression we set earlier.
- **File format**: Leave the default, `Text`.
- **Column delimiter character**: Use the vertical bar (|).

14. Click on the **Columns** tab and set the columns at the left of the editor and rename them, as shown in the following screenshot. Once done, click on **OK** to close the **HDFS File Source Editor**:

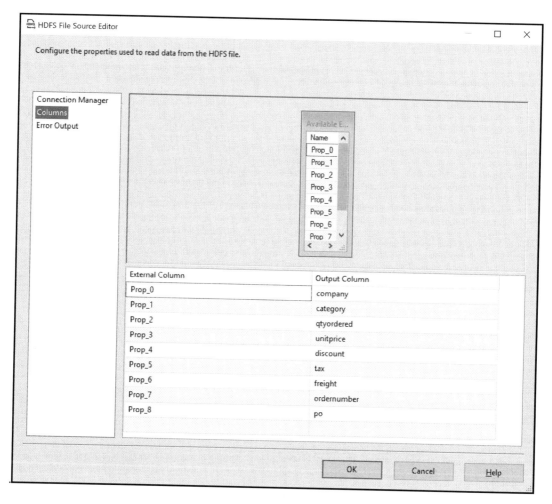

15. Add a **Derived Column** to the data flow task and link it to hfs_src_SSISCookBook_Export.FilePath. Rename it der_LoadExecutionId. Open the **Derived Column Editor** and add a column called LoadExecutionId. Set the value to the **Package::LoadExecutionId** package parameter.

16. Add an **Azure Blob Destination** to the data flow task and rename it `abd_dst_ssiscookbook_import_FactOrdersAggregated`. Link it to the `der_LoadExecutionId` transform.

17. Double-click on it to open the **Azure Blob Destination Editor**. Set its properties as shown in the following screenshot:

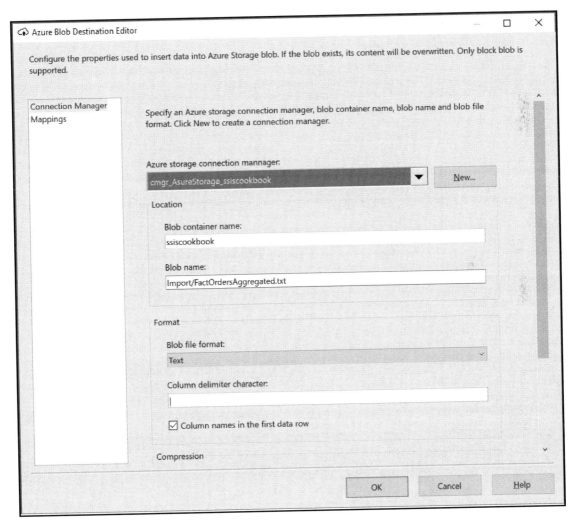

18. Click on the column mapping and verify that our input columns are mapped.

19. The final data flow task should look like the following screenshot:

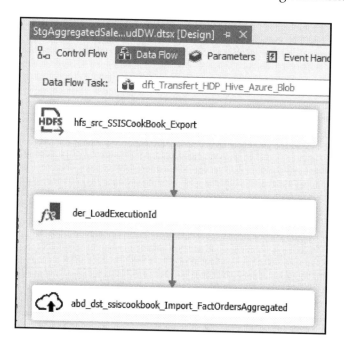

20. Execute the data flow task. Once completed, go to the Azure portal (`portal.azure.com`), go into your **HDInsight cluster | Storage accounts | Blob service**, and click on **Import Blob**. You should have a screen similar to the following screenshot:

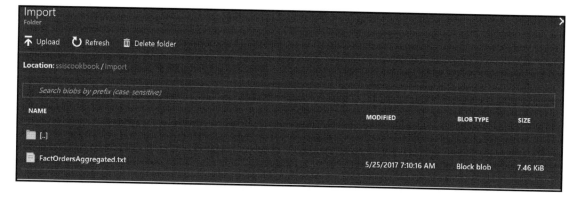

21. Right-click on the `FactOrdersAggergated.txt` file and select **Download**. The content of the file will open in your browser.

That's it! We've transferred the local HDP cluster data to another one. In the following recipe, we'll do something with the transferred data.

Leveraging a HDInsight big data cluster

So far, we've managed Blobs data using SSIS. In this case, the data was at rest and SSIS was used to manipulate it. SSIS was the orchestration service in Azure parlance. As stated in the introduction, SSIS can only be used on- premises and, so far, on a single machine.

The goal of this recipe is to use Azure HDInsight computation services. These services allow us to use (rent) powerful resources as a cluster of machines. These machines can run Linux or Windows according to user choice, but be aware that Windows will be deprecated for the newest version of HDInsight. Such clusters or machines, as fast and powerful as they can be, are very expensive to use. In fact, this is quite normal; we're talking about a potentially large amount of hardware here.

For this reason, unless we want to have these computing resource running continuously, SSIS has a way to create and drop a cluster on demand. The following recipe will show you how to do it.

Getting ready

You will need to have access to an Azure subscription to do this recipe.

How to do it...

1. If not open, open the package we're using from the previous recipe: `ETL_Staging.StgAggregatedSales.dtsx`.
2. Right-click on the **Connection Manager** pane, add **New Connection...**, and select `AzureResourceManager`. Fill out the properties following the instructions provided at the following link: `https://docs.microsoft.com/en-us/azure/azure-resource-manager/resource-group-create-service-principal-portal`.

3. Your connection manager should look like the one in the following screenshot:

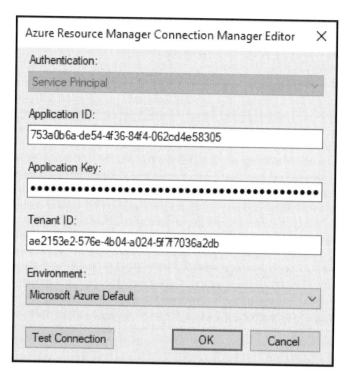

4. Drag and drop an **Azure Create Cluster** task from the SSIS toolbox on the control flow and attach it to the `felc_HDP_Export` Foreach Loop container. Rename the task `acc_ssiscookbook` for **Azure Create Cluster** as `ssiscookbook`.

5. Double-click on it to open the **Azure HDInsight Create Cluster Editor**. Fill the properties as shown in the following screenshot. For the **SubsciptionId**, use your Azure subscription ID. The location depends on where you created your storage account. To avoid extra fees, you should have your cluster created in the same region as the one you used for your storage account:

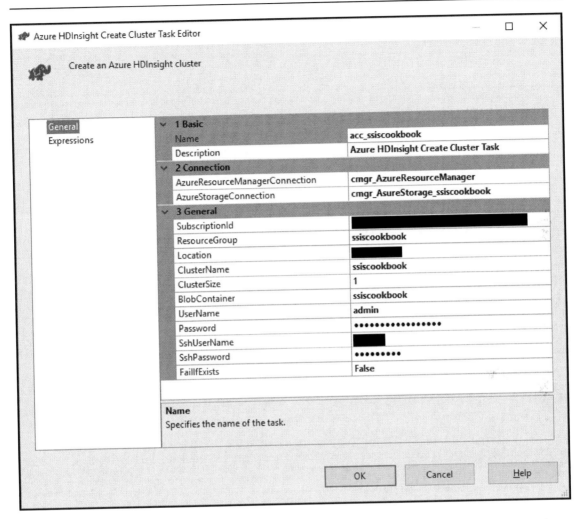

6. Now, for this task to work correctly, you have to parameterize both passwords: cluster password and SSH password.

7. Now we'll test if the cluster creation works. Right-click on the task and select **Execute Task**. The cluster creation starts. This task might take several minutes to complete. In our case, it takes up to 15 minutes.

8. Once completed, open a bash terminal. We will use the one that comes with Windows 10. Go to the Azure portal and look for the HDInsight cluster that has been created. In the overview, there is an option to connect using SSH. Click on it and copy the SSH command. Paste it in the bash terminal. It should consist of a command similar to the following:

```
ssh User@yourcluster-ssh.azurehdinsight.net
```

It is also shown in the following screenshot:

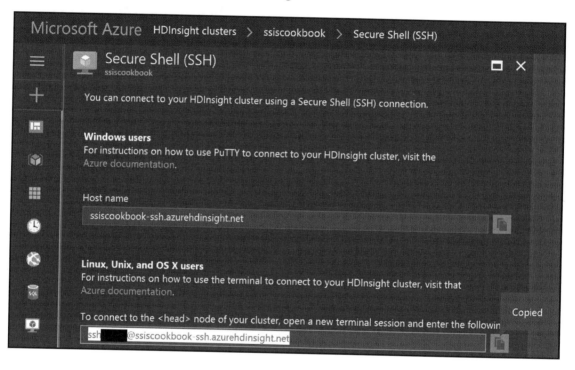

9. Next, we'll add a task to drop the cluster once we've finished with it. From the SSIS toolbox, drag and drop an **Azure HDInsight Delete Cluster Task** on the control flow. Rename it `adc_ssiscookbook`. Double-click on it and set the properties as shown in the following screenshot:

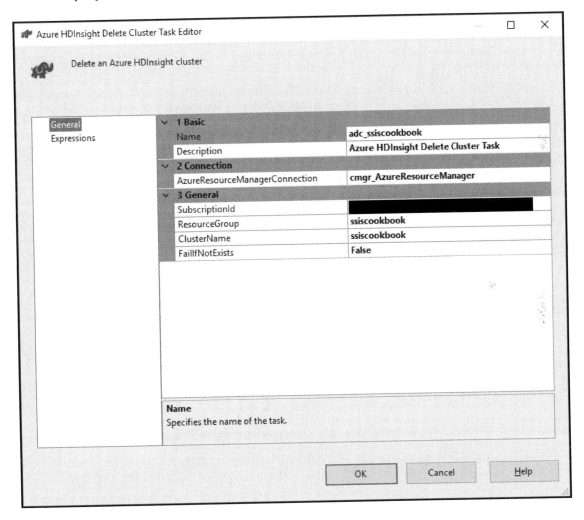

10. Click **OK** to close the `adc_ssiscookbook` task. Right-click on it and select **Execute Task** from the contextual menu that appears. Once executed successfully, go to the Azure portal and verify that the cluster has been dropped.

There's more...

That's it! We can now create and drop clusters on demand. The following recipe will show how we can use the cluster with Pig.

Managing data with Pig Latin

Pig Latin is one of the programs available in big data clusters. The purpose of this program is to run scripts that can accept any type of data. "Pig can eat everything," as the mantra of the creators states.

This recipe is just meant to show you how to call a simple Pig script. No transformations are done. The purpose of the script is to show you how we can use an Azure Pig task with SSIS.

Getting ready

This recipe assumes that you have created a HDInsight cluster successfully.

How to do it...

1. In the `StgAggregatedSales.dtsx` SSIS package, drag and drop an **Azure Pig Task** onto the control flow. Rename it `apt_AggregateData`.

2. Double-click on it to open the **Azure HDInsight Pig Task Editor** and set the properties as shown in the following screenshot:

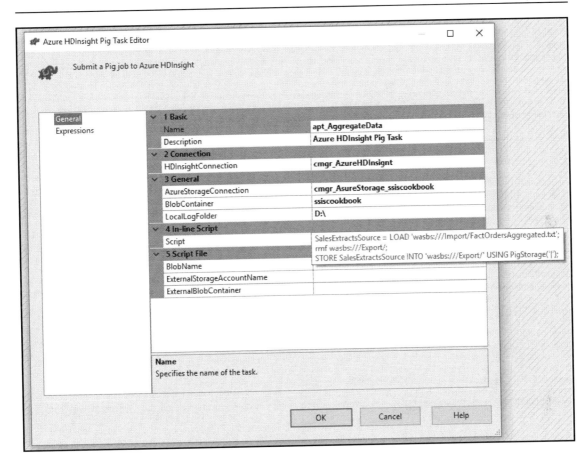

3. In the script property, insert the following code:

```
SalesExtractsSource = LOAD
'wasbs:///Import/FactOrdersAggregated.txt';
rmf wasbs:///Export/;
STORE SalesExtractsSource INTO 'wasbs:///Export/' USING
PigStorage('|');
```

4. The first line holds a reference to the `Import/FactOrdersAggregated.txt` file. The second line removes (deleting) the directory `/Export`. Finally, the data is copied over to a new file in the `/Export` folder using a vertical bar (|) as a delimiter.

5. Right-click on the `apt_AggregateData` and select **Execute Task** from the contextual menu that appears to run the script.

6. Once done successfully, go to the Blob storage in the Azure portal to check that the file has been created.

7. If any error occurs, go to the log file located in the directory that you specified in `apt_AggregateData`.

8. Your package should now look like the following screenshot:

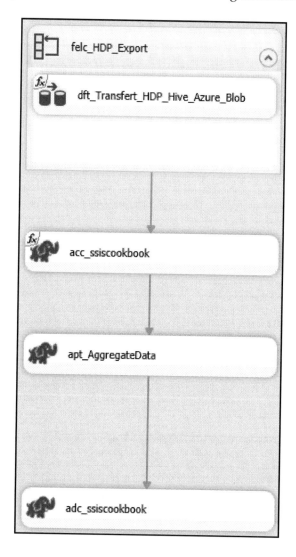

There's more...

You'll notice that the data hasn't been modified, as the purpose of the recipe was to show how to call a Pig script from SSIS.

Importing Azure Blob storage data

So far, we've created and dropped a HDInsight cluster and called a Pig script using the Azure Pig task. This recipe will demonstrate how to import data from an Azure Blob storage to a table in the staging schema.

Getting ready

This recipe assumes that you have completed the previous one.

How to do it...

1. From the SSIS toolbox, drag and drop, and **Execute SQL Task** on the control flow, and rename it `sql_truncate_Staging_StgCloudSales`.

2. Double-click on it to open the **SQL Task Editor**. Set the properties as follows and click on OK:
   - **Connection**: `cmgr_DW`
   - **SQL Statement**: `TRUNCATE TABLE [Staging].[StgCloudSales];`

3. From the SSIS toolbox, drag a **Foreach Loop Container** and rename it `felc_StgCloudSales`.

4. Double-click on it to open the **Foreach Loop Editor**, and assign the properties in the **Collection** pane, as shown in the following screenshot:

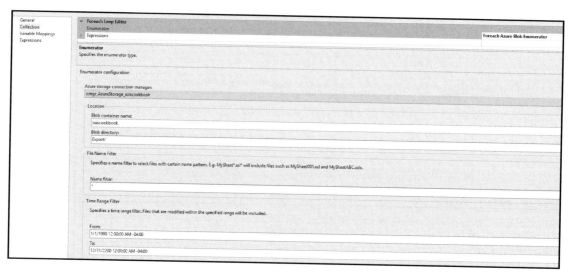

5. Now go to the **Variable Mappings** pane and add a string variable called `User::AzureAggregatedData`. Make sure the scope is at the package level.

6. Drag a **Data Flow Task** into the `felc_StgCloudSales` and rename it `dft_StgCloudSales`.

7. Go into the **Data Flow Task** and drag an **Azure Blob Source** from the SSIS toolbox. Rename it `azure_blob_src_ExportBlob`.

8. Click anywhere on the background of the data flow and go to the **Properties** pane. Select **Expressions**. Click on the ellipsis button (...) and select `[azure_blob_src_ExportBlob].[Blob Name]` from the list. Assign `@[User::AzureAggregatedData]` as the value.

9. Double-click on the `azure_blob_src_ExportBlob` to open the **Azure Blob Source Editor**, and assign the various properties as shown in the following screenshot. And click **OK**.

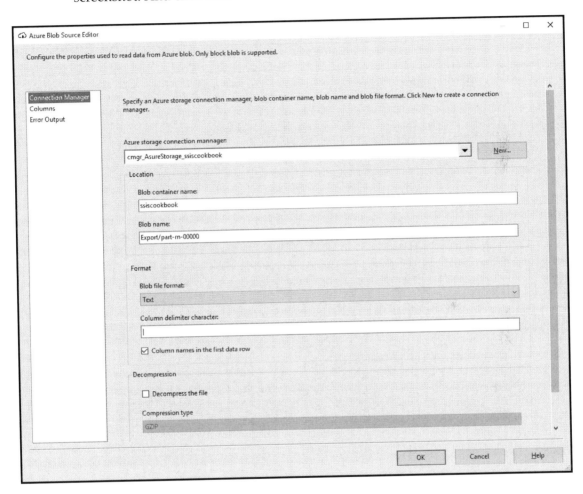

10. Drag an **OLE DB Destination** to the **Data Flow Task** and rename it `ole_dst_Staging_StgCloudSales`. Attach it to `azure_blob_src_ExportBlob`.

11. Double-click on it and set the properties as follows:
    - **OLE DB connection manager**: `c,mgr_DW`
    - **Name of the table or view**: `[Staging].[StgCloudSales]`

12. Go into the **Mappings** panes and make sure that all columns are mapped. Click **OK** to close the editor. Your screen should look like the following screenshot:

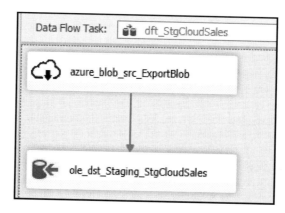

13. Go back to the control flow and right-click on `felc_StgCloudSales`. Select **Execute** from the contextual menu to execute the container.

14. Attach `felc_StgCloudSales` to both the `sql_truncate_Staging_StgCloudSales` and the `apt_AggregateData` tasks. Your final package should look like the following screenshot:

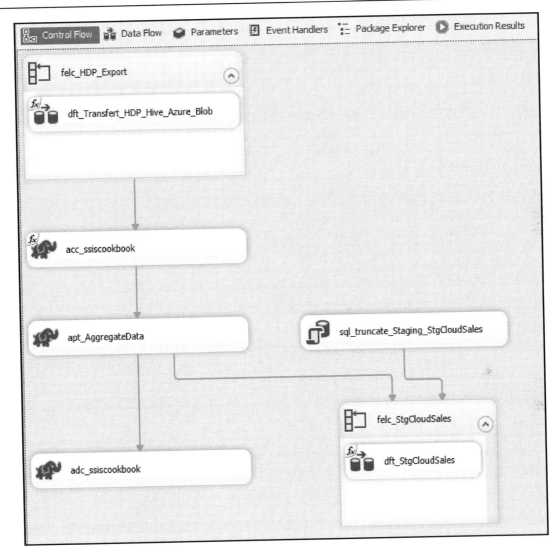

That's it! We now have a package that can read from a local Hadoop cluster, transfer data to and from Azure, and execute Azure HDInsight tasks.

There's more...

This chapter gave a 360° overview of how SSIS can interact with the big data world, be it on-premises or in the clouds. The next section will consist of a brief discussion on the difference between SSIS and the Azure Data Factory.

There is a service available in Azure that can do about as much as SSIS can do with Azure data. In fact, if your data is only in Azure, this is the service you should use in conjunction with SSIS.

Azure Data Factory and SSIS

Azure Data Factory (ADF) is a service that orchestrate data integration using different services available in Azure. Like SSIS, it can move data from one location to another. The main differences are the following:

- SSIS needs a windows machine to run. Even to copy data, the service runs on a windows server. ADF doesn't needs anything to accomplish copy data tasks since the service runs in Azure
- SSIS has a rich toolset integrated into it to transform data; the dataflow task. ADF has nothing that come close to it built-in.
- ADF relies on compute services like HDInsight clusters that can run Hive and Pig scripts to transform data.
- SSIS can transform data on without leaving the package and, without necessarily staging it. It can transform and load data immediately to the destination. ADF calls a service that will transform the data but this service might not be able to load the data directly in a destination.

For example, we need to load data from Oracle, transform and load it into SQL Server. SSIS can do it in one single package. ADF would have to copy the data to an intermediately storage, call a service to transform the data and finally load it into the destination. SSIS 2016 service runs on a Windows OS based machine; ADF runs in Azure where there's no OS to consider.

Generally, when most of your enterprise data is in Azure ecosystem and you barely use data on premises, it makes sense to use ADF. In that case, you are probable making the ETL using ADF and/or TSQL be it stored procedure or DML statements.

But, if your enterprise data is mostly on premises and some of it is in Azure, it makes more sense to use SSIS. Same statement if you're using on-premises Big Data cluster as you saw earlier in this chapter. SSIS now has a lot of connectors to leverage big data clusters on premises as well as in Azure.

Extending SSIS Custom Tasks and Transformations

13

This chapter covers the following recipes:

- Designing a custom task
- Designing a custom transformation
- Managing custom components versions

Introduction

This chapter discusses SSIS customization - the built-in capability of the SSIS platform that allows you to extend the natively provided programmatic elements. In addition to the system-provided tasks and components, including the script task and the script component, the SSIS programming model allows you to implement your own programmatic logic by designing your own control flow tasks (custom tasks) or your own data flow components (custom components).

Typically, a custom task would be needed when none of the system-provided tasks facilitate the specific operation that you need to implement in your SSIS solution; for instance, the built-in **File Transfer Protocol (FTP)** task does not support Secure FTP, so if you need to access remote file locations using the **Secure File Transfer Protocol (SSH FTP)**, you need to design a custom task.

The most frequent uses of the custom component are custom transformations that either provide operations that are not provided by the built-in components, or they encapsulate a series of transformations within a single one. In the latter case, you might also implement the operations by using multiple built-in transformations, but you would prefer to reduce the complexity of the data flow by implementing them as a single component.

Script tasks and components are discussed in more detail in `Chapter 11`, *Unleash the Power of SSIS Script Tasks and Components*. In both cases, the custom code is embedded in the SSIS package definition; you can create and modify it during package development, and it is deployed together with the package.

When using custom tasks or components, the custom code is developed in a separate Visual Studio project. You should create a separate assembly for each custom task, or component; this allows you to develop, modify, and deploy them without having to redeploy any of the packages in which they are used, and independently of any other custom tasks or components.

To decide whether to use scripting, or whether to design a custom task or component, you can use the following rule: use scripting if the complete logic of the task or component can be encapsulated into a single script and if the same script does not need to be used in multiple packages. Otherwise, you are encouraged to consider using custom tasks or components, especially in situations where the same custom logic needs to be implemented in numerous packages.

Designing a custom task

To design a custom control flow task, you create a DOT.NET assembly based on the Class Library Visual Studio template; the task's definition must be placed in a class derived from the `Task` base class, of the `Microsoft.SqlServer.Dts.Runtime` namespace (located in the `Microsoft.SqlServer.ManagedDTS.dll` assembly). This class also needs to implement the `DtsTaskAttribute` that is used to identify the class as an SSIS task and provide the elementary properties used when implementing the custom task in SSIS control flows.

Optionally, you can provide a custom graphical user interface for the custom task, which will be used as the task editor when the task is configured during SSIS package development. If a custom editor is not provided, the custom task can be edited by using the built-in advanced editor.

The task base class provides two methods that you need to override, and in them provide your custom code to:

- Validate the configuration of the task. This method is called automatically by the SSIS control flow designer whenever the task settings are changed, and allows you to communicate with the SSIS package developers to help them understand the task's configuration and help them configure it correctly before it can be used.
- You also need to provide the logic needed to execute the task. This method will be called at runtime, when the package execution reaches the task in the control flow sequence. This method also allows access to various SSIS package resources:
    - The SSIS variables can be read or written
    - The connections accessible to the package can be used to connect to various data sources
    - The custom task may send log entries to the event log
    - You are encouraged to implement events in your custom task, so that its performance can be captured by SSDT at design time, and by the SSIS server after the packages implementing the task have been deployed
    - In the custom task, you can also detect whether the operation is participating in a transaction, and use this information when connecting to a data source

Both the preceding methods return a DTSExecResult value specifying the result of the validation, or the execution; this communicates the outcome of each method to the SSIS package developer, as well as the SSIS execution engine. The following values are supported by the DTSExecResult enumeration:

- Success is used to specify that the validation, or the execution, completed successfully.
- Failure specifies that the validation, or the execution, has failed. Generally, in case of failure, additional events should be returned from the task to provide more information about the failure to the SSIS package developer, or to the administrator of the deployment environment.
- Completion can be used for executions when either Success or Failure are not relevant results, or not specific enough. For instance, if a task completes its work successfully it returns Success, if it fails, it returns Failure, but if no work was performed, even though the configuration was in order, the task might return Completion to communicate a specific result that is neither a success nor failure.

- `Canceled` is used to report to the SSIS execution engine that the execution had to be interrupted; for instance, before even reaching the point in its execution that could be interpreted as any of the other three results.

Normally, only `Success` and `Failure` should be used in the `Validate()` method.

To deploy a custom task - either to the development workstation used in SSIS package development, or to the environment, in which it is going to be used - the assemblies containing the task need to be copied to the following folders:

- `%ProgramFiles%\Microsoft SQL Server\130\DTS\Tasks` - for the 64-bit edition of the assembly
- `%ProgramFiles(x86)%\Microsoft SQL Server\130\DTS\Tasks` - for the 32-bit edition of the assembly

If the assembly is platform-independent, the file needs to be copied to both folders.

The assembly, and all of the assemblies it references, must also be registered in the **Global Assembly Cache (GAC)**. To register the assemblies on the SSIS development workstation, you can use the `gacutil.exe` command-line utility (it is installed together with Visual Studio); however, on a production server `gacutil.exe` might not be available. You can also use an appropriate Windows PowerShell script to perform the registration.

In this recipe, you are going to develop a custom task, deploy it to your development workstation, and use it in an SSIS package.

This custom task is going to use an external library to allow you to perform FTP tasks in SSIS using the (SSH FTP).

 For your convenience, the C# code snippets needed for this chapter are provided in the `Chapter13.txt` file.

Getting ready

Before you begin, you need to install the `WinSCP` class library from the `https://winscp.net/` website; WinSCP is a free tool that you can use in your own solutions, under the terms of the GNU General Public License as published by the Free Software Foundation (`https://www.gnu.org/licenses/gpl.html`).

Please review the WinSCP GNU license, at
https://winscp.net/eng/docs/license.

To install and register the external library on your workstation, follow these steps:

1. Download version **5.9.5** of the **Installation package,** or the **.NET assembly / COM library** of WinSCP from
   https://winscp.net/eng/download.php.
2. We recommend that you use the installation package, which will install the application and the necessary assemblies in a folder expected by the recipes in this chapter.
3. If you decided on using the installation package, run it, and then follow the instructions in the installation wizard to complete the installation.
4. If you prefer to download only the assembly, download the archive file, and then unzip it into the C:\Program Files (x86)\WinSCP\ folder.
5. After the installation has completed successfully, or after you placed the files in the specified folder, use Windows Explorer to navigate to the C:\SSIS2016Cookbook\Chapter13\Scripts folder.
6. Locate the Chapter13_GAC_WinSCPnet.bat command file, and open it in Notepad.
7. Inspect the file, and then close it.
8. In Windows Explorer, right-click the command file, and select **Execute as administrator...** from the shortcut menu.
9. In the **User Account Control** dialog click **OK** to allow the execution.
10. After the execution completes, press any key to close the command prompt window.

You are now ready to design the custom task.

How to do it...

1. Start Visual Studio 2015 and create a new project.
2. In the **New Project** dialog, make sure that **.NET Framework 4.5.2** is selected, and then under **Templates \ Visual C#**, select the **Class Library** template. Use `SSISCustomTasks` as the project name, place it in the `C:\SSIS2016Cookbook\Chapter13\Starter` folder, check **Create directory for solution**, and use `SSISCustomization` as the solution name. Refer to the following screenshot to verify your settings:

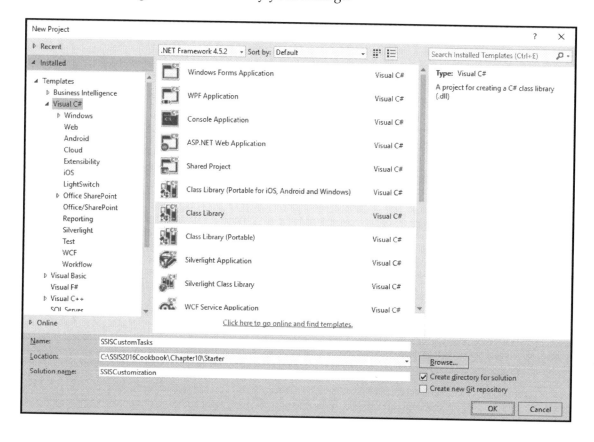

3. Click **OK** to confirm the configuration and create the solution.

4. In the **Solution Explorer**, right-click the newly created `SSISCustomTasks` project, and select **Properties** from the shortcut menu to open the `SSISCustomTasks` properties pane.

5. On the **Application** page, change the default namespace value to `SSIS2016Cookbook`.

6. On the **Signing** page, check **Sign the assembly**, and select **<Browse...>** in the **Choose a strong name key file** selection box.

7. In the **Select File** dialog, navigate to the `C:\SSIS2016Cookbook\Chapter13\Scripts` folder, and select the `SSIS2016Cookbook.snk` strong name key file, as shown in the following screenshot:

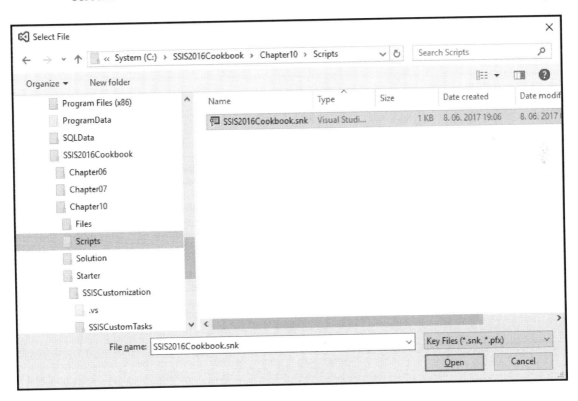

8. Click **Open** to confirm the selection.

9. Save the solution, and then close the project properties pane.

10. In the `Class1.cs` designer pane, change the namespace of the class to `SSIS2016Cookbook`, and change the `Class1` name to `SecureFTP`.

11. In the **Solution Explorer**, change the `Class1.cs` file name to `SecureFTP.cs`, and then save the solution.

12. In the **Solution Explorer**, right-click **References**, and then select **Add Reference...** from the shortcut menu to open the **Reference Manager** dialog.

13. Under **Assemblies / Extensions**, check the `Microsoft.SqlServer.Dts.Design`, `Microsoft.SqlServer.ManagedDTS`, and **WinSCPnet** assemblies, as shown in the following screenshot:

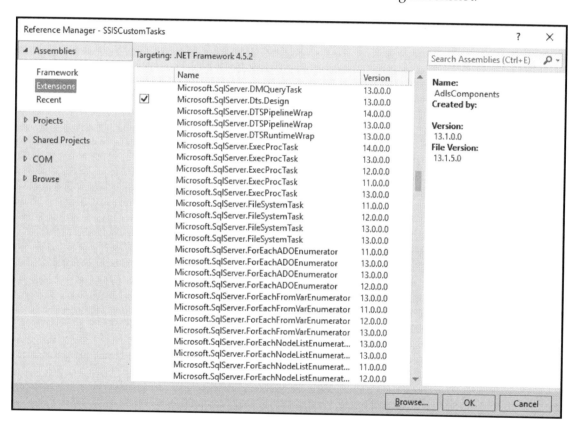

14. Click **OK** to confirm the selection.

15. In the `SecureFTP.cs` file, at the top of the source code, replace all existing namespace references with the following ones:

```
using System;
using Microsoft.SqlServer.Dts.Runtime;
using WinSCP;
```

16. The `SecureFTP` class must be derived from `Microsoft.SqlServer.Dts.Runtime.Task` base class, and it must also implement the `DtsTaskAttribute`:

```
[DtsTaskAttribute
  (
    Description = "Perform FTP operations securely, by using SSH.",
    DisplayName = "Secure FTP Task"
  )]
public class SecureFTP : Task
{
    ...
}
```

The `Microsoft.SqlServer.Dts.Runtime.Task` base class provides the functionalities necessary in any SSIS control flow task, and the `DtsTaskAttribute` allows you to configure some principal properties of the custom task. Together they allow the class in the assembly to be recognized as an SSIS Task, which in turn allows it to be used in an SSIS package.

17. Add the following private constants to the `SecureFTP` class:

```
private const String TASK_NAME = "Secure FTP Task";
private const String FtpProtocolName_MISSING_MESAGE =
"FtpProtocolName has not been set.";
private const String FtpHostName_MISSING_MESAGE = "FtpHostName has
not been set.";
private const String FtpUserName_MISSING_MESAGE = "FtpUserName has
not been set.";
private const String FtpPassword_MISSING_MESAGE = "FtpPassword has
not been set.";
private const String FtpSshHostKeyFingerprint_MISSING_MESAGE =
"FtpSshHostKeyFingerprint has not been set.";
private const String FtpOperationName_MISSING_MESAGE =
"FtpOperationName has not been set.";
private const String FtpLocalPath_MISSING_MESAGE = "FtpLocalPath
has not been set.";
```

```
private const String FtpRemotePath_MISSING_MESAGE = "FtpRemotePath
has not been set.";
private const String REMOVE_ENABLED_MESSAGE = "FtpRemove is set to
TRUE, which means that the file is going to be removed from the
source.";
private const String SESSION_OPEN_MESSAGE = "Session opened
succesfully.";
private const String REMOTE_DIRECTORY_MISSING_MESSAGE_PATTERN =
"The specified remote [{0}] directory is missing.\r\nIt will be
created.";
private const String REMOTE_DIRECTORY_CREATED_MESSAGE_PATTERN =
"The specified remote [{0}] directory has been created.";
private const String REMOTE_FILES_MISSING_MESSAGE_PATTERN = "The
specified remote file(s) [{0}] cannot be found.";
private const String EXCEPTION_MESSAGE_PATTERN = "An error has
occurred:\r\n\r\n{0}";
private const String UNKNOWN_EXCEPTION_MESSAGE = "(No other
information available.)";
```

These constants are going to be used by the custom task's methods to convey information about the state of the task to the SSIS package developers when configuring the task.

18. Create the following public members of the `SecureFTP` class:

```
public String FtpProtocolName { get; set; }
public String FtpHostName { get; set; }
public Int32 FtpPortNumber { get; set; }
public String FtpUserName { get; set; }
public String FtpPassword { get; set; }
public String FtpSshHostKeyFingerprint { get; set; }
public String FtpOperationName { get; set; }
public String FtpLocalPath { get; set; }
public String FtpRemotePath { get; set; }
public Boolean FtpRemove { get; set; }
```

These public members of the `SecureFTP` class will be accessible in the SSDT as task properties, and will allow the SSIS package developers to configure the custom task; in SSDT, the values can be supplied as literal values or by using expressions.

19. Add the following enumeration to the class definition:

```
public enum OperationMode
{
    GetFiles,
    PutFiles
}
```

This enumeration lists the supported modes of operation of the **Secure FTP Task**; two of them are implemented using the code in this recipe: `GetFiles` receives the files from and `PutFiles` sends the files to the specified FTP site. Of course, the enumeration itself does not contain the complete programmatic logic needed to perform these operations.

 You can extend the range by implementing additional functions available in the WinSCP library. You can find more information about the library at `https://winscp.net/eng/docs/start`.

20. Add the following private function to the `SecureFTP` class:

```
private Session EstablishSession()
{
    Session winScpSession = new Session();

    Protocol ftpProtocol = (Protocol)Enum.Parse(typeof(Protocol),
    this.FtpProtocolName);

    SessionOptions winScpSessionOptions = new SessionOptions
    {
        Protocol = ftpProtocol,
        HostName = this.FtpHostName,
        PortNumber = this.FtpPortNumber,
        UserName = this.FtpUserName,
        Password = this.FtpPassword,
        SshHostKeyFingerprint = this.FtpSshHostKeyFingerprint
    };

    winScpSession.Open(winScpSessionOptions);

    return winScpSession;
}
```

This function creates an instance of the `WinSCP Session` class; it connects to the FTP server, establishes the appropriate security context, and allows the operations to be performed against the remote site.

21. Add another private function to the `SecureFTP` class:

```
private DTSExecResult ValidateProperties(ref IDTSComponentEvents
componentEvents)
{
    DTSExecResult result = DTSExecResult.Success;

    if (String.IsNullOrEmpty(this.FtpProtocolName))
    {
        componentEvents.FireError(0, TASK_NAME,
FtpProtocolName_MISSING_MESAGE, String.Empty, 0);
        result = DTSExecResult.Failure;
    }

    if (String.IsNullOrEmpty(this.FtpHostName))
    {
        componentEvents.FireError(0, TASK_NAME,
FtpHostName_MISSING_MESAGE, String.Empty, 0);
        result = DTSExecResult.Failure;
    }

    if (String.IsNullOrEmpty(this.FtpUserName))
    {
        componentEvents.FireError(0, TASK_NAME,
FtpUserName_MISSING_MESAGE, String.Empty, 0);
        result = DTSExecResult.Failure;
    }

    if (String.IsNullOrEmpty(this.FtpPassword))
    {
        componentEvents.FireError(0, TASK_NAME,
FtpPassword_MISSING_MESAGE, String.Empty, 0);
        result = DTSExecResult.Failure;
    }

    if (String.IsNullOrEmpty(this.FtpSshHostKeyFingerprint))
    {
        componentEvents.FireError(0, TASK_NAME,
FtpSshHostKeyFingerprint_MISSING_MESAGE, String.Empty, 0);
        result = DTSExecResult.Failure;
    }

    if (String.IsNullOrEmpty(this.FtpOperationName))
    {
        componentEvents.FireError(0, TASK_NAME,
FtpOperationName_MISSING_MESAGE, String.Empty, 0);
        result = DTSExecResult.Failure;
    }
```

```
    if (String.IsNullOrEmpty(this.FtpLocalPath))
    {
        componentEvents.FireError(0, TASK_NAME,
FtpLocalPath_MISSING_MESAGE, String.Empty, 0);
        result = DTSExecResult.Failure;
    }

    if (String.IsNullOrEmpty(this.FtpRemotePath))
    {
        componentEvents.FireError(0, TASK_NAME,
FtpRemotePath_MISSING_MESAGE, String.Empty, 0);
        result = DTSExecResult.Failure;
    }

    return result;
}
```

This function extends the `Validate()` method of the `Task` base class by encapsulating additional validation rules that need to be performed on the string properties of this particular task. The function reports any string properties that do not have their values set, through SSIS events.

22. Below the `SecureFTP` class public member declarations, create some space, and start typing the `override` directive; Visual Studio Intellisense should list the `Task` base class methods that you can override; select the `Validate()` method.

23. Replace the default definition of the newly overridden method with the following code:

```
Boolean fireAgain = false;

try
{
    // Validate mandatory String properties.
    DTSExecResult propertyValidationResult =
this.ValidateProperties(ref componentEvents);
    if (propertyValidationResult != DTSExecResult.Success)
    {
        return propertyValidationResult;
    }

    // The package developer should know that files will be removed
from the source.
    if (this.FtpRemove)
    {
        componentEvents.FireInformation(0, TASK_NAME,
REMOVE_ENABLED_MESSAGE, String.Empty, 0, ref fireAgain);
    }
```

```csharp
            // Verify the connection.
            using (Session winScpSession = this.EstablishSession())
            {
                componentEvents.FireInformation(0, TASK_NAME,
        SESSION_OPEN_MESSAGE, String.Empty, 0, ref fireAgain);

                // Verify the remote resources.
                OperationMode operation =
        (OperationMode)Enum.Parse(typeof(OperationMode),
        this.FtpOperationName);
                switch (operation)
                {
                    case OperationMode.PutFiles:
                        Boolean remoteDirectoryExists =
        winScpSession.FileExists(this.FtpRemotePath);
                        if (!remoteDirectoryExists)
                        {
                            componentEvents.FireInformation(0, TASK_NAME,
        String.Format(REMOTE_DIRECTORY_MISSING_MESSAGE_PATTERN,
        this.FtpRemotePath), String.Empty, 0, ref fireAgain);
                        }
                        break;
                    case OperationMode.GetFiles:
                    default:
                        Boolean remoteFileExists =
        winScpSession.FileExists(this.FtpRemotePath);
                        if (!remoteFileExists)
                        {
                            componentEvents.FireInformation(0, TASK_NAME,
        String.Format(REMOTE_FILES_MISSING_MESSAGE_PATTERN,
        this.FtpRemotePath), String.Empty, 0, ref fireAgain);
                        }
                        break;
                }
            }

        return DTSExecResult.Success;
    }
    catch (Exception exc)
    {
        String exceptionMessage = exc != null ? exc.Message :
    UNKNOWN_EXCEPTION_MESSAGE;
        componentEvents.FireError(0, TASK_NAME,
    String.Format(EXCEPTION_MESSAGE_PATTERN, exceptionMessage),
    String.Empty, 0);
        return DTSExecResult.Failure;
    }
```

The `Validate()` method is going to be used whenever the SSIS package, in which the task is used, is validated or executed, and will report any incorrect or missing settings, as well as notify the caller of any exceptions returned by the `WinSCP` library. This method also invokes the `ValidateProperties()` method created in step 21.

24. Make some more room below the `Validate()` method definition, and start typing the `override` directive again; this time select the `Execute()` method to override, and replace its default definition with the following code:

```
Boolean fireAgain = false;

try
{
    // Create a new FTP session.
    using (Session winScpSession = this.EstablishSession())
    {
        componentEvents.FireInformation(0, TASK_NAME,
SESSION_OPEN_MESSAGE, String.Empty, 0, ref fireAgain);

        // Determine the operation mode.
        OperationMode operation =
(OperationMode)Enum.Parse(typeof(OperationMode),
this.FtpOperationName);
        switch (operation)
        {
            case OperationMode.PutFiles:
                // When uploading files, make sure that the
destination directory exists.
                Boolean remoteDirectoryExists =
winScpSession.FileExists(this.FtpRemotePath);
                if (!remoteDirectoryExists)
                {
winScpSession.CreateDirectory(this.FtpRemotePath);
                    componentEvents.FireInformation(0, TASK_NAME,
String.Format(REMOTE_DIRECTORY_CREATED_MESSAGE_PATTERN,
this.FtpRemotePath), String.Empty, 0, ref fireAgain);
                }
                winScpSession.PutFiles(this.FtpLocalPath,
this.FtpRemotePath, this.FtpRemove);
                break;
            case OperationMode.GetFiles:
            default:
                winScpSession.GetFiles(this.FtpRemotePath,
this.FtpLocalPath, this.FtpRemove);
                break;
        }
```

```
            return DTSExecResult.Success;
        }
    }
    catch (Exception exc)
    {
        String exceptionMessage = exc == null ?
    UNKNOWN_EXCEPTION_MESSAGE : exc.Message;
        componentEvents.FireError(0, TASK_NAME,
    String.Format(EXCEPTION_MESSAGE_PATTERN, exceptionMessage),
    String.Empty, 0);
        return DTSExecResult.Failure;
    }
```

25. Save the class file and build the `SSISCustomTasks` project. If you followed the preceding instructions correctly, the build should succeed. If the build fails, inspect the **Error List** pane, and check whether any errors have occurred. Investigate each error and resolve it accordingly.

26. In the Visual Studio toolbar, select **Release** in the **Solution Configuration** selection box, as shown in the following screenshot:

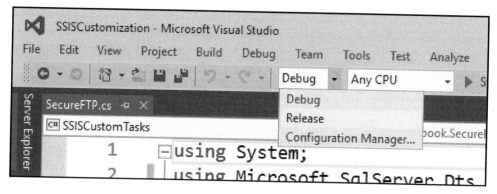

27. Build the `SSISCustomTasks` project again. The files are now created in the release folder and are ready to be deployed.

28. Use Window Explorer to locate the `Chapter13_Deploy_CustomTask.bat` command file in the `C:\SSIS2016Cookbook\Chapter13\Starter\` folder.

29. Run the command file as the administrator. This will copy the custom task assembly to the appropriate folders, and register the assemblies in the Windows GAC, SSDT (at design time), and the SSIS runtime (at runtime), and it needs the relevant assemblies to be registered in GAC.

30. In SSDT, open the `AdventureWorksETL.sln` solution, located in the `C:\SSIS2016Cookbook\Chapter13\Starter\AdventureWorksETL\` folder.

31. Open the `SecureFtpTask.dtsx` SSIS package in the control flow designer.

32. Inspect the package properties and the variables; this package contains most information needed to configure the **Secure FTP Task** that you created earlier in this recipe.

33. Make sure that the control flow designer is active, and inspect the **SSIS Toolbox**. The **Secure FTP Task** should be listed in the **Common** section. If the task is missing, right-click the **SSIS Toolbox**, and select **Refresh Toolbox** from the shortcut menu. If that doesn't help, close SSDT and open the solution again. If not even that helped, close SSDT, and repeat steps 26 to 33.

34. From the **SSIS Toolbox**, drag the **Secure FTP Task** to the control flow designer, and change its name to **Download Files**.

35. Double-click the task to open its editor; the following warning should pop up:

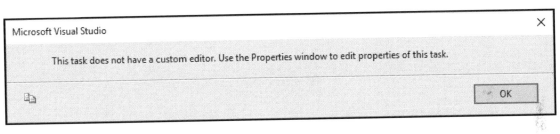

You did not design a custom editor for your custom task; therefore, in order to use the task, you need to configure its properties in the **Properties** pane.

36. While the **Secure FTP Task** is selected in the control flow, inspect its properties in the **Properties** pane. In addition to the base task properties, all of the public members of the `SecureFTP` class that you created in step 18 should be listed in the **Misc** section.

37. Locate the **Expressions** collection, click its text box, and then click the ellipsis icon on the far-right side to start the **Property Expression Editor**.

38. In the **Property Expression Editor**, in the **Property** column select the `FtpHostName` property.

39. Click the ellipsis icon on the far right in the same row to open the **Expression Builder** dialog.

40. In the **Expression Builder**, drag the `$Package::HostName` parameter to the **Expression** text box, and then click **Evaluate** to validate the expression, as shown in the following screenshot:

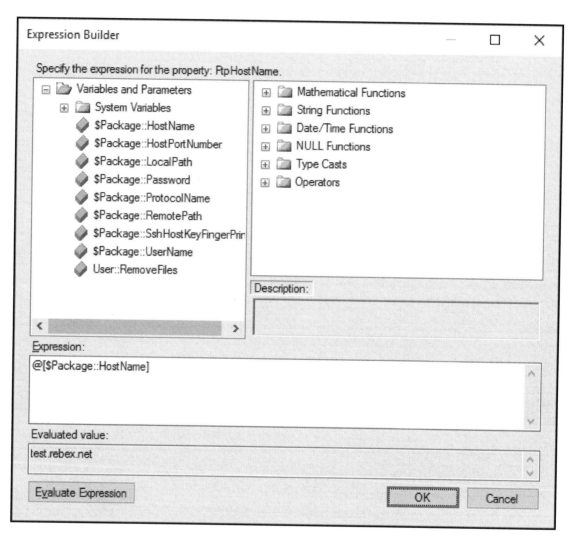

41. Click **OK** to confirm the expression.

42. Repeat steps 38 through 41 for the rest of the properties; use the following settings:

Property	Parameter or variable
FtpLocalPath	$Package::LocalPath
FtpPassword	$Package::Password
FtpPortNumber	$Package::HostPortNumber
FtpProtocolName	$Package::ProtocolName
FtpRemotePath	$Package::RemotePath
FtpRemove	User::RemoveFiles
FtpSshHostKeyFingerprint	$Package::SshHostKeyFingerprint
FtpUserName	$Package::UserName

Use the following screenshot to verify your settings:

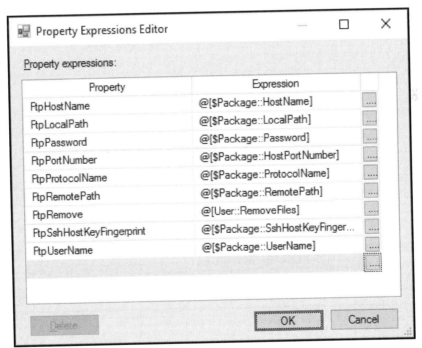

43. Click **OK** to confirm the property expressions.
44. In the **Secure FTP TaskProperties** pane, locate the **FtpOperationName** property and set its value to GetFiles (without the quotation marks).

45. Save the package.

46. Use Windows Explorer to navigate to the
`C:\SSIS2016Cookbook\Chapter13\Files` folder; the folder should not contain any files.

47. In SSDT, execute the `SecureFtpTask.dtsx` SSIS package in debug mode. Observe its execution, and inspect the messages in the **Progress** pane.

> The public FTP site used in this example is hosted on `test.rebex.net`; the site exposes one folder with read-only permissions for the purposes of FTP testing. Several file transfer protocols are supported, and a few files are available in the folder for testing purposes.
> As file access is restricted to read-only, the site cannot be used to upload files. Therefore, in order to test the `PutFiles` operation mode, you need to connect to another site - for instance, create your own FTP server. You can find additional information on the Rebex company website, at `http://www.rebex.net/`.

48. Stop the execution and switch back to Windows Explorer. The folder should now contain 18 PNG files and a `Readme.txt` file.

49. Close the `AdventureWorksETL.sln` solution.

How it works...

In your custom task, the **Secure FTP Task**, you implemented your custom logic in the `Validate()` and `Execute()` methods. You exposed the settings needed to perform the file transfer operations as public members of the `SecureFTP` class.

The `Microsoft.SqlServer.Dts.Runtime.Task` base class allows the task to be used in an SSIS control flow, its public properties are accessible from SSDT, and the custom programmatic logic allows the task to be validated and executed.

If configured correctly, the task can either download files from, or upload them to, an FTP site.

When you used the task in the `SecureFtpTask.dtsx` SSIS package, you were not able to configure it using a custom editor, because this recipe did not cover the design of such an editor. However, you were able to configure the task by accessing its properties directly.

All of the properties were passed into the task using property expressions, except for the `FtpOperationName` property, for which you used a literal value.

When you executed the package, the **Secure FTP Task** connected to the remote server, traversed the files in the remote folder, and downloaded them to the local folder.

Designing a custom transformation

To design a Custom Data Flow Component, you need to create a .NET assembly based on the Class Library Visual Studio template; the class with the component's definition must be derived from the `PipelineComponent` base class of the `Microsoft.SqlServer.Dts.Pipeline` namespace. The class also needs to implement the `DtsPipelineComponentAttribute` that allows the class to be identified as an SSIS component and to provide the essential properties of the component used in the development of SSIS data flows.

If you want to simplify the configuration of the component, you can provide a custom graphical user interface; otherwise, the **Advanced Transformation Editor** will be used to configure the component during SSIS package development.

The component also needs access to the interfaces and classes of the `Microsoft.SqlServer.Dts.Pipeline.Wrapper` namespace. Depending on the functionalities provided by the component, additional references might be needed to the `Microsoft.SqlServer.Dts.Runtime` and `Microsoft.SqlServer.Dts.Runtime.Wrapper` namespaces.

The custom component, be it a source, a destination, or a transformation, must implement two sets of methods of the base class:

- **Design time** methods are used, as the name suggests, at design time; they are called during SSIS package development when the custom component is implemented in the data flow. These methods provide a way for the SSIS package developer to correctly configure the component. They also provide a way for the developer of the component to communicate with the package developers, making sure that they understand how the component is to be used, and to configure it correctly.
- **Run time** methods are used by the execution engine at run time, when the SSIS packages are being executed. These methods provide the programmatic logic needed to perform the operations against the data flow pipeline.

The following design time methods must be provided in order for the custom component to be available and configurable in an SSIS package:

- The `ProvideComponentPorperties()` method is invoked when the component is dropped into the data flow designer. In this method, you provide the configuration of the component's inputs and/or outputs, its custom properties, and any other settings that must be set for the component to be ready for design time configuration.
- The `Validate()` method is used to validate the component and its settings; it is invoked every time the SSIS package developer confirms (or attempts to confirm) the settings during data flow development. Therefore, this method also provides a way for you, the component developer, to communicate with the package developers and to help them configure the component correctly. Use the `FireError()`, `FireWarning()`, and `FireInformation()` methods to notify the package developer of any missing or incorrect settings by using the appropriate error messages or warnings.
- The `ReinitializeMetaData()` method is invoked when, based on the result of the validation, the component's metadata needs to be reset and reinitialized.

The following run time methods are used to provide the principal programmatic logic of the custom component:

- The `PrepareForExecute()` method is used to determine the values of any settings that need to be set before the rows are received from any upstream components, and for any processing that needs, and can be, performed before the rows have been placed into the pipeline. When this method is executed, no additional connections are available yet.
- The `AcquireConnections()` and `ReleaseConnections()` methods are used to manage connections to any additional data sources that are needed in the component and are not provided by any of the component's inputs. Use the former to establish connections to external data sources, and the latter to release them. `AcquireConnections()` is invoked during validation, and again at the beginning of the execution, whereas `ReleaseConnections()` is invoked at the end of the validation, and again at the end of the execution.

- When the `PreExecute()` method is invoked, the rows are already available in the pipeline, and any external connections are also ready, which means that this method can be used to determine any settings that depend on the pipeline data, or the data from the external data sources. If the data acquired from any external sources can be cached (for instance, because its size allows it to be placed completely in memory), this method is also a good alternative to the `ReleaseConnections()` method when you need to close the external connections early to save on resources.

- The `PrimeOutput()` method is used in source components, and in transformations that use asynchronous outputs; it allows these outputs to start consuming data. If the component implements multiple outputs, the method must be capable of preparing each one of them - rows can only be placed into primed outputs. In a source component, this is the principal data processing method.

- The `ProcessInput()` method represents the principal data processing method in transformation and destination components; it is used to consume the data received from the upstream components.

- The rows in the current buffer need to be consumed in a `while` loop with the aid of the `NextRow()` method of the `PipelineBuffer` instance.

    In SSIS data flows, the data is placed into one or more buffers; therefore, the `ProcessInput()` method may be invoked multiple times. In addition, depending on the complexity of the data flow and the availability of resources, the SSIS execution engine can also parallelize the execution of data flow components.

    To make sure that all the upstream rows have been consumed, and to complete the processing of any asynchronous outputs correctly, you also need to check whether more buffers are available with the help of the `EndOfRows()` method of the `PipelineBuffer` instance. This check needs to be made after all the rows of the given buffer instance have been received.

    Synchronous outputs will be closed automatically after all input buffers have been consumed, but asynchronous outputs must be closed explicitly. When no more rows are to be placed into any asynchronous output, you must state this by invoking the `SetEndOfRowset()` method of the output `PipelineBuffer` instance.

    If the component uses multiple inputs, it must also be capable of processing each one of them.

- The `PostExecute()` and `Cleanup()` methods are invoked at the end of the data flow execution; the former is called as soon as all the pipeline data has been consumed, and the latter is invoked last. You should use them to assign values to any writable variables, and complete any unfinished operations.

- The `ReleaseConnections()` method is called after the `PostExecute()` method; therefore, in the `PostExecute()` method you might still have access to any external data sources that you haven't released up to this point in the execution.

- Use the `Cleanup()` method to release any remaining resources that were used in the data flow, in order to make a clean exit from the execution. This is also the last place where variable assignments can be made.

To deploy a custom component - either to the development workstation used in SSIS package development, or to the environment in which it is going to be used - the assemblies containing the component need to be copied to the following folders:

- `%ProgramFiles%\Microsoft SQL Server\130\DTS\PipelineComponents` - for the 64-bit edition of the assembly
- `%ProgramFiles(x86)%\Microsoft SQL Server\130\DTS\PipelineComponents` - for the 32-bit edition of the assembly

If the assembly is platform-independent, the file needs to be copied to both folders.

The assembly, and all of the assemblies it references, must also be registered in the GAC. To register the assemblies on the SSIS development workstation, you can use the `gacutil.exe` command-line utility (it is installed together with Visual Studio); however, on a production server `gacutil.exe` might not be available. You can also use an appropriate Windows PowerShell script to perform the registration.

In this recipe, you are going to port the logic from a script transformation that you developed in Chapter 11, *Unleash the Power of SSIS Script Tasks and Components*, into a custom transformation, deploy it to your development workstation, and use it in an SSIS package.

How to do it...

1. In Visual Studio 2015, open the `SSISCustomization.sln` solution that you created in the previous recipe, *Designing a custom task*; it should be located in the `C:\SSIS2016Cookbook\Chapter13\Starter\SSISCustomization\` folder. In case you have not followed the previous recipe, follow steps 1 through 3 to create the solution.

2. In the **Solution Explorer**, right-click the **Solution** node, and select **Add New Project...** from the shortcut menu to add a new project.

3. In the **Add New Project** dialog, select the **Class Library** template, located in the **Visual C#** template group; use `SSISCustomComponents` as the project name. Refer to the following screenshot to verify your settings:

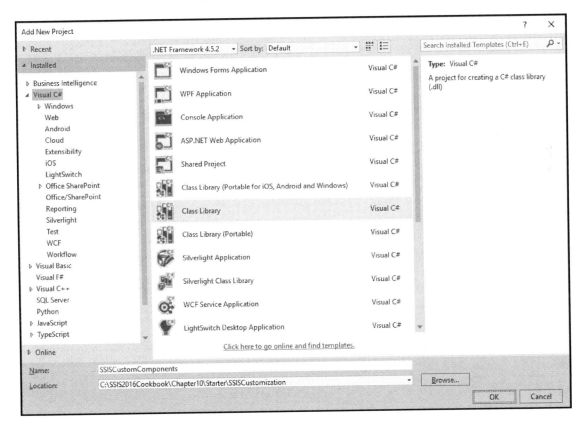

4. Click **OK** to confirm the configuration, and create the project.

5. In the **Solution Explorer**, right-click the newly created `SSISCustomComponents` project, and select **Properties** from the shortcut menu to open the `SSISCustomComponents` properties pane.

6. On the **Application** page, change the default namespace value to `SSIS2016Cookbook`.

7. On the **Signing** page, check **Sign the assembly**, and select **<Browse...>** in the **Choose a strong name key file** selection box.

8. In the **Select File** dialog, navigate to the `C:\SSIS2016Cookbook\Chapter13\Scripts` folder, and select the `SSIS2016Cookbook.snk` strong name key file.

9. Click **Open** to confirm the selection.

10. Save the solution, and then close the project properties pane.

11. In the `Class1.cs` designer pane, change the namespace of the class to `SSIS2016Cookbook`, and change the `Class1` name to `ValidateEmail`.

12. In the **Solution Explorer**, change the `Class1.cs` file name to `ValidateEmail.cs`, and then save the solution.

13. In the **Solution Explorer**, right-click **References**, and then select **Add Reference...** from the shortcut menu to open the **Reference Manager** dialog.

14. Under **Assemblies | Extensions**, check the `Microsoft.SqlServer.PipelineHost`, `Microsoft.SqlServer.DTSPipelineWrap`, and `Microsoft.SQLServer.DTSRuntimeWrap` assemblies, as shown in the following screenshot:

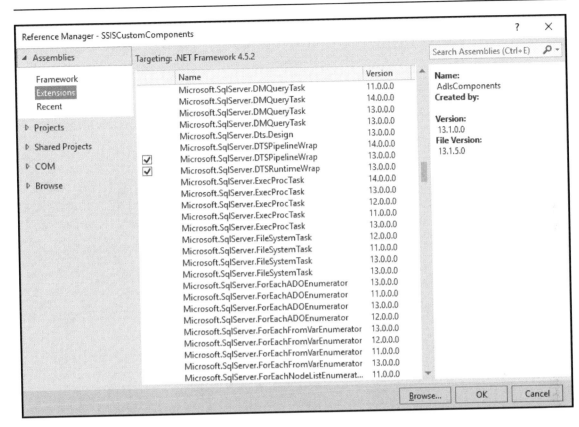

If multiple versions of the same assembly are available, make sure that only
version **13.0.0.0** is checked.

15. Click **OK** to confirm the selection.
16. In the **Solution Explorer**, make sure that the **References** node is expanded.

17. Select the **Microsoft.SqlServer.DTSPipelineWrap** node, locate the Embed Interop Types setting in the assembly's properties, and make sure it is set to **False**, as shown in the following screenshot:

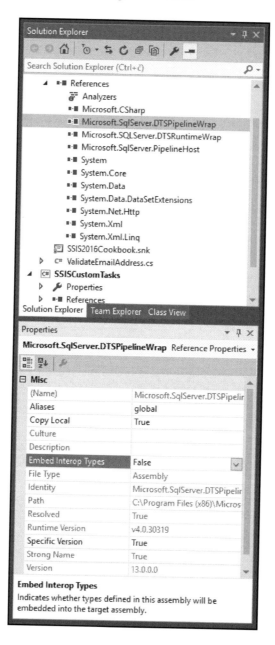

18. Do the same for the `Microsoft.SQLServer.DTSRuntimeWrap` assembly.

19. Save the project.

20. Make sure that `ValidateEmail.cs` is open in the designer, and replace the existing list of assembly references at the top of the definition with the following references:

```
using Microsoft.SqlServer.Dts.Pipeline;
using Microsoft.SqlServer.Dts.Pipeline.Wrapper;
using Microsoft.SqlServer.Dts.Runtime.Wrapper;
using System;
using System.Collections.Generic;
using System.IO;
using System.Linq;
using System.Text;
using System.Text.RegularExpressions;
using System.Xml;
```

The references provide the functionalities needed to develop a complete SSIS component, and to perform its operations.

21. Modify the `ValidateEmail` class definition so that it is derived from the `Microsoft.SqlServer.Dts.Pipeline.PipelineComponent` base class, and implement the `DtsPipelineComponent` attribute:

```
[DtsPipelineComponent
    (
    ComponentType = ComponentType.Transform,
    DisplayName = "Validate Email",
    Description = "Validates email addresses using the
corresponding rule in a data profile file.",
    NoEditor = false
    )]
public class ValidateEmail : PipelineComponent
{
}
```

The base class provides the design-time and run-time functionalities that every SSIS component needs to implement, and the `DtsPipelineComponent` attribute allows the class to be recognized as an SSIS component - at design time as well as run time.

22. Add the following private constant declarations to the `ValidateEmail` class definition:

```
private const String DATA_PROFILE_FILE_NAME_PROPERTY_NAME = "Data
Profile File Name";
private const String DATA_PROFILE_FILE_NAME_PROPERTY_DESCRIPTION =
"Data profile file name (fully qualified).";
private const String DATA_PROFILE_COLUMN_NAME_PROPERTY_NAME = "Data
Profile Column Name";
private const String DATA_PROFILE_COLUMN_NAME_PROPERTY_DESCRIPTION
= "The name of the columns in the data profile.";
private const String INPUT_NAME = "ValidateEmailInput";
private const String INPUT_COLUMN_NAME = "Input Column Name";
private const String INPUT_COLUMN_DESCRIPTION = "The name of the
column to be validated.";
private const String OUTPUT_NAME = "ValidateEmailOutput";
private const String IS_VALID_COLUMN_NAME = "IsValidEmail";
private const String IS_VALID_COLUMN_DESCRIPTION = "True, if the
value of the selected column is a valid email address; otherwise,
False.";
private const String IS_INTERNAL_OBJECT_PROPERTY_NAME =
"isInternal";

private const String TOO_MANY_INPUTS_MESSAGE = "Only a single input
is supported.";
private const String TOO_MANY_OUTPUTS_MESSAGE = "Only a single
output is supported.";
private const String DEFAULT_OUTPUT_MUST_EXIST_MESSAGE = "The
built-in synchronous output cannot be removed.";
private const String USER_DEFINED_COLUMNS_NOT_SUPPORTED = "User-
defined columns are not supported.";
private const String DEFAULT_COLUMNS_MUST_EXIST = "Built-in output
columns cannot be removed";
private const String DATA_PROFILE_FILE_NOT_FOUND_MESSAGE_PATTERN =
"The file [{0}] could not be located.";
private const String DATA_PROFILE_FILE_FOUND_MESSAGE_PATTERN = "The
file [{0}] exists.";
private const String REGEX_PATTERNS_LOADED_MESSAGE_PATTERN = "{0}
Regular Expression patterns loaded.";
private const String DATA_PROFILE_COLUMN_NOT_FOUND_MESSAGE_PATTERN
= "The file [{0}] does not contain a column named [{1}].";
private const String REGEX_PATTERNS_NOT_FOUND_MESSAGE_PATTERN =
"The file [{0}] does not contain any Regular Expressions patterns
data for a column named [{1}].";
private const String INPUT_COLUMN_NOT_SET_MESSAGE = "The input
column has not been set.";
private const String INPUT_COLUMN_NOT_FOUND_MESSAGE_PATTERN = "An
input column named [{0}] cannot be found.";
```

```
private const String INPUT_COLUMN_FOUND_MESSAGE_PATTERN = "The
input column named [{0}] was found.";
private const String
INPUT_COLUMN_DATATYPE_NOT_SUPPORTED_MESSAGE_PATTERN = "The data
type [{0}] of the selected input column [{1}] is not
supported.\r\nPlease, use a column with a supported data type:
DT_NTEXT, DT_TEXT, DT_STR, or DT_WSTR.";

private const String DATA_PROFILE_NAMESPACE =
"http://schemas.microsoft.com/sqlserver/2008/DataDebugger/";
private const String DATA_PROFILE_NAMESPACE_ALIAS = "dp";

private const String DATA_PROFILE_COLUMN_XPATH_PATTERN
    = "/dp:DataProfile/dp:DataProfileOutput/dp:Profiles" +
    "/dp:ColumnPatternProfile[dp:Column[@Name='{0}']]";

private const String REGEX_ELEMENT_XPATH_PATTERN
    = DATA_PROFILE_COLUMN_XPATH_PATTERN +
"/dp:TopRegexPatterns/dp:PatternDistributionItem/dp:RegexText/text(
)";
```

Object names and descriptions are defined in these constants, as well as all the messages used in communicating the current state of the component to the SSIS package developers.

23. Add the following private variables to the `ValidateEmail` class:

```
private String _dataProfileFileName;
private String _dataProfileColumnName;
private String _emailAddressInputColumnName;
private List<String> _regexPatterns = new List<String>();
```

These variables allow the principal settings of the component to be set once, and reused as many times as needed during validation and execution.

24. At the bottom of the `ValidateEmail` class definition, add the following private functions:

```
private Boolean DataProfileColumnExists(String dataProfileName,
String columnName)
{
    Boolean result = true;

    XmlDocument dataProfile = new XmlDocument();
    dataProfile.Load(dataProfileName);
    XmlNamespaceManager dataProfileNSM = new
XmlNamespaceManager(dataProfile.NameTable);
```

```
    dataProfileNSM.AddNamespace(DATA_PROFILE_NAMESPACE_ALIAS,
DATA_PROFILE_NAMESPACE);

    String regexElementXPath =
String.Format(DATA_PROFILE_COLUMN_XPATH_PATTERN, columnName);
    XmlNode dataProfileColumn =
dataProfile.SelectSingleNode(regexElementXPath, dataProfileNSM);
    if (dataProfileColumn == null)
    {
        result = false;
    }

    return result;
}
```

25. This function checks whether the data profile file contains the profile information about the specified column:

```
private List<String> LoadRegularExpressions(String dataProfileName,
String columnName)
{
    List<String> result = new List<String>();

    if (!String.IsNullOrEmpty(dataProfileName) &&
        !String.IsNullOrEmpty(columnName))
    {
        XmlDocument dataProfile = new XmlDocument();
        dataProfile.Load(dataProfileName);
        XmlNamespaceManager dataProfileNSM = new
XmlNamespaceManager(dataProfile.NameTable);
        dataProfileNSM.AddNamespace(DATA_PROFILE_NAMESPACE_ALIAS,
DATA_PROFILE_NAMESPACE);

        String regexElementXPath =
String.Format(REGEX_ELEMENT_XPATH_PATTERN, columnName);
        foreach (XmlNode regexPatternElement in
dataProfile.SelectNodes(regexElementXPath, dataProfileNSM))
        {
            String regexPattern = regexPatternElement.Value;
            if (!result.Contains(regexPattern))
            {
                result.Add(regexPattern);
            }
        }
    }

    return result;
}
```

26. This function extracts the regular expressions patterns for the specified column from the data profile file that can be used to validate the column values:

```
private void ResolveComponentCustomProperties()
{
    _dataProfileFileName =
ComponentMetaData.CustomPropertyCollection[DATA_PROFILE_FILE_NAME_P
ROPERTY_NAME].Value.ToString();
    if (VariableDispenser.Contains(_dataProfileFileName))
    {
        IDTSVariables100 variables = null;
        VariableDispenser.LockOneForRead(_dataProfileFileName, ref
variables);
        _dataProfileFileName = (String)variables[0].Value;
    }

    _dataProfileColumnName =
ComponentMetaData.CustomPropertyCollection[DATA_PROFILE_COLUMN_NAME
_PROPERTY_NAME].Value.ToString();
    if (VariableDispenser.Contains(_dataProfileColumnName))
    {
        IDTSVariables100 variables = null;
        VariableDispenser.LockOneForRead(_dataProfileColumnName,
ref variables);
        _dataProfileColumnName = (String)variables[0].Value;
    }

    _regexPatterns.Clear();
    _regexPatterns =
this.LoadRegularExpressions(_dataProfileFileName,
_dataProfileColumnName);

    _emailAddressInputColumnName =
ComponentMetaData.InputCollection[INPUT_NAME].CustomPropertyCollect
ion[INPUT_COLUMN_NAME].Value.ToString();
}
```

This last private function reads the component properties configured by the SSIS package developer, and stores them in private variables for later use. The function is invoked at package validation and at execution.

Observe the _dataProfileFileName and _dataProfileColumnName variable assignments; if the custom property contains the name of a variable or a parameter, the actual value is retrieved from the corresponding variable or parameter; otherwise, the literal value is used.

27. Immediately before the functions you just added, add the following private function that is going to be used to validate the email addresses:

```
private Boolean IsValidEmail(String emailAddress)
{
    Boolean result = false;

    if (!String.IsNullOrEmpty(emailAddress))
    {
        foreach (String regexPattern in _regexPatterns)
        {
            if (Regex.IsMatch(emailAddress, regexPattern,
RegexOptions.IgnoreCase))
            {
                result = true;
                break;
            }
        }
    }

    return result;
}
```

The IsValidEmail() function in this component is the same as the one used in the *Validating data using regular expressions in a script component* recipe presented in Chapter 11, *Unleash the Power of SSIS Script Tasks and Components*. Compared to the rest of the code of the ValidateEmail class, it might appear insignificant; a lot of programmatic logic is needed to make custom components behave correctly at design and at runtime.

28. Make some space just below the private variable declarations and start typing the override directive; from the list of suggested Microsoft.SqlServer.Dts.Pipeline.PipelineComponent base class overridable methods, select ProvideComponentProperties() and replace its default definition with the following code:

```
base.ProvideComponentProperties();

// Data Profile File name
```

```
IDTSCustomProperty100 dataProfileFileName =
ComponentMetaData.CustomPropertyCollection.New();
dataProfileFileName.Name = DATA_PROFILE_FILE_NAME_PROPERTY_NAME;
dataProfileFileName.Description =
DATA_PROFILE_FILE_NAME_PROPERTY_DESCRIPTION;
dataProfileFileName.State = DTSPersistState.PS_PERSISTASCDATA;
dataProfileFileName.TypeConverter =
typeof(String).AssemblyQualifiedName;
dataProfileFileName.Value = String.Empty;

// Data Profile Column name
IDTSCustomProperty100 dataProfileColumnName =
ComponentMetaData.CustomPropertyCollection.New();
dataProfileColumnName.Name =
DATA_PROFILE_COLUMN_NAME_PROPERTY_NAME;
dataProfileColumnName.Description =
DATA_PROFILE_COLUMN_NAME_PROPERTY_DESCRIPTION;
dataProfileColumnName.State = DTSPersistState.PS_DEFAULT;
dataProfileColumnName.TypeConverter =
typeof(String).AssemblyQualifiedName;
dataProfileColumnName.Value = String.Empty;

// Input
IDTSInput100 input = ComponentMetaData.InputCollection[0];
input.Name = INPUT_NAME;
// Input Column Name
IDTSCustomProperty100 inputColumnName =
input.CustomPropertyCollection.New();
inputColumnName.Name = INPUT_COLUMN_NAME;
inputColumnName.Description = INPUT_COLUMN_DESCRIPTION;
inputColumnName.State = DTSPersistState.PS_DEFAULT;
inputColumnName.TypeConverter =
typeof(String).AssemblyQualifiedName;
inputColumnName.Value = String.Empty;

IDTSCustomProperty100 isInternal;
// Synchronous Output
IDTSOutput100 output = ComponentMetaData.OutputCollection[0];
output.Name = OUTPUT_NAME;
output.SynchronousInputID =
ComponentMetaData.InputCollection[0].ID;
isInternal = output.CustomPropertyCollection.New();
isInternal.Name = IS_INTERNAL_OBJECT_PROPERTY_NAME;
isInternal.State = DTSPersistState.PS_DEFAULT;
isInternal.TypeConverter = typeof(Boolean).AssemblyQualifiedName;
isInternal.Value = true;
// Output column
IDTSOutputColumn100 isVaildEmailColumn =
```

```
output.OutputColumnCollection.New();
isVaildEmailColumn.Name = IS_VALID_COLUMN_NAME;
isVaildEmailColumn.Description = IS_VALID_COLUMN_DESCRIPTION;
isVaildEmailColumn.SetDataTypeProperties(DataType.DT_BOOL, 0, 0, 0,
0);
isInternal = isVaildEmailColumn.CustomPropertyCollection.New();
isInternal.Name = IS_INTERNAL_OBJECT_PROPERTY_NAME;
isInternal.State = DTSPersistState.PS_DEFAULT;
isInternal.TypeConverter = typeof(Boolean).AssemblyQualifiedName;
isInternal.Value = true;
```

The component is defined by the `ProvideComponentProperties()` method—its custom properties, its inputs, and outputs. This method is invoked when the component is placed in the data flow designer during SSIS package development.

29. Below the `ProvideComponentProperties()` method definition you just created, create some more space, and start typing the `override` directive again; this time select the `Validate()` method to override, and replace its default definition with the following commands:

```
Boolean isCanceled = false;
Boolean fireAgain = false;

// Only one input is supported.
if (ComponentMetaData.InputCollection.Count > 1)
{
    ComponentMetaData.FireError(0, ComponentMetaData.Name,
TOO_MANY_INPUTS_MESSAGE, String.Empty, 0, out isCanceled);
    return DTSValidationStatus.VS_ISCORRUPT;
}

// Only one output is supported.
if (ComponentMetaData.OutputCollection.Count > 1)
{
    ComponentMetaData.FireError(0, ComponentMetaData.Name,
TOO_MANY_OUTPUTS_MESSAGE, String.Empty, 0, out isCanceled);
    return DTSValidationStatus.VS_ISCORRUPT;
}

this.ResolveComponentCustomProperties();

// Data profile file must exist.
if (!File.Exists(_dataProfileFileName))
{
    ComponentMetaData.FireError(0, ComponentMetaData.Name,
String.Format(DATA_PROFILE_FILE_NOT_FOUND_MESSAGE_PATTERN,
```

```
_dataProfileFileName), String.Empty, 0, out isCanceled);
    return DTSValidationStatus.VS_ISBROKEN;
}
else
{
    ComponentMetaData.FireInformation(0, ComponentMetaData.Name,
String.Format(DATA_PROFILE_FILE_FOUND_MESSAGE_PATTERN,
_dataProfileFileName), String.Empty, 0, ref fireAgain);

    // Data profile file must contain at least one Regular
Expressions pattern for the specified column name.
    Int32 regexPatternCount = _regexPatterns.Count();
    if (regexPatternCount > 0)
    {
        ComponentMetaData.FireInformation(0,
ComponentMetaData.Name,
String.Format(REGEX_PATTERNS_LOADED_MESSAGE_PATTERN,
regexPatternCount), String.Empty, 0, ref fireAgain);
    }
    else
    {
        if (!this.DataProfileColumnExists(_dataProfileFileName,
_dataProfileColumnName))
        {
            ComponentMetaData.FireWarning(0,
ComponentMetaData.Name,
String.Format(DATA_PROFILE_COLUMN_NOT_FOUND_MESSAGE_PATTERN,
_dataProfileFileName, _dataProfileColumnName), String.Empty, 0);
            return DTSValidationStatus.VS_ISBROKEN;
        }
        else
        {
            ComponentMetaData.FireWarning(0,
ComponentMetaData.Name,
String.Format(REGEX_PATTERNS_NOT_FOUND_MESSAGE_PATTERN,
_dataProfileFileName, _dataProfileColumnName), String.Empty, 0);
            return DTSValidationStatus.VS_ISBROKEN;
        }
    }
}

// The input column must exist and must be of a supported data
type.
if (String.IsNullOrEmpty(_emailAddressInputColumnName))
{
    ComponentMetaData.FireError(0, ComponentMetaData.Name,
INPUT_COLUMN_NOT_SET_MESSAGE, String.Empty, 0, out isCanceled);
    return DTSValidationStatus.VS_ISBROKEN;
```

```
    }
    else
    {
        IDTSInputColumn100 inputColumn =
ComponentMetaData.InputCollection[INPUT_NAME].InputColumnCollection
[_emailAddressInputColumnName];
        if (inputColumn == null)
        {
            ComponentMetaData.FireError(0, ComponentMetaData.Name,
String.Format(INPUT_COLUMN_NOT_FOUND_MESSAGE_PATTERN,
inputColumn.Name), String.Empty, 0, out isCanceled);
            return DTSValidationStatus.VS_ISBROKEN;
        }
        else
        {
            ComponentMetaData.FireInformation(0,
ComponentMetaData.Name,
String.Format(INPUT_COLUMN_FOUND_MESSAGE_PATTERN,
inputColumn.Name), String.Empty, 0, ref fireAgain);

            if (inputColumn.DataType != DataType.DT_NTEXT &&
                inputColumn.DataType != DataType.DT_TEXT &&
                inputColumn.DataType != DataType.DT_STR &&
                inputColumn.DataType != DataType.DT_WSTR)
            {
                ComponentMetaData.FireError(0, ComponentMetaData.Name,
String.Format(INPUT_COLUMN_DATATYPE_NOT_SUPPORTED_MESSAGE_PATTERN,
inputColumn.DataType.ToString(), inputColumn.Name), String.Empty,
0, out isCanceled);
                return DTSValidationStatus.VS_ISBROKEN;
            }
        }
    }
}
return base.Validate();
```

Components are validated whenever the package is loaded in SSDT, when the SSIS developer confirms the component's configuration at the beginning of the execution, and whenever deployed packages are validated explicitly.

30. To guide the SSIS package developers, and prevent them from inadvertently corrupting the component's configuration, add the following overrides to the ValidateEmail class definition:

```
public override IDTSInput100 InsertInput(DTSInsertPlacement
insertPlacement, Int32 inputID)
{
    // Only one input is supported.
```

```
        throw new NotSupportedException(TOO_MANY_INPUTS_MESSAGE);
}
```

This method will prevent the SSIS developers from creating any additional inputs:

```
public override IDTSOutput100 InsertOutput(DTSInsertPlacement
insertPlacement, Int32 outputID)
{
    // Only one output is supported.
    throw new NotSupportedException(TOO_MANY_OUTPUTS_MESSAGE);
}
```

This method will prevent the SSIS developers from creating any additional outputs:

```
public override IDTSOutputColumn100 InsertOutputColumnAt(Int32
outputID, Int32 outputColumnIndex, String name, String
description)
{
    // No additional Output Columns can be added.
    throw new
NotSupportedException(USER_DEFINED_COLUMNS_NOT_SUPPORTED);
}
```

This method will prevent the SSIS developers from adding any additional columns to the default output:

```
public override void DeleteOutput(Int32 outputID)
{
    // The built-in output cannot be removed.
    Boolean isInternal =
(Boolean)(ComponentMetaData.OutputCollection.GetObjectByID(outp
utID).CustomPropertyCollection[IS_INTERNAL_OBJECT_PROPERTY_NAME
].Value);
    if (isInternal)
    {
        throw new
InvalidOperationException(DEFAULT_OUTPUT_MUST_EXIST_MESSAGE);
    }
    else
    {
        base.DeleteOutput(outputID);
    }
}
```

This method will prevent the SSIS developers from removing the default output; it will allow them to remove other outputs, but only theoretically, because adding an output is already prevented by the preceding InsertOutput() method override:

```
public override void DeleteOutputColumn(Int32 outputID, Int32
outputColumnID)
{
    // Built-in output columns cannot be removed.
    Boolean isInternal =
(Boolean)(ComponentMetaData.OutputCollection.GetObjectByID(outp
utID).OutputColumnCollection.GetObjectByID(outputColumnID).Cust
omPropertyCollection[IS_INTERNAL_OBJECT_PROPERTY_NAME].Value);
    if (isInternal)
    {
        throw new
InvalidOperationException(DEFAULT_COLUMNS_MUST_EXIST);
    }
    else
    {
        base.DeleteOutputColumn(outputID, outputColumnID);
    }
}
```

This last override will prevent SSIS developers from removing the built-in output columns. Theoretically, it will allow them to remove user-defined columns; however, the overridden InsertOutputColumnAt() method prevents them from being added at all.

31. By using the same technique as in steps 26 and 27, override the PreExecute() base class method, and use the following code as its definition:

```
base.PreExecute();

this.ResolveComponentCustomProperties();
```

All the settings needed to process the pipeline data are determined in the PreExecute() method.

32. Next, override the `ProcessInput()` method and replace its default definition with the following commands:

```
IDTSInput100 input =
ComponentMetaData.InputCollection.GetObjectByID(inputID);
Int32 emailAddressInputColumnId =
input.InputColumnCollection[_emailAddressInputColumnName].ID;
IDTSInputColumn100 emailAddressInputColumn =
input.InputColumnCollection.GetObjectByID(emailAddressInputColumnId
);
Int32 emailAddressInputColumnIndex =
input.InputColumnCollection.GetObjectIndexByID(emailAddressInputCol
umnId);

IDTSOutput100 output =
ComponentMetaData.OutputCollection[OUTPUT_NAME];
Int32 isValidColumnId =
output.OutputColumnCollection[IS_VALID_COLUMN_NAME].ID;
IDTSOutputColumn100 isValidColumn =
output.OutputColumnCollection.GetObjectByID(isValidColumnId);
Int32 isValidColumnIndex =
BufferManager.FindColumnByLineageID(input.Buffer,
isValidColumn.LineageID);

while (buffer.NextRow())
{
    String emailAddress;
    switch (emailAddressInputColumn.DataType)
    {
        case DataType.DT_NTEXT:
            emailAddress =
Encoding.Unicode.GetString(buffer.GetBlobData(emailAddressInputColu
mnIndex, 0,
(Int32)buffer.GetBlobLength(emailAddressInputColumnIndex)));
            break;
        case DataType.DT_TEXT:
            emailAddress =
Encoding.GetEncoding(emailAddressInputColumn.CodePage).GetString(bu
ffer.GetBlobData(emailAddressInputColumnIndex, 0,
emailAddressInputColumn.Length));
            break;
```

```
        default:
            emailAddress =
buffer.GetString(emailAddressInputColumnIndex);
            break;
    }

    buffer.SetBoolean(isValidColumnIndex,
this.IsValidEmail(emailAddress));
}
```

Column value validation is performed in the `ProcessInput()` method. The data is retrieved from the specified column based on the input column data type - `DT_TEXT` and `DT_NTEXT` large object (LOB) data types require special handling, whereas the data in `DT_STR` and `DT_WSTR` can be read simply with the `GetString()` method.

33. In the overridden `PostExecute()` method, use the following commands:

```
_regexPatterns.Clear();

base.PostExecute();
```

After the rows have been processed, the `PostExecute()` method releases the resources; it clears the regular expressions collection, as it is no longer needed.

34. Save the solution, and build the project by selecting the **Build SSISCustomComponents** command from the **Build** menu - first using **Debug**, and then again using the **Release** solution configuration. If you followed the preceding instructions correctly, the project should build successfully. In case of any errors, inspect the messages in the **Error List** pane and make the appropriate corrections.

35. Use Windows Explorer to navigate to the `C:\SSIS2016Cookbook\Chapter13\Starter` folder, and locate the `Chapter10_Deploy_CustomComponent.bat` command file.

36. Execute the command file as the administrator, observe the messages returned in the **Command Prompt** window, and finally press any key to complete the deployment.

37. In SSDT, open the `AdventureWorksETL.sln` solution, located in the `C:\SSIS2016Cookbook\Chapter13\Starter\AdventureWorksETL\` folder.

38. Open the `RegExValidation.dtsx` package in the control flow; the package is based on a similar package with the same name that you created in the *Validating data using regular expressions in a script component* recipe of `Chapter 11`, *Unleash the Power of SSIS Script Tasks and Components.*

39. Open the **Validate Person Data** task in the data flow designer.

40. From the SSIS toolbox, drag the **Validate Email** transformation to the data flow designer; it should be located in the **Common** section. If the **Validate Email** transformation is not available in the SSIS Toolbox, right-click the toolbox, and select **Refresh Toolbox** from the shortcut menu. If that doesn't help, close SSDT, and open the `AdventureWorksETL.sln` solution again. If not even that resolves the problem, return to the Visual Studio instance with `SSISCustomization.sln` open, and repeat steps 32 through 34 to redeploy the assembly.

41. Connect the regular data path from the **Person Data** source component to the **Validate Email** transformation.

42. Double-click the **Validate Email** transformation to open the **Advanced Editor for Validate Email**.

43. On the **Component Properties** page, use the following settings to configure the component's custom properties:

Property	Value
Data Profile Column Name	EmailAddress
Data Profile File Name	$Package::DataProfileName

Refer to the following screenshot to verify your settings:

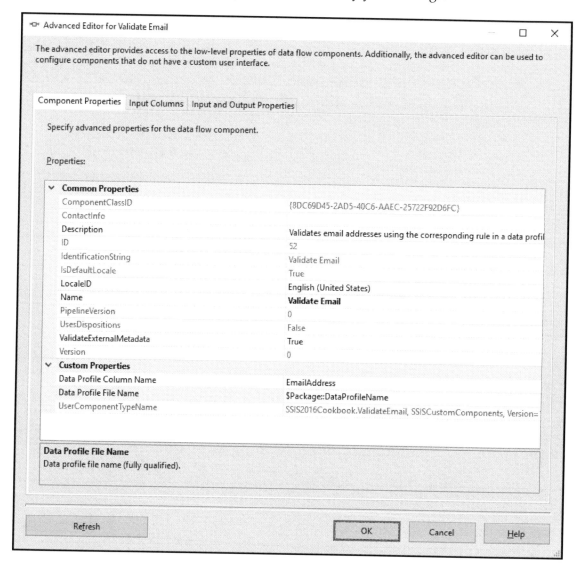

44. On the **Input Columns** page, make sure that all the input columns are selected; leave their **Usage Type** set to **READONLY**.

45. On the **Input and Output Properties** page, locate the **Input Column Name** custom property of the `ValidateEmailInput` input, and use `EmailAddress` as its value, as shown in the following screenshot:

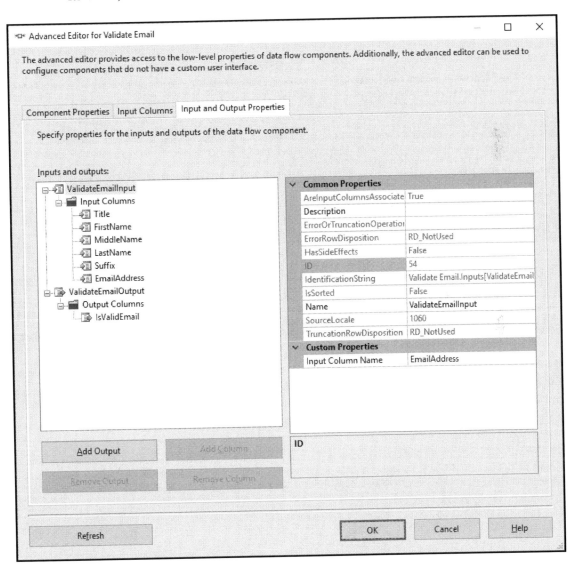

46. Click **OK** to confirm the configuration. If you followed the preceding instructions correctly, no validation errors should be reported. If the component is in error (marked by a red **X** mark), or if there are any warnings (marked by an exclamation mark), inspect the **Error List** pane, investigate each message, and resolve them accordingly.

47. In the data flow designer, connect the regular data path from the **Validate Email** transformation to the **Valid or Invalid Email** transformation.

48. Make sure that the **Data Viewer** is enabled on the regular data path leading from the **Valid or Invalid Email** transformation to the **Multicast** component.

49. Save the RegExValidation.dtsx package, and then execute it in debug mode. 107 rows should be extracted from the source file, and seven rows should be listed in the **Invalid Email Data Viewer**.

50. Stop the debug mode execution, and close the **AdventureWorksETL.sln** solution.

How it works...

To create a custom data flow component, you need to create a class that derives from the Microsoft.SqlServer.Dts.Pipeline.PipelineComponent base class, which provides the functionalities needed to configure the component at design time and perform the operations at run time. By implementing the DtsPipelineComponent attribute, you allow the class to be recognized as an SSIS component by SSDT at design time and by the SSIS execution engine at run time.

By overriding the ProvideComponentProperties() base class method, you established the essential elements of the component: the input, the output, and in it the output column to hold the result of the transformation. You defined the custom properties (two for the component and one for the input) that the SSIS package developers can use to configure the component.

By overriding the Validate() method, and some additional design-time methods, you implemented all the necessary checks needed to guide the SSIS package developer to complete the configuration correctly.

You used the PreExecute() method to prepare the execution of the component - namely, to load the email address validation rules from the Data Profile file you created in Chapter 10, *Dealing with Data Quality*, for the column specified in the **Data Profile Column Name** custom property. You used the PostExecute() method to release these resources after the execution completes.

The principal part of the transformation, however, is implemented in the `ProcessInput()` method, where each row received from the upstream pipeline is validated: data is read from the column specified by the **Input Column Name** custom input property and validated against the Regular Expressions patterns from the Data Profile file. Validation results are then placed in the **IsValidEmail** output column, to be consumed by the downstream components of the data flow.

Managing custom component versions

Over time you might need to make changes to a custom component, for instance, because you needed to optimize or refactor the code, implement new features, or replace the external assemblies. As long as the interface of the component (its custom properties and its inputs and outputs) remain unchanged in a later version, you simply deploy the new version to the destination environments, register it in the GAC, and the new version of the component will be used the next time the package is executed or edited in SSDT. You do not even have to modify its version number.

However, if the change affects the components interface - for instance, if you need to add, remove, or modify any of its custom properties - you need to make the component upgradable. This upgrade is performed automatically - at design time or at run time - by invoking a special design-time method of the `Microsoft.SqlServer.Dts.Pipeline.PipelineComponent` base class, namely the `PerformUpgrade()` method. The method is invoked automatically in SSDT when the SSIS package is being designed or by the SSIS execution engine when the SSIS package is being executed if the `CurrentVersion` property of the `DtsPipelineComponent` attribute was set in the component.

You use the `PerformUpgrade()` method in the later version of the component to make the necessary changes to the properties of the earlier version of the component, for instance by adding a property that was not available in the earlier version, by removing a property that is no longer used, or by modifying an existing property of the earlier version of the component so that it can be used by the later component.

In this recipe, you are going to create version two of the component that you created in the *Designing a custom transformation* recipe earlier in this chapter. The new version is going to use an additional custom parameter and will allow the initial version to be upgraded automatically.

Getting ready

Before you can use this recipe, you need to design the custom component, as described in the *Designing a custom transformation* recipe earlier in this chapter.

Alternatively, you can use the **SSISCustomComponents** project of the SSISCustomization.sln solution, located in the C:\SSIS2016Cookbook\Chapter10\Solution\SSISCustomization\ folder.

How to do it...

1. Open the SSISCustomization.sln solution that you created in the *Designing a custom transformation* recipe, earlier in this chapter.
2. In the SSISCustomComponents project, locate the ValidateEmail.cs file, and open it in the designer.
3. Modify the DtsPipelineComponent attribute of the ValidateEmail class, and add the CurrentVersion property, as shown in the following example:

```
[DtsPipelineComponent
    (
    ComponentType = ComponentType.Transform,
    DisplayName = "Validate Email",
    Description = "Validates email addresses using the
corresponding rule in a data profile file.",
    NoEditor = false,
    CurrentVersion = 2
    )]
```

Do not forget the comma after the NoEditor property declaration! When the CurrentVersion property is set, SSDT at design time and the SSIS execution engine at run time will invoke the PerformUpgrade() base class method, and attempt to upgrade an earlier version of the component used in an SSIS package to the current one registered in the GAC.

4. Add the following private constant declarations to the end of the current list of constants:

```
private const String REGEX_OPTIONS_PROPERTY_NAME = "Regular
Expressions Options";
private const String REGEX_OPTIONS_PROPERTY_DESCRIPTION = "The
Regular Expressions options to be used in email address
validation.";
private const Int64 REGEX_OPTIONS_UPGRADE_VALUE = 513;
private const String REGEX_OPTIONS_UNKNOWN_MESSAGE_PATTERN =
"The value of {0} does not represent a valid RegexOptions
value.";
```

These constants contain some of the settings needed by version two of the component: object names, descriptions, and messages.

5. Another private variable is required; place it next to the existing ones:

```
private Int64 _regexOptionsNumber;
```

6. Modify the `ProvideComponentProperties()` method, and add the following new custom property declaration:

```
// Regular Expressions Options
IDTSCustomProperty100 regularExpressionsOptions =
ComponentMetaData.CustomPropertyCollection.New();
regularExpressionsOptions.Name = REGEX_OPTIONS_PROPERTY_NAME;
regularExpressionsOptions.Description =
REGEX_OPTIONS_PROPERTY_DESCRIPTION;
regularExpressionsOptions.State = DTSPersistState.PS_DEFAULT;
regularExpressionsOptions.TypeConverter =
typeof(Int64).AssemblyQualifiedName;
regularExpressionsOptions.Value = (Int64)0;
```

This property will allow the SSIS package developers to not only specify which regular expressions patterns to use, and against which column, but also which regular expressions options to use for matching.

7. Extend the `Validate()` method by adding the following test at the end of the method's definition (before the `return` command):

```
try
{
    RegexOptions regexOptions = (RegexOptions)_regexOptionsNumber;
    Regex regex = new Regex(@".", regexOptions);
}
catch (ArgumentOutOfRangeException)
{
    ComponentMetaData.FireError(0, ComponentMetaData.Name,
String.Format(REGEX_OPTIONS_UNKNOWN_MESSAGE_PATTERN,
_regexOptionsNumber.ToString()), String.Empty, 0, out isCanceled);
    return DTSValidationStatus.VS_ISBROKEN;
}
```

8. Extend the `ResolveComponentCustomProperties()` private function by adding the following variable assignment to its definition:

```
_regexOptionsNumber =
(Int64)(ComponentMetaData.CustomPropertyCollection[REGEX_OPTIONS_PR
OPERTY_NAME].Value);
```

9. In the `IsValidEmail()` private function, amend the call to the `Regex.IsMatch()` method so that the Regular Expressions options can be passed to it dynamically, as shown in the following example:

```
if (Regex.IsMatch(emailAddress, regexPattern,
(RegexOptions)_regexOptionsNumber))
```

10. Make some space below the `PostExecute()` method definition, and start typing the override directive; from the list of possible overrides, select the `PerformUpgrade()` method. Use the following code to replace the method's default definition:

```
DtsPipelineComponentAttribute pipelineComponentAttribute =
(DtsPipelineComponentAttribute)Attribute.GetCustomAttribute(this.Ge
tType(), typeof(DtsPipelineComponentAttribute), false);
Int32 componentLatestVersion =
pipelineComponentAttribute.CurrentVersion;

Int32 activeComponentVersion = ComponentMetaData.Version;
if (activeComponentVersion < componentLatestVersion)
{
    try
    {
        IDTSCustomProperty100 existingRegularExpressionsOptions =
```

```
ComponentMetaData.CustomPropertyCollection[REGEX_OPTIONS_PROPERTY_N
AME];
    }
    catch (Exception)
    {
        IDTSCustomProperty100 regularExpressionsOptions =
ComponentMetaData.CustomPropertyCollection.New();
        regularExpressionsOptions.Name =
REGEX_OPTIONS_PROPERTY_NAME;
        regularExpressionsOptions.Description =
REGEX_OPTIONS_PROPERTY_DESCRIPTION;
        regularExpressionsOptions.State =
DTSPersistState.PS_DEFAULT;
        regularExpressionsOptions.TypeConverter =
typeof(Int64).AssemblyQualifiedName;
        regularExpressionsOptions.Value =
REGEX_OPTIONS_UPGRADE_VALUE;
    }
}

ComponentMetaData.Version = componentLatestVersion;
```

11. Save the project, and build it - first using the **Debug**, and then again using **Release** solution configuration. In case of any errors, inspect the messages in the **Error List** pane and make the appropriate corrections.

12. Use Windows Explorer to navigate to the `C:\SSIS2016Cookbook\Chapter13\Starter` folder, and locate the `Chapter10_Deploy_CustomComponent.bat` command file.

13. Execute the command file as the administrator, observe the messages returned in the **Command Prompt** window, and finally press any key to complete the deployment.

14. In SSDT, open the `AdventureWorksETL.sln` solution, located in the `C:\SSIS2016Cookbook\Chapter13\Starter\AdventureWorksETL\` folder.

15. Open the `RegExValidation.dtsx` package in the control flow, and then open the **Validate Person Data** task in the data flow designer. In case you did not use the previous recipe, follow steps 38 through 46 of the *Designing a custom transformation* recipe to complete the data flow; otherwise, the **Validate Email** transformation should already be in place.

16. In the **Advanced Editor for the Validate Email** transformation, under **Custom Properties**, the new **Regular Expressions Options** property should be available with the default value of 513 (the value represents the case-insensitive, and culture-invariant, regular expressions matching options). This value is applied during the upgrade. Refer to the following screenshot to verify your settings:

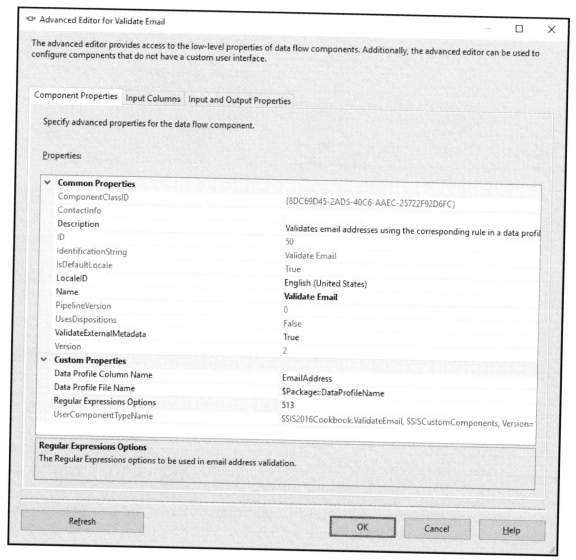

17. Click **OK** to confirm the configuration.
18. Save the package and execute it in debug mode. Out of 107 source rows, seven should fail the **EmailAddress** column validation.
19. Stop the debug mode execution.
20. Close the AdventureWorksETL.sln and SSISCustomization.sln solutions.

How it works...

By specifying the version number of the custom component, in the DtsPipelineComponent attribute, you mark the new version of the component; a new version is needed only if the exposed properties, inputs, and/or outputs, have been modified.

Of course, setting the new version number is not enough to allow the earlier versions of the component that are already in use in deployed SSIS packages to be upgraded accordingly. The upgrade is performed by overriding the PerformUpgrade() base class method. In the preceding example, a new component custom property is added.

After the upgrade, the component's version number is changed as well, to the version number of the component currently registered in the GAC.

When the new version of the component is deployed and registered, any SSIS package that uses the component will be upgraded, either the next time you edit it in SSDT or the next time it is executed.

14
Scale Out with SSIS 2017

This chapter will cover the following recipes:

- SQL Server 2017 download and setup
- SQL Server client tools setup
- SSIS configuration for scale out executions
- Scaling out a package execution

Introduction

Since its inception, SSIS was meant to execute on a single machine running Windows. The service by itself could not scale on multiple machines. Although it would have been possible to call package execution with custom orchestration mechanism, it didn't have anything built in. You needed to manually develop an orchestration service and that was tedious to do and maintain. See this article for a custom scale-out pattern with SSIS: `https://msdn.microsoft.com/en-us/dn887191.aspx`.

What lots of developers wanted was a way to use SSIS a bit like the way Hadoop works: call a package execution from a master server and scale it on multiple workers (servers). The SSIS team is delivering a similar functionality in 2017, enabling us to enhance scalability and performance in our package executions.

As mentioned before, the scale out functionality is like Hadoop. The difference is that we use tools we have more knowledge of. It's also a lot easier to work with SSIS since we are on the Windows filesystem. As we saw in `Chapter 12`, *On-Premises and Azure Big Data Integration*, on big data, we needed to use ssh to connect to the machine where the files were copied and produced. Another advantage is that we can consume data at the source. We don't have to copy it to another machine and SSIS can connect to lots of different sources.

We do not pretend that the SSIS scale out functionality is a replacement for Hadoop. In many situations, it might be a good option before exploring other solutions such as Hadoop/HDInsight or Azure SQL Data Warehouse.

SQL Server 2017 download and setup

This recipe will cover the following subtopics:

- Download SQL Server 2017
- Set up SQL Server with SSIS scale out options

Getting ready

This recipe assumes that you have the necessary permissions to install SQL Server on your machine.

How to do it...

1. Open your web browser and navigate to `https://www.microsoft.com/en-us/sql-server/sql-server-2017`.
2. Select **Download the preview**, as shown in the following screenshot:

3. On the page that appears, select **Windows** in the platform menus at the right and click on **Install on Windows**, as shown in this screenshot:

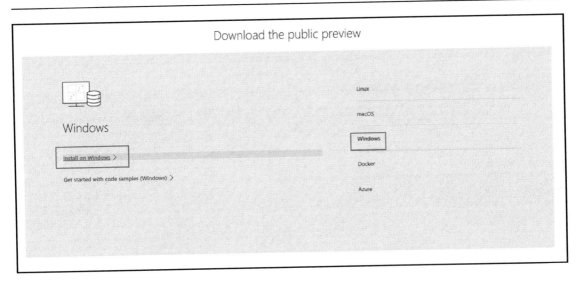

4. As shown in the following screenshot, fill in the form and click on **Continue**:

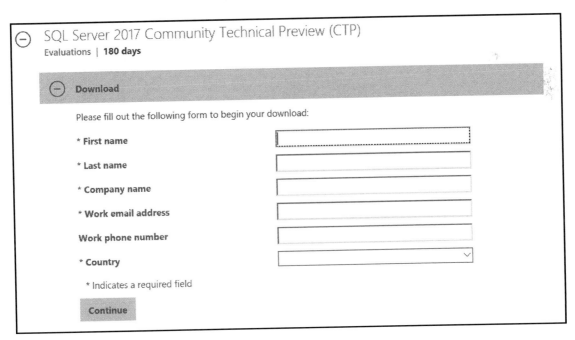

5. Choose **ISO** and click on **Continue**, as shown here:

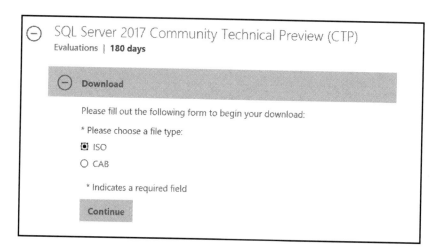

6. Choose the language (we selected **English**) and click on **Download**, as shown in the following screenshot:

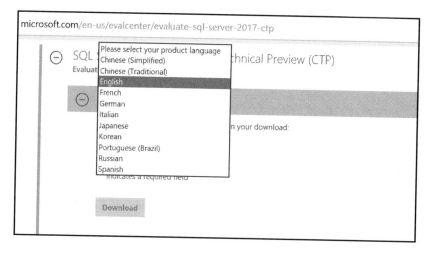

7. The download will now start. Once completed, navigate to the folder where you saved the file named `SQLServer2017CTP2.1-x64-ENU.iso` and double-click on it. Select **setup.exe** to proceed with the SQL Server 2017 CTP 2.1 installation, as shown in the following screenshot:

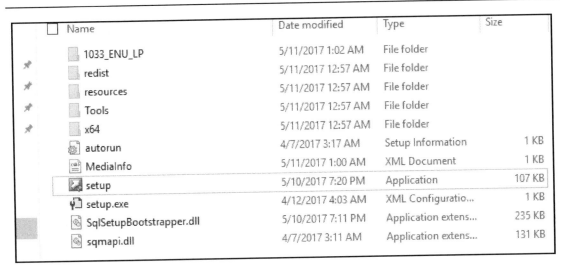

8. Once **SQL Server Installation Center** appears, click on **New SQL Server stand-alone installation or add features to an existing installation**. The **SQL Server 2017 CTP 2.1 Setup** window appears, as shown in the following screenshot. Click on **Next**.

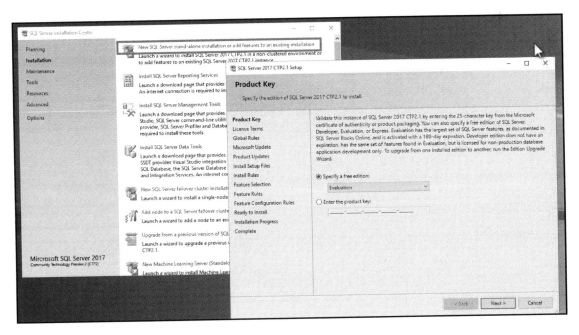

9. Accept the **License Terms** and click on **Next**:

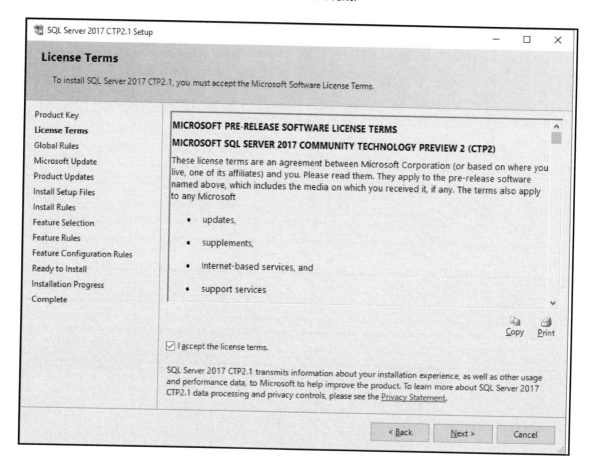

10. As shown in the following screenshot, allow **Microsoft Update** to run and click on **Next**:

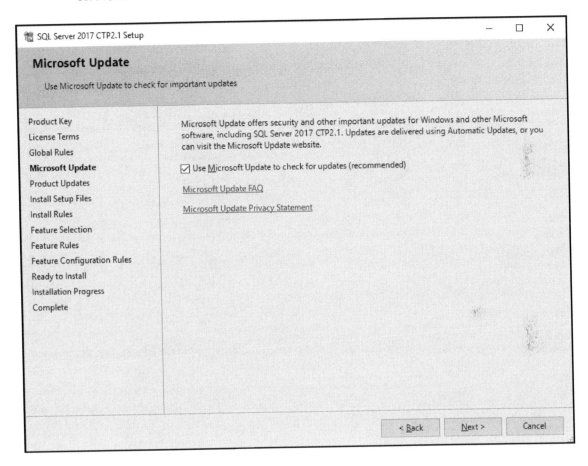

11. Once **Initial Setup Files** completes, as shown in this screenshot, click on **Next**:

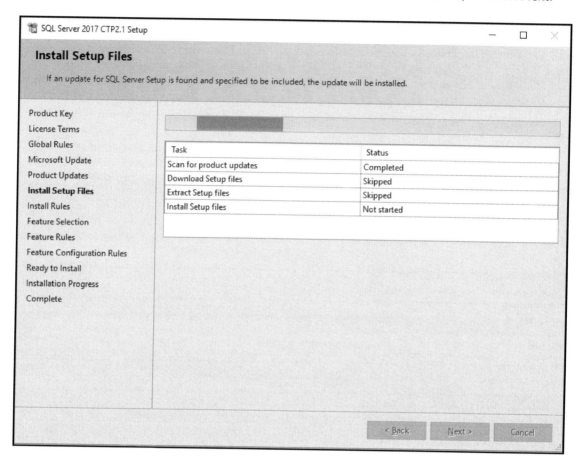

12. Once the updates are done, the **Install Rules** window appears; click on **Next** on this one once the rules check is completed. As shown in the next screenshot, there's always a firewall warning. Since we're working on an all-in-one configuration, this warning can be skipped:

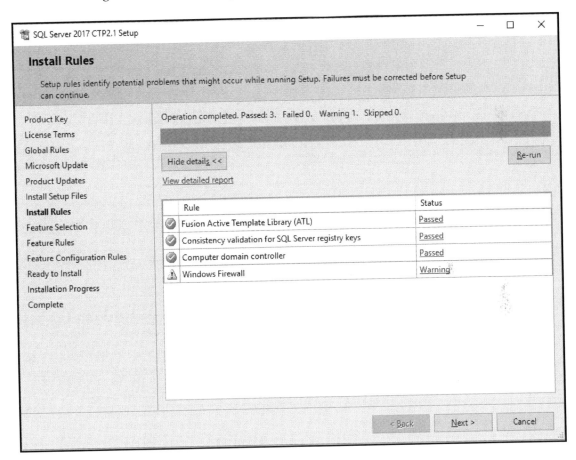

13. The **Feature Selection** window appears. In our case, we'll only install the database engine and SSIS. You'll notice that we select both **Scale Out Master** and **Worker** in **Integration Services**, the new features we're interested in. Select the features shown in the following screenshot and click on **Next**:

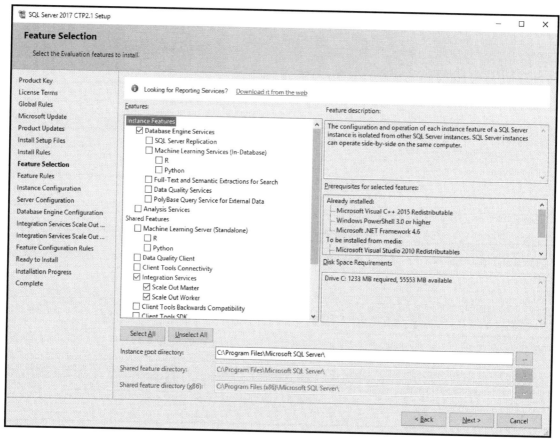

14. The **Instance Configuration** window appears; since we might have multiple instances of SQL Server 2017 until the final release, we'll use a named instance. This creates separate sets of services for each version of SQL Server installed on a machine. Be aware that each instance of SQL Server consumes resources, and the PC where it is installed might have performance issues if you install too many versions and run them at same time. Enter MSSQL2017_21 for MSSQL 2017 CTP 2.1 in the **Named instance** textbox and click on **Next**:

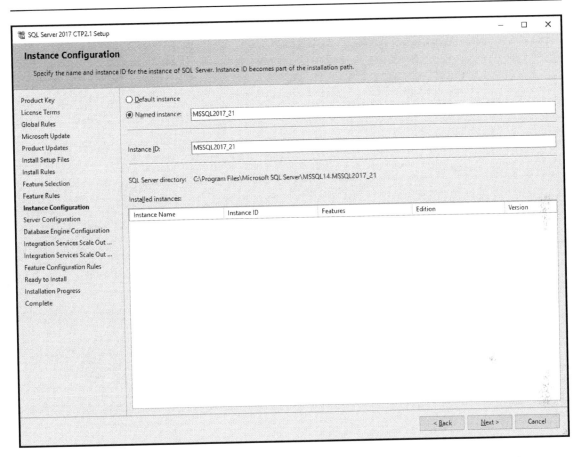

15. In the **Server Configuration** window, click on the **Collation** tab and set the collation to **Latin1_General_100_CI_AI**, as shown in the following screenshot. You might want to refer to `Chapter 7`, *SSIS Setup* for an explanation of the collation choice and definition. Click on **Next**:

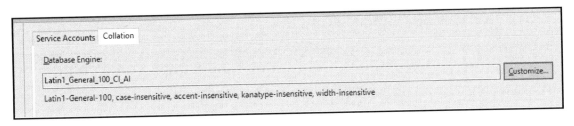

16. The **Database Engine Configuration** window appears. In the **Server Configuration** tab, select **Mixed Mode** as the authentication mode. Enter a password for the SA account. The **Mixed Mode** authentication is required by **Scale Out Workers (SSIS)** to be able to write into SSISDB. Add the current user (you) also as an SQL Server Administrator, as shown in the following screenshot. Leave the other settings as default and click on **Next**:

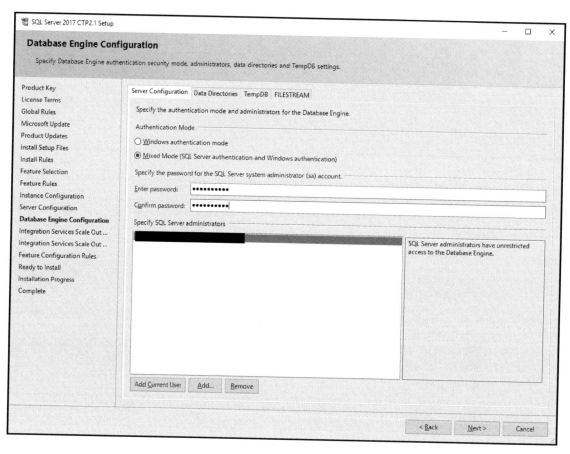

17. We are now directed to **Integration Services Scale Out Configuration - Master Node**. Since we're using an all-in-one sample configuration, which means the master node will reside on the same machine as the worker node, the port configuration is not very important. We currently don't have any SSL Certificate handy. Leave the settings to their default values and click on **Next**.

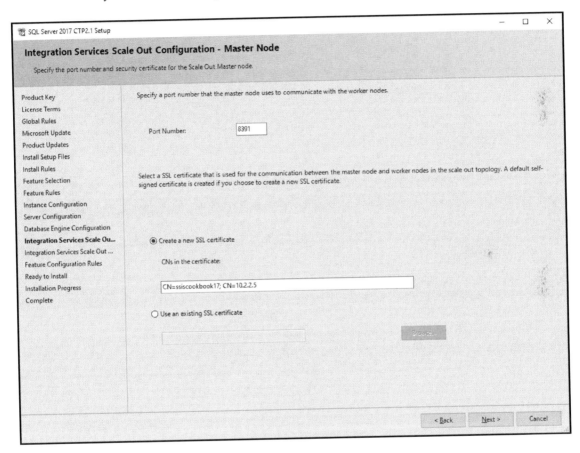

18. The **Integration Services Scale Out Configuration - Worker Node** window appears. As highlighted in the following screenshot, this step is useful when we install separate worker nodes on different machines. In these cases, we need to specify the trusted certificate used to authenticate to the master worker node. In an all-in-one configuration, this step is facultative. Click on **Next** to continue.

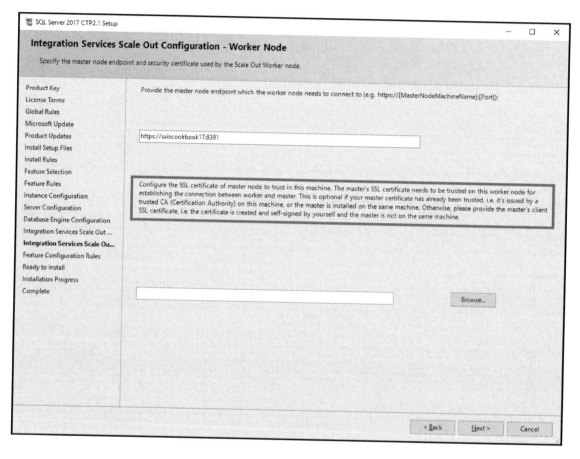

19. The **Ready to Install** window appears. As shown in the following screenshot, this step allows you to review what will be installed. We can always click on **< Back** to change anything that we selected before. In our case, everything is fine; click on **Install** to start installing SQL Server 2017 CTP1.

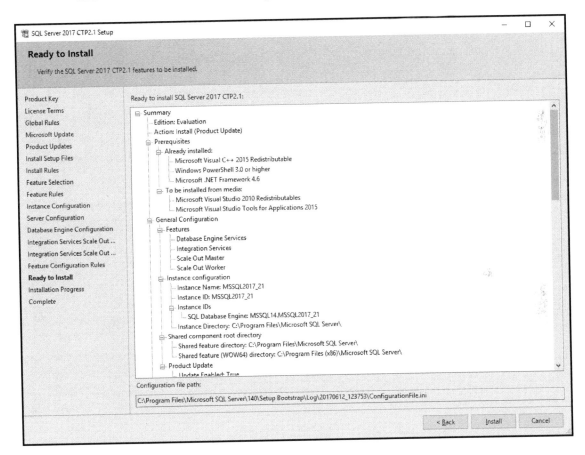

20. The **Installation Progress** window appears. It might take several minutes to complete. As shown in the following screenshot, there's a progress bar that tells us the progress of the installation:

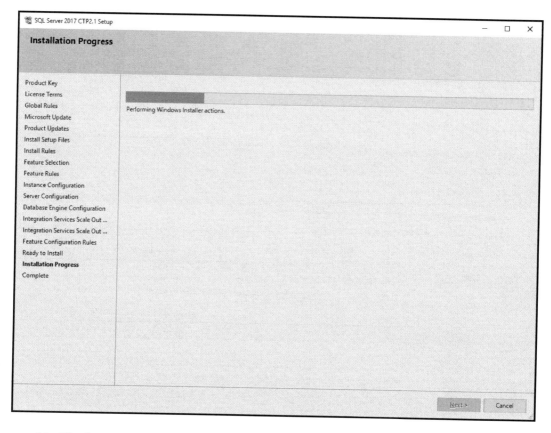

21. The last step will show you that the installation is complete.

There's more...

We have now installed the server portion of SQL Server. The next steps will show you how to install **SQL Server Management Studio (SSMS)** and **SQL Server Data Tools (SSDT)**.

SQL Server client tools setup

We will see how to setup SQL Server client tools.

Getting ready

This recipe assumes that you have access to the internet and you have the necessary rights to install the software on your PC.

How to do it...

1. From **SQL Server Installation Center**, click on **Install SQL Server Management Tools**, as highlighted in the following screenshot:

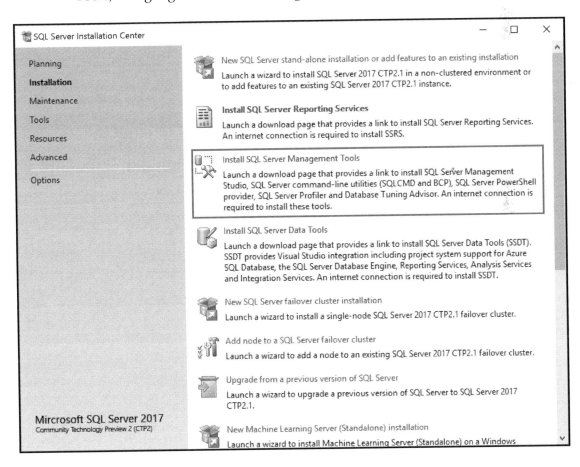

2. A browser opens and the following page opens. Select version 17.1 (the latest version available at the time of writing this book), highlighted in the following screenshot:

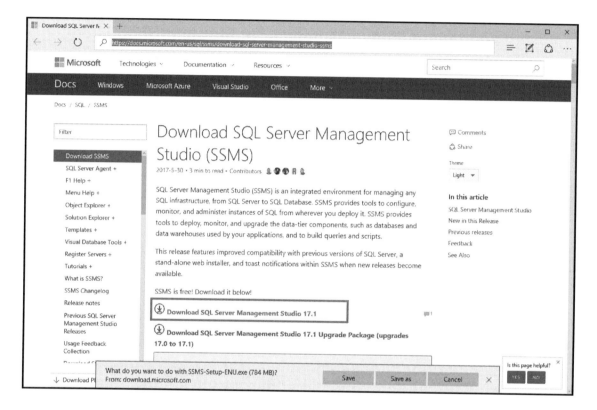

3. Once the download completes, double-click on the downloaded file to start the installation process. Once completed, you get a window similar as the one shown in the following screenshot:

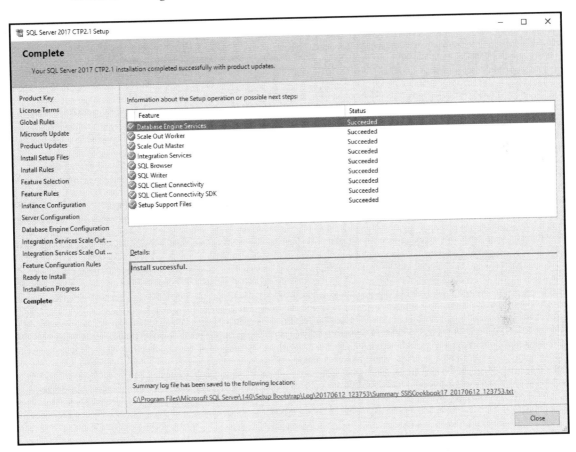

4. Go back to **SQL Server Installation Center**, and this time, click on **Install SQL Server Data Tools**, as highlighted in this screenshot:

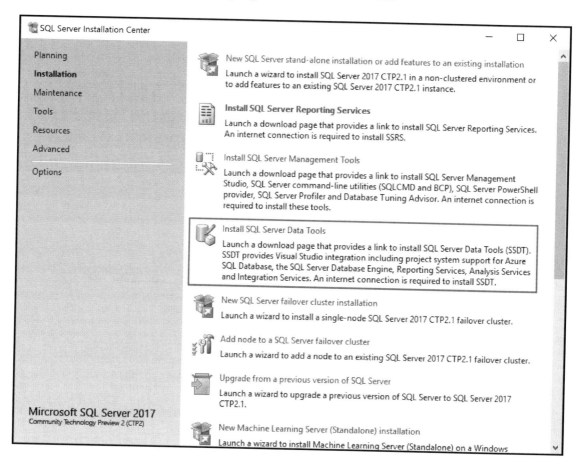

5. You are directed to the SSDT website. As shown in the following screenshot, download the latest version (17.1 at the time of writing) of SSDT:

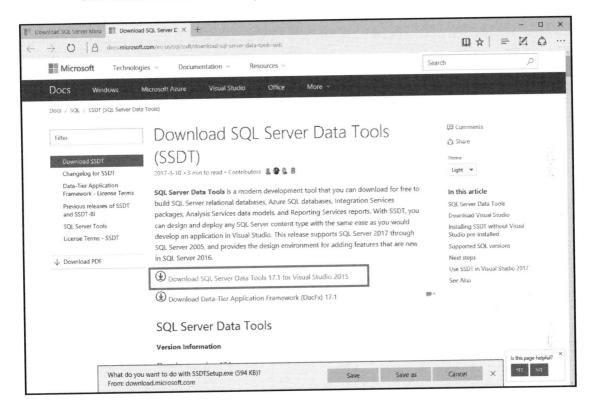

6. The SSDT installer appears as shown in the following screenshot. Although only **SQL Server Integration Services** is necessary for this chapter, it doesn't hurt to install the other component as you might want to use it later. Click on **Next** to start the installation:

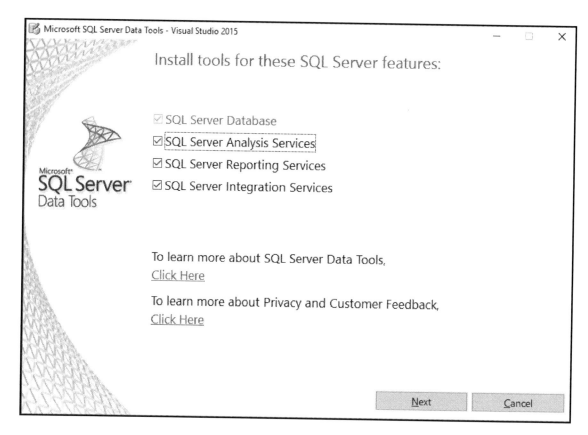

7. The **Microsoft Software License Terms** page appears. Check **I agree to the license terms and conditions** and click on the **Install** button, as shown in the following screenshot:

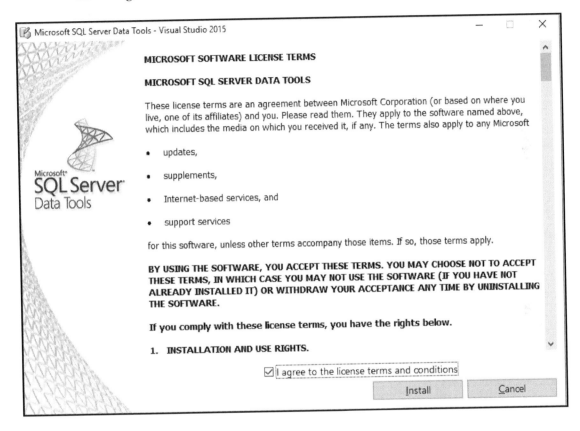

8. The **Setup Progress** page appears as SSTD gets installed, as shown in the following screenshot:

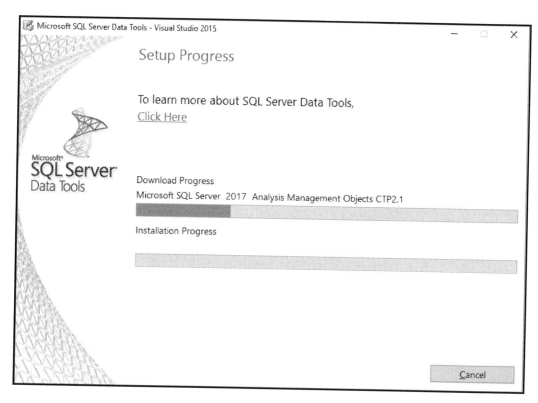

9. Once the installation completes, we're ready to proceed to the setup of SSIS to run in scale out mode.

Configuring SSIS for scale out executions

We'll now configure the SSIS catalog and workers to be able to use scale out executions with SSIS.

Getting ready

This recipe assumes that you've installed SQL Server 2017, SSIS in scale out mode as well as SSMS 17.1 or later.

How to do it...

1. Open **SQL Server Management Studio** and connect to the newly installed SQL Server 2017 instance.
2. In the **Object Explorer**, right-click on the **Integration Services Catalogs** node and select **Create Catalog**.
3. The **Create Catalog** window appears. As shown in the following screenshot, check the **Enable this server as SSIS scale out master** option as well as providing a password for the catalog. Click on **OK** when finished.

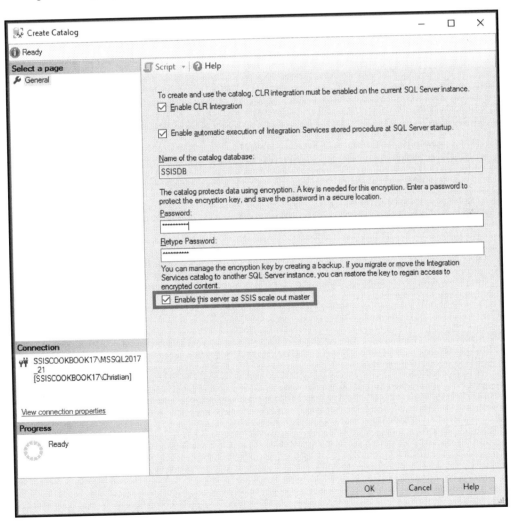

4. Still in SSMS, run the following SQL statements. The first statement lists the workers available. Copy the **WorkerAgentId** into the clipboard by right-clicking on the value in the grid and select **Copy**.
Type the second SQL statement and use the clipboard's content as parameter (the grayed-out shape in the screenshot). This will enable this specific worker.

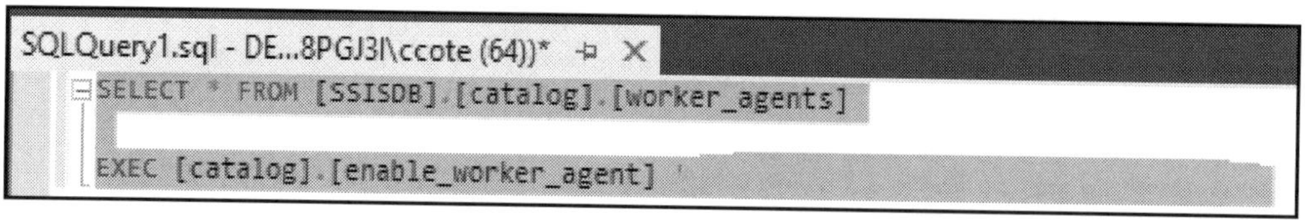

5. We'll now create a simple database to hold our test scale out data. In **SQL Server Object Explorer**, right-click on the **Databases** folder and select **Create Database**. Name it `TestSSISScaleOut` and click on **OK**.

6. By default, the workers run under the `NT Service\SSISScaleOutWorker140` Windows user. This user is not a login in SQL Server. In **SQL Server Object Explorer**, expand the **Security** folder and right-click on the **Logins** folder; select **New Login** from the contextual menu. The **Login - New** window appears. As shown in the following screenshot, type `NT SERVICE\SSISScaleOutWorker140` in the login name:

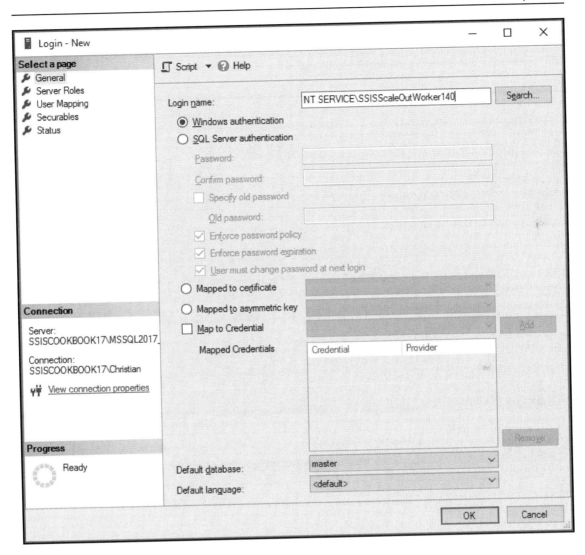

7. Click on **User Mapping** in the upper-left pane.

8. As shown in the following screenshot, select the **TestSSISScaleOut** database and assign both **db_datareader** and **db_datawriter** database roles to the login. Click on **OK** to complete the login creation.

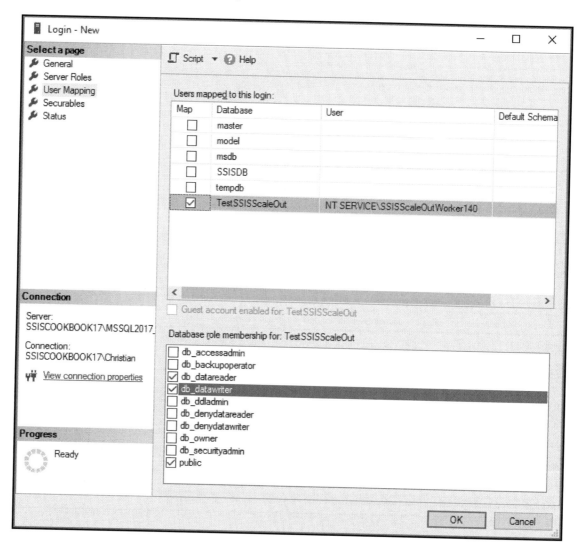

9. The last operation ensures that the worker will have access to the database objects in read/write mode.

There's more...

SSIS is now configured for scale out executions. The next recipe will just show how we can execute a package in scale out mode.

Executing a package using scale out functionality

Finally, we're able to do the real work: creating a simple package and execute it in scale out mode.

Getting ready

You will need SQL Server 2017, SSIS 2017, SSDT, and SSMS 2017 to complete this recipe. It is also assumed that you have configured SSIS in the previous recipe.

How to do it...

1. Open SSDT and create a new SSIS project named `SSISCookBookScaleOut`, as shown in the following screenshot. Click on **OK** to create it:

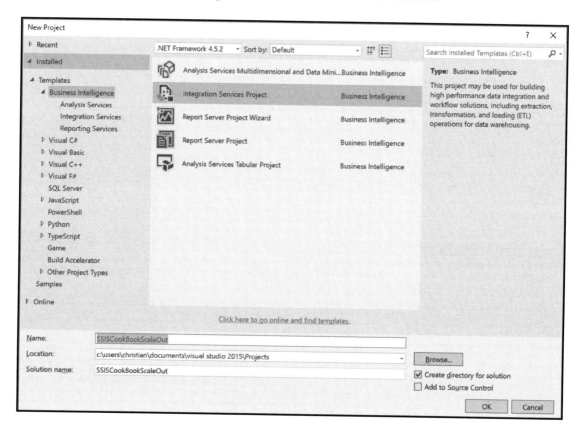

2. In the **Solution Explorer**, right-click on the **Package.dtsx** that is created with the project and select **Delete**, as shown in this screenshot:

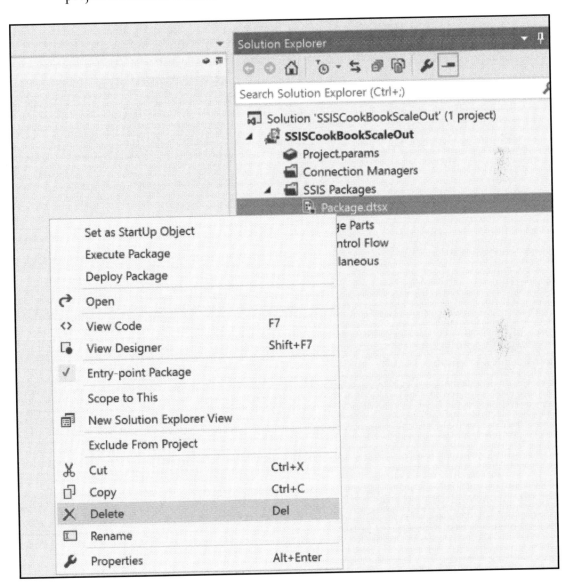

3. Right-click on the project and select **Properties** from the contextual menu. As shown in the following screenshot, change the **ProtectionLevel** property of the project to **Do not save sensitive data** and click on **OK** in both windows. You'll get a warning telling you that you'll have to do the same for all packages in the project. We don't have any, so we simply get rid of the warning dialog. Sensitive data means usernames and passwords. It's better to use parameters instead of relying on SSIS to keep this information. It doesn't hurt to leave this property as default, but we'll get annoying warnings at deployment time. So, the best practice is to use parameters and not the **Encrypt sensitive data with user key** setting.

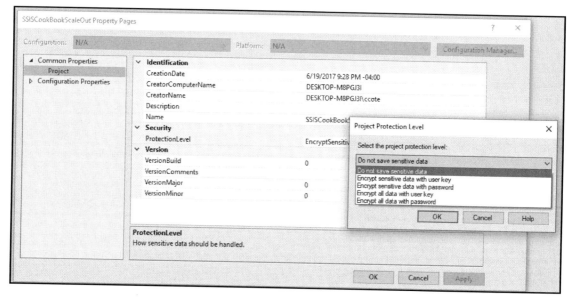

4. Now, right-click on the project and select **New SSIS package** from the contextual menu. Rename it ScaleOut.

5. From the SSIS toolbox, drag and drop a data flow task on the control flow of the package. Name it dft_SSISScaleOut and double-click on it to go into the data flow task.

6. From the connection managers pane, right-click and select **New OLEDB Connection Manager**. In the configure OLEDB **Connection Manager** window, click on **New** and set the properties as shown in the following screenshot:

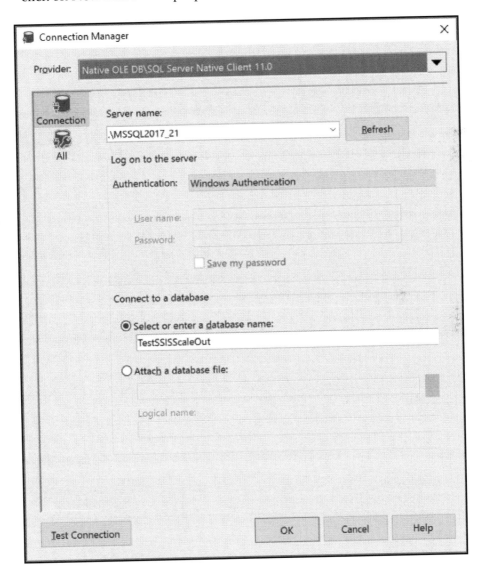

7. Click on the **Test Connection** button to test the connection. If everything is okay, get rid of the test dialog box and click on **OK** to create the connection manager.

8. Rename it as `cmgr_TestSSISScaleOut`.

9. From the **SSIS toolbox | Other sources**, drag and drop an OLEDB source. Rename it `ole_src_AddRows`. Double-click on it and enter the following query:

```
SELECT 1 AS Id, 'Test Scale out' AS ProcessName
```

10. Add a derived component to the data flow. Rename it to `der_ServerExecutionId` and tie it to the `ole_src_AddRow` source. Open it. Add a column, `ServerExecutionId`, and set its expression to `@[System::ServerExecutionID]`. Leave other columns as they are and click on **OK** to close the **Derived Column Transformation Editor**.

11. From the **SSIS toolbox | Other destinations**, drag and drop an OLEDB destination onto the data flow surface. Rename it as `ole_dst_SSISScaleOut`. Open it and click on the **New** button beside the table or view dropdown. Instead of choosing an existing table, since we don't have any yet, we'll create a new one.

12. As shown in the following screenshot, adapt the T-SQL, create the table script to remove the `ole_dst_`, and click on **OK**.

The query is as follows:

```
CREATE TABLE [SSISScaleOut] (
    [Id] int,
    [ProcessName] varchar(14),
    [ServerExecutionId] bigint
)
```

13. Click on the **Mappings** tab to set the links between pipeline and table columns. Click on **OK** in the **OLE DB Destination Editor** to close it. Your data flow should look like the following screenshot:

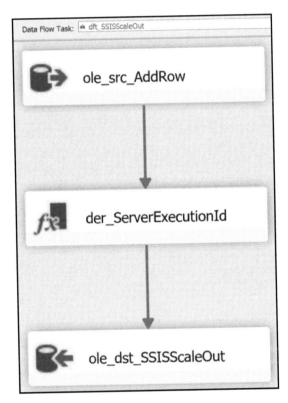

14. Test the package, ensuring that everything works correctly.
15. We'll now deploy the project. In the **Solution Explorer**, right-click on the SSIS and deploy it in the SSIS Catalog created in the previous recipe.

16. Once deployed, open SSMS; expand to the **Integration Services Catalogs** until you get to the **ScaleOut.dtsx** package. Right-click on it and select **Execute in Scale Out...** from the contextual menu, as shown in the following screenshot:

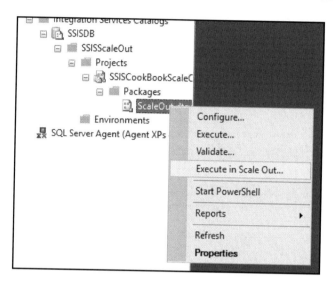

17. The **Execute Package In Scale Out** window opens, as shown here:

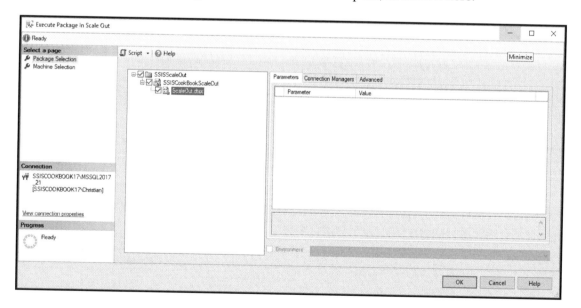

18. Click on **Machine Selection** in the upper-left pane. You can see that the worker we registered in the previous recipe is there. By default, **Allow any machine to execute the selected package** is checked. Since we have only one worker registered, we'll leave it checked. Modifying this setting would be useful if we had many workers and we'd like to be able to choose from among them the worker(s) to execute the package.

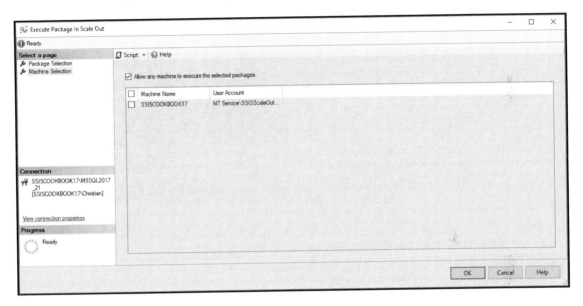

19. Click on **OK** and you'll get a message, as the following screenshot shows. This confirms that the package execution has been queued to execute. Click on **OK** to close this dialog box.

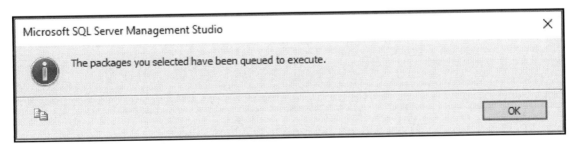

20. In the **SQL Server Object Explorer**, right-click again on the **ScaleOut.dtsx** package. As shown in the following screenshot, go to **Report | Standard Reports | All Executions** from the contextual menu:

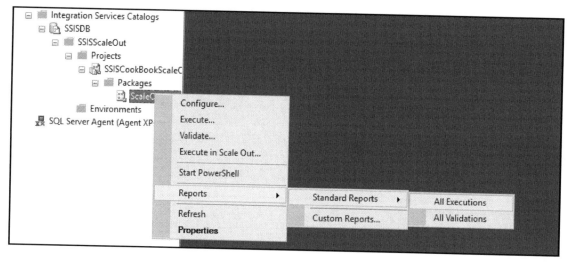

21. The report opens and you can see that the execution has succeeded, as shown in the following screenshot. Click on the **All Message** link under the **Report** column.

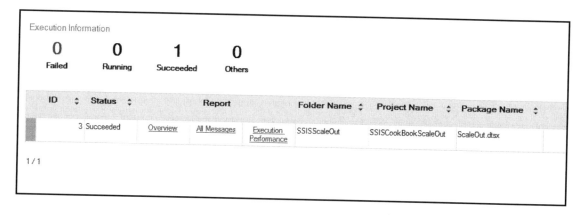

22. The report messages are now detailed. As highlighted in the following screenshot, we can see that SSIS tried to scale out the insertion in the destination, even though it was a very simple package.

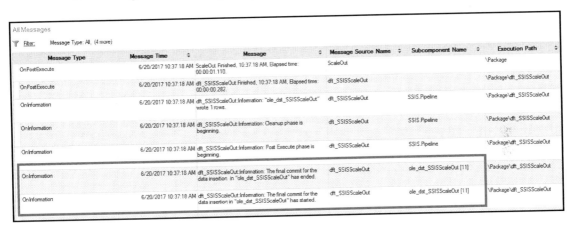

That's it! We've run the SSIS package using scale out mode. That completes the recipe.

Other Books You May Enjoy

If you enjoyed this book, you may be interested in these other books by Packt:

SQL Server 2017 Administrator's Guide
Marek Chmel, Vladimír Mužný

ISBN: 978-1-78646-254-1

- Learn about the new features of SQL Server 2017 and how to implement them
- Build a stable and fast SQL Server environment
- Fix performance issues by optimizing queries and making use of indexes
- Perform a health check of an existing troublesome database environment
- Design and use an optimal database management strategy
- Implement efficient backup and recovery techniques in-line with security policies
- Combine SQL Server 2017 and Azure and manage your solution using various automation techniques
- Perform data migration, cluster upgrades and server consolidation

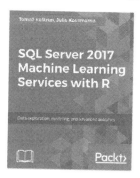

SQL Server 2017 Machine Learning Services with R
Tomaž Kaštrun, Julie Koesmarno

ISBN: 978-1-78728-357-2

- Get an overview of SQL Server 2017 Machine Learning Services with R
- Manage SQL Server Machine Learning Services from installation to configuration and maintenance
- Handle and operationalize R code
- Explore RevoScaleR R algorithms and create predictive models
- Deploy, manage, and monitor database solutions with R
- Extend R with SQL Server 2017 features
- Explore the power of R for database administrators

Leave a review - let other readers know what you think

Please share your thoughts on this book with others by leaving a review on the site that you bought it from. If you purchased the book from Amazon, please leave us an honest review on this book's Amazon page. This is vital so that other potential readers can see and use your unbiased opinion to make purchasing decisions, we can understand what our customers think about our products, and our authors can see your feedback on the title that they have worked with Packt to create. It will only take a few minutes of your time, but is valuable to other potential customers, our authors, and Packt. Thank you!

Index